John Hunter Smith

Greek Testament Lessons for Colleges, Schools and Private Students

Consisting chiefly of the Sermon on the Mount and the Parables of Our Lord

John Hunter Smith

Greek Testament Lessons for Colleges, Schools and Private Students
Consisting chiefly of the Sermon on the Mount and the Parables of Our Lord

ISBN/EAN: 9783744762120

Printed in Europe, USA, Canada, Australia, Japan

Cover: Foto ©Lupo / pixelio.de

More available books at **www.hansebooks.com**

GREEK TESTAMENT LESSONS

FOR

Colleges, Schools, and Private Students

CONSISTING CHIEFLY OF

THE SERMON ON THE MOUNT, AND THE PARABLES OF OUR LORD

WITH NOTES AND ESSAYS

BY THE

REV. J. HUNTER SMITH, M.A.

FIRST ASSISTANT-MASTER OF KING EDWARD'S HIGH SCHOOL, BIRMINGHAM;
FORMERLY SCHOLAR OF MERTON COLLEGE, OXFORD

WILLIAM BLACKWOOD AND SONS
EDINBURGH AND LONDON
MDCCCLXXXIV

LIST OF MAPS AND PLANS.

Τοῖς μαθηταῖς

τῶν μαθημάτων μνημεῖα.

PREFACE.

THIS book has little or no claim to originality, excepting in design and method. The chief objects aimed at have been, to present to intelligent boys, of fourteen and upwards, such a view of Christian Ethics as may make a lasting impression upon them, and to connect the study of the Greek Testament with the other studies of a public-school boy, and the trivial round of his everyday life. An attempt has also been made, so far as was possible in such narrow limits, to place this teaching in its proper historical and geographical setting, to show its relation to that of the writers of the Old Testament, and to illustrate it from the sayings of teachers of morality of ancient and modern times.

It is hoped that the book may prove useful to others besides boys,—to theological students, and perhaps to some teachers and ministers of religion who may not have had leisure or opportunity for the study of the authorities from which are derived the thoughts contained in this volume.

The works principally used have been the com-

mentaries of Meyer, Godet, Trench, Tholuck, Westcott, Lightfoot, Farrar, Carr, Wordsworth, Morrison,
R. Nicholson, and T. Evans; the lives of Christ by
Edersheim, Farrar, Geikie, and Keim; Bruce on the
Parabolic Teaching of Christ; Brace's Gesta Christi,
Lecky's History of European Morals; the sermons
of the late Professor Mozley; Martineau's Hours
of Thought; Davidson's Introduction to the New
Testament; and the works of Mr Prebendary Row,
the late Dean Stanley, Dr E. A. Abbott, and Professor Seeley. I have not hesitated to adopt the
language of my authorities where it suited my purpose to do so.

I have to thank Professors Westcott and Hort for
their kindness in permitting me to use their text.
After consultation with Dr Westcott, I have ventured to depart from the spelling adopted in his
edition when it seemed that the strangeness of the
forms would tend to create difficulties for boys without affording them any compensating instruction.
In one or two instances I have even ventured, for a
similar reason, to depart from the readings : these,
however, will be found in footnotes.

My thanks are also due to Mr Carr for his courtesy in permitting me to make use of his valuable
notes on the Gospels of St Matthew and St Luke; to
Professor J. Massie, the scholarly contributor to the
'Expositor,' for much important assistance; and to
several friends for aid rendered me in looking over
the proofs as they passed through the press.

CONTENTS.

GREEK TESTAMENT LESSONS.

LESSON I.

St Luke ii. 40-52.

THE VISIT OF JESUS, WHEN A BOY, TO JERUSALEM.

40 Τὸ δὲ παιδίον ηὔξανεν καὶ ἐκραταιοῦτο πληρού-
μενον σοφίᾳ, καὶ χάρις θεοῦ ἦν ἐπ᾽ αὐτό.

41 Καὶ ἐπορεύοντο οἱ γονεῖς αὐτοῦ κατ᾽ ἔτος εἰς
Ἰερουσαλὴμ τῇ ἑορτῇ τοῦ πάσχα. 42 καὶ ὅτε
ἐγένετο ἐτῶν δώδεκα, ἀναβαινόντων αὐτῶν κατὰ τὸ
ἔθος τῆς ἑορτῆς 43 καὶ τελειωσάντων τὰς ἡμέρας, ἐν
τῷ ὑποστρέφειν αὐτοὺς ὑπέμεινεν Ἰησοῦς ὁ παῖς ἐν
Ἰερουσαλήμ, καὶ οὐκ ἔγνωσαν οἱ γονεῖς αὐτοῦ. 44
νομίσαντες δὲ αὐτὸν εἶναι ἐν τῇ συνοδίᾳ ἦλθον ἡμέρας
ὁδὸν καὶ ἀνεζήτουν αὐτὸν ἐν τοῖς συγγενεῦσιν καὶ
τοῖς γνωστοῖς, 45 καὶ μὴ εὑρόντες ὑπέστρεψαν εἰς
Ἰερουσαλὴμ ἀναζητοῦντες αὐτόν. 46 καὶ ἐγένετο
μετὰ ἡμέρας τρεῖς εὗρον αὐτὸν ἐν τῷ ἱερῷ καθεζόμενον
ἐν μέσῳ τῶν διδασκάλων καὶ ἀκούοντα αὐτῶν καὶ
ἐπερωτῶντα αὐτούς· 47 ἐξίσταντο δὲ πάντες οἱ
ἀκούοντες αὐτοῦ ἐπὶ τῇ συνέσει καὶ ταῖς ἀποκρίσεσιν
αὐτοῦ. 48 καὶ ἰδόντες αὐτὸν ἐξεπλάγησαν, καὶ εἶπεν
πρὸς αὐτὸν ἡ μήτηρ αὐτοῦ Τέκνον, τί ἐποίησας
ἡμῖν οὕτως; ἰδοὺ ὁ πατήρ σου καὶ ἐγὼ ὀδυνώμενοι

ζητοῦμέν σε. 49 καὶ εἶπεν πρὸς αὐτούς Τί ὅτι
ἐζητεῖτέ με ; οὐκ ᾔδειτε ὅτι ἐν τοῖς τοῦ πατρός μου
δεῖ εἶναί με ; 50 καὶ αὐτοὶ οὐ συνῆκαν τὸ ῥῆμα ὃ
ἐλάλησεν αὐτοῖς. 51 καὶ κατέβη μετ' αὐτῶν καὶ
ἦλθεν εἰς Ναζαρέτ, καὶ ἦν ὑποτασσόμενος αὐτοῖς.
καὶ ἡ μήτηρ αὐτοῦ διετήρει πάντα τὰ ῥήματα ἐν τῇ
καρδίᾳ αὐτῆς. 52 Καὶ Ἰησοῦς προέκοπτεν
τῇ σοφίᾳ καὶ ἡλικίᾳ καὶ χάριτι παρὰ θεῷ καὶ
ἀνθρώποις.

THE COUNTRY AND HOME OF JESUS.

**PALESTINE : its central position and seclusion :
advantages of this.**—Jesus was born in Palestine, and
His home was at Nazareth, or perhaps we should say
Nazara, in the province of Galilee, in that country.
Palestine is a very small country, about the size of Wales,
less than 140 miles in length, and barely 40 in average
breadth : its influence on the history of the world is
due rather to its geographical position, the character of
its people, and their remarkable training, than to its
size. There are two chief points to be remembered about
its geographical position : (1) that it was secluded ; (2)
that it was central. The first advantage kept the
Israelites for many years comparatively safe from the
polluting influences of other nations, so that while these
last were given up to various forms of idolatry, the
better part at least of the Israelitish nation retained
that great truth which distinguished them from the
other nations — that God is One, is a Person, is a
Spirit, and is Holy : the second advantage enabled
them, when the time was fully come, to communicate
this truth and the Gospel to the civilised world.

Its boundaries.—A glance at the map will show that
Palestine is a strip of country on the extreme frontier of

the East, and pushing out towards the West into the
Mediterranean: its position is at once a central one
between the East and West, and yet secluded and cut
off from both by the natural barriers of desert, mountain,
and sea. When the chosen people first conquered
Palestine, the East was still the world, the Western
empires had not yet risen. Now Palestine was cut off
from the great Eastern empires, first, by the deep fissure
of the Jordan valley; secondly, by the eastern desert.
It was cut off from Egypt on the south by the "great
and terrible wilderness," which rolled like a sea between
the valley of the Nile and that of the Jordan, and this
wilderness could only be reached by formidable passes.
On the west it was protected by the Mediterranean
(which was navigated at that time by none but the
Phœnicians), and by its own inhospitable seaboard,
whose long line was broken only by one bay, the bay of
Acre, and never had more than three harbours, and those
bad ones, Joppa, Acre, and Haifa—the last unknown to
the ancient world. On the northern frontier the ranges
of Libanus and Anti-Libanus, the White Mountain or
Mont Blanc of Syria, formed two not insignificant ram-
parts. Between them ran the long fertile valley to
which the Greeks after the time of Alexander gave
the name of Cœle (Hollow) Syria, and which the
Hebrews called Bukâ'a, the Cleft—a name it still re-
tains, and which aptly describes the great contrast
between its ordinary width (seven or eight miles) and
its great length (100 miles). Through this narrow
pass, as through a gate, the hosts of Syria and Assyria
would pour into Palestine.

Its contact with the great empires.—In Ezek. v. 5
it is said, "I have set Jerusalem in the midst of the
nations and countries that are round about her," and in
later times this was taken literally. When Ezekiel
wrote, Palestine was really the vanguard of the Eastern,

and therefore of the civilised world; but now civilisation
has swept westwards : then, however, she stood midway
between the two great seats of ancient empires, Babylon
and Egypt; and the whole history of Palestine between
the return from the captivity and the Christian era is a
history of the contest between the kings of the north
and the kings of the south, the descendants of Seleucus
and Ptolemy, for the possession of the country. Palestine, in fact, was to Assyria and Egypt what Sicily was
afterwards to Rome and Carthage—their football.

Such was the position of Palestine with respect to
other nations—cut off from them, yet ever reminded of
them by the view of the sea, which could be obtained
from elevations in all parts of the land, stretching to the
outline of Chittim or Cyprus just visible in the clear
evening horizon.[1]

Its internal condition.—If we endeavour to realise
the internal condition of Palestine as it was in Jesus'
time, we must be careful not to think of it as accurately
divided among the tribes as in Old Testament times.
Some of the districts, indeed, still retained the names of
the ancient tribes which formerly occupied them, but a
comparatively small number of the exiles had returned
to Palestine under Ezra and Nehemiah. We have no
proof that any of these were descendants of the former
inhabitants of the ten tribes; they were for the most
part from the tribes of Judah and Benjamin. Henceforth the name of Israel gave way to that of Judæan or
Jew.

Its divisions.—Palestine from north to south may
be represented by four parallel bands—the seaboard,
the hill country, the Jordan valley, and the trans-
Jordanic range. On the east the long solid wall
of the Moab and Gilead mountains is always in sight,
and forms the background to almost every view. There

[1] Num. xxiv. 24 ; Isa. xxiii. 1-12.

are many eminences in the highlands which command the view of both frontiers at the same time—the eastern mountains of Gilead with the Jordan at their feet on the one hand, on the other the Western sea with its line of white sand and its blue expanse. Armies of the great empires marching by the seaboard did not care to penetrate into the highlands, which seemed to them an insurmountable wall.

Samaria.—In the time of Jesus, Palestine, east of the Jordan, could not be regarded as Jewish, the majority of the people being Syrians and Greeks, rude barbarians and heathens. The west, under the Roman rule, was divided into the provinces of Galilee, Samaria, and Judæa; but of these, Samaria was like a foreign country, intercepting Galilee on the north from Judæa on the south. For after the ten tribes were carried away in B.C. 721, an Assyrian king, probably Esarhaddon, had transplanted the Israelites who dwelt in Samaria, and peopled it with idolatrous Assyrians and nations that had been subjugated by the Assyrians. In B.C. 409, one Manasseh, a man of priestly lineage, on being expelled from Jerusalem by Nehemiah for an unlawful marriage, took refuge with the Samaritans, and obtained leave from the Persian king to build a temple on Mount Gerizim for that people. Thus the animosity that naturally existed between two neighbouring nations of different races was intensified by the existence of a rival temple and rival religious rites. In the time of our Lord political jealousy had added fuel to the flames; for the Samaritans had been loyal to the Roman conqueror and to Herod the Great, and had been specially favoured above the Jews by both. Herod had married a Samaritan woman, and indulged in Samaria his Roman tastes, so hated in Judæa; had embellished and almost rebuilt the capital, to which he gave the name Sebaste (Augusta), in honour of the Emperor

Augustus, to whom also he dedicated a magnificent temple built within its walls. In this city thus distinguished by a detested heathen name, he found rest when weary of his struggles with the Jews, and against them he made it a fortress: and after his death the Samaritans remained quiet, while Judæa and Galilee took up arms against the son of a Samaritan woman, and were rewarded by being relieved of a fourth part of their taxes, which the Romans added to the burdens of the Jews. Between the Galileans and the Samaritans prevailed bitter feuds resembling those once carried on on the frontiers of England and Scotland (Tac. Ann., xii. 54).

Judæa.—Between the provinces of Galilee and Judæa there was a contrast in respect both to their scenery and to the character of the inhabitants. "Judæa was the true home of Judaism, Galilee of Christianity." The landscapes of Judæa, at least towards the east, were comparatively barren, her hills bare and rocky, her wildernesses lonely; and her religious views were not dissimilar—hard, unsympathetic, and gloomy. She was full of "solemn doctors, hypocritical devotees, stern sticklers for the letter of the Law."

Galilee.—Galilee, on the contrary,—at least in the southern district, which Jesus for the most part made His home,—was "very verdant, sylvan, and smiling. During the two months of March and April the country is a carpet of flowers of extraordinary diversity of colour." The province lay three days' journey from Jerusalem. The name means "circuit," and was originally applied to the little circuit of country round Kedesh-Naphtali, in which were situated the twenty towns given by Solomon to Hiram, king of Tyre, as payment for his work in conveying timber from Lebanon to Jerusalem. They were then or subsequently occupied by strangers, who increased in number, and became during the captivity the great body of the inhabitants. After the return, the Jewish colonists gradually extended their settlements again, even in the north; so that in our Lord's time Galilee still professed the faith of Israel, although surrounded by foreign countries. But the population was a very mixed one, consisting, besides Jews, of Phœnicians, Syrians, Greeks, and Arabians; and the Galilean Jews were despised by those of Judæa, because they lived at a distance from the temple, and from the Scribes, the authoritative teachers, because their religious observances were indifferent, and their way of speaking provincial (Matt. xxvi. 73). Hence the province was spoken of as "Galilee of the Gentiles" (Matt. iv. 15); Γαλιλαία ἀλλοφύλων (1 Macc. v. 15). The term "Galileans" was a distinctive one, cf. Acts i. 11. They, however, had a reputation for bravery, which had been proved in many a tumult at the Jerusalem feasts, and many a border foray; and in the Jewish war they were the first to offer resistance to the Roman armies, and among the last to defend the ruins of Jerusalem. From Galilee, too, came the first token of the poetic spirit of Israel, in the outpourings of Deborah after the victory of Barak: here too, perhaps, was composed the Song of Songs, the Jewish idyl; and here was born the prophet Hosea, who first gave emphatic expression to Jehovah's essential attribute as "Love."

Nazareth : the house where Jesus lived.—Let us now try to place ourselves in Nazareth, and think of the world as it would appear to a boy in the time of Jesus. First, let us picture His home in its external surroundings. And this we are well able to do on account of the description given us by a modern traveller of the homes of Nazareth as they are now; and there is no reason to suppose that they have greatly altered. "We can see," he says, "the streets where He played as a boy in the stony footpaths or little crossways which separate the dwellings. The house of Joseph doubtless much resembled those poor shops lighted by the door, serving at once for shop, kitchen, and bedroom, having for furniture a mat, some cushions on the ground, one or two clay pots, and a painted chest. The population of Nazareth is from 3000 to 4000, and it can never have varied much."

The social position of His family.—"Joseph was a carpenter, and Jesus, too, seems to have worked at Joseph's trade. In the cities the carpenters would be Greeks and skilled workmen: the carpenter of a provincial village can only have held a very humble position, and secured a very moderate competence. But we need not think of the family as suffering either from a degrading or a grinding poverty. Mechanical trade was not among the Jews regarded with contempt, as it was among the Greeks and Romans. Among the Jews every boy was compelled to learn a trade; but the Rabbis had no respect for trade unless accompanied by a knowledge of the Law. The life then led by the holy family, though it would necessitate self-denial, would not be one of penury or of much anxiety. Indeed, in Palestine, the extreme simplicity of life makes the privilege of riches almost useless, and leads nearly every one to be voluntarily poor. Again, the total want of taste for the arts and for the things which contribute to the elegance of material life, gives even to the house of one who is in need of nothing an aspect of destitution. We must remember, too, that in the delicious climate of Galilee it would be possible to live much more in the open air than it is in our uncertain climate. In such a home, then, we may think of Jesus learning to make and making ploughs and yokes."

Geographical position of Nazareth.—A glance at the map will show that half-way up the coast the maritime plain is suddenly interrupted by a long ridge thrown out from the central mass, rising considerably above the general level, and terminating in a bold promontory on the very edge of the Mediterranean. This ridge is Mount Carmel. On its northern side, the plain, as if to compensate for its temporary displacement, invades the centre of the country, and forms an undulating hollow right across it from the Mediterranean to the Jordan valley. This central lowland, which divides with its broad depression the mountains of Ephraim from the mountains of Galilee, is the plain of Esdraelon or Jezreel, the great battle-field of Palestine.

Almost in the centre of the northern or Galilean chain of hills there is a singular cleft in the limestone, forming the entrance to a little valley. As the traveller leaves the plain he will ride up a steep and narrow pathway, bordered with grass and flowers, through infinitely beautiful and picturesque scenery. Beneath him on his right-hand side the vale will gradually widen until it becomes a quarter of a mile in breadth. The basin of the valley is divided by hedges of cactus into little fields and gardens, which about the fall of the spring rains wear an aspect of indescribable calm, and glow with a tint of the richest green. Beside the narrow pathway, at no great distance from each other, are two wells, and the women who draw water there are more beautiful, and the ruddy, bright-eyed, shepherd boys who sit or play by the well-side in their gay-coloured, oriental costume, are a happier, bolder, brighter-looking race than the traveller will have seen elsewhere. Gradually the valley opens into a little natural amphitheatre of hills, supposed by some to be the crater of an extinct volcano; and there, clinging to the hollows of a hill which rises to the height of some 500 feet above it, lie like a handful of pearls in a goblet of emerald the flat roofs and narrow streets of a little Eastern town.

Natural scenery of Nazareth.—In spring everything about the place looks indescribably bright and soft: doves murmur in the trees; the hoopoe flits about in ceaseless activity; the crested lark alights almost at the feet of the traveller; the bright blue roller-bird, the commonest and loveliest bird of Palestine, flashes, like a living sapphire, over fields which are enamelled with innumerable flowers; storks, with modest and grave deportment, approach the wayfarer with fearlessness and familiarity. Such is Nazareth; and along the narrow mountain-path above described the feet of Jesus must have often trod, for it is the only approach by which, in returning northwards from Jerusalem, He could have reached the home of His infancy, youth, and manhood. The surrounding heights vary in altitude, some of them rising above it to 400 or 500 feet, like foliage round a rose. They have rounded tops, are composed of the glittering limestone which is so common in the country, and though, on the whole, barren and unattractive in appearance, present not an unpleasing aspect, diversified as they are with the foliage of fig-trees and wild shrubs, and with the verdure of occasional fields of grain. Our familiar hollyhock is one of the gay flowers which grow wild here. Being so sheltered by hills, Nazareth enjoys a mild atmosphere and climate. Hence all the fruits of the country—as pomegranates, oranges, figs, and olives—ripen early and attain a rare perfection. The village is still called En-Nazerah.

The famous view from the back of Nazareth.—Such a mountain village would be likely, from its pure air, to produce inhabitants with healthy bodies; from its retirement, to foster meditation; from the beauty of its position, its views, and its animal life, to kindle a thoughtful and peaceful love of nature. But a retired village life will often produce narrowness of mind and a want of sympathy with those who differ from the code of manners and morals adopted by the little community. The inhabitant of Nazareth was protected from this evil by its propinquity to cities, and to great caravan roads, but, above all, by a view of rare extent and beauty that can be seen from a hill at the back of the town. This view must have been constantly before the eyes of Jesus, and must have suggested thoughts of the "other sheep" which were to be gathered into the flock, and of the religious and historical associations of His country. Hence He would see its three famous mountains: *Tabor* on the east, six or eight miles off, with its round top, about 1000 feet high, on which Barak had assembled his forces before the contest with Sisera; in the distant north, 60 miles off, *Hermon's* white summit, 10,000 feet above the sea-level, the boundary of Palestine in that direction; to the west, ranging from 600 to 1600 feet, the hills and headland of *Carmel* crowned with woods of oaks and fig-trees, the scene of Elijah's contest with the prophets of Baal; below it, and closing the western view, the blue waters of the Mediterranean. On the south and south-east the plain of Esdraelon or Jezreel, the battle-field of Palestine; beyond this, on the south, the hills of Samaria.

The well—At Nazareth travellers are shown many memorials of more than doubtful authenticity connected with the lives of Mary and Jesus. Of one, however, there can be no doubt, and that is the well situated at the north-eastern extremity of the town. This must have been the evening rendezvous to which the women of Nazareth came with their pitchers on their heads to draw water and talk together. And hither Jesus must have often come with His mother.

The " brothers " of Jesus.—In Matt. xiii. 55, 56, and Mark vi. 3, mention is made of four brothers of Jesus, whose names are given as James, Joses, Simon, and Judas, and also of sisters. Some have thought these were really cousins of Jesus, not brothers; but it does not seem probable that cousins would always be spoken of without any qualification as brothers. On the other hand, if they were the sons of Mary it seems very strange that Jesus in their lifetime should have committed the care of His mother to John (John xix. 26). It is most likely, therefore, that they were the sons of Joseph by a former marriage. In this case they would have occupied the same home with Jesus; but we know nothing of His relations to them excepting that during His lifetime they did not believe in Him. We may, however, probably assume, from the allusions to them in the subsequent history, that they were men of considerable force of character. It is possible that James and Jude were the authors of the epistles that go by their names.

His education.—It is uncertain whether Jesus ever went to school: in towns, the synagogues usually had schools attached to them; but Nazareth was probably too small a community for this. Jesus probably gained His education from Joseph and Mary, from the synagogue, and from solitary meditation. That there was uninterrupted affection between Him and Joseph and Mary, we may assume from the pictures of home and childhood we find in His teaching. The allusion to the playing of the children in the market-place, and the assumption of a father's willingness to grant his children's prayers, are suggestions of a happy childhood surrounded by loving influences.

He would be taught at home by His parents in the Law, and the short proverbial sayings in use among the Rabbis.

It would be chiefly, however, from the synagogue that He would gain His knowledge of Scripture. Thither,

probably, from the time He was five years old, He would
go week by week and hear, at least every Sabbath,
a portion of the Law, followed by a portion of the
Prophets, read and explained.

The language He spoke.—He would probably write,
or rather print, Hebrew, and quote the sacred writings in
that tongue; but the language He ordinarily employed
was Aramaic, which the Jews had learnt during the
captivity in Babylon, and by contact with the Aramaic
population who were their immediate neighbours.

LESSON II.

JERUSALEM AND THE TEMPLE.

Situation of the city.—Jerusalem is a mountain city, whose highest point is 2600 feet above the level of the sea : it breathes a mountain air, and is enthroned on a mountain fastness, and possesses a mountainous character unrivalled by any important city that has ever existed on earth. Like Rome, it was situated on a cluster of steep hills, with nearer and more remote hills as protecting barriers, with Mount Olivet for its Janiculum, and the hills of Mizpch, Gibeon, and Ramah for its distant Alban and Apennine mountains. But whereas Rome was in a well-watered plain, leading direct to the sea, Jerusalem was on a bare table-land in the heart of the country, on the watershed between the Mediterranean and the Jordan, 32 miles distant from the sea, and 18 from the river.

Its ravines.—The approach to Jerusalem from the north is a continual ascent from the plain of Esdraelon : the city itself stands on the southern termination of a table-land, which is cut off from the country round it on its west, south, and east sides by two deep and precipitous ravines, encompassing it like a great natural fosse.

Jehoshaphat and Hinnom.—These ravines leave the level of the table-land, the one on the west and the other on the north-east of the city, and after a fall of as much as 672 feet each, form a junction below its south-

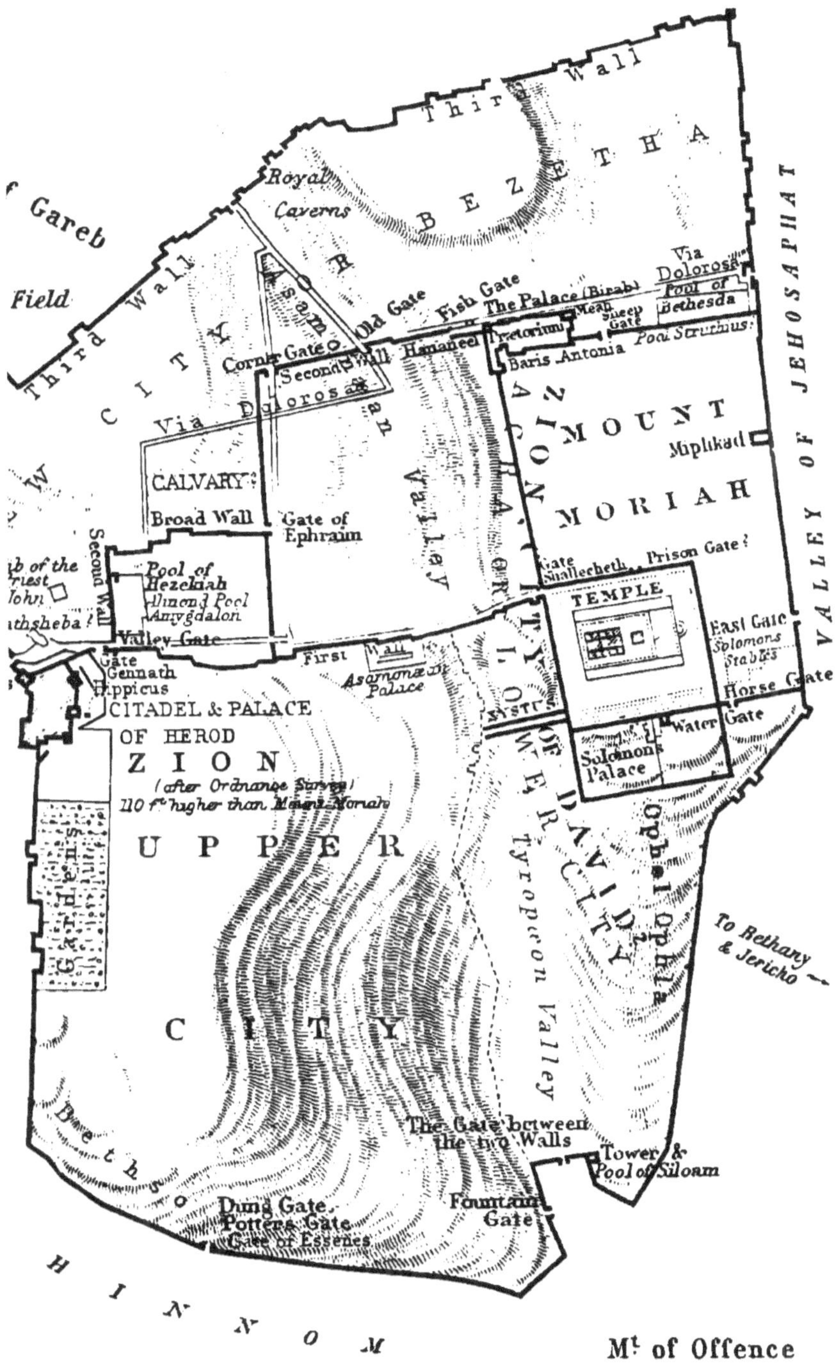
Gareb
Field
Third Wall
Royal Caverns
THIRD WALL
BEZETHA
Via Dolorosa
Old Gate
Fish Gate
The Palace (Birah)
Pool of Bethesda
Corner Gate
Second Wall
Hananeel
Meah
Sheep Gate
Via Dolorosa
Pretorium
Pool Struthius
Baris Antonia
CITY
CALVARY?
MOUNT
MORIAH
Mipkhad
Broad Wall
Gate of Ephraim
Tomb of the Priest John
Pool of Hezekiah
Almond Pool Amygdalon
Gate Shallecheth
Prison Gate?
Bathsheba?
Second Wall
TEMPLE
Valley Gate
First Wall
East Gate
Solomons Stables
Gate Gennath
Asamona Palace
Horse Gate
Hippicus
XYSTUS
Water Gate
CITADEL & PALACE
OF HEROD
Solomons Palace
ZION
(after Ordnance Survey)
110 ft higher than Mount Moriah
UPPER
LOWER CITY
TOWER OF DAVID
Ophel
To Bethany & Jericho
Gardens
CITY
Tyropeon Valley
Bethso
The Gate between the two Walls
Tower & Pool of Siloam
Dung Gate
Potters Gate
Gate of Essenes
Fountain Gate
HINNOM
Mt of Offence
VALLEY OF JEHOSAPHAT

east corner. The eastern runs straight from north to south : it is commonly called the valley of Jehoshaphat, or the valley of Kedron—*i.e.*, the black torrent, so called either from the obscure depth of the ravine, or the blackness of the torrent's waters.

The western valley—the valley of Hinnom—runs south for a time, and then takes a sudden bend to the east until it meets the valley of Jehoshaphat.

The Tyropœon.—These deep ravines give the city the appearance of a promontory joined to the main table-land only on the north-west. And this promontory is itself divided by a longitudinal ravine running up it from south to north, rising gradually from the south like the external ravines, till at last it arrives at the level of the upper plateau. This valley was called the Tyropœon, or " valley of the cheesemongers " (Τῶν τυροποιῶν). It is both shallower and broader than the other ravines, its depth averaging only from 100 to 150 feet below the height of the ridges. In it the streets range in terraces up the steep sides of the hills, side lanes climbing here and there to the top, the whole being a busy scene of traffic, and filled with bazaars; the streets being narrow and paved with white marble, and named mostly after the gates to which they led or from the various bazaars.

The hills.—The hill on the west of the ravine is divided into two summits by a kind of dell or theatre-shaped depression, extending westward for not more than 300 yards, and measuring not quite 200 yards north and south. These two heights are joined by a narrow saddle. The southernmost is the largest and most lofty—its highest part, which is towards the west, being 2520 feet, and its northernmost having an extreme altitude of 2490 feet above the Mediterranean.

The eastern and western hills, into which the Tyropœon ravine divides the city, presented in the time of Jesus in their main features striking illustrations of its double character. On the eastern stood the Temple, enclosed with its various courts; on the western, on the southern height, stood the palace of Herod, environed by its parks and gardens. The one hill was the symbol of Judaism, the other of paganism and the Roman conquest. Forbearing to enter into disputed questions, we can picture to ourselves very fairly the aspect these two different sides of the city must have presented.

The lower or northern hill on the west appears to have been called indifferently the lower city, or Akra. This was separated from the upper city on the south by the wall of David, high above which rose the three famous castles, Hippicus, Phasælus, and Mariamne, built by Herod the Great, and named after his brother, his friend, and his wife. These were of white marble, and, towering respectively 120, 130, and 75 feet above the high wall which crowned the crest of a lofty hill, must have presented a majestic appearance.

Herod's palace on the western hill.—Under the protection of these splendid structures rose the new palace of Herod, the magnificence of which Josephus says was indescribable, and surpassed even that of the Temple itself. It was subsequently occupied by Pilate the Procurator. It was situated on the loftier or southern of the two hills on the west, a great part of which was enclosed within its park walls, themselves a second line of defence, forty-five feet in height, with strong towers rising at equal distances along their broad tops. Its spacious rooms, with elaborately carved walls and ceilings, many of them crusted with precious stones, often of great rarity, were capable of affording sleeping accommodation to a hundred guests at a time. The furniture was superb, and most of the vessels were of silver and gold. Outside, between its colossal wings of white marble, was an open space commanding a noble view of Jerusalem. Here porticoes, with curious pillars of costly stone, offered shady retreats. Groves and gardens stretched on all sides, intermingled with pools and artificial rivers, bordered by long delightful walks, and adorned with statues which must have filled all pious Jews with horror. About these promenades tame doves found a delightful asylum.

The amphitheatre.—In this part of the city too, apparently, was the theatre which Herod had built, to the horror of the nation: and outside, at a little distance, was the amphitheatre, an object of still greater aversion; for in it men were made to fight with wild beasts or with one another, and chariot-races and musical contests were celebrated by foreigners gathered from all parts of the world.

The Xystus.—At the opposite or north-eastern corner of the upper city was the palace of the High Priest. South of this, and opposite the Temple, was a market-place called Xystus ($\Xi v\sigma\tau\acute{o}s$, from $\xi\acute{v}\omega$, to polish, on account of its polished floor), surrounded by a covered colonnade, 600 feet in length, under cover of which the athletes exercised themselves in the winter. Here on great occasions the populace was harangued. It fronted half the western side of the Temple courts. It had been built by Antiochus Epiphanes as a place of exercise when he was seeking to introduce Hellenic exercises into Palestine. Behind it, on the south, was the palace of Agrippa, the ancient palace of the Maccabees.

Such were the chief features of the western, or what we may call the paganised side of the holy city, comprising as it did the palatial residence and parks, and the theatre of the detested foreigner—even its superior height above the eastern hill on which the Temple was built serving to emphasise his supremacy; while the strength of its walls and the pagan fashion of its decorations, both internal and external, served as a constant memorial to the holy people of the subjugation and desecration of their Holy Land.

The Castle of Antonia.—But even the sacred or eastern hill of Moriah itself was not free from an obtrusive symbol of the Roman power. This was the citadel of Antonia (so called after the triumvir Antony, Herod's friend), a place of extraordinary strength, which had been built by the Maccabees to protect the Temple, and in which were deposited the sacred vestments of the High Priest. It was built upon a rock 75 feet high, at the end of the cloisters leading from the north-west angle of the Temple. It was a square, and had a castle in the centre and towers at three corners—the one at the south-east corner being 105 feet high—and from these the whole Temple might be viewed. Its interior had the form and size of a palace, and was divided into all kinds of rooms, for receptions, bathing, &c., with open spaces for soldiers to be quartered. On the corner, where it joined the cloisters of the Temple, it had passages down to them both, through which the guard went, arms in hand, on the Jewish festivities, to watch the people and prevent disturbances. For the Temple was a fortress which guarded the lower city, just as the Antonia did the Temple.

The Temple area.—The eastern hill, or Moriah, on which stood the Temple, was, as we have said, lower than the western mounts. The plateau on which the Temple stood had been artificially levelled at immense labour and cost, and enlarged by gigantic substructures. This was done at the expense of Herod the Great. Thus enlarged, the Temple area occupied an elongated square of from 925 to 950 feet and upwards. Roughly calculating it at about 1000 feet, this would give an extent more than one-half greater than the length of St Peter's at Rome, which measures 613 feet, and nearly double our own St Paul's, whose extreme length is $520\frac{1}{2}$ feet.

This square, each side of which was 1000 feet long, was enclosed by a gigantic wall, the dimensions of which are best realised by a comparison. The southern face of the wall is at present nearly the length of the Crystal Palace, and the height of the transept. The area within these walls was more extensive than Lincoln's Inn Fields or Grosvenor Square, and the south wall offered a larger frontage and far greater height than the Chelsea Hospital.

The Temple itself, however, stood not in the centre of this square but towards the north-west, and its courts were not on a level but rose terrace above terrace, till the sacred edifice itself was reached, its porch protruding shoulder-like on each side, and covering the holy and most holy places.

The gates to the Temple.—Access to the Temple area was obtained on the west through four gates, one of which led to the Akra, or lower city, by a subterranean tunnel, the road descending down into the valley from the Temple by a great number of steps, and thence up again. A second led over a great causeway which joined the first wall of the city to the Temple, and led over the valley to King Herod's palace in the upper city; and the other two led to the suburbs. On the south side, again, there were two gates; on the east side was the gate Shushan by which the High Priest made his exit to Mount Olivet on the great day of atonement: Jesus probably entered Jerusalem by it on the day of His triumphal entry. On the north was a gate which led by a secret passage to the Castle of Antonia.

Worshippers would approach the Temple area from a bridge over the Tyropœon valley at the south-west corner; they would then find themselves in the Court of the Gentiles, or, as the Jews called it, the Mountain of the House. The area of this was 180,000 feet, as nearly as may be equal to the area of the portion appropriated exclusively to the Jews. This court was the addition to the Temple made by Herod.

The Royal Porch.—The great glory of this outer court was the Stoa Basilica, or Royal Porch. It was 600 feet long, 100 wide, supported by 162 Corinthian columns, which divided it into three aisles, the centre one of which was 100 feet. We may form some idea of this if we fancy the transepts taken off the sides of York Minster, and added to the ends.

On the other three sides also were double porticoes, but of less height and inferior magnificence to the Stoa Basilica: that on the east facing the main entrance to the Temple was called Solomon's Porch, as having been built by the wise king.

The Court of the Gentiles.—The Court of the Gentiles was paved with the finest variegated marble. In it tradition places eating and sleeping apartments for the Levites, and a synagogue. In it the oxen, sheep, and doves selected as fit for sacrifice were sold as in a market; and here were the tables of the money-changers. At a short distance within the court, a marble screen $4\frac{1}{2}$ feet high, and beautifully ornamented, bore Greek and Latin inscriptions warning Gentiles not to proceed on pain of death. That in Greek has been recently found. The walls of the court were of white marble.

The gates.—Within this outer court rose the huge castellated wall which enclosed the Temple. It had nine gateways, with towers 50 feet high. The great entrance was by the eastern gate, sometimes called Beautiful; sometimes, from a Maccabean hero, Nicanor's gate. The other gates were sheeted with gold or silver; the bronze of this one shone almost with an equal splendour.

Every evening it was carefully closed: twenty men were needed to roll its heavy doors, and drive down into the rock its iron bolts and bars. It was regarded as the portcullis of the divine castle.

PLAN OF THE TEMPLE.

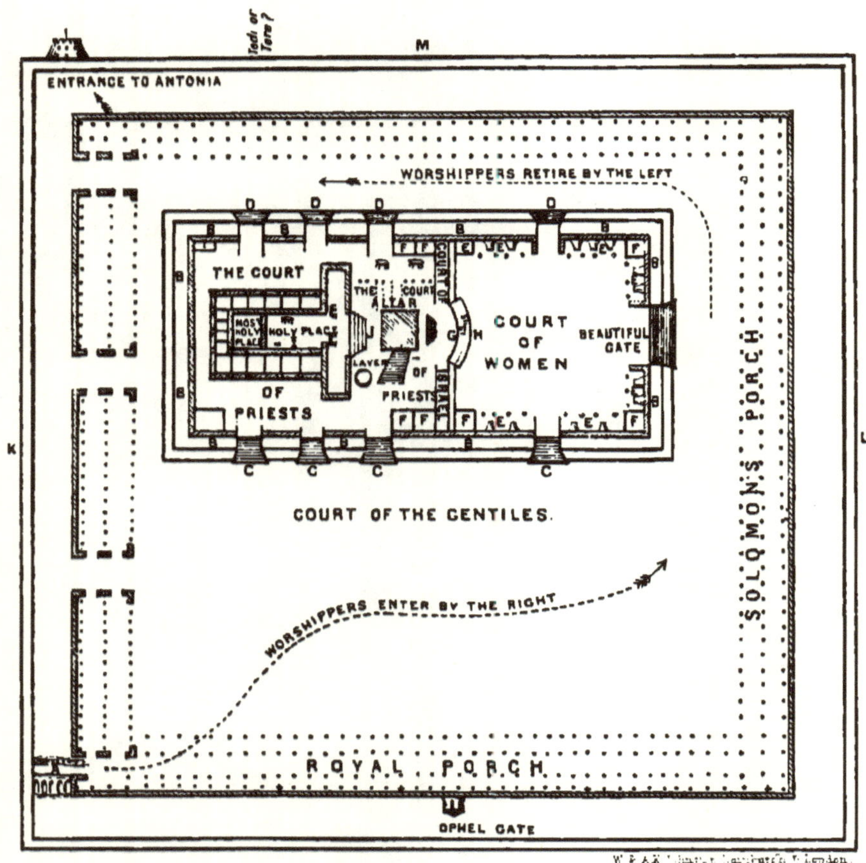

A. Royal Tyropœon Bridge.

B B. etc. Terrace, or Chel, outside of which tradition places a low enclosure, called the Soreg.

C C C. South Side Gates, the second on the right hand being the ancient Water Gate.

D D D. North Side Gates.

E E E E. Money Chests.

F F. Courts and Chambers.

G. Nicanor Gate.

H. Fifteen Steps of the Levites.

I. House of Stoves.

J. Steps of the Priests.

K. To Mount Zion.

L. Shushan Gate, with arched roadway, to Mount of Olives (?)

M. To Bezetha.

Copied by permission from Edersheim's " Temple and its Services," published by the Religious Tract Society.

The Court of the Women.—On penetrating through this sacred entrance, a platform was entered called "The Court of the Women." At the sides of this were the treasuries. Thirteen receptacles of money were placed there like inverted trumpets. The women sat round in galleries, as they do still in Jewish synagogues.

The Court of the Priests.—From this platform, by fifteen steps, the worshipper ascended into the Court of the Priests. In the first part of it was the standing-place for the people to look at the sacrifices, divided by a rail from the rest. The chambers round this court were occupied by the priestly guard, and contained the shambles for the slaughter of the victims. In the centre was the altar; in the south-west corner was the Gazith, or "Chamber of the Squares," where sat the Great Council, with a door opening on the one side into the outer court, on the other into this inner precinct.

The Temple.—Immediately beyond the altar was the Temple itself, encased with white marble studded with golden spikes, which dazzlingly reflected the rays of the sun. The porch had two vast wings, and was in dimensions and proportions about the same size as the façade of Lincoln Cathedral.

In the porch hung the colossal golden vine, resting on cedar beams, and spreading its branches under the cornices.

The doors of the Temple stood open, but a curtain prevented any from looking into the interior. This curtain was of Babylonian texture, blue, scarlet, white, and purple, and on it were embroidered the constellations of heaven.

Within the Temple was the table of Judas Maccabeus, and the seven-branched candlestick which was afterwards carried away by Titus, and may be seen to this day engraved on the arch of Titus at Rome. Within the dark recess of the Holy of Holies was nothing but the stone on which the High Priest laid his censer.

Appearance of the city.—The city itself must have seemed very uninviting to strangers, especially to Romans accustomed to the more varied life of their own towns—the baths, the circus, the piazzas, and the market-places. Yet it must have claimed an interest from the peculiarity of its population. The priests, whose number Josephus estimates at 20,000, formed no small part of the inhabitants: then there were the Levites, recognised by their pointed caps and the pocket which contained their book of the Law; the Pharisees, with their broad phylacteries and deep fringes; the Essenes, with their solemn white dresses and prophetic manner; Herodian courtiers, and Roman soldiers.

Even when there were no feasts going on, the life in the sanctuary did not cease. In the interior courts there were the throng of sacrificers, women after childbed with their doves, lepers who had been cured with their birds or lambs, Nazarites with their hair grown long. Then there was the recitation of prayers and formularies, the genuflexions and gestures, the slaughtering of sheep, the lowing of the oxen, and the whirling columns of smoke from the burnt-offerings.

Appearance of the Temple.—The Temple itself must have formed one of the most splendid architectural combinations to be found in the ancient world. The appearance of its triple courts must have been very striking: the lower court, standing on its magnificent terraces; the inner court, surrounded by its embattled towers and gateways; within this, again, the sacred building itself, with its snow-white walls and glittering pinnacles of gold rising out of this singular group, and crowning the view; and the whole scene soaring out of the deep and dark abyss of the precipitous glen which lay beneath it.

LESSON III.

INTRODUCTION TO THE SERMON ON THE MOUNT.

THE watchword of Jesus when He first went forth to preach was—"Repent, for the kingdom of heaven is at hand." But this had been the watchword of John the Baptist also, and the Old Testament is full of the idea of a "kingdom of God" upon earth—cf. Exod. xix. 5, "All the earth is mine;" and Ps. ciii. 19, "The Lord hath prepared His throne in the heavens, and His kingdom ruleth over all." Later prophets had looked forward to a time when the kingdom of God should extend from Jerusalem over all the earth—Zech. xiv. 8, 9; Isa. ii. 2; ix. 6, 7; xi. 1-10; Dan. vii. 9-14.

In what respect, then, was the watchword of Jesus in advance of the watchwords of the old prophets and of John the Baptist? What was the meaning of His summons? We find an answer in the Sermon on the Mount.

When the Jews thought of the kingdom of God, they thought of the kingdom which had been lost at the captivity, and their dream was of its restoration to Jerusalem and to David in the person of the Messiah, who should be his descendant, and of the subsequent submission of the Gentiles to his authority—Isa. ix. 6, 7; xi. 1-10. This kingdom was to be accompanied by universal godliness, but its form was Jewish and earthly. Many of the better spirits connected redemption with the forgiveness of sins, and the pure worship of God, and liberty and peace to indulge in it; but the prevailing thought was that of redemption from their enemies, and triumph over them.

John the Baptist taught that the kingdom could not come without repentance and reformation, and so put the earthly triumph in the background. Hence the Pharisees and the patriotic party did not submit to his baptism.

Earnest-minded Jews would expect the delivering Messiah to found the kingdom by appearing riding on the clouds of heaven, encompassed by thousands of angels taking vengeance upon the enemies of Sion, according to the words of the prophet Daniel (vii. 9-14); or else coming as a kingly warrior like another David riding at the head of his ten thousands, or ruling the Gentiles with a rod of iron and breaking them in pieces like a potter's vessel; or in the guise of Elijah or Elisha calling down fire from heaven for a sign or for the destruction of his enemies.

Jesus, in the Sermon on the Mount, explained what He meant by "the kingdom of heaven," and introduced a new ideal for the world, the kingdom of Love. The opening beatitudes describe the character of the kingdom, and the prayer He taught His disciples is an expression of the desire for it. The former characterises the members of the new kingdom. They are those that in the spirit of love are teachable, because they have a lowly opinion of themselves; whose love makes them mourn for the shortcomings of themselves and of their fellow-men; makes them patient under suffering, whether it seem to come from God or man; makes them long for all that is noble and good; makes them merciful, and undistracted in their love to God and their duty, and ever ready to make peace.

After describing the members, Jesus proceeds to describe the statutes of the new kingdom. And here He sought to correct an evil which had grown upon His countrymen and hearers out of the Mosaic legislation itself, and out of the interpretation put upon it by the teachers who were His contemporaries. That legislation contained not only moral precepts, but political institutions and enactments for ceremonial rites, and these came to be regarded as all of equal importance. The Jew was therefore not always able to discern the difference in value between obedience to a ceremonial ordinance and to the instincts even of humanity. A father might hesitate to save his child's life when carried away by a torrent if the day of the disaster was the Sabbath, which the Law forbade him to break. Again, as all the details of his life were dictated to him by the Law, there was no play for his own conscience : he was a kind of moral automaton ; he had not to reflect for himself whether any course were right or wrong—he consulted the Law or a Scribe, had his duty thus dictated to him, and then obeyed. He came to think of the external act as everything—of the motive as unimportant. In harmony with this spirit, we find in the apocryphal and other writings, which give us the thoughts of some of the best Jews near the time of Jesus, religion is regarded as consisting mainly in external acts rather than in a state of the heart or soul. Thus Daniel's piety is marked by his choosing a particular kind of diet (Dan. i. 8); Judith is praised for fasting during her widowhood (Judith viii. 6); the giving of alms is said to deliver from death and purge away all sin (Tobit xii. 9).

Jesus sought to correct these evils by declaring that the Law applies to the thoughts of the heart as well as to the act, and by checking the excessive reverence for alms and fasting, by the prohibition of an ostentatious display of those practices. The Law of Moses commanded men what they should *do;* Jesus set before them what they should *be.*

THE SERMON ON THE MOUNT.

Matt. v. 1-16.—The Character, Privileges, and Responsibilities
of the Members of the Kingdom of God.

1 Ἰδὼν δὲ τοὺς ὄχλους ἀνέβη εἰς τὸ ὄρος· καὶ καθίσαντος αὐτοῦ προσῆλθον [αὐτῷ] οἱ μαθηταὶ αὐτοῦ· 2 καὶ ἀνοίξας τὸ στόμα αὐτοῦ ἐδίδασκεν αὐτοὺς λέγων

3 Μακάριοι οἱ πτωχοὶ τῷ πνεύματι, ὅτι αὐτῶν ἐστὶν ἡ βασιλεία τῶν οὐρανῶν.

4 μακάριοι οἱ πενθοῦντες, ὅτι αὐτοὶ παρακληθήσονται.

5 μακάριοι οἱ πραεῖς, ὅτι αὐτοὶ κληρονομήσουσι τὴν γῆν.

6 μακάριοι οἱ πεινῶντες καὶ διψῶντες τὴν δικαιοσύνην, ὅτι αὐτοὶ χορτασθήσονται.

7 μακάριοι οἱ ἐλεήμονες, ὅτι αὐτοὶ ἐλεηθήσονται.

8 μακάριοι οἱ καθαροὶ τῇ καρδίᾳ, ὅτι αὐτοὶ τὸν θεὸν ὄψονται.

9 μακάριοι οἱ εἰρηνοποιοί, ὅτι [αὐτοὶ] υἱοὶ θεοῦ κληθήσονται.

10 μακάριοι οἱ δεδιωγμένοι ἕνεκεν δικαιοσύνης, ὅτι αὐτῶν ἐστὶν ἡ βασιλεία τῶν οὐρανῶν.

11 μακάριοί ἐστε ὅταν ὀνειδίσωσιν ὑμᾶς καὶ διώξωσιν καὶ εἴπωσιν πᾶν πονηρὸν καθ᾽ ὑμῶν ψευδόμενοι ἕνεκεν ἐμοῦ· 12 χαίρετε καὶ ἀγαλλιᾶσθε, ὅτι ὁ μισθὸς ὑμῶν πολὺς ἐν τοῖς οὐρανοῖς· οὕτως γὰρ ἐδίωξαν τοὺς προφήτας τοὺς πρὸ ὑμῶν.

13 Ὑμεῖς ἐστὲ τὸ ἅλας τῆς γῆς· ἐὰν δὲ τὸ ἅλας μωρανθῇ, ἐν τίνι ἁλισθήσεται; εἰς οὐδὲν ἰσχύει ἔτι εἰ μὴ βληθὲν ἔξω καταπατεῖσθαι ὑπὸ τῶν ἀνθρώπων. 14 ὑμεῖς ἐστὲ τὸ φῶς τοῦ κόσμου. οὐ δύναται πόλις

κρυβῆναι ἐπάνω ὄρους κειμένη· 15 οὐδὲ καίουσιν λύχνον καὶ τιθέασιν αὐτὸν ὑπὸ τὸν μόδιον ἀλλ᾽ ἐπὶ τὴν λυχνίαν, καὶ λάμπει πᾶσιν τοῖς ἐν τῇ οἰκίᾳ. 16 οὕτως λαμψάτω τὸ φῶς ὑμῶν ἔμπροσθεν τῶν ἀνθρώπων, ὅπως ἴδωσιν ὑμῶν τὰ καλὰ ἔργα καὶ δοξάσωσιν τὸν πατέρα ὑμῶν τὸν ἐν τοῖς οὐρανοῖς.

LESSON IV.

ON THE STYLE AND METHOD OF JESUS' TEACHING.

The form of the sentences.—Justin Martyr, who lived in the second century, thus describes the teaching of Jesus: "The words that fell from Him were brief and concise, for He was not a Sophist, but His speech was the power of God."

As far as the form of Jesus' teaching is concerned, this refers to the fact that He did not deliver sentences *subordinated* to one another, after the manner of Greek and Latin, but *co-ordinated* in the Semitic fashion. A good illustration of this, from a merely grammatical point of view, will be found by comparing Matt. vii. 25 with Luke vi. 48. St Luke wrote for Gentile readers, and naturally, in reporting the words of Jesus, used more classical language. St Matthew wrote earlier, and probably reports more literally. Now contrast the repeated καί in St Matthew: καὶ κατέβη ἡ βροχὴ καὶ ἦλθον οἱ ποταμοὶ καὶ ἔπνευσαν οἱ ἄνεμοι καὶ προσέπεσον τῇ οἰκίᾳ ἐκείνῃ, καὶ οὐκ ἔπεσεν, τεθεμελίωτο γὰρ ἐπὶ τὴν πέτραν—with the genitive absolute and the διά in St Luke: πλημμύρης δὲ γενομένης προσέρρηξεν ὁ ποταμὸς τῇ οἰκίᾳ ἐκείνῃ, καὶ οὐκ ἴσχυσεν σαλεῦσαι αὐτὴν διὰ τὸ καλῶς οἰκοδομῆσθαι αὐτήν.

If we examine even the continuous discourses of Jesus, we shall find this sententious style running through them. Thus, in the long discourse against the

Pharisees in Matt. xxiii., we find " brief and concise" sayings that have become current coin in our literature,—as, "they say and do not ;" "binding heavy burdens on men's shoulders which they themselves will not move with a finger;" "doing their works to be seen of men;" "loving the chief seats ;" "compassing sea and land to make one proselyte ;" "tithing mint, and anise, and cummin, and neglecting the weightier matters of the Law ;" "these ought ye to have done, and not to have left the other undone ;" "straining out the gnat and swallowing the camel ;" "cleaning the outside of the cup and the platter ;" "whited sepulchres."

It would probably be impossible to collect from the same length of speech from any other source so many brief and.telling sentences.

The sayings of the Scribes.—In adopting such a method of teaching, Jesus was conforming to the custom of the Scribes and the traditions of the national literature.

There is in the Talmud a tract called " Pirqe Aboth," or "Chapters of the Fathers," consisting, to a great extent, of maxims of the Jewish Scribes relating to practical morality.　It is used at certain seasons of the year in the Jewish synagogue.　It contains sayings, some of which must have been on the lips and in the hearts of Jesus' contemporaries.　Some of them are very noble ; but they are far inferior to the sayings of Jesus, both in the form, which is less figurative than His, and in the matter, which is narrower and more Judaistic.　Here are some of them :—

"Be deliberate in judgment; and raise up many disciples ; and make a fence to the Thorah " (the Law).

"On three things the world is stayed : on the Thorah, and on the Worship, and on the bestowal of kindnesses."

"Be not as slaves that minister to the lord with a view to receive recompense, but be as slaves that minister to the lord without a view to receive recompense; and let the fear of Heaven be upon you."

"Let thy house be a meeting-house for the wise; and powder thyself in the dust of their feet; and drink their words with thirstiness."

"Make unto thyself a master; and possess thyself of an associate; and judge every man in the scale of merit."

It is to be observed that these sentences usually have prefixed to them the name of their author, with the formula, "He received from so and so."   Thus Antigonus of Soko received from " Shimeon ha-Çaddiq,"—*i.e.*, he was his pupil.   This refers to the fact that each great Rabbi was regarded as the successor of a preceding great Rabbi, and as basing his teaching on his master's authority. This explains the passage where, after the Sermon on the Mount, the Jews expressed astonishment at Jesus because He "spake as one having authority, and not as the Scribes" (Matt. vii. 29).

But it was not merely in contrast to the Scribes that Jesus' method of teaching displayed authority.   The proverbial or gnomic method is the authoritative method: it does not argue, but states a truth that is likely to be self-evident to the listener, either because it is the result of past experience, though for the first time expressed in a terse and forcible manner, or because it appeals to the higher consciousness of the listener, and wins at once a hearing, owing to the truth of the matter combined with the winsomeness of the manner.

Proverbs in Israel.—Such a method of teaching seems first to have been popularised among the Israelites in the time of Solomon, who is said to have composed 3000 proverbs.   That it existed before Solomon's time is, however, clear from the maxim quoted by David as an ancient proverb (1 Sam. xxiv. 13), "Wickedness proceedeth from the wicked."   The canonical Book of Proverbs has embodied the proverbial wisdom of Solomon and of some others, while the apocryphal Book of Ecclesiasticus gathers up the maxims of the wise men among the Jews from the time of Solomon to that of Jesus the son of Sirach, the editor, who is supposed to have lived about B.C. 200.   So that there seems to have been an uninterrupted flow of proverbial wisdom among the Israelites for centuries, and we may reasonably suppose that such utterances were the common talk of every household.

Proverbial sayings of Jesus.—If now we turn to those sayings of Jesus which are recorded by all the three first evangelists, we shall find them frequently taking this proverbial form: "The whole have no need of a physician, but they that are sick;" "No one puts new wine into old skins;" "Whosoever hath, to him shall be given; and whosoever hath not, from him even what he hath shall be taken away;" "God is not the God of the dead, but of the living;" "Whosoever wishes to save his life shall lose it; and whosoever shall lose his life for my sake, shall save it;" "The last shall be first, and the first last;" "Render unto Cæsar the things that are Cæsar's, and to God the things that are God's."

Figurative sayings in the Old Testament.—But again, in the Books of Proverbs and Ecclesiasticus the maxims are often put in a figurative form, sometimes almost as riddles—the object being sometimes, perhaps, to display the skill of the composer, sometimes to tax the ingenuity of the hearer or to fix the maxim in his memory.   Thus in Prov. xxv. 16, "Hast thou found honey?   Eat so much as is sufficient for thee, lest thou be filled therewith, and vomit it."   The honey is a figure for pleasure which cloys when indulged in to excess.

And as used by Jesus.—Such figurative modes of speech were common with Jesus, not merely because He was an Oriental, and therefore naturally adopted figure, but because also such figures awakened the attention and stimulated the curiosity of the hearer, and the lessons they conveyed would be retained in their memories. If we turn once more to the common narrative of the three evangelists, we find such figures abounding in the short sayings of Jesus, as well as in His parables : "I will make you fishers of men ;" "Can the children of the bride-chamber fast while the bridegroom is with them ?" "Beware of the leaven of the Phar   ;" "Whosoever will come after me, let him   himself, and take up his cross and follow me ;" Salt is good ; but if the salt have lost its savour, wherewith shall it be seasoned ?" "Whosoever shall not receive the kingdom of God as a little child, he shall not enter therein ;" "It is easier for a camel to pass through the eye of a needle, than for a rich man to enter into the kingdom of God."

Jesus compared with the Prophets.—Though it can perhaps be shown that many of the utterances of Jesus were of the nature of Hebrew poetry, we must bear in mind that He spoke neither as an orator nor as a poet. The aim of the orator is to influence his hearers by means of art ; the aim of the poet is to please. The prophet-poets of the Old Testament did indeed combine both objects : in their orations they composed exalted prose—sometimes even, as in Isaiah v., changing their discourse into song. But Jesus spoke with a higher aim and greater authority, and therefore is His style simpler than theirs. He appealed straight to men's consciences and to their noblest intuitions, which had been crusted over with ignorance and prejudice. Most of us have from our earliest childhood been so accustomed to His thoughts and words, or are so surrounded by the atmosphere they have produced, that we cannot realise fully how startling their effect must have been on His hearers. The very simplicity of

His teaching was the cause why His words "pierced like a sword." He had to teach the weak to know their strength, and the strong to know their weakness; to teach all to know themselves. Yet he was not addressing, like Socrates, a select audience of the educated, but a mixed audience of the simple and uneducated, who, however much some of them might love Him, for the most part expected impossibilities from Him: and out of this material he had to found His Church, the Christians who were to mould the world. Sometimes, again, He addressed an audience of teachers who hated Him, and whom He had to convict of unreality before the people and to their own consciences.

Hyperboles and paradoxes.—In order to startle His hearers into attention and fix His words on their minds, He sometimes speaks hyperbolically—that is, with exaggeration; as when He says, " It is easier for a camel to go through a needle's eye than for a rich man to enter the kingdom of heaven; " " If ye have faith as a grain of mustard-seed, ye shall say unto this mountain, Remove hence to yonder place, and it shall remove ; " " Resist not evil ; but to him that smites thee on the right cheek, turn to him also the left." And paradoxically ($\pi a\rho\acute{a}$, $\delta\acute{o}\xi a$—contrary to received opinion), as when He says, " The first shall be last, and the last first ; " " He that would be great among you shall be your minister ; " " Whosoever hath, it shall be given to him; and from him that hath not, shall be taken away even that which he hath ; " " Whosoever will save his life shall lose it, and whosoever shall lose his life for my sake shall save it."

Similes.—Sometimes we find a simile or short parable which is elsewhere amplified : thus perhaps the parable of the master returning to his house (Luke xii. 35-38) is amplified into the parable of the ten virgins in Matt.

xxv.   The parable of the lost sheep in Luke xv. 4-10, is expanded into the allegory of the good shepherd in John x. 1-16.

Parables.—The parable is the most distinguishing feature of Jesus' teaching.   It was a familiar method in the East, but no parables have ever had so much influence as those of Jesus.

The fable and the parable.—The earliest instance of anything like a parable in the Old Testament is that told by Jotham in Judges ix. 7-15.   But that is a fable rather than a parable, the differences between the two being these—(1) The parable dwells on truths which are spiritual and heavenly, which concern man's relations to God, and those relations to his fellow-man which arise out of his being made in the image of God; whereas the fable concerns man's relations to man in points which he shares with the beasts, which belong to his lower nature, as pride, indolence, cunning, and the like.   (2) Again, in the fable, animals, and even inanimate things (as the trees in Jotham's fable), are represented as having the attributes of men; in the parable they act in accordance with their own nature.   (3) Again, in the fable we find irony, raillery, sarcasm; but the parable is ordinarily too earnest and kindly to indulge in these.

The next instance of a parable in the Old Testament is that uttered by Nathan to David in 2 Sam. xii. 1-4. Perhaps the most beautiful is that of the deceitful vine-yard in Isaiah v. 1-7.

The allegory and the parable.—It has been observed that there are no allegories in the Synoptic Gospels, and no parables in the fourth Gospel, in which are found two allegories, that of the good shepherd in John x., and that of the vine in John xv.

The difference between an allegory and a parable is this: in the parable, the story takes a form that has a value independent of the moral application; in the allegory, the application is perceived immediately through each trait of the story. Thus, in the parable of the sower the story has a value, and is a whole in itself, apart from the interpretation : in the allegory of the good shepherd there is no point in the story apart from that which it is intended to illustrate. In the parable, the threads of the illustration and of the truth illustrated are separate ; in the allegory they are interwoven. The parable is a picture, the allegory a transparency.

Reasons for teaching in parables.—Jesus gives His reason for teaching in parables in a somewhat difficult passage in Matt. xiii. 13-15, where what He seems to imply is this—that the parable captivates the mind even of the dull, and, like the riddles of old (Prov. i. 6), awakens their curiosity to know the meaning. But this is the case only with the disciples. The unimpressionable multitude do not come to inquire. Jesus pities them, and applies to them the message uttered to their forefathers by Isaiah (vi. 9, 10). But as, no doubt, that message was intended to awaken those who heard it from their spiritual sloth, so Jesus is in hope that hereafter His story may be remembered by, and enforce its lesson on, some of those on whom at present it had no influence. The fact that so many of His parables are recorded shows how they imprinted themselves on His hearers' minds.

Stories.—The narratives of the Publican and Pharisee, the good Samaritan, the rich man and Lazarus, are perhaps hardly to be called parables, since in them there are no imaginary actors : the persons are real types of classes, and the stories give direct patterns for actions.

Parallelism.—In the form of His sentences Jesus is influenced by the style of the writers of the Old Testament.

In Hebrew poetry there was probably no rhyme or metre ; but the form adopted both in poetry and in exalted prose is what is called Parallelism, in which one clause repeats another more or less exactly. Here is a simple example from Ps. ii. 3, 4 : "He that sitteth in the heavens shall laugh : the Lord shall have them in derision." Here "He that sitteth in the heavens" is defined in the second clause as "the Lord"; and the second clause adds no new idea, nothing but emphasis, to the first.

This is true very largely in the Ovidian couplet, in which, as the sense is nearly always completed in two lines, it frequently happens that the pentameter only repeats the idea of the hexameter in a new form, or amplifies it. Thus, take a couplet from "The Death of Corinna's Parrot," Amores ii. 6. 13—

> " Plena fuit vobis omni concordia vitâ,
>   Et stetit ad finem longa tenaxque fides."

Here the pentameter introduces no new idea,—merely amplifies the idea contained in the hexameter.

Parallelism probably had its origin in the religious services, in which the sacred hymns were alternately sung by opposite choirs. Thus in 1 Sam. xviii. 7, the one choir of women sang, "Saul hath slain his thousands," the other answering, "And David his ten thousands."

Bishop Lowth has divided parallelism into three species : *synonymous*, when the same sentiment is repeated in different but equivalent terms ; the *antithetic*, when a sentiment is illustrated by its opposite being opposed to it ; the *synthetic* or *constructive*, in which the sentences answer to each other, not by the iteration of the same image or sentiment, or the opposition of contraries, but merely by the form of construction, such as noun answering to noun, verb to verb, interrogative to interrogative.

Bishop Jebb has shown this parallelism running throughout the New Testament.   Here is an instance of the *synonymous* kind (Matt. v. 42) :—

> "To him that asketh thee give ;
>   And him that would borrow from thee turn not away."

Here of the *antithetic* (Matt. xvi. 19) :—

> "Whatsoever thou shalt bind on earth shall be bound in heaven ;
> And whatsoever thou shalt loose on earth shall be loosed in heaven."

In Matt. vii. 24-27, we have two stanzas antithetically opposed to each other, each consisting of seven lines, in which the fourth, fifth, sixth, and seventh are instances of synthetical parallelism.   They may be construed and arranged thus :—

> "Every one that heareth these my words, and doeth them, shall
>   be likened to a prudent man,
>   That built his house upon the rock :
>   And down came the rain,
>   And on rushed the torrents,
>   And blew the winds,
>   And struck upon that house ;
>   And it fell not, for it was founded upon the rock.

> "And every one hearing these my words, and doing them not,
>   shall be likened to a foolish man,
>   That built his house upon the sand :
>   And down came the rain,
>   And on rushed the torrents,
>   And blew the winds,
>   And struck upon that house ;
>   And it fell, and the fall thereof was great."

Chiasmus.—There is a rhetorical figure sometimes used by Jesus which aids us occasionally in interpreting His sayings.   This is the figure called Chiasmus, from the Greek letter χ, where words or sentences are arranged crosswise like that letter, as—

Ratio consentit.

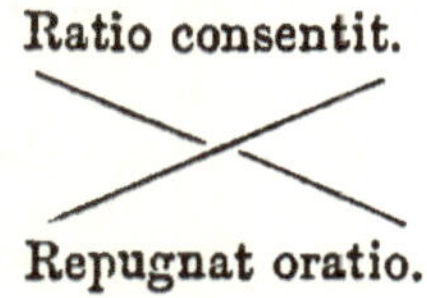

Repugnat oratio.

The following is a more lengthened instance :—

"We have piped unto you, and ye have not danced ;
  We have mourned unto you, and ye have not lamented.
    For John came neither eating nor drinking, and they
      say, He hath a devil.
The Son of Man came eating and drinking, and they say, Behold
    a man gluttonous and a winebibber," &c.

Here the first line corresponds with the fourth, and the second with the third.

Stanzas.—Again, sometimes in teaching, Jesus first stated a truth, then illustrated it, and then restated it again, the whole passage making a stanza,—cf. Matt. vii. 16-20, the passage beginning, "By their fruits shall ye know them," and ending, "By their fruits therefore shall ye know them ;" and Matt. vi. 24, where "No servant can serve two masters" corresponds with "Ye cannot serve God and mammon ;" and in the intermediate clauses there is a chiasmus.

Jesus spoke Aramaic.—The question has been raised whether Jesus in His teaching spoke Greek or Aramaic. Aramaic, under the Persian empire, was a sort of official language for the western provinces ; and the Hebrews, being in constant contact with Aramaic populations, gradually, after the return from captivity, lost the use of their own language, and acquired that of their neighbours—the language of the many superseding that of the few. It is probable that the Jews, and more especially those in Galilee, were bilingual—*i.e.*, spoke two languages. But the scanty evidence we derive from Jesus' own words goes to prove that He habitually used Aramaic. Thus He named His Galilean disciples Cephas and Boanerges ; He uses such phrases as *Talitha cumi* and *Ephphatha* (Mark v. 41; vii. 34); in His own prayer He uses the word Abba, Father (Mark xiv. 36); and His last utterance is recorded in Aramaic (Matt. xxvii. 46 ; Mark xv. 34).

The testimony of Josephus fortifies this view. Though a man of education, he declares it cost him a great deal of pains to learn Greek, and that he had never learnt to pronounce the language with correctness ; and though he translated his 'Wars' into Greek, he wrote them originally in Aramaic. This he did not only for the sake of his countrymen in Judæa, but also for that of " Parthians, Babylonians, and remotest Arabians, and those of our nation beyond the Euphrates and the Adiabeni." It is evident, therefore, that a large number of readers in the East would be more likely to read Aramaic than Greek.

LESSON V.

St Matthew v. 17-32.

CHRISTIANITY A DEVELOPMENT OF THE MORAL LAW.

17 Μὴ νομίσητε ὅτι ἦλθον καταλῦσαι τὸν νόμον ἢ τοὺς προφήτας· οὐκ ἦλθον καταλῦσαι ἀλλὰ πληρῶσαι. 18 ἀμὴν γὰρ λέγω ὑμῖν, ἕως ἂν παρέλθῃ ὁ οὐρανὸς καὶ ἡ γῆ, ἰῶτα ἓν ἢ μία κεραία οὐ μὴ παρέλθῃ ἀπὸ τοῦ νόμου, ἕως [ἂν] πάντα γένηται. 19 ὃς ἐὰν οὖν λύσῃ μίαν τῶν ἐντολῶν τούτων τῶν ἐλαχίστων καὶ διδάξῃ οὕτως τοὺς ἀνθρώπους ἐλάχιστος κληθήσεται ἐν τῇ βασιλείᾳ τῶν οὐρανῶν· ὃς δ' ἂν ποιήσῃ καὶ διδάξῃ, οὗτος μέγας κληθήσεται ἐν τῇ βασιλείᾳ τῶν οὐρανῶν. 20 λέγω γὰρ ὑμῖν ὅτι ἐὰν μὴ περισσεύσῃ ὑμῶν ἡ δικαιοσύνη πλεῖον τῶν γραμματέων καὶ Φαρισαίων, οὐ μὴ εἰσέλθητε εἰς τὴν βασιλείαν τῶν οὐρανῶν. 21 Ἠκούσατε ὅτι ἐρρέθη τοῖς ἀρχαίοις· οὐ φονεύσεις· ὃς δ' ἂν φονεύσῃ, ἔνοχος ἔσται τῇ κρίσει. 22 ἐγὼ δὲ λέγω ὑμῖν ὅτι πᾶς ὁ ὀργιζόμενος τῷ ἀδελφῷ αὐτοῦ ἔνοχος ἔσται τῇ κρίσει· ὃς δ' ἂν εἴπῃ τῷ ἀδελφῷ αὐτοῦ, Ρακά, ἔνοχος ἔσται τῷ συνεδρίῳ· ὃς δ' ἂν εἴπῃ, Μωρέ, ἔνοχος ἔσται εἰς τὴν γέενναν τοῦ πυρός. 23 ἐὰν οὖν προσφέρῃς τὸ δῶρόν σου ἐπὶ τὸ θυσιαστήριον κἀκεῖ μνησθῇς ὅτι ὁ ἀδελφός σου ἔχει τι κατὰ σοῦ, 24 ἄφες ἐκεῖ τὸ δῶρόν σου ἔμπροσθεν τοῦ θυσιαστηρίου, καὶ ὕπαγε πρῶτον, διαλλάγηθι τῷ ἀδελφῷ σου, καὶ τότε ἐλθὼν πρόσφερε

τὸ δῶρόν σου. 25 ἴσθι εὐνοῶν τῷ ἀντιδίκῳ σου ταχὺ
ἕως ὅτου εἶ μετ᾽ αὐτοῦ ἐν τῇ ὁδῷ· μήποτέ σε παραδῷ
ὁ ἀντίδικος τῷ κριτῇ καὶ ὁ κριτὴς τῷ ὑπηρέτῃ, καὶ
εἰς φυλακὴν βληθήσῃ. 26 ἀμὴν λέγω σοι, οὐ μὴ
ἐξέλθῃς ἐκεῖθεν ἕως ἂν ἀποδῷς τὸν ἔσχατον κοδράντην.
27 Ἠκούσατε ὅτι ἐρρέθη· οὐ μοιχεύσεις. 28 ἐγὼ
δὲ λέγω ὑμῖν ὅτι πᾶς ὁ βλέπων γυναῖκα πρὸς τὸ
ἐπιθυμῆσαι ἤδη ἐμοίχευσεν αὐτὴν ἐν τῇ καρδίᾳ αὐτοῦ.
29 εἰ δὲ ὁ ὀφθαλμός σου ὁ δεξιὸς σκανδαλίζει σε,
ἔξελε αὐτὸν καὶ βάλε ἀπὸ σοῦ· συμφέρει γάρ σοι
ἵνα ἀπόληται ἓν τῶν μελῶν σου καὶ μὴ ὅλον τὸ σῶμά
σου βληθῇ εἰς γέενναν. 30 καὶ εἰ ἡ δεξιά σου χεὶρ
σκανδαλίζει σε, ἔκκοψον αὐτὴν καὶ βάλε ἀπὸ σοῦ·
συμφέρει γάρ σοι ἵνα ἀπόληται ἓν τῶν μελῶν σου
καὶ μὴ ὅλον τὸ σῶμά σου εἰς γέενναν ἀπέλθῃ. 31
Ἐρρέθη δέ· ὃς ἂν ἀπολύσῃ τὴν γυναῖκα αὐτοῦ,
δότω αὐτῇ ἀποστάσιον. 32 ἐγὼ δὲ λέγω ὑμῖν
ὅτι πᾶς ὁ ἀπολύων τὴν γυναῖκα αὐτοῦ παρεκτὸς
λόγου πορνείας, ποιεῖ αὐτὴν μοιχευθῆναι [καὶ ὃς ἐὰν
ἀπολελυμένην γαμήσῃ μοιχᾶται].

THE SCRIBES.

In the time of David the term "scribe" seems to
have meant a sort of secretary to the king, whose office
it was to write his letters, draw up his decrees, and man-
age his finances. But the zeal of Hezekiah led him to
foster the growth of a body of men whose work was to
transcribe old records, or put in writing what had been
handed down orally (Prov. xxv. 1). After this period
the term no longer designates only an officer of the king's
court but a class, students and interpreters of the Law,
boasting of their wisdom (Jer. viii. 18).

The years of the captivity gave a fresh glory to
the name. The exiles would be anxious above all
things to preserve the sacred books, the hymns, the

prophecies of the past. The necessities of the time demanded a man or class of men who should know what was worth preserving, transcribe the older Hebrew documents accurately, and explain what was hard and obscure, at a time when the spoken language of the people was passing into Aramaic. Such a person was Ezra the Scribe, who combined the priesthood with that office. He and his fellow-Scribes would probably read and expound the Law, and perhaps translate it from Hebrew into Aramaic; they would compile excerpts and epitomes of larger histories, as in the two books of the Chronicles (1 Chron. xxix. 29; 2 Chron. ix. 29). The phrase "story" of the prophet Iddo mentioned in 2 Chron. xiii. 22 probably means commentary, and shows that the work of commenting and expounding had begun as early as the days of Jeroboam.

The only Scribe of whose name we have a record besides that of Ezra is Zadok. The men by whose agency the Scriptures of the Old Testament were written in their present characters, compiled in their present form, and limited to their present number, remain unknown to us. The one aim of these early Scribes was to promote reverence for the Law, and to make it the groundwork of men's lives. They would write nothing of their own, lest less worthy words should be raised to a level with those of the oracles of God. They maintained the principle of an unwritten teaching up to the destruction of the Temple. Their work is described in Neh. viii. 8: "So they read in the book, in the law of God, distinctly, and gave the sense, and caused them to understand the reading." They devoted themselves to recitation and the careful study of the text, and laid down rules for transcribing it with the most careful precision.

But this reverence for the letter led to those evil results which our Lord condemned. The infinite variety of life presented cases which had not been contemplated

by the code. A Roman or Greek jurist would have dealt
with them on principles of equity or polity. The Jewish
teacher could recognise no principles beyond the precepts
of the Law. To him these all stood on the same footing,
were all equally divine. All possible cases must be
brought within their range, decided by their authority.
As fresh cases occurred, they were decided by the authority
of the Scribes' interpretation of the Law. These decisions
passed into precepts, and as they more precisely fitted
into the circumstances of men's lives than the old did,
they came practically to take their place, though still
transmitted orally. The "words of the Scribes" were
honoured above the Law. It was a greater crime to offend
against them than against the Law. They were as wine,
while the precepts of the Law were as water. The principle of the Scribes was that there can be no indifferent
action, that there must be a right or wrong even for the
commonest necessities of life, and that it was the work
of the teacher to formulate that principle into rules.
The right relation of moral and ceremonial laws was not
only forgotten but absolutely inverted.

After the death of Ezra, Jerusalem appears to have
been the chief seat of the Scribes, and their central assembly there to have been called " the Great Synagogue."
This flourished till about the year 200 b.c. The following statement contains the views of the Jewish Rabbis
about the relation of the Law to the Great Synagogue :—

"Moses received the Thorah (Law) from Sinai and
delivered it to Jehoshua, and Jehoshua to the elders, and
the elders to the prophets, and the prophets to the
men of the Great Synagogue. They said three things :
Be deliberate in judgment, and raise up many disciples,
and make a fence for the Thorah." This last phrase
refers to the precepts of the oral law, which, by their
prohibitions and requirements, hindered the Law from
being broken or trampled on : just as the prohibition to

schoolboys to sit together would be a "fence" against their copying from one another.

Outside Palestine the influence of the Scribes was extended by means of the synagogues, in which they read and expounded the Law, and through their agency every Jew could know something of his religion.

After the death of Simeon the Just, the last representative of the Great Synagogue, he was replaced by Antigonus of Soko, who seems to have flourished as the most eminent Scribe in the first half of the third century B.C. After him two men always perpetuated "the Thorah" or tradition at the same time; they are sometimes called the pairs (*zûgóth*). There were five such pairs at the head of the Scribes in Jerusalem before our Lord's time. Of these the first pair flourished from B.C. 140-130, and were named Joses ben-Joezer and Joses ben-Joachan. To them is assigned the contemptuous phrase "people of the earth," applied to all who did not strictly observe the Thorah. The chief precept associated with the name of the former is,—"Let thy house be the assembly for the wise; dust thyself with the dust of their feet; drink eagerly of their words." They set themselves to secure the absolute isolation of Israel and the preservation of the people from the taint of Hellenism. With this object they declared glass vessels and the soil of Gentile lands unclean—preventing, by the first of these decisions, all social intercourse with Gentiles in Palestine, and by the second, all emigration from it. This legalised and intentional unsociability was called in Greek ἀμιξία, and in Syriac Perîshoth, and is the origin of the famous name of Pharisee or Separatist.

The most famous, however, of all the Rabbis was Hillel, with whom was coupled, at first, Menahem, and afterwards Shammai. Hillel became the head (Nasi) of the school and of the Sanhedrim in B.C. 30, and is said to have died A.D. 10.

The presidency of the school, and to a certain extent the high-priesthood, remained for ten generations with his posterity, among whom was his grandson Gamaliel, probably the same as St Paul's teacher (Acts xxii. 3).

Hillel and Shammai did not teach, as their predecessors had done, in entire harmony with one another. Shammai was much more rigid than Hillel in his teaching about the observance of the Law, though he was said himself to be rich, luxurious, and self-indulgent. Their disciples formed two distinct schools. Those of Shammai were conspicuous for their fierceness, appealed to popular passions, and used the sword to decide their controversies. Those of Hillel were, like their master (cf. the conduct of Gamaliel in Acts v. 34-40), cautious, gentle, tolerant, unwilling to make enemies, content to let things take their course. Shammai's school resisted, Hillel was disposed to foster, the study of Greek literature; Shammai's sought to impose on the Gentiles the full burden of the Law, Hillel to treat them with sympathy and indulgence.

Dr Farrar has very pointedly put the difference between the teaching of Jesus and Hillel in this way: Hillel rested on precedent; Jesus spoke with authority. Hillel spoke in the schools to students and select audiences; Jesus in the streets and by the roadsides to publicans and sinners. Hillel confined his teaching to Jerusalem; Jesus traversed the length and breadth of Palestine. Hillel mainly occupied himself with the Levitical law, and modified its regulations to make them more easy and more palatable; Jesus taught only the moral law, and extended its application from external actions to the thoughts of the heart.

There were grave flaws in the moral teaching and conduct of Hillel. There is reason to suppose that he taught that a man might put away his wife even if she had merely burnt the food in cooking his dinner: this expression, however, he may have used as a figure of speech for bringing disgrace on the house.   But there seems no doubt of the truth of the story, that once when he caused a sacrifice to be slain in the outer court of the Temple, he declared, in order to avoid a dispute with the Shammaites, that the ox was a cow, and craftily covered the animal with the skirts of his dress.

The most famous of his sayings was, "What is unpleasing to thee, do not to thy neighbour."

Much of his teaching, however, dwelt on trivial matters of ceremonial.   For instance, he wrote an elaborate treatise on the question, whether one might or might not eat an egg which a hen had laid on a feast-day, when the feast came in connection with a Sabbath. The kind of topics he discussed were these: Whether, when you are carrying perfumed oil and myrtles, you ought to bless first the myrtles and then the oil; whether you ought to take off your phylacteries or not in certain places of daily resort; whether you ought first to wash your hands and then fill the glasses, or *vice versâ;* whether you ought to lay the napkin on the table or on the seat.   Such was the frivolous character of the teaching of this famous Rabbi.   From such trivialities it was that Jesus sought to divert the minds of the people by enunciating the great principles contained in the Sermon on the Mount.

LESSON VI.

St Matthew v. 33-48.

ON THE LOVE OF OUR NEIGHBOURS AND OF OUR ENEMIES.

33 Πάλιν ἠκούσατε ὅτι ἐρρέθη τοῖς ἀρχαίοις· οὐκ ἐπιορκήσεις, ἀποδώσεις δὲ τῷ κυρίῳ τοὺς ὅρκους σου. 34 ἐγὼ δὲ λέγω ὑμῖν μὴ ὀμόσαι ὅλως· μήτε ἐν τῷ οὐρανῷ, ὅτι θρόνος ἐστὶν τοῦ θεοῦ· 35 μήτε ἐν τῇ γῇ, ὅτι ὑποπόδιόν ἐστιν τῶν ποδῶν αὐτοῦ· μήτε εἰς Ἱεροσόλυμα, ὅτι πόλις ἐστὶν τοῦ μεγάλου βασιλέως· 36 μήτε ἐν τῇ κεφαλῇ σου ὀμόσῃς ὅτι οὐ δύνασαι μίαν τρίχα λευκὴν ποιῆσαι ἢ μέλαιναν. 37 ἔστω δὲ ὁ λόγος ὑμῶν ναὶ ναί, οὒ οὔ· τὸ δὲ περισσὸν τούτων ἐκ τοῦ πονηροῦ ἐστίν. 38 Ἠκούσατε ὅτι ἐρρέθη· ὀφθαλμὸν ἀντὶ ὀφθαλμοῦ καὶ ὀδόντα ἀντὶ ὀδόντος. 39 ἐγὼ δὲ λέγω ὑμῖν μὴ ἀντιστῆναι τῷ πονηρῷ· ἀλλ' ὅστις σε ῥαπίζει εἰς τὴν δεξιὰν σιαγόνα, στρέψον αὐτῷ καὶ τὴν ἄλλην· 40 καὶ τῷ θέλοντί σοι κριθῆναι καὶ τὸν χιτῶνά σου λαβεῖν, ἄφες αὐτῷ καὶ τὸ ἱμάτιον· 41 καὶ ὅστις σε ἀγγαρεύσει μίλιον ἕν, ὕπαγε μετ' αὐτοῦ δύο. 42 τῷ αἰτοῦντί σε δός, καὶ τὸν θέλοντα ἀπὸ σοῦ δανίσασθαι μὴ ἀποστραφῇς. 43 Ἠκούσατε ὅτι ἐρρέθη· ἀγαπήσεις τὸν πλησίον σου καὶ μισήσεις τὸν ἐχθρόν σου. 44 ἐγὼ δὲ λέγω ὑμῖν, ἀγαπᾶτε τοὺς ἐχθροὺς ὑμῶν καὶ προσεύχεσθε

ὑπὲρ τῶν διωκόντων ὑμᾶς· 45 ὅπως γένησθε υἱοὶ τοῦ
πατρὸς ὑμῶν τοῦ ἐν οὐρανοῖς, ὅτι τὸν ἥλιον αὐτοῦ
ἀνατέλλει ἐπὶ πονηροὺς καὶ ἀγαθοὺς καὶ βρέχει ἐπὶ
δικαίους καὶ ἀδίκους. 46 ἐὰν γὰρ ἀγαπήσητε τοὺς
ἀγαπῶντας ὑμᾶς, τίνα μισθὸν ἔχετε; οὐχὶ καὶ οἱ
τελῶναι τὸ αὐτὸ ποιοῦσιν; 47 καὶ ἐὰν ἀσπάσησθε
τοὺς ἀδελφοὺς ὑμῶν μόνον, τί περισσὸν ποιεῖτε; οὐχὶ
καὶ οἱ ἐθνικοὶ τὸ αὐτὸ ποιοῦσιν; 48 ἔσεσθε οὖν ὑμεῖς
τέλειοι ὡς ὁ πατὴρ ὑμῶν ὁ οὐράνιος τέλειός ἐστιν.

The love of our neighbour.—At first sight it seems
impossible that we should love our neighbour as ourselves,—and perhaps in the very strictest sense it is so.
Jesus was not speaking as a logician. He appealed to
the heart, and not to the head. Love would interpret
the hyperbole without nicely calculating less or more.
This particular precept was given as a summary of those
of the Ten Commandments which relate to our duty to
our neighbour, and presents a kind of standard by which
we may measure our obedience to them in detail. For
example, the commandment tells us not to steal; the
precept, "Love your neighbour as yourself," checks us
from taking an unfair advantage in making a bargain
with a neighbour,—bids us tell him if there is any
defect in the article we are selling, of which, if we were
buyers, we should have liked to be informed.

But it has been said that the precept, "Love your
neighbour as yourself," may be carried to extravagance,
and a word has been invented to express this regard for
our neighbour as opposed to regard for ourselves,—Altruism (from *alter*), as opposed to Egoism.

Altruism is best represented in its utter excess perhaps in the story of Gautama, the Buddha, offering
himself to a famishing tigress that she might satisfy her
hunger with his flesh. This we may assume to be a
legend. But daily experience might point to more ordi-

nary examples. A father for the sake of his children may deny himself all recreation, and overwork himself to such an extent as at once to cut his own life short, and to leave his children unprovided for. Or again, for the sake of an idle, dissolute brother, a man endowed with all the qualities calculated to make him a useful citizen, perhaps to make some discovery that would benefit the whole human race, overtasks his strength, and by an untimely death deprives his brother of his assistance, and the world of his genius and attainments. We may say he has left the world the example of his self-sacrifice,—but has the example been a wise or salutary one ?

The answer perhaps to this difficulty is this, that life is an art, and for the conduct of life Jesus left us not only precepts, but a wise example, and the spirit of love and wisdom. He, we know, took needful rest, and urged His disciples to do so ; and though ready to die for others, showed needful discretion, that He might not incite His enemies to slay Him prematurely.

And the spirit He has bequeathed us is the spirit of unselfishness. We are indeed to live for others ; but this implies that we must take care of our health, cultivate our talents, take needful rest and recreation, seek to prolong our lives that we may prolong our usefulness. The care for others is not necessarily unpleasant ; and if it be painful, there is a natural satisfaction in unselfish actions which softens the pain. The fact is, there is a limit to self-indulgence beyond which even the most selfish begin caring for others. Few can utterly eradicate from their nature the love of children, or friendship in some superficial form. But the Christian finds his happiness, and therefore his egoism, in altruism. He seeks to be " perfect as his heavenly Father is perfect," by making thinking and acting for others natural, so that in these he finds his happiness. But for the sake of others he husbands his resources : he does not overwork himself till he loses his buoyancy and becomes irritable; is not so lavishly generous to others as to ruin their character by making them self-ish or idle. He finds out the best means of spending for his fellows, and uses those means with the same care and discretion as though he were spending for himself.

The love of our enemies.—The difficulty of loving our enemies will be great in proportion to the cause of the enmity and the quality of our own dispositions. Superficial characters forgive, or seem to forgive, with greater ease than the more earnest. The enmity may originate from our own fault, from that of our enemy, or from a misunderstanding. It is only in the second case that a display of affection on our part is unlikely to succeed in dissipating the enmity. At the time when Jesus was preaching, such displays of love were rare. The word *rival*, from *rivus*, a stream, expressing the enmity between neighbours contending for the use of the waters of the same brook, is an indication of the natural hostility all foreigners had for one another, even when separated by very slight boundaries. The word *hostis* originally meant a stranger. Enmity to the foreigner was almost, and among very many, abso-lutely regarded as a duty. When Jesus bade His fol-lowers act in contradiction to the general sentiment of the men of His time, He knew they would suffer, and He warned them of the fact. Their conduct, so unusual, would be misunderstood, and even suspected. They were the martyrs of reform. But, on the whole, love wins — for it is at the bottom more natural than hate. For mankind recognise in one another a common humanity, and to this recognition love appeals. Jesus called on His disciples to recognise more than this common humanity—to recognise the divine in all men, even the most morose and the most degraded ; and for the sake of this divinity, and for His sake who called Himself the Son of Man and regarded all men as His brothers, He bids His disciples lay aside hate, and strive to conquer enmity by love.

LESSON VII.

St Matthew vi. 1-18.

ON ALMSGIVING, PRAYER, AND FASTING.

1 Προσέχετε [δὲ] τὴν δικαιοσύνην ὑμῶν μὴ ποιεῖν ἔμπροσθεν τῶν ἀνθρώπων πρὸς τὸ θεαθῆναι αὐτοῖς· εἰ δὲ μήγε, μισθὸν οὐκ ἔχετε παρὰ τῷ πατρὶ ὑμῶν τῷ ἐν τοῖς οὐρανοῖς.   2 Ὅταν οὖν ποιῇς ἐλεημοσύνην, μὴ σαλπίσῃς ἔμπροσθέν σου, ὥσπερ οἱ ὑποκριταὶ ποιοῦσιν ἐν ταῖς συναγωγαῖς καὶ ἐν ταῖς ῥύμαις, ὅπως δοξασθῶσιν ὑπὸ τῶν ἀνθρώπων· ἀμὴν λέγω ὑμῖν, ἀπέχουσιν τὸν μισθὸν αὐτῶν. 3 σοῦ δὲ ποιοῦντος ἐλεημοσύνην μὴ γνώτω ἡ ἀριστερά σου τί ποιεῖ ἡ δεξιά σου, 4 ὅπως ᾖ σου ἡ ἐλεημοσύνη ἐν τῷ κρυπτῷ· καὶ ὁ πατήρ σου ὁ βλέπων ἐν τῷ κρυπτῷ ἀποδώσει σοι.   5 Καὶ ὅταν προσεύχησθε, οὐκ ἔσεσθε ὡς οἱ ὑποκριταί· ὅτι φιλοῦσιν ἐν ταῖς συναγωγαῖς καὶ ἐν ταῖς γωνίαις τῶν πλατειῶν ἑστῶτες προσεύχεσθαι, ὅπως φανῶσιν τοῖς ἀνθρώποις· ἀμὴν λέγω ὑμῖν, ἀπέχουσι τὸν μισθὸν αὐτῶν. 6 σὺ δὲ ὅταν προσεύχῃ, εἴσελθε εἰς τὸ ταμεῖόν σου καὶ κλείσας τὴν θύραν σου πρόσευξαι τῷ πατρί σου τῷ ἐν τῷ κρυπτῷ· καὶ ὁ πατήρ σου ὁ βλέπων ἐν τῷ κρυπτῷ ἀποδώσει σοι· 7 Προσευχόμενοι δὲ μὴ βατταλογήσητε ὥσπερ οἱ ἐθνικοί, δοκοῦσιν γὰρ ὅτι ἐν τῇ πολυλογίᾳ αὐτῶν εἰσακουσθήσονται· 8 μὴ οὖν ὁμοιωθῆτε αὐτοῖς, οἶδεν γὰρ [ὁ θεὸς] ὁ πατὴρ

ὑμῶν ὧν χρείαν ἔχετε πρὸ τοῦ ὑμᾶς αἰτῆσαι αὐτόν.
9 Οὕτως οὖν προσεύχεσθε ὑμεῖς

Πάτερ ἡμῶν ὁ ἐν τοῖς οὐρανοῖς·
ʽΑγιασθήτω τὸ ὄνομά σου,
10 ἐλθέτω ἡ βασιλεία σου,
γενηθήτω τὸ θέλημά σου,
ὡς ἐν οὐρανῷ καὶ ἐπὶ γῆς·
11 Τὸν ἄρτον ἡμῶν τὸν ἐπιούσιον
δὸς ἡμῖν σήμερον.
12 καὶ ἄφες ἡμῖν τὰ ὀφειλήματα ἡμῶν
ὡς καὶ ἡμεῖς ἀφήκαμεν τοῖς ὀφειλέταις ἡμῶν.
13 καὶ μὴ εἰσενέγκῃς ἡμᾶς εἰς πειρασμόν,
ἀλλὰ ῥῦσαι ἡμᾶς ἀπὸ τοῦ πονηροῦ·

14 Ἐὰν γὰρ ἀφῆτε τοῖς ἀνθρώποις τὰ παραπτώματα αὐτῶν, ἀφήσει καὶ ὑμῖν ὁ πατὴρ ὑμῶν ὁ οὐράνιος· 15 ἐὰν δὲ μὴ ἀφῆτε τοῖς ἀνθρώποις τὰ παραπτώματα αὐτῶν, οὐδὲ ὁ πατὴρ ὑμῶν ἀφήσει τὰ παραπτώματα ὑμῶν.

16 ὅταν δὲ νηστεύητε, μὴ γίνεσθε ὡς οἱ ὑποκριταὶ σκυθρωποί, ἀφανίζουσιν γὰρ τὰ πρόσωπα αὐτῶν ὅπως φανῶσιν τοῖς ἀνθρώποις νηστεύοντες· ἀμὴν λέγω ὑμῖν, ἀπέχουσιν τὸν μισθὸν αὐτῶν. 17 σὺ δὲ νηστεύων ἄλειψαί σου τὴν κεφαλὴν καὶ τὸ πρόσωπόν σου νίψαι, 18 ὅπως μὴ φανῇς τοῖς ἀνθρώποις νηστεύων ἀλλὰ τῷ πατρί σου τῷ ἐν τῷ κρυφαίῳ· καὶ ὁ πατήρ σου ὁ βλέπων ἐν τῳ κρυφαίῳ ἀποδώσει σοι.

LESSON VIII.

St Matthew vi. 19-34.

ON ANXIETY FOR THE FUTURE, AND SEEKING FIRST THE KINGDOM OF GOD.

19 Μὴ θησαυρίζετε ὑμῖν θησαυροὺς ἐπὶ τῆς γῆς, ὅπου σὴς καὶ βρῶσις ἀφανίζει, καὶ ὅπου κλέπται διορύσσουσιν καὶ κλέπτουσιν· 20 θησαυρίζετε δὲ ὑμῖν θησαυροὺς ἐν οὐρανῷ, ὅπου οὔτε σὴς οὔτε βρῶσις ἀφανίζει, καὶ ὅπου κλέπται οὐ διορύσσουσιν οὐδὲ κλέπτουσιν. 21 ὅπου γάρ ἐστιν ὁ θησαυρός σου, ἐκεῖ ἔσται [καὶ] ἡ καρδία σου. 22 Ὁ λύχνος τοῦ σώματός ἐστιν ὁ ὀφθαλμός. ἐὰν οὖν ᾖ ὁ ὀφθαλμός σου ἁπλοῦς, ὅλον τὸ σῶμά σου φωτεινὸν ἔσται· 23 ἐὰν δὲ ὁ ὀφθαλμός σου πονηρὸς ᾖ, ὅλον τὸ σῶμά σου σκοτεινὸν ἔσται. εἰ οὖν τὸ φῶς τὸ ἐν σοὶ σκότος ἐστίν, τὸ σκότος πόσον. 24 Οὐδεὶς δύναται δυσὶ κυρίοις δουλεύειν· ἢ γὰρ τὸν ἕνα μισήσει καὶ τὸν ἕτερον ἀγαπήσει, ἢ ἑνὸς ἀνθέξεται καὶ τοῦ ἑτέρου καταφρονήσει. οὐ δύνασθε θεῷ δουλεύειν καὶ μαμωνᾷ 25 Διὰ τοῦτο λέγω ὑμῖν, μὴ μεριμνᾶτε τῇ ψυχῇ ὑμῶν τί φάγητε, μηδὲ τῷ σώματι ὑμῶν τί ἐνδύσησθε. οὐχὶ ἡ ψυχὴ πλεῖόν ἐστιν τῆς τροφῆς καὶ τὸ σῶμα τοῦ ἐνδύματος; 26 ἐμβλέψατε εἰς τὰ πετεινὰ τοῦ οὐρανοῦ, ὅτι οὐ σπείρουσιν οὐδὲ θερίζουσιν οὐδὲ συνάγουσιν εἰς ἀποθήκας, καὶ ὁ πατὴρ ὑμῶν ὁ οὐράνιος τρέφει αὐτά· οὐχ ὑμεῖς μᾶλλον διαφέρετε αὐτῶν;

27 τίς δὲ ἐξ ὑμῶν μεριμνῶν δύναται προσθεῖναι ἐπὶ τὴν ἡλικίαν αὐτοῦ πῆχυν ἕνα; 28 καὶ περὶ ἐνδύματος τί μεριμνᾶτε; καταμάθετε τὰ κρίνα τοῦ ἀγροῦ πῶς αὐξάνουσιν· οὐ κοπιῶσιν οὐδὲ νήθουσιν. 29 λέγω δὲ ὑμῖν ὅτι οὐδὲ Σολομὼν ἐν πάσῃ τῇ δόξῃ αὐτοῦ περιεβάλετο ὡς ἓν τούτων. 30 εἰ δὲ τὸν χόρτον τοῦ ἀγροῦ σήμερον ὄντα καὶ αὔριον εἰς κλίβανον βαλλόμενον ὁ θεὸς οὕτως ἀμφιέννυσιν, οὐ πολλῷ μᾶλλον ὑμᾶς ὀλιγόπιστοι; 31 μὴ οὖν μεριμνήσητε λέγοντες· τί φάγωμεν ἢ τί πίωμεν ἢ τί περιβαλώμεθα; 32 πάντα γὰρ ταῦτα τὰ ἔθνη ἐπιζητοῦσιν· οἶδεν γὰρ ὁ πατὴρ ὑμῶν ὁ οὐράνιος ὅτι χρῄζετε τούτων ἁπάντων. 33 ζητεῖτε δὲ πρῶτον τὴν βασιλείαν καὶ τὴν δικαιοσύνην αὐτοῦ, καὶ ταῦτα πάντα προστεθήσεται ὑμῖν· 34 μὴ οὖν μεριμνήσητε εἰς τὴν αὔριον· ἡ γὰρ αὔριον μεριμνήσει ἑαυτῆς. ἀρκετὸν τῇ ἡμέρᾳ ἡ κακία αὐτῆς.

What does Jesus mean when He tells us not to be anxious about the morrow, and not to be anxious about our life, and to take an example from the careless freedom of the birds, and comfort from the unbought apparel of the lilies? Are we to sit idle and expect the ravens to come and feed us? or to retire to the desert, into caves, or into monasteries, and give ourselves up to contemplation and to living on the most frugal fare, like the old hermits and monks? At first sight His words seem romancing, or at least useless for the busy nineteenth century, however they may have been adapted for the lives of the Galilean peasants. We are tempted to put them aside as unintelligible, or as at least only to be acted upon by people who have not to work for their daily bread, and can afford to devote themselves to the luxury of a religious life.

. Some would translate the phrase μὴ μεριμνᾶτε, not " be not anxious," as our revised version does, but " be not over anxious"; or speak of "toilsome anxiety" and "carking care." The old version was, "Take no thought for the morrow," the word "thought" having a stronger meaning in the literature of the period when that translation was made than it has now. Thus Bishop Ridley said, "No person of any honesty, without thinking, could abide to hear the lie spoken by a most vile varlet"; and Shakespeare sums up the powerlessness of Antony to foil the conspiracy for the assassination of Cæsar in these words—

> " If he love Cæsar, all that he can do
> Is to himself take thought, and die for Cæsar."

Again, Bacon speaks of a man as "dying of thought [*i.e.*, of over-anxiety] and anguish."

But neither in classic nor in Hellenistic Greek do μεριμνάω and μέριμνα always imply anxious thought. In Œd. Tyr., 1124, Œdipus asks the shepherd what his employment under King Laius had been,—ἔργον μεριμνῶν ποῖον ἢ βίον τίνα;—*i.e.*, "caring for," or "following what work or what manner of life?" Again, Pindar describes the enthusiasm for athletic renown as κρέσσονα πλούτου μέριμναν,—"a care better than the care for riches."

The "care concerning this world" (Matt. xiii. 22) and the "cares of this life" (Luke xxi. 34) signify nothing more than ordinary worldly carefulness (cf. 1 Cor. xii. 25; Phil. ii. 20).

Since, then, μεριμνάω may mean nothing more than "providence of every kind," we must search for Jesus' meaning in the context. Now in what *precedes*, He bids His disciples "look upon the birds of heaven, that they sow not, neither do they reap, nor gather into barns, and your heavenly Father feedeth them."

But the birds are not idle in quest of food or of shelter; indeed they are almost incessantly occupied in providing themselves with either one or the other. Yet we cannot apply the word $\mu\epsilon\rho\iota\mu\nu\acute{\alpha}\omega$ to them, for they do not act from intelligent foresight, but from instinct; neither are there any higher thoughts or occupations from which they are distracted by the gratification of their appetites.

If, therefore, we imitate the birds, we shall not neglect provision for our animal wants, nor overlook the change of the seasons as affecting them; yet while we *provide for* the morrow, we shall *take no thought for* the morrow. As the food of the birds is easily attainable because it is simple, so if we please may ours be. It is the procuring of the luxuries rather than of the necessaries of life that leads to anxiety. If we desire better things than luxuries, we shall avoid this anxiety. Instinct limits the desires of the birds: it is left to our will to limit ours.

Again, the birds are free from anxiety because they act unconsciously: what instinct does for them, habit may do for us. If we limit our desires, as far as material wants are concerned, to what can be gained by routine work, we may leave ourselves time and energy for nobler pursuits than the satisfaction of them. The rule of Jesus then is this—" Seek ye your physical good unconsciously, by strictness of habit: seek ye spiritual good with full consciousness and intensity of will." [1]

But this brings us to what *follows in* the context, " Seek first the kingdom of God."

This does not mean we are to abandon all worldly pursuits. The kingdom of God is not a business set up in rivalry with worldly business, but a divine law regulating, and a divine temper pervading, the pursuits of worldly business. St Paul defines the Christian's duty

---

[1] J. Martineau, to whom, and to the late Professor Mozeley, many of the thoughts in this essay are due.

thus—" Not slothful in business, fervent in spirit, serving the Lord." He who seeks after " what he shall eat and what he shall drink," is one whose chief conscious aim is to get such things. He who seeks first the kingdom of God, is one whose chief conscious aim is not to get them unworthily. We must be more concerned with what we are than with what we get.

And Jesus encourages us to prefer the principles of the kingdom of God to our worldly interests by the thought that our heavenly Father cares for us. Not, indeed, that honesty is always the best policy in this world, but because it brings most happiness, since it is in harmony with the laws of the universe, of which the Maker is righteous and loving. By being just we not only promote our own happiness by keeping a clear conscience, but the happiness of all around us also,—for injustice begets injustice, and therefore unhappiness. Nay, acts of injustice not only hinder the wrong-doer himself from attaining the kingdom, but impede the formation of the renewed society in which the precepts of Jesus shall be uniformly carried out, and the promise, " All these things shall be added unto you," shall be fulfilled without even an apparent exception.

We shall obey the precept, therefore, *first*, if when we have to choose between our worldly interests and our spiritual character, we prefer the latter; *secondly*, by being industrious and prudent without being anxious or fussy.

There are plenty of opportunities in school life for practising ourselves in this obedience. To give one example that will come home to boys : marks in class are to them what coin is to grown-up people, the test and outward sign of success; and they present as many opportunities for cheating as money does. Now a boy seeks first the kingdom of God when he prefers apparent failure to cheating, even though, as may happen, his schoolfellows are winning marks unfairly without detection. The temptation is strong to provide for the morrow first, and the kingdom of God second : that is to say, to follow the multitude to do evil in order to ensure success at the end of the term. Jesus warns us against succumbing to this temptation. Even from a worldly point of view, to yield is unwise. For the sure sign of success is not the marks a boy gets, but the knowledge and power of grappling with problems he has attained. But his moral and spiritual nature are more important parts of him than his intellectual. It will be better for him, hard as it may seem, to lose his place in class than to train himself in deceit, and perhaps form a deceitful character for the rest of his life. Such trials are part of his education. He finds no temptations at school which he will not find in the world for which school is training him. In all departments of life he will find men apparently the losers— because they prefer their integrity of character to success, because they " seek first the kingdom of God."

Then as to the other point of view from which we may regard the phrase, " Be not anxious for the morrow." It warns us against that nervousness and fussiness in our ordinary occupations which is an impediment to our own work and that of others. When we have any work to do, or danger to face, it bids us take all necessary preparation, and then check our minds from dwelling uselessly on the subject.

Jesus Himself sets us an example of this composure, this restraining of the natural feelings of anxiety or terror. He foresaw that the Jews would slay Him, and because He was holy, and gentle, and loving, not rude and coarse, the thought of pain and death, and, above all, of facing the hatred and scorn of the rough and violent, was very terrible to Him. This partly explains the mysterious scene of the agony in the garden at

Gethsemane.   But He did not allow this dread and terror to hinder Him from calmly pursuing His course, and making all necessary preparations for the future. That, however, He had a struggle for fortitude we can see from the remarkable passage in Mark x. 32, where we are told that as the disciples were going up to Jerusalem, Jesus went before them "like a dauntless leader;" and that as He meditated on the certainty of the death that awaited Him at the end of His journey some were amazed, and others, following at a distance, were afraid, so striking was His bearing in its sorrow and resolution. And so completely was He master of His feelings, so long as action was necessary, that the agony at Gethsemane was preceded by the long calm conversations contained in John xii.-xvii., in which He prepared His disciples for the approaching time when they would be left to propagate His religion without Him.

Such is the example of calmness conquering dread by which Jesus teaches us not to be anxious about the morrow which brings death.   There is another morrow, however, about which men may reasonably be still more anxious, and that is the morrow of mystery, the morrow after death.   Here, too, Jesus sets us an example of trust in God's providence conquering doubt and dread. In the midst of the physical agonies and the spiritual terrors of the crucifixion He was heard to cry, "My God, my God, why hast Thou forsaken me?"   Whatever may be the full depth of meaning of these mysterious words, they at least imply that for a moment the horror of death and the sense of desolation had overcome the spirit of Jesus, as they may those of all men as they walk alone the last journey.

It has been thought that Jesus, when He uttered these words, had in His mind all the words of the Psalm (xxii.), though He had strength to utter only the first verse. Now the Psalm rises from sadness to exultation, and continues at last thus : " I will declare Thy name unto my brethren : in the midst of the congregation will I praise Thee. . . . For He hath not despised nor abhorred the affliction of the afflicted; neither hath He hid His face from him, but when he cried unto Him, He heard." But, however this may be, Jesus is at last conqueror over the doubt and despair of imminent death, and ends His life with the same trust in His heavenly Father with which He sought to inspire His followers, battling down the anxiety for the morrow after death in His last words, " Father, into Thy hands I commend my spirit."

LESSON IX.

St Matthew vii. 1-14.

FALSE JUDGMENT AND PRAYER.

1 Μὴ κρίνετε, ἵνα μὴ κριθῆτε· 2 ἐν ᾧ γὰρ κρίματι κρίνετε κριθήσεσθε, καὶ ἐν ᾧ μέτρῳ μετρεῖτε μετρηθήσεται ὑμῖν. 3 τί δὲ βλέπεις τὸ κάρφος τὸ ἐν τῷ ὀφθαλμῷ τοῦ ἀδελφοῦ σου, τὴν δὲ ἐν τῷ σῷ ὀφθαλμῷ δοκὸν οὐ κατανοεῖς; 4 ἢ πῶς ἐρεῖς τῷ ἀδελφῷ σου Ἄφες ἐκβάλω τὸ κάρφος ἐκ τοῦ ὀφθαλμοῦ σου, καὶ ἰδοὺ ἡ δοκὸς ἐν τῷ ὀφθαλμῷ σοῦ; 5 ὑποκριτά, ἔκβαλε πρῶτον ἐκ τοῦ ὀφθαλμοῦ σου τὴν δοκόν, καὶ τότε διαβλέψεις ἐκβαλεῖν τὸ κάρφος ἐκ τοῦ ὀφθαλμοῦ τοῦ ἀδελφοῦ σου. 6 Μὴ δῶτε τὸ ἅγιον τοῖς κυσίν, μηδὲ βάλητε τοὺς μαργαρίτας ὑμῶν ἔμπροσθεν τῶν χοίρων, μή ποτε καταπατήσουσιν αὐτοὺς ἐν τοῖς ποσὶν αὐτῶν καὶ στραφέντες ῥήξωσιν ὑμᾶς. 7 Αἰτεῖτε, καὶ δοθήσεται ὑμῖν· ζητεῖτε, καὶ εὑρήσετε· κρούετε, καὶ ἀνοιγήσεται ὑμῖν. 8 πᾶς γὰρ ὁ αἰτῶν λαμβάνει καὶ ὁ ζητῶν εὑρίσκει καὶ τῷ κρούοντι ἀνοιγήσεται. 9 ἢ τίς ἐξ ὑμῶν ἄνθρωπος, ὃν αἰτήσει ὁ υἱὸς αὐτοῦ ἄρτον—μὴ λίθον ἐπιδώσει αὐτῷ; 10 ἢ καὶ ἰχθὺν αἰτήσει—μὴ ὄφιν ἐπιδώσει αὐτῷ; 11 εἰ οὖν ὑμεῖς πονηροὶ ὄντες οἴδατε δόματα ἀγαθὰ διδόναι τοῖς τέκνοις ὑμῶν, πόσῳ μᾶλλον ὁ πατὴρ ὑμῶν ὁ ἐν τοῖς οὐρανοῖς δώσει ἀγαθὰ τοῖς αἰτοῦσιν αὐτόν; 12 Πάντα οὖν ὅσα ἐὰν θέλητε ἵνα ποιῶσιν ὑμῖν οἱ ἄνθ-

ρωποι, οὕτως καὶ ὑμεῖς ποιεῖτε αὐτοῖς· οὗτος γάρ
ἐστιν ὁ νόμος καὶ οἱ προφῆται.

13 Εἰσέλθετε διὰ τῆς στενῆς πύλης· ὅτι πλατεῖα
καὶ εὐρύχωρος ἡ ὁδὸς ἡ ἀπάγουσα εἰς τὴν ἀπώλειαν,
καὶ πολλοί εἰσιν οἱ εἰσερχόμενοι δι' αὐτῆς· 14 ὅτι
στενὴ ἡ πύλη καὶ τεθλιμμένη ἡ ὁδὸς ἡ ἀπάγουσα εἰς
τὴν ζωήν, καὶ ὀλίγοι εἰσὶν οἱ εὑρίσκοντες αὐτήν.

ON PRAYER.

Jesus in His sayings on Prayer breathes the same
hopeful spirit as in His sayings on Nature. In spite of
the cruelties that pervade the external universe and the
difficulties connected with its government, He had drawn
from it lessons of hope and cheerfulness while He argued
that the same heavenly Father who provided for the food
of the birds and the beautiful robes of the flowers would
provide also for the food and clothing of man under
whose feet birds and flowers were put in subjection.
In a similar spirit He bids man take courage from the
example of earthly fathers towards their children to
believe that the heavenly Father will listen with kindly
wisdom to His children's prayers.

When Jesus tells His hearers to " ask and it shall
be given them," we may be quite sure they would not
suppose that He meant to tell them that every prayer
of each hearer could be granted on every occasion,
or that by their prayers they could stay the course
of the sun. The Jews of His time were taught by the
Scribes to regard God as a jealous Being who must be
served by the punctilious devotion of every minute
to the observance of some ritual in connection with
His law. The ordinary people could not, from their
circumstances, pay homage to God in this way ; and
so they were in danger of regarding Him as a hard
taskmaster whom they could not please, and the idea

of whom filled them with despair. The words of Jesus were intended to fill them with new hope, so that they might feel they could pour out their inmost thoughts and wishes to God, and pursue their daily avocations cheerfully as under His eye and protection. In all ages of the world since, and among all classes of men, the words of Jesus have had this effect, and men and women on sea and on land, in trouble and in danger, and in the ordinary course of their daily life, have poured out their thoughts to the heavenly Father with these words of Jesus in their hearts. Yet they have not taken the words literally, but in the spirit of the context, and of the words of Jesus Himself when in the garden of Gethsemane He prayed, "O my Father, if it be possible, let this cup pass from me : nevertheless not as I will, but as Thou wilt" (Matt. xxvi. 39).

The words in the 11th verse, $\dot{a}\gamma a\theta\dot{a}$, may be rendered "wholesome" gifts, as opposed to the unwholesome gifts of the stone and the serpent mentioned above. The words are still further explained in Luke xi. 13 as "the Holy Spirit;"[1] and if we look at the clauses of the Lord's Prayer we shall see that one only, that for "daily bread," or as it should, perhaps, be rendered, "to-morrow's bread," or "bread enough for our sustenance," refers to material advantages.

Prayer, so far as it means petition, may refer either to material or to spiritual blessings—that is, its objects may be things that affect either our physical or our spiritual life. On the one hand, bread, money, friends, health, a change in the weather, and so on; on the other hand, an increase of humility, patience, hope, love, and so on : or we may pray for the former class for the sake of the latter,—for health, because ill health affects our temper; for money, because poverty tempts us to dishonesty; for

---

[1] There is, however, a well-supported reading, $\dot{a}\gamma a\theta\dot{o}\nu$ $\delta\dot{o}\mu a$, in this passage.

friends, because our acquaintances degrade our character instead of elevating it.

But there are certain things we do not ask of God, because we do not expect to obtain them. We do not pray that the sun may not rise, or that the ground may not be hard, or that we may never die,—because we believe that on such matters the will of God is fixed. Probably, too, we pray for fewer things of a material character as we grow older, partly because we come to believe that God's will is fixed on a larger number of such matters, partly because our childish notions of God become enlarged as we learn more of His greatness, from our increasing knowledge of the vastness of the universe. But we need not suppose that our childish prayers offended the majesty of our heavenly Father. Little children ask of their earthly fathers things that cannot or ought not to be given them; but their earthly fathers are not offended at their innocent requests, and sometimes leave them to learn by experience the reasons why they cannot be granted.

In a similar way, as the world advances in knowledge people are learning to limit the things they may legitimately ask of their heavenly Father, and to see that there are many things it is better they should seek to gain by the use of the spirit of wisdom and knowledge which He has bestowed on them, than by asking Him to give them. Thus men will not now pray that a disease may be healed which can certainly be cured by a simple remedy; or that a friend a thousand miles away may be moved to come at once to help them, when the telegraph can send a message in an hour; or that a calm may give place to a wind when they are in a steam-vessel, whose engines only await orders to get to work.

Jesus sought to make men feel that they lived constantly in the presence of the heavenly Father, and that He cares for all His children. As men realise this presence more and more, their prayers naturally become less selfish, and are less concerned with material matters. They feel that not only they, but all the family of the human race, are in the presence of the Father, and expressing their thoughts and desires to Him. If, therefore, they pray for material blessings, they will do so always with the reservation that their own receiving them be not injurious to others, and this will put a limit on their prayers. They will feel that to pray for results that may benefit themselves at the expense of their neighbours is unworthy; that to pray for results that can easily be secured by action is trifling. They will be afraid and ashamed to pray to the holy and omnipotent Father for anything that is mean and base.

Again, though it is necessary, on account of our weakness, to have fixed periods for prayer, what we have to aim at is to live so constantly in the presence of God, that all our time is one long prayer, because we are never absent from the thought of Him,—and this is probably what St Paul meant when he speaks of "praying without ceasing" (1 Thess. v. 17). And again, though our weakness makes it necessary that we should put our desires into the form of words when addressing God, yet the more we habituate ourselves to feel His presence the less this will be necessary: all our thoughts will become more and more prayers to God, just as children can express their feelings to their parents by their looks, without the need of words.

Again, as our views of prayer become ennobled, we shall always remember when we are praying that all good men everywhere are doing so too, and this will make us feel more fraternally towards our brother-men, who have a common Father with us; and thus, as Tennyson says—

> "The whole round earth is every way
>   Bound by gold chains about the feet of God."

The prayers of all men praying for themselves and their brothers are breathed up to God, and return from Him to spread peace and love on the earth.

Lastly, we must remember that the word "prayer" is not restricted in the Bible to petitioning, but is used also of thanksgiving and praise, both of which are expressions natural to children who are happy in the love of their Father, and in the bounties and beautiful things He provides them.

LESSON X.

St Matthew vii. 15-29.

THE WARNING AGAINST FALSE PROPHETS—THE WISE AND FOOLISH BUILDER—THE TEACHING OF JESUS IN RELATION TO NATURE.

15 Προσέχετε ἀπὸ τῶν ψευδοπροφητῶν, οἵτινες ἔρχονται πρὸς ὑμᾶς ἐν ἐνδύμασι προβάτων, ἔσωθεν δέ εἰσιν λύκοι ἅρπαγες. 16 ἀπὸ τῶν καρπῶν αὐτῶν ἐπιγνώσεσθε αὐτούς· μήτι συλλέγουσιν ἀπὸ ἀκανθῶν σταφυλὰς ἢ ἀπὸ τριβόλων σῦκα; 17 οὕτω πᾶν δένδρον ἀγαθὸν καρποὺς καλοὺς ποιεῖ, τὸ δὲ σαπρὸν δένδρον καρποὺς πονηροὺς ποιεῖ· 18 οὐ δύναται δένδρον ἀγαθὸν καρποὺς πονηροὺς ἐνεγκεῖν, οὐδὲ δένδρον σαπρὸν καρποὺς καλοὺς ποιεῖν. 19 πᾶν δένδρον μὴ ποιοῦν καρπὸν καλὸν ἐκκόπτεται καὶ εἰς πῦρ βάλλεται. 20 ἄραγε ἀπὸ τῶν καρπῶν αὐτῶν ἐπιγνώσεσθε αὐτούς. 21 Οὐ πᾶς ὁ λέγων μοι, Κύριε, κύριε, εἰσελεύσεται εἰς τὴν βασιλείαν τῶν οὐρανῶν, ἀλλ' ὁ ποιῶν τὸ θέλημα τοῦ πατρός μου τοῦ ἐν τοῖς οὐρανοῖς· 22 πολλοὶ ἐροῦσίν μοι ἐν ἐκείνῃ τῇ ἡμέρᾳ, Κύριε, κύριε, οὐ τῷ σῷ ὀνόματι ἐπροφητεύσαμεν, καὶ τῷ σῷ ὀνόματι δαιμόνια ἐξεβάλομεν, καὶ τῷ σῷ ὀνόματι δυνάμεις πολλὰς ἐποιήσαμεν; 23 καὶ τότε ὁμολογήσω αὐτοῖς ὅτι Οὐδέποτε ἔγνων ὑμᾶς· ἀποχωρεῖτε ἀπ' ἐμοῦ οἱ ἐργαζόμενοι τὴν ἀνομίαν.

24 Πᾶς οὖν ὅστις ἀκούει μου τοὺς λόγους [τούτους] καὶ ποιεῖ αὐτούς, ὁμοιωθήσεται ἀνδρὶ φρονίμῳ, ὅστις ᾠκοδόμησεν αὐτοῦ τὴν οἰκίαν ἐπὶ τὴν πέτραν. 25 καὶ κατέβη ἡ βροχὴ καὶ ἦλθον οἱ ποταμοὶ καὶ ἔπνευσαν οἱ ἄνεμοι καὶ προσέπεσον τῇ οἰκίᾳ ἐκείνῃ, καὶ οὐκ ἔπεσεν, τεθεμελίωτο γὰρ ἐπὶ τὴν πέτραν. 26 Καὶ πᾶς ὁ ἀκούων μου τοὺς λόγους τούτους καὶ μὴ ποιῶν αὐτοὺς ὁμοιωθήσεται ἀνδρὶ μωρῷ, ὅστις ᾠκοδόμησεν αὐτοῦ τὴν οἰκίαν ἐπὶ τὴν ἄμμον. 27 καὶ κατέβη ἡ βροχὴ καὶ ἦλθον οἱ ποταμοὶ καὶ ἔπνευσαν οἱ ἄνεμοι καὶ προσέκοψαν τῇ οἰκίᾳ ἐκείνῃ, καὶ ἔπεσεν, καὶ ἦν ἡ πτῶσις αὐτῆς μεγάλη.

28 Καὶ ἐγένετο ὅτε ἐτέλεσεν ὁ Ἰησοῦς τους λογους τούτους, ἐξεπλήσσοντο οἱ ὄχλοι ἐπὶ τῇ διδαχῇ αὐτοῦ· 29 ἦν γὰρ διδάσκων αὐτοὺς ὡς ἐξουσίαν ἔχων καὶ οὐχ ὡς οἱ γραμματεῖς αὐτῶν.

THE TEACHING OF JESUS IN RELATION TO NATURE.

The word *Nature* has a variety of meanings more or less extensive. In its widest sense it is a collective name for all facts and processes, actual and possible. In another sense it is opposed to art, and the natural to the artificial, and means, not everything which happens, but only what takes place without the voluntary and intentional agency of man. Again, it is often personified and spoken of as if it had some real existence. If we analyse what we mean by this personification, we shall find it is a convenient and picturesque way of speaking of the universe outside ourselves. And this universe we are in the habit of regarding from two points of view: we look upon it either in the light of cause and effect, and apply our reason to investigate the laws by which it is controlled ; and this investigation we call physical science, and often, but improperly, Science : or else we look upon the universe as a thing of beauty, and as beautiful in its details, and we find our emotions touched by it, and are awestruck, or admire, or are pensive, or glad at its sights and sounds, and seek carefully and faithfully to reproduce what we see, and this reproduction we call Art. Then, again, since we believe God created the earth, we think by our investigations and observations we learn something of His nature—that He loves order, that He is grand, that He is infinite; and we speak of Him in terms borrowed from His works. So Milton makes Adam say—

> " These are Thy glorious works, Parent of good,
> Almighty ! Thine this universal frame
> Thus wondrous fair : Thyself how wondrous then ! "

This being the case, we are naturally led to ask, What did Jesus think and teach about nature ? How did His teaching differ from that of those who preceded Him ? And what influence has it had on the thoughts of men since ?

Now if we turn to the Old Testament, we shall find several psalms devoted to the subject of the universe outside ourselves : we shall find many references to the subject in the prophets, and a large portion of the Book of Job given up to a description of its wonders as displaying the greatness of the Creator.

Thus the 29th Psalm contains the praise of Jehovah in the storm ; the 19th, the praise of Jehovah in the firmament and in the law ; the 104th, which has been called the natural history of a day, the praise of Jehovah as the almighty Creator of the world. The 26th chapter of the Book of Job, after an animated description of some of the wonders of the universe, ends thus :[1] " Lo, these are the edges of His way, and how slight a whisper hath been heard of Him ! but the thunder of His power who can understand ? "

[1] After an amended version by Mr Cox.

The attributes of God alluded to are His glory, His majesty, His wisdom, and, incidentally, His goodness. The spirit in which the Psalmist speaks of natural objects is that of joy and praise. He delights in the thunderstorm, and in the calm bright sky, because they exhibit the glory of the God of Israel; he joys in his God because His works are manifold, and all made in wisdom : earth and sea are full of His riches.

God seemed so near to the ancient Israelite that he expressed no fear at the most awful phenomena of nature—only awe of God, whose immediate presence he recognised in them.

If now we turn to the teaching of Jesus, we shall find that His views of nature are pervaded by hope, and love, and tenderness. Everything in nature tells Him something of the heavenly Father. He has a "quiet eye" for every object, and draws His teaching from the sights around Him. It has been said[1] that had He lived in England, His imagery would have been our rural cottages and the alleys of our towns, the redbreast, the dog-rose, and bramble—as in Galilee they were the rock and sand built houses, the ravens, and the lilies of the field. He moved amid the sights and sounds of nature as if in His Father's home, and in them all He saw tokens of His Father's love, and He sought to make men more loving and hopeful by the teachings He drew from them. He made the earth a picture-book illustrating the love and goodness of God. The birds of the air and the grass of the field living all careless beneath the fostering hand of God, told that the same God would provide for the wants of man; the sunshine and the rain enjoyed by the good and wicked alike, taught men to love their enemies as well as their friends; the shepherd going in quest of the lost sheep portrayed the Father's

---

[1] Harriet Martineau's Eastern Life.

love for the erring sinner; the maternal love of the hen, His own ardour to save His people.

It is clear from His recorded sayings that He delighted in the beauties of nature, and looked on her operations as revealing something of the Father's attributes.

It is true there is a darker side of nature on which He does not dwell—for there are cruelties as well as kindnesses in nature. There are hurricanes and earthquakes, poisonous reptiles and herbs, and parasites that prey upon and destroy animal life. In a word, there is the mystery of pain in the world. We can no more deny that nature is cruel than that she is bountiful and beautiful; and we cannot fathom the mystery of her cruelty. But with regard to non-human nature, we may choose to adopt nobler or baser thoughts and actions, as we can with regard to men. Jesus taught us to think the best we can of the latter, and to strive gently to rectify what is evil. So with regard to the external world, we may regard it with despair and moroseness or with hope and love. Hope and love was Jesus' feeling towards it; and hope and love have been the thoughts of the noblest of His disciples. Where she is cruel they have sought to soften her cruelty; and they have striven faithfully to observe and understand her beauty. Her cruelty may be softened by the study of her laws, —that is the work of science; the appreciation of her beauties leads to poetry and art. By the one pursuit the Christian is worshipping the heavenly Father, by studying the laws by which He works; by the other he is worshipping Him by reverently admiring their result, —and this last is the most appropriate and innocent recreation for the Christian to pursue.

If we seek for illustrations of the Christian way of regarding nature, perhaps the most striking imitation of the method of Jesus is that exhibited by St Francis d'Assisi, who was born in the year 1182. So filled was he with love towards God and all His creatures, that it was his habit to call the latter his brothers and sisters. To express this idea he wrote a poem, one of the earliest in the Italian tongue, called sometimes the "Song of the Sun," sometimes the "Song of the Creatures," which has been translated as follows :—

" Praised be the Lord my God
  By Messer Sun, my brother, above all,
  Who by his rays lights us and lights the day—
  Radiant is she, with his great splendour stored,
       Thy glory, Lord, confessing.
  By sister Moon and Stars my Lord is praised,
  Where clear and fair they in the heavens are raised.
  By brother Wind, my Lord, Thy praise is said,
  By air and clouds and the blue sky o'erhead,
  By which Thy creatures all are kept and fed.
  By one most humble, useful, precious, chaste,
  By sister Water, O my Lord, Thou art praised.
       And praisèd is my Lord
  By brother Fire—he who lights up the night ;
  Jocund, robust is he, and strong and bright.
  Praisèd art Thou, my Lord, by Mother Earth—
  Thou who sustainest her and governest,
  And to her flowers, fruit, herbs, dost colour give and birth."

This song gives expression to the idea that the universe is man's home, and all its phenomena the offspring of the same heavenly Father as man, but the expression is vague and broad. It was not till comparatively modern times that the idea received fuller development in the writings of Rousseau, Goethe, Schiller, Chateaubriand, Coleridge, Shelley, and Byron, till at last it found its prophets in Wordsworth the poet, Turner the painter, and Ruskin the critic.

Wordsworth may fairly be taken as the best exponent of the noblest views that a Christian can take of nature, though in some respects we must regard his theories as matters of speculation. Thus he seems to believe that the souls of children existed, before they entered their bodies, in a world superior to ours, and that the sights and sounds of the universe remind them in their purest hours of those past glories: that, for instance, a rainbow, a cuckoo's cry, or a sunset of extraordinary beauty, will renew for the child the sense of vision and nearness to the spiritual world from which he has recently come.

But apart from this speculation, Wordsworth has represented nature as especially adapted for man, and man for nature. Nature, he declared, sympathises with man and solemnises him, and man's spirit is adapted to sympathise with and be influenced in its moods by nature.

Pope and the men of his time had, for their amusement, described natural scenes, but they had done so carelessly, without faithful or accurate study, making even the flowers of different seasons to bloom together, and birds of different seasons to sing together. Scott and others took a deeper view of the poet's work, and dutifully and accurately studied the objects of nature before they attempted to describe them. Wordsworth did this, and did it more intensely; but he did more. He regarded every scene, almost every object, as having a *genius loci*, and as capable of influencing, temporarily or permanently, the spirit of the gazer. Nature filled him with happiness, and therefore with love to, and faith in, God the Creator. He lived constantly amid some of the most beautiful scenery—not, indeed, the most sublime or the grandest, but the varied scenery of the English Lake country. He lived among the mountains as in the home of his heavenly Father, all whose works were worthy of reverent study, and taught him something of his Father's attributes—His sternness and the inflexibility of His laws, as well as His glories and His love.

The most appropriate passage in illustration to quote

from his works for the purposes of this book is the following, in which are described the feelings of a boy towards nature, at first purely animal delight, but succeeded almost unconsciously by a deep and abiding sentiment :—

" There was a boy ; ye knew him well, ye cliffs
   And islands of Winander ! Many a time,
   At evening, when the earliest stars began
   To move along the edges of the hills,
   Rising or setting, would he stand alone,
   Beneath the trees, or by the glimmering lake ;
   And there, with fingers interwoven, both hands
   Pressed closely palm to palm and to his mouth
   Uplifted, he, as through an instrument,
   Blew mimic hootings to the silent owls,
   That they might answer him.   And they would shout
   Across the watery vale, and shout again,
   Responsive to his call,—with quivering peals,
   And long halloos, and screams, and echoes loud
   Redoubled and redoubled ; concourse wild
   Of mirth and jocund din ! *And, when it chanced*
   That pauses of deep silence mocked his skill,
   Then, sometimes, in that silence, while he hung
   Listening, a gentle shock of mild surprise
   Has carried far into his heart the voice
   Of mountain torrents ; or the visible scene
   Would enter unawares into his mind
   With all its solemn imagery, its rocks,
   Its woods, and that uncertain heaven, received
   Into the bosom of the steady lake."

The despondency caused by the darker view of human nature has been expressed in " In Memoriam," stanzas liv., lv. After alluding to "the cloven worm," and " the moth with vain desire, shrivelled in a fruitless fire," the poet concludes with this expression of hopefulness, all the grander because the grounds for despondency are fully recognised :—

" The wish, that of the living whole
No life may fail beyond the grave,
Derives it not from what we have
The likest God within the soul ?

Are God and Nature then at strife
That Nature lends such evil dreams
So careful of the type she seems,
So careless of the single life ;

That I, considering everywhere
Her secret meaning in her deeds,
And finding that of fifty seeds
She often brings but one to bear,

I falter where I firmly trod,
And falling with my weight of cares
Upon the great world's altar stairs
That slope through darkness up to God,

I stretch lame hands of faith, and grope,
And gather dust and chaff, and call
To what I feel is Lord of all,
And faintly trust the larger hope."

If, then, we sum up the result of Jesus' teaching on His noblest disciples so far, we shall find—(1) That they regard nature as revealing God, indeed, but this revelation as attended with great difficulties, because nature often seems both cruel and wasteful.   Nevertheless, the glories as well as the beneficence of nature have led them to hope and trust in spite of these difficulties.   (2) That they regard the faithful study of the beauties of nature as the most pure and purifying recreation for a Christian.   (3) That they regard the beauties of nature as a means God has of speaking with man, and consider that the spirit of man has been so constituted that he is ready to listen to this speech, so that all men have always been affected by the same emotions, whether awe, solemnity, love, joy, peace, or hope, by the same features of nature everywhere.

Lastly, there is another speculation which can only just be alluded to here, and that is this, that all the glories of earth are but types or shadows of the glories of heaven, and were constituted to be so—a thought put into the lips of an angel by Milton :—

> " What if earth
> Be but the shadow of heaven, and things therein
> Each to other like, more than on earth is thought ?"

LESSON XI.

THE SCENE OF JESUS' MINISTRY—THE LAKE OF GALILEE AND ITS TOWNS.

Capernaum. — In Judæa, Jesus' ministry was hindered by the influence and prejudices of the Scribes and Pharisees. The chief part of His time was spent in Galilee, and He took up His residence at Capernaum. Nazareth, His native town, was in too quiet a mountain district, and too remote from the main thoroughfare of life, to give scope to His work, and, moreover, His fellow-townsmen there appear to have violently rejected His teaching (Luke iv. 16-30).

In Capernaum He seems to have dwelt for the most part at the house of Peter, who lived with his brother Andrew and his mother-in-law. The house appears to have been only one storey high, to have had a courtyard before it (Mark ii. 2, 4), and to have been on the strand. John and James also had a house in the town.

The place was a busy centre of travel and traffic. There was a custom-house, a garrison, a synagogue, and probably a harbour; and a Roman road passed close by it, leading from Egypt and the south to Damascus and the north. By this road news could be carried of new teaching, as of seditions, not only to Egypt and Damascus, but to the seaports of Cæsarea and Ptolemäis, and thence even to Rome. Nor would the tidings travel slowly, for

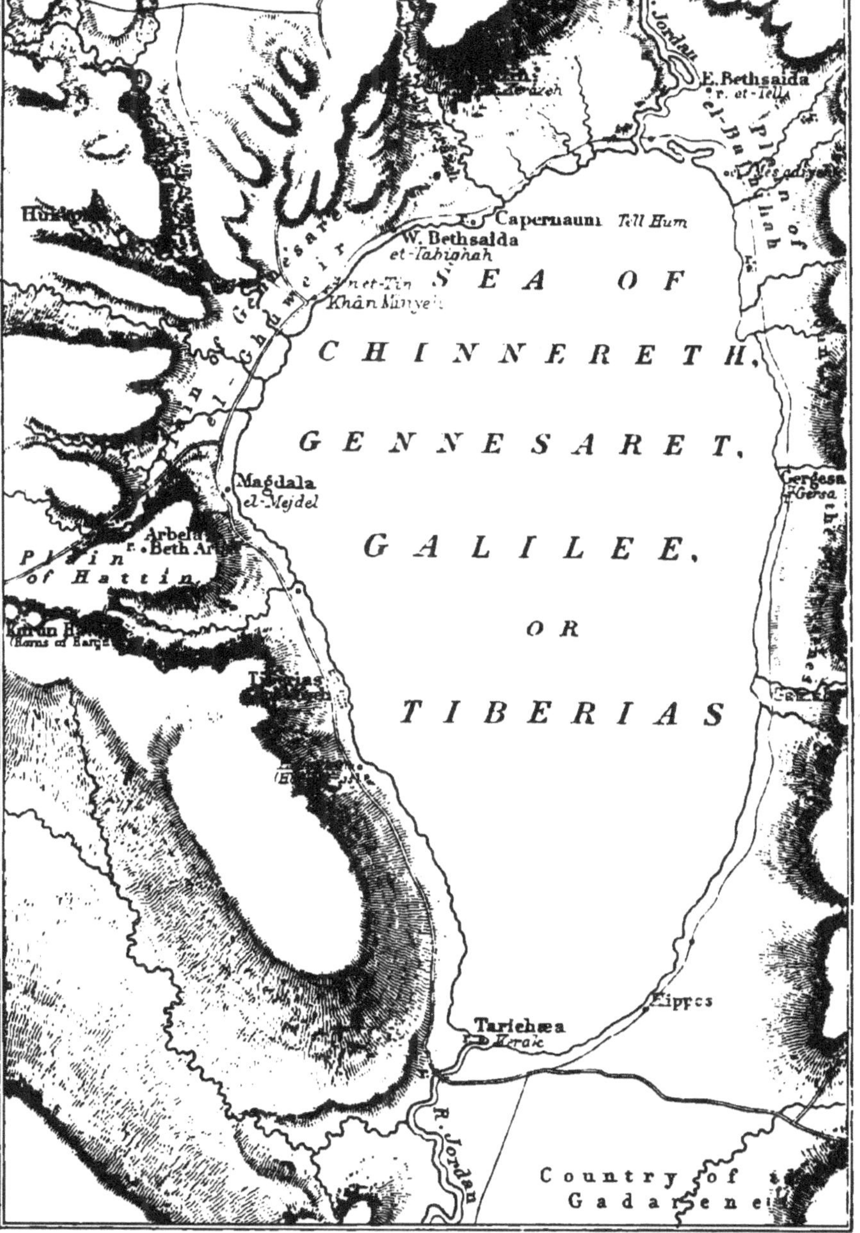

Huttin
R. Jordan
E. Bethsaida
or. et-Tell
el-Bu...
Plain of Batiha
Yarzeh
Capernaum Tell Hum
W. Bethsaida
et-Tabighah
Ghweir
Plain el
net-Tin
Khân Minyeh
SEA OF
CHINNERETH,
GENNESARET,
Magdala
el-Mejdel
GALILEE,
Gergesa
or Gersa
Arbela
r. Beth Arbel
Plain
of Hattin
OR
Kurûn Hattin
(Horns of Hattin)
TIBERIAS
Tiberias
(Hammam)
Hippos
Taricheæa
Kerak
R. Jordan
Country of the
Gadarenes

along the well-formed roads men could travel in twenty-four hours 100 or even 200 miles.

In the time of Jesus, Capernaum was for population and activity "the manufacturing district" of Palestine, and the waters of its lake were ploughed by 4000 vessels of every description, from the war-vessel of the Romans to the rough fisher-boats of Bethsaida and the gilded pinnaces from Herod's palace. All along the western shores of Gennesaret Jews and Gentiles were strangely mingled, and there might be seen the wild Arabs of the desert side by side with the enterprising Phœnicians, the Romans—the proud *terrarum domini*—the effeminate Syrians, and the still intellectual though corrupted Greeks.

As Capernaum was the boundary town between the territories of Herod Antipas and Philip, Jesus could easily by taking boat pass from the territories of the former, who often showed himself hostile, and place Himself under the juster and gentler rule of the latter.

The Sea of Galilee.—From it Jesus visited the towns and villages of Galilee, and especially those situated on the lake. This sheet of water is, therefore, sacred to Christians, and travellers have vied with one another in describing it, though their accounts greatly vary, some speaking of the scenery as exquisite, others as dreary in the extreme. This discrepancy arises partly, probably, from a difference in the travellers' moods, partly from a difference in the time of year in which it was visited. In the summer the vegetation is burnt up by the heat, which is almost torrid, and terribly depressing. Even in our own Lake country it is possible to find dreariness and depression one day, and beauty and exhilaration on the next.

The lake is about thirteen miles long, and in its broadest parts six miles wide—that is, about the same length as Windermere, but of a considerably greater breadth. But what makes it unlike any of our English lakes is the deep depression, for it is nearly 700 feet below the level of the Mediterranean. It is of volcanic origin, and is surrounded by hills. Those on the eastern side are nearly 2000 feet high, destitute of verdure and foliage, deeply furrowed by ravines, but quite flat along the summit. Those on the west, especially the northern end, are more varied in form.

Along the edge of the lake runs, the whole way round from north to south, a level beach—at the southern end roughly strewn with the black and white stones peculiar to the district, but the central or northern part formed of smooth sand, or of a texture of shells and pebbles so minute as to resemble sand. Shrubs, too, of the tropical thorn, fringe the greater part of the line of shore, mingled here and there with the bright pink colours of the oleander. On this beach, which can be discerned running like a white line all round the lake, the hills plant their dark base, descending nowhere precipitously, but almost everywhere presenting an alternation of soft grassy slopes and rocky cliffs.

In the Old Testament the lake is called the Sea of Chinneroth, perhaps from its harp-like shape.

Bethsaida Julias.—We shall best understand the connection of the lake and its towns with the history of Jesus if we take an imaginary tour part of the way round it from the north to the south by the west coast. At the extreme north the Jordan flows into and forms it. Near the inlet, a little to the north of the sea, are some insignificant ruins called **et Tell,** which are supposed to indicate the site of **Bethsaida Julias,** though some think the site is further to the south, at a ruined village called **Mes'-adîyeh,** a name resembling Bethsaida in sound but not in meaning. If we accept this latter site, we must suppose the course of the Jordan to have shifted westward. This town had been rebuilt by Philip, and was named after

Julia, the beautiful but infamous daughter of Augustus. It is the only Bethsaida named outside the New Testament, and is placed by Josephus on the east side of the Jordan, while the New Testament speaks of a Bethsaida of Galilee (John xii. 21). Many have therefore supposed that there were two Bethsaidas on the lake; and as the word means "home of fish," this is possible, though improbable. On the other hand, Bethsaida Julias may have had some of its houses on the west bank; or "Bethsaida of Galilee" may mean simply the Galilean part of the town, just as London south of the Thames is used, not as a geographical definition of London, but as a designation of districts which have grown up on the other side of the river.[1]

St John tells us that Bethsaida was the city of Philip, Andrew, and Peter. As the synoptists tell us that Simon and Andrew had a home at Capernaum (Mark i. 21, 29; Matt. viii. 5, 14), we may perhaps look on the house at Bethsaida as merely a fishing-station.

Tell Hum.—Passing along the coast in a south-westerly direction, we next arrive at the ruins of Tell Hum, regarded by many as the site of **Capernaum.** This theory has arisen partly from the name, which was supposed to be a corruption of Caphar-Nahum (the village of Nahum, the prophet, or perhaps a Rabbi, who was buried there). But Tell Hum means "black mound," and refers to the colour of the basalt stone. Here are the ruins of a large synagogue, which it has been thought might be that mentioned in Luke vii. 6 as having been built by the centurion; but there is nothing to fix its date to the time of Jesus. The objections to Tell Hum as the site of Capernaum are,—the fact that the Roman road does not pass it; the absence of a harbourage, though it would seem that Jesus landed at Capernaum—and of a fountain,

---

[1] Nicholson.

F

though Josephus especially mentions a fountain near Capernaum (B. J., iii. 10, § 8).

Kerâzeh.—About two miles north of Tell Hum we come to some ruins called Kerazeh, standing on a rocky spur about 900 feet above the lake. This is supposed to have been **Chorazin,** named after the Corâcin fish which are mentioned by Josephus as found in the neighbourhood.

Khân Minyeh.—Two miles and a half south of Tell Hum we come on the ruins which dispute its claim to the site of the ancient **Capernaum.** These are called Khân Minyeh. Khân means an "inn," and here are the ruins of one which appears to have been built in the middle ages. The Minai or "sorcerers" are mentioned in the Talmud, and by this title the Jews stigmatised the early Christians, and these Minai are called in one passage "sons of Capernaum." There is thus a close connection between this Minyeh—named from the Minai —and the site of Capernaum. In favour of the site are the facts that the Roman road passes it, that it is close on the lake, has a harbourage, is on the plain of Gennesaret, and is within two miles of "the round spring" or fount of Capernaum mentioned by Josephus.

The Plain of Gennesaret.—After leaving Khân Minyeh we enter upon the famous "plain of Gennesaret," now called the Ghuweir, or little plain. Here the mountains suddenly recede inland, leaving a level plain of one mile wide, and three to four miles long. Gennesaret probably means "paradise or garden," and this plain is the garden of North Palestine. Josephus said of it in his time that " there is no plant whose growth it refuses to sustain, such is its fertility. In countless quantities grows there the hardy walnut-tree, but none the less the palm, which flourishes in hot climates ; close to it fig and olive trees, for which a gentler temperature is fitted." Modern travellers describe it as watered by four springs, which pour forth their almost full-grown rivers: the richness of the soil displays itself in magnificent corn-fields: along the shore rises a thick jungle of thorn and oleander: the wild doves, hawks, and jays of brilliant plumage, with which Galilee abounds, are congregated in unusual numbers over the whole plain.

Along this plain Jesus must often have passed, making His way from Magdala to Capernaum and Bethsaida; and we may, as far as external nature is concerned, reproduce the frame of His life upon it,—the morning, when the plain was awakened under the first rays of the sun, with all the brightness of flowers and all the murmur of birds; the evening, when the golden lights of his setting brought out again the softness of the contour of the mountains; the night, when the heaven was covered with as many stars as the earth is studded with flowers, and the calm lake reflected them almost without diminishing their brightness. But whereas now the plain is desolate, in the time of Jesus it was crowded with towns and villages. Yet from this dense population He could easily pass into solitude by climbing the hills at the beach on the west, or crossing over in a boat to the still wilder mountains on the east.

Mejdel.—At the southern extremity of the plain is a place called Mejdel, the ancient *Magdala*, probably the home of Mary Magdalene. The word means watch-tower: there was probably a tower here to guard the entrance of the plain. Nothing now remains but a few mud hovels and a solitary thorn-bush.

Tiberias. — Leaving Mejdel, three miles of rough rocks and ravines must be crossed, which form a natural frontier between the plain of Gennesaret and that of Tiberias. There is no record of Jesus ever having been in the latter town. It does not follow that He was never in it, for we have not a complete record of His doings. He may, however, have avoided it, lest by entering it He should put Himself into the power of Antipas, or because of its worldly character, or, as some think, because it was ceremonially unclean, though there is little evidence that He cared for such things. Herod Antipas rebuilt the town some time between A.D. 20 and 27, and named it after the Emperor Tiberius. He built a palace in it, and an amphitheatre, and adorned it with Grecian colonnades and marble statues. Here were splendid villas of his nobles, and a synagogue, one of the finest in the province of Galilee, and a castle, the ruins of which still remain, in which were stored arms for a garrison of 70,000 men. As some portion of the ground it was built on had been a cemetery, the thought of residing there was repulsive to the Jews. Herod compelled many by force to be inhabitants. For fifty years after, Tiberias was the capital of Galilee, and, Cæsarea excepted, the finest city in Palestine. After the fall of Jerusalem, in the second century, it became the home of the Jewish council, the Sanhedrin; and the Mishna, or second *corpus juris* of Rabbinical precepts, was compiled there by the great Rabbi, Judah Hakko-desh (A.D. 190).

Influence on the teaching of Jesus.—Such was the character and scenery of the lake which was the chief centre of the ministry of Jesus, and they have left their impression on His words, for He constantly drew His lessons from the objects around Him. The men, the fields, and the valleys round the lake are immortalised by their association with Him. There were the vineyards on the hill-slopes, round which their lord planted a hedge, and in which he built a watch-tower and dug a wine-press (Matt. xxi. 33). The plain of Gennesaret was the enamelled meadow, on which, in spring, ten thousand lilies were robed in more than the glory of Solomon, and where, in winter, the grass was cast into the oven (Luke xii. 27, 28). It was on such pastures as those

around that the shepherd left the ninety and nine
sheep to seek in the mountains the one that was
lost, and carried it back on his shoulders, rejoicing
(Luke xv. 4, 5). The ravens, that have neither store-
house nor barn, daily sailed over from the cliffs of
Arbela, at the back of Magdala, to seek their food on
the shore of the lake; and from the same cliffs, from
time to time, flew forth the hawks, to make the terrified
hen gather her chickens under her wings (Matt. xxiii.
37). The orchards were there in which the fig-tree
grew on which the dresser of the vineyard, in three
years, found no fruit (Luke xiii. 7), and in which the
grain of mustard-seed grew into so great a shrub that
the fowls of the air lodged in its branches (Matt. xiii.
31, 32). Across the lake rose the hills of Gaulonitis,
from which men watched for signs of weather. A
murky red, seen above them in the morning, was a sign
of foul weather; whereas when the sun sank red and
glowing behind the hills in the west, it was a sign of
fair weather on the morrow (Matt. xvi. 2, 3).

The daily business of Capernaum itself supplied Jesus
with many of the illustrations found in His discourses.
He might see in the bazaar of the town, or on the
street, the rich travelling merchant, who exchanged
perhaps a heavy load of Babylonian carpets for the one
lustrous pearl (Matt. xiii. 46), that had, it may be,
found its way to the lake from the Persian Gulf.
Fishermen, and publicans, and dressers of vineyards
passed and repassed each moment. To the north, in
Julias, the favourite town of the tetrarch Philip; to
the south, in Tiberias, at the court of Antipas, were
those who lived in kings' houses and wore soft raiment [1]
(Matt. xi. 8).

[1] Geikie.

LESSON XII.

St Matthew xiii. 1-23.

THE PARABLE OF THE SOWER—THE RISE OF THE KINGDOM.

1 Ἐν τῇ ἡμέρᾳ ἐκείνῃ ἐξελθὼν ὁ Ἰησοῦς τῆς οἰκίας ἐκάθητο παρὰ τὴν θάλασσαν· 2 καὶ συνήχθησαν πρὸς αὐτὸν ὄχλοι πολλοί, ὥστε αὐτὸν εἰς πλοῖον ἐμβάντα καθῆσθαι, καὶ πᾶς ὁ ὄχλος ἐπὶ τὸν αἰγιαλὸν εἱστήκει. 3 καὶ ἐλάλησεν αὐτοῖς πολλὰ ἐν παραβολαῖς λέγων Ἰδοὺ ἐξῆλθεν ὁ σπείρων τοῦ σπείρειν. 4 καὶ ἐν τῷ σπείρειν αὐτὸν ἃ μὲν ἔπεσεν παρὰ τὴν ὁδόν, καὶ ἐλθόντα τὰ πετεινὰ κατέφαγεν αὐτά. 5 ἄλλα δὲ ἔπεσεν ἐπὶ τὰ πετρώδη ὅπου οὐκ εἶχεν γῆν πολλήν, καὶ εὐθέως ἐξανέτειλεν διὰ τὸ μὴ ἔχειν βάθος γῆς, 6 ἡλίου δὲ ἀνατείλαντος ἐκαυματίσθη καὶ διὰ τὸ μὴ ἔχειν ῥίζαν ἐξηράνθη. 7 ἄλλα δὲ ἔπεσεν ἐπὶ τὰς ἀκάνθας, καὶ ἀνέβησαν αἱ ἄκανθαι καὶ ἀπέπνιξαν αὐτά. 8 ἄλλα δὲ ἔπεσεν ἐπὶ τὴν γῆν τὴν καλὴν καὶ ἐδίδου καρπόν, ὃ μὲν ἑκατὸν ὃ δὲ ἑξήκοντα ὃ δὲ τριάκοντα. 9 Ὁ ἔχων ὦτα ἀκουέτω. 10 Καὶ προσελθόντες οἱ μαθηταὶ εἶπον αὐτῷ Διὰ τί ἐν παραβολαῖς λαλεῖς αὐτοῖς; 11 ὁ δὲ ἀποκριθεὶς εἶπεν, ὅτι Ὑμῖν δέδοται γνῶναι τὰ μυστήρια τῆς βασιλείας τῶν οὐρανῶν, ἐκείνοις δὲ οὐ δέδοται. 12 ὅστις γὰρ ἔχει, δοθήσεται αὐτῷ καὶ περισσευθήσεται· ὅστις δὲ οὐκ ἔχει, καὶ ὃ ἔχει ἀρθήσεται ἀπ᾽ αὐτοῦ. 13 διὰ

τοῦτο ἐν παραβολαῖς αὐτοῖς λαλῶ, ὅτι βλέποντες
οὐ βλέπουσιν καὶ ἀκούοντες οὐκ ἀκούουσιν οὐδὲ
συνίουσιν· 14 καὶ ἀναπληροῦται αὐτοῖς ἡ προφητεία
Ἡσαίου ἡ λέγουσα,

    ἀκοῇ ἀκούσετε καὶ οὐ μὴ συνῆτε,
    καὶ βλέποντες βλέψετε καὶ οὐ μὴ ἴδητε.
15 ἐπαχύνθη γὰρ ἡ καρδία τοῦ λαοῦ τούτου,
    καὶ τοῖς ὠσὶν βαρέως ἤκουσαν,
      καὶ τοὺς ὀφθαλμοὺς αὐτῶν ἐκάμμυσαν·
    μὴ πότε ἴδωσιν τοῖς ὀφθαλμοῖς
    καὶ τοῖς ὠσὶν ἀκούσωσίν
    καὶ τῇ καρδίᾳ συνῶσιν καὶ ἐπιστρέψωσιν
    καὶ ἰάσομαι αὐτούς.

16 ὑμῶν δὲ μακάριοι οἱ ὀφθαλμοὶ ὅτι βλέπουσιν, καὶ
τὰ ὦτα [ὑμῶν] ὅτι ἀκούουσιν. 17 ἀμὴν γὰρ λέγω
ὑμῖν ὅτι πολλοὶ προφῆται καὶ δίκαιοι ἐπεθύμησαν
ἰδεῖν ἃ βλέπετε καὶ οὐκ εἶδον, καὶ ἀκοῦσαι ἃ ἀκούετε
καὶ οὐκ ἤκουσαν. 18 Ὑμεῖς οὖν ἀκούσατε
τὴν παραβολὴν τοῦ σπείραντος. 19 Παντὸς ἀκούον-
τος τὸν λόγον τῆς βασιλείας καὶ μὴ συνιέντος, ἔρχεται ὁ πονηρὸς καὶ ἁρπάζει τὸ ἐσπαρμένον ἐν τῇ
καρδίᾳ αὐτοῦ· οὗτός ἐστιν ὁ παρὰ τὴν ὁδὸν σπαρείς.
20 ὁ δὲ ἐπὶ τὰ πετρώδη σπαρείς, οὗτός ἐστιν ὁ τὸν
λόγον ἀκούων καὶ εὐθὺς μετὰ χαρᾶς λαμβάνων αὐτόν·
21 οὐκ ἔχει δὲ ῥίζαν ἐν ἑαυτῷ ἀλλὰ πρόσκαιρός ἐστιν,
γενομένης δὲ θλίψεως ἢ διωγμοῦ διὰ τὸν λόγον εὐθὺς
σκανδαλίζεται. 22 ὁ δὲ εἰς τὰς ἀκάνθας σπαρείς,
οὗτός ἐστιν ὁ τὸν λόγον ἀκούων καὶ ἡ μέριμνα τοῦ
αἰῶνος καὶ ἡ ἀπάτη τοῦ πλούτου συμπνίγει τὸν
λόγον, καὶ ἄκαρπος γίνεται. 23 ὁ δὲ ἐπὶ τὴν καλὴν
γῆν σπαρείς, οὗτός ἐστιν ὁ τὸν λόγον ἀκούων καὶ
συνιείς, ὃς δὴ καρποφορεῖ καὶ ποιεῖ ὃ μὲν ἑκατὸν ὃ
δὲ ἑξήκοντα ὃ δὲ τριάκοντα.

LESSON XIII.

St Matthew xiii. 24-43.

THE PARABLE OF THE TARES, OF THE MUSTARD SEED, AND OF THE LEAVEN.

24 Ἄλλην παραβολὴν παρέθηκεν αὐτοῖς λέγων· ὡμοιώθη ἡ βασιλεία τῶν οὐρανῶν ἀνθρώπῳ σπείραντι καλὸν σπέρμα ἐν τῷ ἀγρῷ αὐτοῦ. 25 ἐν δὲ τῷ καθεύδειν τοὺς ἀνθρώπους ἦλθεν αὐτοῦ ὁ ἐχθρὸς καὶ ἐπέσπειρεν ζιζάνια ἀνὰ μέσον τοῦ σίτου καὶ ἀπῆλθεν. 26 ὅτε δὲ ἐβλάστησεν ὁ χόρτος καὶ καρπὸν ἐποίησεν, τότε ἐφάνη καὶ τὰ ζιζάνια. 27 προσελθόντες δὲ οἱ δοῦλοι τοῦ οἰκοδεσπότου εἶπον αὐτῷ· Κύριε, οὐχὶ καλὸν σπέρμα ἔσπειρας ἐν τῷ σῷ ἀγρῷ; πόθεν οὖν ἔχει ζιζάνια; 28 ὁ δὲ ἔφη αὐτοῖς· ἐχθρὸς ἄνθρωπος τοῦτο ἐποίησεν. οἱ δὲ αὐτῷ λέγουσιν· θέλεις οὖν ἀπελθόντες συλλέξωμεν αὐτά; 29 ὁ δὲ φησίν· οὔ, μήποτε συλλέγοντες τὰ ζιζάνια ἐκριζώσητε ἅμα αὐτοῖς τὸν σῖτον. 30 ἄφετε συναυξάνεσθαι ἀμφότερα ἕως τοῦ θερισμοῦ, καὶ ἐν καιρῷ τοῦ θερισμοῦ ἐρῶ τοῖς θερισταῖς· συλλέξατε πρῶτον τὰ ζιζάνια καὶ δήσατε αὐτὰ εἰς δεσμὰς πρὸς τὸ κατακαῦσαι αὐτά, τὸν δὲ σῖτον συναγάγετε εἰς τὴν ἀποθήκην μου.

31 Ἄλλην παραβολὴν παρέθηκεν αὐτοῖς λέγων· ὁμοία ἐστὶν ἡ βασιλεία τῶν οὐρανῶν κόκκῳ σινάπεως ὃν λαβὼν ἄνθρωπος ἔσπειρεν ἐν τῷ ἀγρῷ αὐτοῦ· 32 ὃ μικρότερον μέν ἐστιν πάντων τῶν σπερμάτων, ὅταν

δὲ αὐξηθῇ, μεῖζον τῶν λαχάνων ἐστὶν καὶ γίνεται δένδρον, ὥστε ἐλθεῖν τὰ πετεινὰ τοῦ οὐρανοῦ καὶ κατασκηνοῦν ἐν τοῖς κλάδοις αὐτοῦ. 33 Ἄλλην παραβολὴν ἐλάλησεν αὐτοῖς· ὁμοία ἐστὶν ἡ βασιλεία τῶν οὐρανῶν ζύμῃ, ἣν λαβοῦσα γυνὴ ἐνέκρυψεν εἰς ἀλεύρου σάτα τρία, ἕως οὗ ἐζυμώθη ὅλον.

34 Ταῦτα πάντα ἐλάλησεν ὁ Ἰησοῦς ἐν παραβολαῖς τοῖς ὄχλοις, καὶ χωρὶς παραβολῆς οὐδὲν ἐλάλει αὐτοῖς, 35 ὅπως πληρωθῇ τὸ ῥηθὲν διὰ τοῦ προφήτου λέγοντος· ἀνοίξω ἐν παραβολαῖς τὸ στόμα μου, ἐρεύξομαι κεκρυμμένα ἀπὸ καταβολῆς.

36 Τότε ἀφεὶς τοὺς ὄχλους ἦλθεν εἰς τὴν οἰκίαν. καὶ προσῆλθον αὐτῷ οἱ μαθηταὶ αὐτοῦ λέγοντες· διασάφησον ἡμῖν τὴν παραβολὴν τῶν ζιζανίων τοῦ ἀγροῦ. 37 ὁ δὲ ἀποκριθεὶς εἶπεν· ὁ σπείρων τὸ καλὸν σπέρμα ἐστὶν ὁ υἱὸς τοῦ ἀνθρώπου, 38 ὁ δὲ ἀγρός ἐστιν ὁ κόσμος· τὸ δὲ καλὸν σπέρμα, οὗτοί εἰσιν οἱ υἱοὶ τῆς βασιλείας· τὰ δὲ ζιζάνιά εἰσιν οἱ υἱοὶ τοῦ πονηροῦ, 39 ὁ δὲ ἐχθρὸς ὁ σπείρας αὐτά ἐστιν ὁ διάβολος· ὁ δὲ θερισμὸς συντέλεια αἰῶνός ἐστιν, οἱ δὲ θερισταὶ ἄγγελοί εἰσιν. 40 ὥσπερ οὖν συλλέγεται τὰ ζιζάνια καὶ πυρὶ κατακαίεται, οὕτως ἔσται ἐν τῇ συντελείᾳ τοῦ αἰῶνος. 41 ἀποστελεῖ ὁ υἱὸς τοῦ ἀνθρώπου τοὺς ἀγγέλους αὐτοῦ, καὶ συλλέξουσιν ἐκ τῆς βασιλείας αὐτοῦ πάντα τὰ σκάνδαλα καὶ τοὺς ποιοῦντας τὴν ἀνομίαν, 42 καὶ βαλοῦσιν αὐτοὺς εἰς τὴν κάμινον τοῦ πυρός· ἐκεῖ ἔσται ὁ κλαυθμὸς καὶ ὁ βρυγμὸς τῶν ὀδόντων. 43 τότε οἱ δίκαιοι ἐκλάμψουσιν ὡς ὁ ἥλιος ἐν τῇ βασιλείᾳ τοῦ πατρὸς αὐτῶν. ὁ ἔχων ὦτα ἀκουέτω.

ON THE PARABLE OF THE TARES—EVIL IN THE KINGDOM.

False notions of the kingdom.—As the multitudes listened to the words of Jesus, who by this time had attained great fame as a teacher and healer, many would begin to think of Him as the Messiah; and when their thoughts took this direction, and they reflected on the kingdom of heaven that He had proclaimed, they would look to Him to fulfil the dreams which they entertained about this kingdom; and, above all, they would begin to look to Him to extinguish all evil from the world. But they did not all regard evil in the same light. Many thought those men evil who did not keep the law, and who, therefore, were polluted; or who, like the Romans, persecuted the holy nation, and were therefore destined to be exterminated by the Messiah. For the picture the Messiah presented to their expectation was that of a king who should be infinitely greater than all other kings had been, because God should endow him with an irresistible might by which to crush all opposition, and to put all enemies under his feet. Force and compulsion were to be the weapons of the king of the Jews, as they had been the weapons of all kings before him. The words of the Psalmist seemed to be a fitting prophecy of his unchecked progress (Psalm xlv. 3)— "Gird thy sword upon thy thigh; ride on, and thy right hand shall teach thee terrible things." The author of the so-called Psalms of Solomon (a work composed probably about the year B.C. 40) looked for the Messiah as a king "who should break in pieces the unjust rulers, cleanse Jerusalem from the heathen who tread it under foot, thrust out the sinners from his inheritance, grind to dust the haughtiness of the transgressors, and shatter in pieces all their strength, as a potter's vessel is shattered by a rod of iron." When Jesus, then, though professing to found a kingdom, declined to wield a king's weapons, those who regarded themselves as the enlightened among His countrymen rejected Him; the humbler populace continually looked for, and even sometimes sought to thrust upon Him, the assertion of His power; and even His most loyal disciples felt His reserve as a stumbling-block. These last, indeed, with the exception of Judas Iscariot, were all Galileans, a people who ever showed a gallant readiness to fight for a Messiah, or against the Gentile; and we find this fierce spirit of patriotism displayed in John and James when they asked leave on one occasion to call down fire on a Samaritan village that had refused to receive their Master (Luke ix. 54).

How evil is to be cured.——From such false notions of Jesus' kingship, and of His method of dealing with evil and evil men, the disciples had to be delivered; and with this end in view, He read them the lesson of the tares. Evil was not to be cured by violence and the sword, but, so far as it could be cured, by patience and love. The Messiah was not to gather together in one great secular state all who acknowledged His authority, or to commission His servants to destroy all who rejected Him. His " power over all flesh " was not to mean the extermination of those who did not obey His laws. His kingdom was to be unlike any other kingdom. It was not to be a separate nationality, an organised imperial power, maintaining open war against all who were hostile to it. His true and loyal subjects were to live among those who were disobedient to Him—the wheat and the tares were to grow together. The kingdom was to be a kingdom over hearts: Jesus would rule by consent, not by coercion, and hence the lesson for all succeeding ages. When the disciples of Mahomet sought to propagate their religion by the sword, they were following the example and obeying the precepts of their teacher. When the disciples of Jesus seek to win obedience to His laws by other methods than loving persuasion, they are disloyal to the precepts and example of their Founder, who preferred a shameful death at the hands of the foreigner to establishing His kingdom by the deliverance of His countrymen from the foreigner's yoke.

Evil will exist in spite of all.—But we may fairly suppose that Jesus in this parable had in His view the thoughts of others besides those who looked to Him to found an external rule, and who regarded those as tares who would not show allegiance to it. Others there would be who, though they did not expect His kingdom to be established by violence, or that He would found by the sword a universal empire, would yet expect that this kingdom should very speedily exhibit within its own bounds a condition of ideal virtue, and would be impatient to banish from it all members who did not attain to the ideal standard they had formed. Jesus had to prepare these disciples for the disappointment of these hopes. Evil was not to be speedily destroyed by His influence, but would continue to exist even within His kingdom and among its citizens. How, then, was it to be dealt with? When Jesus said, "Let both grow together until the harvest," are we to suppose that He meant there was to be no discipline among His followers, but that, however impure and openly wicked men might be, they were still to be regarded as Christians if they chose to adhere to their profession, and Christians were still to regard them as fellow-members with themselves? We know that the most active disciple of Jesus did not accept the words in this sense, for St Paul admonishes the Corinthian disciples in 1 Cor. v. 11, "I have written unto you not to keep company, if any man that is called a brother [*i.e.*, is a Christian] be a fornicator, or covetous, or an idolater, or a railer, or a drunkard, or an extortioner; with such an one no not to eat."

How offending members are to be dealt with.—Neither here, nor when He said, "Swear not at all," and "Take no thought for the morrow," is Jesus laying down a rigid rule. He is warning against the *spirit* of impatience

and spiritual pride, inculcating the spirit of patience and
love. The first thought in a Christian community when
a brother sins is to be, not his expulsion, but his reformation and redemption to a better life. St Paul lays down
the principle in Gal. vi. 1: "Brethren, if a man be over-
taken in a fault, ye which are spiritual restore such an
one in the spirit of meekness; considering thyself, lest
thou also be tempted." When St Paul thus wrote, he
had probably been just dealing with a grave offender in
the Church at Corinth. In his first epistle to that Church,
he had appealed to the brotherhood to punish the guilty
person. The appeal had not only been answered, but
answered with so much promptness that it was necessary
to intercede for the offender. He commended their zeal,
and the punishment they had inflicted, but now they
must forgive and comfort their erring brother, lest he be
swallowed up with overmuch sorrow.

We could have no better illustration of a method of
dealing with the Christian tares.

In Jesus' words we seem to see Him reading the hearts
of His disciples in all ages,—warning against self-satisfaction in their own goodness—a trait we see even in
children—against hasty judgment, and against indulging
malice and envy under the pretext of a zeal for godliness
and religion. His kingdom was not to be a luxurious
abode of pious souls uncontaminated by evil, but rather
a busy workshop to reclaim the evil, and in which the
despair of such redemption was not to enter. There are
very few so hopelessly wicked that the influence of the
good cannot reclaim them, if it be exercised lovingly,
unassumingly, and persistently. It may be that Jesus
kept Judas by His side so long, in hopes that, by His
gentle and loving treatment of him, He might win over
his gloomy and sordid spirit.

ON THE PARABLES OF THE MUSTARD-SEED AND THE LEAVEN—THE GROWTH OF THE KINGDOM.

In the parables of the sower and the tares Jesus had presented the dark side of the prospects of the kingdom. His followers were not to be beguiled by the numbers who were thronging to hear Him into an expectation of great and immediate success. Out of all those multitudes very few would grasp the principles and be initiated into the mysteries of the kingdom, and after it had been established, so far from being a perfect or stainless community it would contain evil within it—evil members with difficulty distinguishable from the good, and imperfection in the characters of the members themselves.

The parables of the mustard-seed and the leaven, on the other hand, describe the bright side of the prospects of the kingdom. Its beginnings, indeed, were destined to be small, but its progress was to be certain and great.

The external growth by organisations.—The parable of the mustard-seed portrays the external and visible development, that of the leaven the internal influence, of the kingdom. The former refers to Christian organisations, the latter to the Christian spirit.

At the moment Jesus was speaking, His disciples watching the multitudes might feel that their Master was speaking too disparagingly of the kingdom when He spoke of its beginnings as the tiniest of all seeds; but it seemed tiny, indeed, during the last few days of His life, when one upper chamber appeared capable of containing all His disciples; and faint was the hope of its growth, when even these all forsook Him and fled, and one had betrayed and another openly denied Him. But very soon the seed began to develop into a tree, when on the day of Pentecost 3000 new disciples were enrolled (Acts ii. 41), and all fear of its growth had passed away when St Paul carried the faith beyond the boundaries of Judea, and the name of Christians was given to the disciples at Antioch (Acts xi. 26). And now we may discern its wide-spreading branches and thick foliage in the Christian churches, chapels, schools, and charitable buildings that are to be seen in almost every habitable portion of the globe, and in the multitudes who profess Christianity, and the organisations that are established for promulgating the creed and promoting charitable purposes in the name of Christ. Perhaps the most notable outward sign of the height to which it has grown is the bronze statue of St Peter that has stood for centuries upon the triumphal column of Trajan, and of St Paul upon that of Marcus Aurelius, in the centre of Rome, the venerable capital of paganism.

The internal growth through the influence of the Spirit.—The parable of the leaven teaches that the influence of Christianity is to spread, but that it is to spread by the influence of its spirit, not by any external means. As leaven works from the centre to the circumference, and by the method of contagion, so the spirit of Christianity takes possession first of the heart, the seat of life, and thence proceeds outwards to exercise sway over conduct, and communicates itself from mind to mind by the contagious power of sympathy.

The spirit took possession first of the hearts of a few simple fishermen, tax-gatherers, and sinful women turned from their sins, and it was destined to spread over the whole of the Roman empire, and of the civilised world. The spirit itself is invisible as the leaven, but its influence on the world is as evident as the influence of the leaven on bread. The spirit is defined by Jesus as the spirit of *love*,—"By this shall men know that ye are my disciples, if ye have love one to another" (John xiii. 35).

The antagonistic spirit of Rome.—Nothing could be more opposed to this spirit in all its manifestations than the spirit that leavened the Roman empire at the time that Jesus spoke. In Europe, now, there are the spirits of many nations to leaven the world, and this leaven spreads rapidly by means of the press. In the time of Jesus one nation was pre-eminent, and had won its pre-eminence by the brutalising method of conquest. The spirit of this nation was leavening the whole civilised world. It claimed its descent from a wolf, and throughout its history had shown the savage spirit of its fabled ancestress, a spirit, hard, tameless, inexorable, unbending, and callous. The Romans had crushed the Samnites, wiped Carthage off the face of the earth, and in turning their arms against one another had deluged Italy and the civilised world with blood. Their leading men were distinguished, with but few exceptions, by the qualities of sternness and hardness. These qualities characterise their laws, their customs, and their amusements. The Roman father at first had the power to punish, sell, or even slay his son; he had absolute power over his wife, whom he divorced with a freedom unrestrained by sentiment or the associations of domestic life. He was hardened by the mastery he exercised over his slaves, and rendered callous to suffering by his daily treatment of them, and by his chief recreation and amusement, the spectacle of the gladiatorial shows.

Not, indeed, that there were no instances throughout the empire of softer manners, or that what was permissible was rigorously carried into practice. Wives, indeed, were divorced, but grown-up sons were not slain. Men were found like Seneca, the Stoic philosopher, to treat slaves as members of their family; and the comedies of Plautus and Terence show us that the slave was often on intimate and confidential terms with his master.

It was left, however, for Christianity to introduce new principles into the world which should leaven not merely the sentiments of the enlightened few, but should alter the whole tone and practices of society.

Leaven of the spirit of Christian brotherhood.— Thus, by upholding that all men were brothers, Christianity ameliorated the condition of the slave, gave him a share in religion from which he had been excluded, and finally struck off his chains.

Leaven of the spirit of reverence for human life. —Again, Christianity leavened society with loftier ideas of the sanctity of human life, and this had practical influences on social customs.

Among the Greeks, Plato recommended that in order to keep down the population, no infant should be reared that did not promise to be strong and healthy, but that the weakly and diseased should be painlessly destroyed. Among the Romans it was quite a common practice, and strictly legal, for female children to be destroyed ; and the destruction of male children was forbidden only till they reached the third year.

Such exposed children Christians sought to save by rearing them at first by private charity, and afterwards in hospitals founded to receive them.

Again, the first Christian emperor, Constantine, published the first edict condemning the gladiatorial shows : a Christian monk, named Telemachus, is said, by a heroic deed, to have led the Emperor Honorius to abolish them altogether.   The story runs that this noble martyr travelled from the East to Rome for the purpose of protesting against these shows, leapt into the arena, and attempted to separate the combatants.   The infuriated spectators stoned him to death, but afterwards so far repented of their conduct as willingly to acquiesce in a decree of the Emperor Honorius abolishing the games for ever (A.D. 404).

Again, the leaven of Christianity has done much to mitigate the horrors of war.

In ancient times, after a battle was over, the wounded of the vanquished, if not taken captive to be made slaves of, were left to their sufferings on the field, or put to death by the victors. Our own days have witnessed the signature of an international code for the purpose of relieving the wounded in time of active warfare (after a congress held in Geneva, 1864), and the establishment of "The Red Cross Society" for that purpose, whose flag during the Franco - Prussian war in 1870 was recognised as neutral.

In ancient times, prisoners of war were made slaves or gladiators, or slain in cold blood. In the early days of Christianity, benevolent Christian ladies used to redeem captives, and church plate was sold for that purpose. In the thirteenth century, civilised nations began to exchange their prisoners. After the treaty of Münster (1648), it became the general custom of European nations to release all prisoners at the end of the war, without ransom.

It is now a recognised principle among civilised nations that only those actively engaged in war, or discharging public duties, are to be regarded as enemies; that philanthropic and scientific buildings are not to be plundered, and that piracy and privateering are not permissible. Arbitration is resorted to in order to avoid war, as in our dispute with the United States about the Alabama (1872).

Again, in the barbaric societies with which Christianity was brought into contact, the leaven worked by the abolition of feuds, and the substitution of fines paid to the king. For Christian legislation found that private injury was revenged at once on the person of the enemy; and since the wrongs of the injured were regarded as wrongs done to the family, these feuds were continued from one generation to another. It substituted for the death of the injurer, first a payment of blood-money to

the person injured or his relatives ; then the payment of
a fine to the prince, as a surety of peace, and to atone
for injury done to the community.

Again, in the middle ages, the frightful calamities
brought about by private wars were mitigated by the
establishment on the part of the clergy and the mercantile community of what was called "The Peace of
God."   In the tenth and eleventh centuries, to counter-
act the effect of these wars, which were depopulating
the cities, and reducing the fields to solitude, the clergy
preached peace ; religious enthusiasts went from village
to village proclaiming it in the name of the " Prince of
Peace ; " great councils were held to spread abroad the
ideas of brotherly amity ; and the Popes wrote letters and
published encyclicals to recommend the vows and habits
of concord to all Christian nations.   In the fourteenth
century, pilgrims, with white bands round their necks,
marched through various lands, preaching the duty of
a Christian peace.   No less than thirty councils in
different parts of Europe proclaimed the truce of God.
At last, in the fifteenth century, Charles VI. put forth
a law absolutely forbidding private war in France.
In Germany it lingered till the end of the sixteenth
century.

The leaven of Christian love has had an influence, too,
on the infliction of punishment.   The old codes of law
were filled with sentences of torture, mutilation, and
hideous forms of death.   The Roman law admitted torture in the examination, first of slaves, and subsequently
of freemen.   The early Christian Church opposed this
cruel practice, but the later Church adopted it under the
influence of bigotry, and of the revival of the study of
Roman law, and for centuries it was practised by the
Inquisition.   It fell before the promulgation of the
Scriptures at the time of the Reformation.

The punishment of death has now been abolished

formally by some civilised countries; and in Belgium, Prussia, Bavaria, Denmark, and Sweden, though not abolished, has practically ceased.

Government by force in the State, in the army, and in the school, is gradually yielding to government by sympathy.

Thus slowly, as Jesus foresaw, but surely, the leaven of Christian love has operated, and is operating, on the tone and institutions of society.

LESSON XIV.

St Matthew xiii. 44-52.

THE PARABLES OF THE HID TREASURE, OF THE PEARL, AND OF THE NET — THE APPROPRIATION OF THE KINGDOM BY MANKIND, AND THE FINAL SELECTION OF ITS MEMBERS.

44 Ὁμοία ἐστὶν ἡ βασιλεία τῶν οὐρανῶν θησαυρῷ κεκρυμμένῳ ἐν τῷ ἀγρῷ, ὃν εὑρὼν ἄνθρωπος ἔκρυψεν, καὶ ἀπὸ τῆς χαρᾶς αὐτοῦ ὑπάγει καὶ πωλεῖ ὅσα ἔχει καὶ ἀγοράζει τὸν ἀγρὸν ἐκεῖνον. 45 Πάλιν ὁμοία ἐστὶν ἡ βασιλεία τῶν οὐρανῶν ἐμπόρῳ ζητοῦντι καλοὺς μαργαρίτας· 46 εὑρὼν δὲ ἕνα πολύτιμον μαργαρίτην ἀπελθὼν πέπρακεν πάντα ὅσα εἶχεν καὶ ἠγόρασεν αὐτόν.

47 Πάλιν ὁμοία ἐστὶν ἡ βασιλεία τῶν οὐρανῶν σαγήνῃ βληθείσῃ εἰς τὴν θάλασσαν καὶ ἐκ παντὸς γένους συναγαγούσῃ· 48 ἣν ὅτε ἐπληρώθη ἀναβιβάσαντες ἐπὶ τὸν αἰγιαλὸν, καὶ καθίσαντες, συνέλεξαν τὰ καλὰ εἰς ἄγγη, τὰ δὲ σαπρὰ ἔξω ἔβαλον. 49 οὕτως ἔσται ἐν τῇ συντελείᾳ τοῦ αἰῶνος· ἐξελεύσονται οἱ ἄγγελοι καὶ ἀφοριοῦσιν τοὺς πονηροὺς ἐκ μέσου τῶν δικαίων 50 καὶ βαλοῦσιν αὐτοὺς εἰς τὴν κάμινον τοῦ πυρός· ἐκεῖ ἔσται ὁ κλαυθμὸς καὶ ὁ βρυγμὸς τῶν ὀδόντων. 51 Συνήκατε ταῦτα πάντα; λέγουσιν αὐτῷ Ναί. 52 ὁ δὲ εἶπεν αὐτοῖς Διὰ τοῦτο πᾶς γραμματεὺς μαθητευθεὶς τῇ βασιλείᾳ τῶν οὐρανῶν

ὅμοιός ἐστιν ἀνθρώπῳ οἰκοδεσπότῃ ὅστις ἐκβάλλει
ἐκ τοῦ θησαυροῦ αὐτοῦ καινὰ καὶ παλαιά.

St Mark iv. 26-29.   *

THE PARABLE OF THE SEED GROWING SECRETLY AND
   SLOWLY—THE SLOW AND SECRET GROWTH OF
   THE KINGDOM.

26 Καὶ ἔλεγεν   Οὕτως ἐστὶν ἡ βασιλεία τοῦ θεοῦ
ὡς [ἐὰν] ἄνθρωπος βάλῃ τὸν σπόρον ἐπὶ τῆς γῆς
27 καὶ καθεύδῃ καὶ ἐγείρηται νύκτα καὶ ἡμέραν, καὶ
ὁ σπόρος βλαστάνῃ καὶ μηκύνηται ὡς οὐκ οἶδεν αὐτός.
28 αὐτομάτη ἡ γῆ καρποφορεῖ, πρῶτον χόρτον,
εἶτα στάχυν, εἶτα πλήρη σῖτον ἐν τῷ στάχυϊ.   29
ὅταν δε παραδοῖ ὁ καρπός, εὐθὺς ἀποστέλλει τὸ
δρέπανον, ὅτι παρέστηκεν ὁ θερισμός.

(1.) *The Parables of the Hid Treasure and of the Pearl.*

The appropriation of the kingdom by mankind.—
These two parables teach the priceless value of the kingdom—*i.e.*, of Christianity—as compared with everything
else in the world, and enjoin the sacrifice of all else for
the sake of it.   They contain at once a prophecy that men
will be willing to make such sacrifices, and a precept
that they should do so.   The possessions that men sell
or of which they rid themselves may be external, as
property—or internal, as opinions, usages, tendencies, by
which their life has been swayed.

The history of Christianity affords many examples of
those who so acted, the first and chief being that of the
apostles themselves.   They not only embraced, for the
most part, a life of poverty in order to be with Jesus,
but for His sake separated themselves from their fellow-

countrymen and cut themselves off from their religion. They recognised in Jesus such a divine nature that they declared their belief in Him and clung to Him when nearly all the Rabbis, and the pious, and the learned had rejected Him, when the patriots or Galileans had cast Him off, and none but a few of the lowest class, sinners and publicans, were on His side. Thus they cut themselves off, for the sake of this treasure and pearl, from all they had held dear or venerated, abandoning the traditions of their forefathers handed down through many hundreds of years, and the Law for which many generations of their countrymen had fought and died —seeming even to reject the authority of Moses, which was regarded by every pious Jew as invested with the most awful sanctity. Such vast sacrifices they were willing to incur, induced by the words and character of Jesus, and His loving and winning bearing.

The difference between the two parables is this: the discoverer of the treasure lights upon it accidentally; he who finds the pearl is in search of pearls. The latter is making it his business to find some system of wisdom or philosophy that will satisfy him; the former is occupied in his ordinary business, and lights upon Christianity, which he finds so precious that he is willing to abandon all for it. Or again, we may say that two classes of men are described into which the world may roughly be divided. The one, the seekers after pearls, those who with a divine discontent desire to find out what is the best in the world—the best thoughts, the best system of life, the best principles on which to base their actions; the others, the finders of the treasure, those who have never thought about methods of managing their lives or principles on which to base their actions, but follow contentedly the traditions of their parents, and adopt the habits and ways of thinking prevalent in the society in which they were brought up, until, apparently by accident, novel methods and principles are brought to their notice. In the time of Jesus we may regard, as finders of the treasure, Zaccheus the publican and the woman of Samaria; as seekers after pearls, Anne and Simeon, and others who "waited for the consolation of Israel" (Luke ii. 25-36). In the apostolic age the finders of the treasure are such as the jailer at Philippi (Acts xvi. 30); the seekers of pearls, the eunuch of Ethiopia (Acts viii. 27-37), and Lydia (Acts xvi. 14, 15, 40).

In a later age the life of Augustine illustrates both parables. He found a hidden treasure in the works of Cicero, for from the perusal of them he was first awakened to a desire for truth and wisdom. He then became a seeker after pearls; he sought for happiness in the works of Plato, in Manichæism (a belief in the existence of two principles, one of good, the other of evil), and at last found the *unio*, the one pearl of great price, when he was converted to Christianity by hearing St Ambrose preach and by reading the epistles of St Paul. Thereupon he threw up his profession as a rhetorician, and gave himself up to retirement till he had qualified himself for active service in the cause of his adopted faith.

(2.) *The Parable of the Seed growing secretly and slowly.*

The slow and secret influence of the kingdom.—The object of this parable seems to be to warn the disciples that the results of preaching and teaching will be slow and unseen, as the processes of nature are. The contemporaries of Jesus expected results that should be immediate, and accompanied with great external signs and parade. Thus, on another occasion (Luke xvii. 20), the Pharisees demanded of Jesus when the kingdom of God should come. He answered them, " The kingdom of God cometh not with observation: neither shall they say,

Lo here! or, lo there! for, behold, the kingdom of God is within you," *or* "among you" ($\dot{\epsilon}\nu\tau\grave{o}\varsigma\ \dot{\upsilon}\mu\hat{\omega}\nu$).

The parable is a complement to that of the tares. In the latter Jesus prepared His disciples for imperfection in the kingdom; in this He prepares them for its slow and unostentatious development.

They were looking forward to immediate triumph and visible honour in an external kingdom. Thus two of His most intimate disciples ask that they may sit the one on His left, the other on His right hand, when He enters into His kingdom (Matt. xx. 21)—and this on the last journey to Jerusalem, where, as He had shortly before told them, He was to be shamefully put to death. After the crucifixion they were still discussing whether Jesus would restore again the kingdom to Israel—*i.e.*, they were still dreaming of a swiftly established and visible dominion (Acts i. 6).

The reply of Jesus on that occasion was in the spirit of this parable: "It is not for you to know the times or the seasons, which the Father hath put in His own power. But ye shall receive power, after that the Holy Ghost is come upon you: and ye shall be witnesses unto me both in Jerusalem, and in all Judea, and in Samaria, and unto the uttermost part of the earth."

He foresaw that His dominion was to extend, but it was to be a dominion to which men's hearts and spirits should submit voluntarily—a more real dominion than one established by force, and therefore established more slowly.

It is comparatively easy to control men's actions, but to win men's hearts and control their wills is a slower process.

This slowness and secrecy in the influence of Christianity is seen both in society at large and in the individual human spirit.

In society at large.—Christianity was preached first

in Palestine, far away from Rome, the great centre of civilisation—and in Galilee rather than in Jerusalem, the religious capital, and to a few peasants and fishermen, not to statesmen or philosophers. And these humble followers, this "little flock," required a long and patient training before they understood the principles of the kingdom. Jesus shrank from that kind of publicity which makes a preacher or teacher merely fashionable, and brings crowds to listen to him, who come not to be influenced by him but for the sake of the sensation, and because others come. This trait in His character is best illustrated from Matt. xii. 15-19: "A great multitude followed Him, and He healed them all; and charged them that they should not make Him known: that it might be fulfilled which was spoken by Esaias the prophet, saying, Behold my servant, whom I have chosen; my beloved, in whom my soul is well pleased: I will put my spirit upon Him, and He shall show judgment to the Gentiles. He shall not strive, nor cry; neither shall any man hear His voice in the streets. A bruised reed shall He not break, and smoking flax shall He not quench, till He send forth judgment unto victory."

Many times Jesus sought secrecy and forbade the proclamation of His acts, lest He should win notoriety; and though, contrary to the tone of the passage above and the parable before us, He seemed to be leading a life in public and to be making rapid progress, He knew that His progress was slower than it seemed to be. The multitudes that followed Him were in very few instances genuine disciples: the seed that He had sown was indeed growing, but not in this open fashion, as was seen at the time of His death, when He was misunderstood and finally forsaken, even by the eleven.

And after His death His religion won its way secretly and gradually, and principally among the humble and obscure, among the slaves, and in the dregs of the mixed populations of the cities of the empire.

Even now Christianity is very far from being the prevailing religion in the world: the Buddhists, for instance, are more numerous than Christians.

This parable, therefore, and the life of Jesus Himself, teach patience and trust to preachers and teachers, and to all who have to deal with the human will. They are not to expect quick or visible results, nor to distrust their existence because they are not speedy or visible.

There is a fine illustration of the lesson of the parable in Prescott's ' History of Mexico.' When the conqueror Cortes wished to convert the inhabitants of Tlascala in a single day, by throwing down their idols and forcing them to vow allegiance to Christ, he was deterred by the wiser counsels of Father Olmedo who accompanied him. The priest had "no relish for forced conversions. They could hardly be lasting. The growth of an hour might well die with an hour. Of what use was it to overturn the altar, if the idol remained enthroned in the heart? or to destroy the idol itself, if it were only to make room for another? Better to wait patiently the effect of time and teaching to soften the heart and open the under-standing, without which there could be no assurance of a sound and permanent conviction."

In individual Christians.—And as in society at large, so in individual Christians, the influence of Christianity is. secret and gradual. The noisy convert is rarely to be trusted to maintain his faith or his morality. Jesus Himself ever showed sobriety and temperance in His conduct and teaching. Impulsive enthusiasts He would warn, as He did Peter, of the sifting test of danger (Matt. xxvi. 33); or apply to them the touch-stone of a call to self-denial, as He did to the rich young man who asked Him what he should do to inherit the kingdom of heaven, and to the man who avowed he was ready to follow Him whithersoever He went (Luke xviii. 18-22, ix. 57, 58).

It does not follow that there is no religious feeling because men do not talk loudly of their religion. The man who has a high ideal before him distrusts himself. In this spirit St Paul, towards the close of his career, writing to the Philippians, says (Phil. iii. 12-14), "Not as though I had already attained, either were already perfect ; but I follow after, if that I may apprehend that for which also I am apprehended of Christ Jesus. Brethren, I count not myself to have apprehended : but this one thing I do, forgetting those things which are behind, and reaching forth unto those things which are before, I press toward the mark, for the prize of the high calling of God in Christ Jesus."

LESSON XV.

St Matthew xviii. 1-14.

THE PARABLE OF THE LITTLE CHILD—THE LITTLE ONES OF THE KINGDOM.

1 Ἐν ἐκείνῃ τῇ ὥρᾳ προσῆλθον οἱ μαθηταὶ τῷ Ἰησοῦ λέγοντες Τίς ἄρα μείζων ἐστὶν ἐν τῇ βασιλείᾳ τῶν οὐρανῶν; 2 καὶ προσκαλεσάμενος παιδίον ἔστησεν αὐτὸ ἐν μέσῳ αὐτῶν 3 καὶ εἶπεν Ἀμὴν λέγω ὑμῖν, ἐὰν μὴ στραφῆτε καὶ γένησθε ὡς τὰ παιδία, οὐ μὴ εἰσέλθητε εἰς τὴν βασιλείαν τῶν οὐρανῶν. 4 ὅστις οὖν ταπεινώσει ἑαυτὸν ὡς τὸ παιδίον τοῦτο, οὗτός ἐστιν ὁ μείζων ἐν τῇ βασιλείᾳ τῶν οὐρανῶν· 5 καὶ ὃς ἐὰν δέξηται ἓν παιδίον τοιοῦτο ἐπὶ τῷ ὀνόματί μου, ἐμὲ δέχεται· 6 ὃς δ’ ἂν σκανδαλίσῃ ἕνα τῶν μικρῶν τούτων τῶν πιστευόντων εἰς ἐμέ, συμφέρει αὐτῷ ἵνα κρεμασθῇ μύλος ὀνικὸς περὶ τὸν τράχηλον αὐτοῦ καὶ καταποντισθῇ ἐν τῷ πελάγει τῆς θαλάσσης. 7 Οὐαὶ τῷ κόσμῳ ἀπὸ τῶν σκανδάλων· ἀνάγκη γὰρ ἐλθεῖν τὰ σκάνδαλα, πλὴν οὐαὶ τῷ ἀνθρώπῳ δι’ οὗ τὸ σκάνδαλον ἔρχεται. 8 Εἰ δὲ ἡ χείρ σου ἢ ὁ πούς σου σκανδαλίζει σε, ἔκκοψον αὐτὸν καὶ βάλε ἀπὸ σοῦ· καλόν σοί ἐστιν εἰσελθεῖν εἰς τὴν ζωὴν κυλλὸν ἢ χωλόν, ἢ δύο χεῖρας ἢ δύο πόδας ἔχοντα βληθῆναι εἰς τὸ πῦρ τὸ αἰώνιον. 9 καὶ εἰ ὁ ὀφθαλμός σου σκανδαλίζει σε, ἔξελε αὐτὸν καὶ βάλε ἀπὸ σοῦ· καλόν σοί ἐστιν μονόφθαλμον εἰς

τὴν ζωὴν εἰσελθεῖν, ἢ δύο ὀφθαλμοὺς ἔχοντα βληθῆναι εἰς τὴν γέενναν τοῦ πυρός.   10 Ὁρᾶτε
μὴ καταφρονήσητε ἑνὸς τῶν μικρῶν τούτων, λέγω
γὰρ ὑμῖν ὅτι οἱ ἄγγελοι αὐτῶν ἐν οὐρανοῖς διὰ παντὸς βλέπουσι τὸ πρόσωπον τοῦ πατρός μου τοῦ ἐν
οὐρανοῖς.   12 τί ὑμῖν δοκεῖ; ἐὰν γένηταί τινι ἀνθρώπῳ ἑκατὸν πρόβατα καὶ πλανηθῇ ἓν ἐξ αὐτῶν, οὐχὶ
ἀφήσει τὰ ἐνενήκοντα ἐννέα ἐπὶ τὰ ὄρη καὶ πορευθεὶς
ζητεῖ τὸ πλανώμενον;   13 καὶ ἐὰν γένηται εὑρεῖν
αὐτό, ἀμὴν λέγω ὑμῖν ὅτι χαίρει ἐπ᾽ αὐτῷ μᾶλλον ἢ
ἐπὶ τοῖς ἐνενήκοντα ἐννέα τοῖς μὴ πεπλανημένοις.
14 οὕτως οὐκ ἔστιν θέλημα ἔμπροσθεν τοῦ πατρός
μου τοῦ ἐν οὐρανοῖς ἵνα ἀπόληται εἷς τῶν μικρῶν
τούτων.

LESSON XVI.

THE PAGAN AND CHRISTIAN IDEALS OF VIRTUE.

Virtue, manlike and childlike.—When Jesus declares
to His disciples that greatness is to be achieved in His
kingdom by those only who are humble and childlike,
He is introducing a new ideal of virtue into the world.
With both Greeks and Romans virtue and manliness
were nearly synonymous : ἀρετή is connected with
Ἄρης, the war-god, and *virtus* with *vir*. Homer represents this manly courage as that which confers pre-
eminence among men, αἰὲν ἀριστεύειν καὶ ὑπείροχον
ἔμμεναι ἄλλων (Il. vi. 208).

The qualities of manhood are courage, firmness, resolution, independence, self-respect, sense of honour : the
qualities of childhood are submission, obedience, modesty,
humility, meekness, gentleness, trustfulness.

In what way, then, is it good for the world that the
latter rather than the former should be represented as
having claim to eminence in the kingdom of heaven ?
Are we not inclined at heart to revolt from these words
of Jesus, as we do from some of His other difficult sayings —as that we resist not evil, but turn our left cheek
to him who smites us on the right ? We find it difficult
not to prefer the knight to the monk or the trader :
goodness as represented by Jesus seems to us passive
rather than active, and to consist in innocence rather
than nobleness : we are tempted to contrast unfavour-

ably the μικροί of Jesus with the μεγαλόψυχος of Aristotle.

The μεγαλόψυχος "thinks himself worthy of high honours because he is worthy of them; will not court little dangers, but will incur great ones; does kindnesses, but is ashamed to receive them; is concerned in few things, and those great and famous; does not bear malice, nor care to be praised himself, nor to have others blamed, because this is inconsistent with self-respect."

Above all, perhaps, we seem to miss in the teaching of Jesus any reference to the virtue patriotism; whereas among the Greeks and Romans, at least in their best days, the words patriot and good man were almost synonymous.

Let us consider if we can find any reason for these apparent defects, and if the records of history lead us to conclude that the teaching of Christ has impaired the manliness of the world, and that Christians have shown themselves less manly or less patriotic than other men.

Now it was reasonable to expect that Jesus in His precepts should have regard to the thoughts and condition of those whom He was addressing, and to the times in which He lived. He addressed mainly Jews, partly Romans, and to some extent Greeks and people of other nationalities, whom it is not necessary to mention in detail, as they have had but little influence on the world.

The Roman type of character.—Now the Romans were the ruling nation of the world, and they had become so by the display of what may be called the heroic virtues, as firmness, resolution, courage, patriotism, and justice.

The type of character thus produced was majestic and solid, but it cannot be said to be pleasing on the whole, or graceful. It was usually austere, simple, unemotional, and unsentimental, even among the noblest

spirits; and among ordinary men, coarse and even brutal.
There were, indeed, exceptions to this type, as, notably,
Virgil, whose influence even in modern times is felt as
a softening power; and before Virgil's time, Cicero
showed something of the sentiment of a modern gentleman.

But in the time of Jesus, the Romans had degenerated
even in the practice of the virtues for which they were
most conspicuous. The days of the Punic wars, when,
on the return of the defeated consul from the battle
of Cannæ, the Senate thanked him for not despairing
of the commonwealth, and had refused to ransom the
prisoners or to listen to terms of peace, had been succeeded by the days of Jugurtha, when Roman generals
had received bribes from the enemy—by the horrors of
the civil wars—and finally by a despotism which made
patriotism impossible.

That lofty ideal of patriotism which implied the utter
abnegation of self for the sake of the community, and
connected all religious rites with the State, had degenerated into a worship of the emperor. This, indeed, was
the only tangible form that patriotism could assume
when once the empire had embraced peoples of all
creeds and all nationalities.

Greek patriotism.—The Greeks in the time of Jesus
had fallen, as far as external rule was concerned, under
the dominion of Rome, though, as far as the intellect
was concerned, they had led their conquerors captive.

Græcia capta ferum victorem cepit.

When we look back on their history we are tempted,
however, to regard them as affording greater examples of
patriotism than Christianity has been able to present.
We think of Leonidas and his three hundred perishing
in perfect composure, and with no hope of future happiness, at the sacred call of duty in defence of their
country; of Pericles, who raised Athens to be not only

the first Hellenic State of her time, but to take her place among the very few States that have had an abiding influence on the history of the world, and who served his country in spite of her capricious treatment of him, never giving way to envy or anger, notwithstanding the greatness of his power, and who died declaring that the most honourable part of his character was this, that no Athenian through his means ever put on mourning; of Callicratidas, who, at a time when the animosity between Sparta and Athens was bitterest, nobly sought to unite them against the Persian, and died fighting in the execution of his duty for a cause he was too great to admire; of Demosthenes bravely contending against the supineness of his countrymen, and by his eloquence and spirit keeping alive for a time the Pan-Hellenic spirit against the barbarian. But there is another side to the picture. We see men like Themistocles, Pausanias, and Alcibiades, in alliance with the bitterest foes of their countrymen, receiving bribes from them, and fighting on their side in a manner we cannot easily imagine possible in Christendom, especially when we recollect that that foe was an Eastern. Modern heroes have been pirates, like the great Elizabethan naval heroes; have plotted against the sovereign who trusted them, as Marlborough did. But it would be very difficult in modern times to find any parallel in which a statesman of Western descent has served under the banner of an Eastern monarch against his own countrymen with the shamelessness of these Greek politicians.

Jewish patriotism.—If we turn now from Greece and Rome to the countrymen of Jesus, we shall find their patriotism as obstinate as it was hopeless and misguided. This was proved subsequently by the issue of the war with Titus. It was hopeless not only on account of the enormous power of Rome, and the paucity of the Jewish population, but also of the quarrels of the Jews among themselves. In fact, a far-seeing patriot in those days must have felt not only that resistance was hopeless, but that the most desirable position for the Jews was submission. The Romans were on the whole more prepared and more likely to deal justly by them than they were by one another.

The times demanded a milder ideal.—But besides all this, we must remember that the heroic or manly virtues are pre-eminently the virtues of the early ages of man, while nations were fighting for superiority, forming themselves and their characters by the struggle, and proving which was to be the conqueror. The more amiable virtues belonged to the future or the more civilised ages, and it was to these ages that Christianity adapted itself.

The Romans had finished the conquest of the civilised world, and with that conquest had lost the scope for the manly virtues, and though still retaining much of their ancient greatness, were falling to decay and corruption for lack of the amiable virtues and an inspiring motive: the Greeks had already fallen into decay, partly from restlessness and caprice, partly because with them lust had taken the place of love: the Jew was approaching to his destruction, because with him religion had become a selfish and fanatical expectation of immediate conquest, or of future reward and happiness.

It was among such a population that Jesus uttered the words, "Whosoever shall humble himself as this little child, the same is greatest in the kingdom of heaven."

That is to say, a new type of character was to be introduced—a type, indeed, that had already been partially prepared for by such men as Euripides and Virgil, and was destined to find noble pagan representatives in such men as Epictetus and Marcus Aurelius—a type in which the consciousness of an unattainable standard would foster humility and dependence upon God, rather than self-reliance and pride in the greatness of humanity.

But that the milder virtues do not necessarily exclude the heroic we can show from the example of Jesus Himself and of His followers.

Jesus Himself, throughout His life, displayed in harmonious proportions the heroic and the amiable virtues —often, indeed, passing, apparently without an effort, from a display of the one to a display of the other.

The patriotism of Jesus.—As a patriot, He saw the uselessness of a contest with Rome; but by His teaching and example He expanded the notion of patriotism. Demosthenes was a patriot when he sought to awaken his countrymen to their danger from Philip; Jeremiah was no less a patriot when he counselled his countrymen to submit to Babylon; Socrates was a patriot not only when he fought for his country, and when, for the sake of his country, he refused to obey an angry mob calling upon him to commit an act of injustice, but also when, day by day, he strove to awaken in them an intellectual conscience and a desire for truth. Jesus showed the patriotism of Jeremiah when He refused to countenance a hopeless struggle. against the invincible legions of Rome. He betrayed the true patriot's yearning over His country in His exclamation, " O Jerusalem, Jerusalem, . . . how often would I have gathered thy children together, even as a hen gathereth her chickens under her wings, and ye would not ! " (Matt. xxiii. 37); and in His words to the women who followed Him weeping to the place of crucifixion, " Daughters of Jerusalem, weep not for me, but weep for yourselves, and for your children " (Luke xxiii. 28). But He showed a loftier patriotism when He strove to persuade His fellow-countrymen that a moral and spiritual regeneration was more important even than political freedom; that it is the truth that makes free; and that to lose life for the sake of others is nobler than to save it. In such teaching were the germs of all freedom and safety, for a lofty moral tone conduces to national deliverance as much as physical force does; for " where the carcass is [*i.e.*, where moral corruption is], there are the vultures gathered together " (Matt. xxiv. 28).

The manliness of Jesus.—If, again, we review the life of Jesus, we shall find, though on the whole it was distinguished by the amiable virtues of gentleness and meekness, there was no defect of heroism and manly vigour when occasion required. Gentle with the sinner who erred from weakness, He showed strong and right-eous resentment against the Pharisee, whose self-satisfied hypocrisy was an injury to the nation.

In the same hour in which, as a patriot, He wept over His native city, whose doom He foresaw, He drove indignantly from the Temple those who bought and sold. The very evening He was betrayed He is repre-sented by the Gospel as spending in calm discourse with His disciples. He is calm before His betrayer, before Pilate, before Herod. After outrage and torture, and while His weakened frame faints under the burden of the cross, He has words of comfort for the women who follow Him. Amid the agonies of the crucifixion, He prays that His enemies may be forgiven. Yet for Himself He will not plead. During and after His trial, injustice, indignity, and outrage extort from Him no word of undignified complaint; and for two long sol-emn hours, while His enemies watch or taunt Him on the cross, His heroic silence is unbroken.

Neither do we find unmanly weakness among His disciples : witness the conduct of Peter and John before the Sanhedrim (Acts iv. 19), of Stephen, and of the vigorous and fearless St Paul.

But it has been said the courage of the early Christians was shown only in the propagation of the faith, and in the endurance of persecution on behalf of it; while they held aloof from public affairs, and at first sight would appear to have shown themselves bad patriots, or at least to have transferred their allegiance from their country to their creed. The fact was, their religion debarred them from taking part in public life, for nearly every act of duty performed by a public officer was preceded by a sacrifice to false gods.

Patriotic courage of the early Christians.—But the time came when opportunities of serving their fellow-countrymen in other ways presented themselves, and then the Christians did not show themselves wanting. During the pestilences that desolated Carthage in A.D. 326, and Alexandria in the reign of Maximin, A.D. 312, while the pagans fled panic-stricken from the contagion, the Christians extorted the admiration of their fellow-countrymen by the courage with which they rallied round their bishops, consoled the last hours of the sufferers, and buried the abandoned dead.

Extension of the civic virtues.—In point of fact, the teaching of Jesus and His disciples is so far from disparaging the civic and manly virtues, that it has rather found new scope and fresh motives for them.

For in ancient times civic virtues bore reference only to the upper and middle classes of society: those who performed the manual labour of the world, being slaves, were excluded from all participation in civic life. Though we cannot ascribe to Christianity all the credit of the elevation and emancipation of slaves, much is due to its influence; and, above all, much to the example of the monk Benedict (born A.D. 480), who, by enjoining manual labour on the community he founded, was the first to make such labour honourable. And, as time went on, the labourer so honoured gained freedom, and with freedom a share in public life, and scope for the exercise of civic virtues.

Christian courage.—Again, the Christians displayed the manly virtues in contending with the sufferings of humanity, even those of a most loathsome description, not shrinking even from contact with the leper, or with those smitten with the plague. One of the most notable displays of Christian courage which resulted in a great public advantage was that of the monk Telemachus, mentioned in the essay on the parable of the leaven.

Examples of civic virtue in Christians. — That Christianity is far from being incompatible, however, with the display of the civic virtues in the strictest sense, might be shown from the life of Louis IX. of France (1226-1270), whose gentleness, honesty, and piety make his renown rival that of the stoic Marcus Aurelius (138-161); of our own Alfred the Great (869-901), who was superior as a ruler to Louis in that he never forsook his duty at home for enterprises abroad, and of whom it has been said that he was a saint without superstition, a scholar without ostentation, a warrior all whose wars were fought in the defence of his country, a conqueror whose laurels were never stained by cruelty, a prince never cast down by adversity, never lifted up to insolence in the hour of triumph, whose character was always distinguished by pure, simple, and almost childlike disinterestedness; of Washington, again, who never, through resentment or jealousy, swerved from the task his lofty and serene sense of duty imposed, never in war or peace felt the touch of a meaner ambition, and knew no aim save that of guarding the freedom of his fellow-country-men, and no personal longing save that of returning to his own fireside when that freedom was secured; of Joan of Arc, who, inspired by piety and patriot-ism, faced wounds and death with manly courage, and yet never abandoned her gentle womanly character; and of John Hampden, who combined courtesy, humility, and affability with iron resolution in council and fearless courage on the field. Other names will occur, but all these are names of Christians who displayed, in lives spent in intense activity, a combination of the heroic and amiable virtues such as, if we except the great Marcus Aurelius, we find in none of the heroes of antiquity.

Still, however, we have not yet really touched the essential point of difference in the exhibition of the manly virtues by pagans and by Christians, which is this, that the virtues of paganism were adapted only for great occasions, while those of Christianity can be exhibited in the humblest sphere of life.

Christian virtue displayed in humble spheres.—In the time of Jesus, religion had little or no influence on the minds of Romans. It had become a mere ceremonial, necessary to divert the anger of the gods, but having no reference to conduct. Conduct was influenced by the Stoic philosophy, which, noble as it was, rarely penetrated below the upper classes of society. It was a school for heroes, not for ordinary people. But all men cannot lead the lives of heroes in the sense of passing their lives amid great public actions. When manual labour came to be performed by freemen, and was no longer the monopoly of the slave, a creature regarded as a tool and outside the pale of human sympathy; when women and the lives and work of women were, under the influence of Christianity, estimated at a higher value, the manly and heroic virtues found an ampler scope for action, and could be displayed not only by statesmen and warriors, but wherever there was work to be done or suffering to be endured or alleviated—at the plough, in the mine, on the sea, in the shop, in the manufactory, in the counting-house. Christianity, by adding new dignity to human life, added new dignity to human employments. The invention of printing, and the publicity given to all notable actions in our time, bring before our notice the heroic actions of the humblest ; and there is an increasing readiness everywhere to recognise heroic deeds performed even by the lowliest of the community, especially when heroism and modesty, manliness and amiability, are combined.

LESSON XVII.

St Matthew xviii. 15-35.

ON CONFLICTS IN THE KINGDOM, AND THE PARABLE OF THE UNFORGIVING DEBTOR.

15 Ἐὰν δὲ ἁμαρτήσῃ ὁ ἀδελφός σου, ὕπαγε ἔλεγξον αὐτὸν μεταξὺ σοῦ καὶ αὐτοῦ μόνου. ἐάν σου ἀκούσῃ, ἐκέρδησας τὸν ἀδελφόν σου· 16 ἐὰν δὲ μὴ ἀκούσῃ, παράλαβε μετὰ σοῦ ἔτι ἕνα ἢ δύο, ἵνα ἐπὶ στόματος δύο μαρτύρων ἢ τριῶν σταθῇ πᾶν ῥῆμα· 17 ἐὰν δὲ παρακούσῃ αὐτῶν, εἰπὸν τῇ ἐκκλησίᾳ· ἐὰν δὲ καὶ τῆς ἐκκλησίας παρακούσῃ, ἔστω σοι ὥσπερ ὁ ἐθνικὸς καὶ ὁ τελώνης. 18 Ἀμὴν λέγω ὑμῖν, ὅσα ἐὰν δήσητε ἐπὶ τῆς γῆς ἔσται δεδεμένα ἐν οὐρανῷ καὶ ὅσα ἐὰν λύσητε ἐπὶ τῆς γῆς ἔσται λελυμένα ἐν οὐρανῷ. 19 Πάλιν [ἀμὴν] λέγω ὑμῖν ὅτι ἐὰν δύο συμφωνήσωσιν ἐξ ὑμῶν ἐπὶ τῆς γῆς περὶ παντὸς πράγματος οὗ ἐὰν αἰτήσωνται, γενήσεται αὐτοῖς παρὰ τοῦ πατρός μου τοῦ ἐν οὐρανοῖς. 20 οὗ γάρ εἰσιν δύο ἢ τρεῖς συνηγμένοι εἰς τὸ ἐμὸν ὄνομα, ἐκεῖ εἰμὶ ἐν μέσῳ αὐτῶν.

21 Τότε προσελθὼν ὁ Πέτρος εἶπεν [αὐτῷ] Κύριε, ποσάκις ἁμαρτήσει εἰς ἐμὲ ὁ ἀδελφός μου καὶ ἀφήσω αὐτῷ; ἕως ἑπτάκις; 22 λέγει αὐτῷ ὁ Ἰησοῦς Οὐ λέγω σοι ἕως ἑπτάκις ἀλλὰ ἕως ἑβδομηκοντάκις ἑπτά. 23 Διὰ τοῦτο ὡμοιώθη ἡ βασιλεία τῶν οὐρανῶν ἀνθρώπῳ βασιλεῖ ὃς ἠθέλησεν συνᾶραι λόγον μετὰ τῶν δούλων

αὐτοῦ· 24 ἀρξαμένου δὲ αὐτοῦ συναίρειν προσήχθη εἷς αὐτῷ ὀφειλέτης μυρίων ταλάντων. 25 μὴ ἔχοντος δὲ αὐτοῦ ἀποδοῦναι ἐκέλευσεν αὐτὸν ὁ κύριος πραθῆναι καὶ τὴν γυναῖκα καὶ τὰ τέκνα καὶ πάντα ὅσα ἔχει καὶ ἀποδοθῆναι. 26 πεσὼν οὖν ὁ δοῦλος προσεκύνει αὐτῷ λέγων Μακροθύμησον ἐπ’ ἐμοί, καὶ πάντα ἀποδώσω σοι. 27 σπλαγχνισθεὶς δὲ ὁ κύριος τοῦ δούλου [ἐκείνου] ἀπέλυσεν αὐτόν, καὶ τὸ δάνειον ἀφῆκεν αὐτῷ. 28 ἐξελθὼν δὲ ὁ δοῦλος ἐκεῖνος εὖρεν ἕνα τῶν συνδούλων αὐτοῦ ὃς ὤφειλεν αὐτῷ ἑκατόν δηνάρια, καὶ κρατήσας αὐτὸν ἔπνιγεν λέγων Ἀπόδος εἴ τι ὀφείλεις. 29 πεσὼν οὖν ὁ σύνδουλος αὐτοῦ παρεκάλει αὐτὸν λέγων Μακροθύμησον ἐπ’ ἐμοί, καὶ ἀποδώσω σοι. 30 ὁ δὲ οὐκ ἤθελεν, ἀλλὰ ἀπελθὼν ἔβαλεν αὐτὸν εἰς φυλακὴν ἕως ἀποδῷ τὸ ὀφειλόμενον. 31 ἰδόντες οὖν οἱ σύνδουλοι αὐτοῦ τὰ γινόμενα ἐλυπήθησαν σφόδρα, καὶ ἐλθόντες διεσάφησαν τῷ κυρίῳ ἑαυτῶν πάντα τὰ γενόμενα. 32 τότε προσκαλεσάμενος αὐτὸν ὁ κύριος αὐτοῦ λέγει αὐτῷ· Δοῦλε πονηρέ, πᾶσαν τὴν ὀφειλὴν ἐκείνην ἀφῆκά σοι, ἐπεὶ παρεκάλεσάς με· 33 οὐκ ἔδει καὶ σὲ ἐλεῆσαι τὸν σύνδουλόν σου, ὡς κἀγὼ σὲ ἠλέησα; 34 καὶ ὀργισθεὶς ὁ κύριος αὐτοῦ παρέδωκεν αὐτὸν τοῖς βασανισταῖς ἕως οὗ ἀποδῷ πᾶν τὸ ὀφειλόμενον. 35 οὕτως καὶ ὁ πατήρ μου ὁ οὐράνιος ποιήσει ὑμῖν, ἐὰν μὴ ἀφῆτε ἕκαστος τῷ ἀδελφῷ αὐτοῦ ἀπὸ τῶν καρδιῶν ὑμῶν.

LESSON XVIII.

FORGIVENESS.

To understand the teaching of Jesus on the subject of forgiveness, we must compare His sayings on different occasions, and recall His own conduct towards sinners and His enemies.

In the Sermon on the Mount He was addressing a popular audience early in His career as a teacher, and in the usual oriental fashion He employed striking particular examples to convey general principles of conduct.

Thus, when He bade His hearers, when smitten on the right cheek, turn the other also, they might perhaps recall the saying of one of their Rabbis, "If thy neighbour calls thee an ass, put on the ass's saddle." In both cases they would understand that this exaggerated instance of non-resistance conveyed a strong lesson against the vindictive spirit, but it is not likely that they thought of literal obedience to either precept.

In John xviii. 22, 23, we read how Jesus acted when He was smitten; and it is curious that the same word occurs there as here, though in that passage it is doubtful whether the blow was given with the rod or with the hand. When one of the officers ἔδωκεν ῥάπισμα τῷ Ἰησοῦ, He did not offer Himself to be smitten again, but calmly, without any appearance of anger, reasoned with the man, saying, "If I spake evil, bear witness of the evil; but if well, why smitest thou me?"

It is, indeed, quite possible to conceive a man obeying the precept and disobeying the principle, and disobeying the precept yet carrying out the principle. It would be possible to turn the other cheek and yet have deadly hate at the heart, and to knock a man down and yet be in perfect charity with him.

Later in His career, and amid His own disciples, when His community was organised, Jesus gave the more detailed directions for their conduct when injured which are recorded in verses 15-17 of the passage which stands at the head of this essay.

In this admonition He bids the offended person to be the first to seek reconciliation—thus declaring that he has the vantage-ground, for it is the giving offence that places a Christian in a position of inferiority. He orders a private interview first, to avoid exposure, and scandal, and unnecessary bitterness : if that fails, the two or three witnesses will, by their impartiality, eliminate misrepresentations or exaggerations arising from self-love : the church—that is, the officers of the church —will at last decide the quarrel authoritatively.

Though there may at first sight seem a difficulty in carrying this out at the present day in many Christian communities, yet, practically, men may almost always carry out the spirit of it. Even boyish quarrels might often be so settled, though not so easily as those of grown-up people, for boys can seldom accurately weigh evidence, or express themselves with care. On the other hand, they are not so apt as grown-up people to be vindictive, or to cherish long animosities. The precept, however, is practically carried out whenever friends seek to reconcile their friends.

Some have thought that the precept, "Not to resist evil," was intended for the conduct of Christians towards the heathen—that by this attitude of non-resistance the latter might. be taught the principles of Christian forgiveness, to which, from ignorance, they could not be expected to conform.　Curiosity and amazement would lead to a revulsion of feeling, to inquiry, and to knowledge.

The records, however, which we possess of the conduct of Jesus' disciples during His life and afterwards are not sufficiently full to enable us to decide whether they did ever literally carry out this precept before the Gentiles.

In Jesus Himself we see righteous contempt for low cunning expressing itself in sarcasm, as when He spoke of Herod Antipas as "a fox" (Luke xiii. 32); and righteous indignation against hypocrisy in His invectives against the Pharisees in Matt. xxiii., culminating in verse 33, "Ye serpents, ye offspring of vipers, how shall ye escape the judgment of Gehenna?"　Notwithstanding, a few days after, amid the agonies of the cross, He prays to His Father to forgive His enemies, "for they know not what they do" (Luke xxiii. 34); and that this prayer does not refer only to the Roman soldiers, but may have extended to all the Pharisees, and even to men so diabolical as Caiaphas and Annas, seems admissible from the speech of St Peter in Acts iii. 17,—"And now, brethren, I know that in ignorance ye did it" ("slew the Prince of life"), "as did also your rulers;" and his previous speech in Acts ii. 23, where he speaks of the Roman soldiers as "wicked *hands*."　So also the first martyr Stephen, though, immediately before he was stoned, he had uttered the strongest invectives against his hearers (Acts vii. 51), calling them stiff-necked and uncircumcised, betrayers and murderers; yet in his dying agonies he cries, "Lord, lay not this sin to their charge."

How are we to reconcile these uncompromising denunciations with these final prayers of forgiveness?

In *the first place*, the denunciations refer to sins

against others—the prayer for forgiveness to the offence against the speaker: *secondly*, in the hour of death the speaker sees himself already before the tribunal of God —the judgment on the offenders can no longer be averted by any effort on his part to change their conduct, neither can he hinder its influence on others by strong words throwing light on its wickedness: *thirdly*, the hour of death, like all supreme events, has a clearing and softening influence,—"life's fitful fever" is over, all harsher passions melt into pity and love, while the soul itself welcomes peace and rest.   There is no difficulty in conceiving the warrior who, in the midst of battle, under a strong sense of fighting for the right, had been unsparingly dealing death and wounds, as dying soon after with a prayer for his enemies on his lips.

In order to understand the true meaning of forgiveness, however, we must analyse still further.

Injuries in relation to forgiveness may be classified (1) as those that affect us as individuals, (2) those we have to deal with as members of society.

(1) As regards the first class, the parable of the unforgiving servant related to St Peter, in Matt. xviii. 23-35, enforces a principle that had already been expressed, though more feebly, by the author of the Book of Ecclesiasticus (xxviii. 3, 4),—" One man beareth hatred against another; and doth he seek pardon from the Lord? He showeth no mercy to a man who is like himself; and doth he ask forgiveness of his own sins?"   As we gain higher conceptions of the holiness of God, we are filled with a greater sense of our own sinfulness, and this will make us more lenient towards the weaknesses of others.

But Jesus introduced another element into the notion of forgiveness, the desire for the improvement of others. Righteous indignation may be salutary for strong and wilful offenders, but His own words, "They know not what they do," and St Peter's, "Through ignorance ye did it," teach us that it is often the offender rather than the offended who is the sufferer, and introduce an element of pitifulness for the Christian who, by injuring his brother, mars his Christian character. Such a man the offended Christian will seek to reclaim by gentleness and sympathy. In point of fact there is no true forgiveness, in a Christian sense, without sympathy. The forgiveness accompanied by contempt, or indifference, or mistrust, is a bastard form of forgiveness. It does not fulfil Christ's condition of "coming from the heart."

On the other hand, for the good of the offender, he who is wronged, though he forgives, may yet punish or demand restitution. The man who has been robbed may forgive the thief and yet enforce repayment. Brutus may have forgiven his sons as a father and executed them afterwards as a judge.

But supposing the offender does not repent? Jesus has told us how to act in Matt. xviii. 15-17. But in the parable that follows, He teaches us that even with the unrepentant we must not be vindictive, must be ready to be reconciled with the offender, and must strive to put ourselves in his place.

But are we to forgive all offences, even the most villanous and deadly, against which our whole moral being revolts?

It is evident there are many offences and sins that those who have no strong moral feelings more readily forgive than those whose moral sense is developed. In this sense, shallow natures forgive more easily than the deeper. But the forgiveness of the Christian will be more cordial and sympathetic in proportion to the greatness of the offence, because he sees in the repentant offender the image of what he might have been had he not fallen so low, and because he expects the sinner's repentance to be bitter in proportion to the greatness of his offence. His love for his fellow-Christians will make him long to make reconciliation easy to him, and to remove from him the feeling of degradation that depresses him and mars his character.

(2) But this love will not hinder him from prosecuting and punishing the offender, if it be necessary for the good or for the protection of society. Jesus, indeed, laid down no law with regard to this, for while He was founding His church He knew that His followers for a long time would be outcasts from the laws, and unable to avail themselves of them. We find St Paul, however, appealing to the emperor against his enemies; and no such objections exist now to the settlement of disputes by the law as existed in the early days of Christianity.

Finally, the principles of Jesus' teaching seem to bid us have some feeling of forgiveness and pity even for the monsters of humanity who have themselves been most pitiless and worked most harm,—even for the Caligulas, the Neros, and the Domitians; even for Philip of Spain and Alva; even for Judas and Caiaphas. We must feel sorry that they mistook their path in life, missed the treasury of the world's love, and forfeited the nobility of their own characters, and we think with dread and horror of their possible future: at the least, we shudder at the thought that in eternity "they should be themselves and know themselves to be." Jesus seems to forbid us to pursue beyond the grave such men (brothers as they were in the great human family) with hatred or rancour, with a desire to punish for the sake of punishing, not of bettering. Even *they* must have had some virtue in them which different circumstances might have developed,—may, perchance, develop yet. They must have had some pity or truthfulness, love of the young, one or two good hours.

And if Jesus inspires us with such feelings towards

these dead monsters who seem to be past doing further harm, must He not much more desire us to entertain them towards the living who are susceptible yet to kindly influences? So that the Christian who seeks to imitate his Master will strive (hard though it be in proportion to his sense of right and indignation at wrong) to be tender towards the hard, patient with the impatient, kindly to the selfish, and philanthropic towards the misanthropic, imitating the perfection of the heavenly Father who makes His sun to shine on the just and the unjust, and His seas to float the pirate as well as the trader.

LESSON XIX.

St Luke x. 25-42.

ON DOING AND BEING—THE PARABLE OF THE GOOD SAMARITAN—MARY AND MARTHA.

25 Καὶ ἰδοὺ νομικός τις ἀνέστη ἐκπειράζων αὐτόν, λέγων· Διδάσκαλε, τί ποιήσας ζωὴν αἰώνιον κληρονομήσω; 26 ὁ δὲ εἶπεν πρὸς αὐτόν· ἐν τῷ νόμῳ τί γέγραπται; πῶς ἀναγινώσκεις; 27 ὁ δὲ ἀποκριθεὶς εἶπεν· ἀγαπήσεις κύριον τὸν θεόν σου ἐξ ὅλης τῆς καρδίας σου καὶ ἐν ὅλῃ τῇ ψυχῇ καὶ ἐν ὅλῃ τῇ ἰσχύϊ σου καὶ ἐν ὅλῃ τῇ διανοίᾳ σου, καὶ τὸν πλησίον σου ὡς σεαυτόν. 28 εἶπεν δὲ αὐτῷ· ὀρθῶς ἀπεκρίθης· τοῦτο ποίει, καὶ ζήσῃ. 29 ὁ δὲ θέλων δικαιῶσαι ἑαυτὸν εἶπεν πρὸς τὸν Ἰησοῦν Καὶ τίς ἐστίν μου πλησίον; 30 ὑπολαβὼν ὁ Ἰησοῦς εἶπεν Ἄνθρωπός τις κατέβαινεν ἀπὸ Ἰερουσαλὴμ εἰς Ἰερειχὼ καὶ λῃσταῖς περιέπεσεν, οἳ καὶ ἐκδύσαντες αὐτὸν καὶ πληγὰς ἐπιθέντες ἀπῆλθον ἀφέντες ἡμιθανῆ. 31 κατὰ συγκυρίαν δὲ ἱερεύς τις κατέβαινεν [ἐν] τῇ ὁδῷ ἐκείνῃ, καὶ ἰδὼν αὐτὸν ἀντιπαρῆλθεν· 32 ὁμοίως δὲ καὶ Λευείτης κατὰ τὸν τόπον ἐλθὼν καὶ ἰδὼν ἀντιπαρῆλθεν. 33 Σαμαρείτης δέ τις ὁδεύων ἦλθεν κατ᾽ αὐτὸν καὶ ἰδὼν ἐσπλαγχνίσθη, 34 καὶ προσελθὼν κατέδησεν τὰ τραύματα αὐτοῦ ἐπιχέων ἔλαιον καὶ οἶνον, ἐπιβιβάσας δὲ αὐτὸν ἐπὶ τὸ ἴδιον κτῆνος ἤγαγεν αὐτὸν εἰς πανδοχεῖον καὶ

ἐπεμελήθη αὐτοῦ. 35 καὶ ἐπὶ τὴν αὔριον ἐκβαλὼν δύο δηνάρια ἔδωκεν τῷ πανδοχεῖ καὶ εἶπεν Ἐπιμελήθητι αὐτοῦ, καὶ ὅτι ἂν προσδαπανήσῃς ἐγὼ ἐν τῷ ἐπανέρχεσθαί με ἀποδώσω σοι. 36 τίς τούτων τῶν τριῶν πλησίον δοκεῖ σοι γεγονέναι τοῦ ἐμπεσόντος εἰς τοὺς λῃστάς; ὁ δὲ εἶπεν 37 Ὁ ποιήσας τὸ ἔλεος μετ᾽ αὐτοῦ. εἶπεν δὲ αὐτῷ [ὁ] Ἰησοῦς Πορεύου καὶ σὺ ποίει ὁμοίως.

38 Ἐν δὲ τῷ πορεύεσθαι αὐτοὺς αὐτὸς εἰσῆλθεν εἰς κώμην τινά· γυνὴ δέ τις ὀνόματι Μάρθα ὑπεδέξατο αὐτὸν εἰς τὴν οἰκίαν. 39 καὶ τῇδε ἦν ἀδελφὴ καλουμένη Μαριάμ, [ἣ] καὶ παρακαθεσθεῖσα πρὸς τοὺς πόδας τοῦ κυρίου ἤκουεν τὸν λόγον αὐτοῦ. 40 ἡ δὲ Μάρθα περιεσπᾶτο περὶ πολλὴν διακονίαν· ἐπιστᾶσα δὲ εἶπεν Κύριε, οὐ μέλει σοι ὅτι ἡ ἀδελφή μου μόνην με κατέλειπεν διακονεῖν; εἰπὸν οὖν αὐτῇ ἵνα μοι συναντιλάβηται. 41 ἀποκριθεὶς δὲ εἶπεν αὐτῇ ὁ κύριος Μάρθα Μάρθα, μεριμνᾷς καὶ θορυβάζῃ περὶ πολλά, ὀλίγων δέ ἐστιν χρεία ἢ ἑνός· 42 Μαριὰμ γὰρ τὴν ἀγαθὴν μερίδα ἐξελέξατο ἥτις οὐκ ἀφαιρεθήσεται αὐτῆς.

LESSON XX.

THE SAMARITANS—RELIGIOUS INTOLERANCE.

THE Samaritans were the descendants of the Assyrians who were settled, probably by Esar-Haddon, in the deserted territory of the ten tribes, after these last had been transported to Babylon (2 Kings xvii. 24). In the course of time they had combined with the remnant of Israel, and the exiled Judeans expelled from Jerusalem in its long party contests, to form a separate Mosaic community. When the Jews returned from Babylon they refused to allow these people, who had not Jewish blood in their veins, to share in the rebuilding of the Temple, and thus commenced a feud which was perpetuated and intensified by deadly contests. The nickname of Cuthæans, derived from Cuth, one of the countries from which their ancestors came, expressed the Jewish contempt for their origin. In B.C. 110, John Hyrcanus, the Maccabean ruler, destroyed their capital, and even brought down streams of water over the ruins, that no Samaritan might ever settle upon the hills again. The town lay in ruins for more than half a century, and the Jews held a special feast in celebration of the destruction of Samaria.

The Samaritans had built on Mount Gerizim a rival temple to that of Jerusalem, but this too had been levelled to the ground by John Hyrcanus, and a synagogue was erected in its stead at Neapolis. They refused to acknowledge as canonical the books which had been first collected during, or after, the exile, and limited themselves to the Pentateuch, for their copy of which they claimed an authority and antiquity above any possessed by the Jews. They regarded themselves as the descendants of the true patriarchs, with memorials of whom their land was full. They believed the genuine vessels of the tabernacle to be buried under Mount Gerizim, and in the time of Pilate all Samaria flocked thither at the summons of a sorcerer. "When the Cuthæans," said a Rabbi, "renounce Mount Gerizim, praise Israel, and believe in the resurrection of the dead, there may be unity again between them and Jerusalem." Not only, however, did they differ seriously from the Jews in the extent of their religious beliefs, but they incurred the contempt of that steadfast people by the facility with which they became renegades to their faith when occasion served, becoming now Sidonian, now Persian, now Median, and allowing their god to be called now by Jewish and now by Hellenic names. This contempt finds strong expression in the Book of Ecclesiasticus (l. 25, 26), in these terms : "There be two manner of nations which my heart abhorreth, and the third nation is no nation ; they that sit on the mountain of Samaria, and they that dwell among the Philistines, and that foolish people that dwell in Sidon."

With the advent of the Romans fresh fuel was added to this national hatred. Pompey restored Samaria under the name of Gabinopolis, and Herod conferred on it the prouder name of Sebaste. The Idumean Herod was as much beloved in Samaria as he was hated in Jerusalem. With the Samaritans he took counsel, and conducted war, and to them he betook himself when Jerusalem no longer pleased him. All his Roman proclivities, which the Rabbis of Judea considered a crime in him, he could satisfy in Sebaste. And the Jews, with increasing disgust, saw this town fortified against themselves, and adorned with a heathen theatre and temple. Herod married Malthace, a Samaritan woman, and after his death, when Judea and Galilee took up arms against her sons, the Samaritans remained quiet; and as a reward for this, Rome took off the fourth part of their taxes, and then added this amount to that paid by the Jewish population,—a new ground of hatred for the people of Judea.

Then, while the Jews were always in a hostile attitude towards the Roman influence, and strove by every means in their power to put a stop to the introduction of all that was foreign, the Samaritans rejoiced over their new importance. Their unrestrained commerce with the nations of the coast, and the mixed population of their settlements, made them less steadfast in their religion, and less hard and bigoted also. And it is this trait in their character that Jesus is alluding to in this parable. But they were capable of showing intense and active hatred against the Jews. In more ancient times, the priests at Jerusalem had been accustomed to give warning of the Easter new moon to those who dwelt in the country by fire-signals upon the mountains; but the Samaritans caused such confusion among the country population by signals too early or too late, that finally another method of communication had to be found. In the year A.D. 10, several Samaritans stole up to Jerusalem, and after the commencement of the feast, when the priests, garments, and vessels, had all been thoroughly purified, strewed human bones in the courts of the Temple to pollute them, so that in the morning the crowd of celebrants had to be turned away at the door of the outer court, and the feast was discontinued in order that the people might not be defiled.

The Jews paid back this hatred with interest. Under the Roman procurators raids were made into the Samaritan border, villages set on fire, and the inhabitants slain without regard to age.   The name of Samaritan became a term of derision.   "We know that Thou art a Samaritan and hast a devil," the Jews say to Jesus in the Gospel according to St John (viii. 48).   The Galileans took a circuitous route to the feasts at Jerusalem, for the towns of Samaria were considered impure, and it was forbidden to ask help or to receive food from the inhabitants.   The Rabbis said, "He who takes bread of the Samaritan is like unto him who eats the flesh of swine." Every contract made in the presence of a Samaritan was void.   The Samaritan was publicly cursed in the synagogue.   The Jews declared that he had no part in the resurrection of the dead, and earnestly desired never to see a member of the nation.

And it was one of this hated nation whom Jesus, in the parable of the Good Samaritan, set before a member of that profession among the Jews, which would hate it most intensely, as an example of kindness and benevolence to his enemy when in distress.   For although the fact is not mentioned, we may fairly assume from the general tone of the parable, and from the direction he was going, that the wounded traveller is to be regarded as a Jew.   The lesson taught by the parable, therefore, is not only that of charity, but also that of charity to those whose religious opinions differ from our own, and therefore of religious tolerance. Unhappy examples of the contrary spirit among Christians are to be found in religious persecutions, and in the excesses perpetrated in the name of Christ by the Crusaders.   "Many," said the old Athenians, "are the wand-bearers, but few the true worshippers of Bacchus.   "Many," may Christians say, "have been the worshippers of Christ; few those who have cared to understand His spirit."   Tertullian encouraging the Christian martyrs who suffered in the amphitheatre with

the future prospect of being spectators, in a vaster amphitheatre, of the eternal torments of their foes; Godfrey
and his Crusaders riding up to the porch of the Temple
at Jerusalem with their horses up to the knees in the
stream of their enemies' blood, while the shrieks of the
Jews being burnt alive in their synagogues rang in their
ears; the horrors of the Inquisition,—these are terrible
instances out of many in the history of Christianity, of
the failure of His disciples to understand the spirit of
Jesus.

In the words of Lord Bacon, " Lucretius, the poet,
when he beheld the act of Agamemnon that could
endure the sacrificing of his own daughter, concludes
with this verse—

> 'Tantum religio potuit suadere malorum.'

But what would he have done if he had known of
the massacre of St Bartholomew's Day, or of the Gun-
powder Plot?   It was a great blasphemy when the devil
said, ' I will ascend and be like the highest ;' but it is a
greater blasphemy if they make God to say, ' I will descend and be like the Prince of Darkness ;' and it is no
better when they make the cause of religion descend to
the execrable actions of murdering of princes, butchery
of people, and firing of states.   Neither is there such a
sin against the Holy Ghost (if one should take it literally) as, instead of the likeness of a dove, to bring Him
down in the likeness of a vulture or raven.   Therefore,
in all counsels concerning religion, that counsel of the
apostle should be prefixed, ' Ira hominis non implet
justitiam Dei.' "

There is a fine historic irony in the fact that the Jews
who were the authors have been the worst victims of
religious intolerance.   They, however, are less to blame
than their imitators, inasmuch as it was their mission
(and they nobly fulfilled it) to defend the pure and spir-

itual religion of a God they regarded as jealous from being defiled by the corrupting influence of the religions of mightier nations which hemmed in their narrow territory on nearly every side; whereas the Christians who have imitated them enjoy the privilege of professing a religion nominally adopted by the majority of the civilised nations of the earth, and of belief in a Founder who sought to promote the sentiment of universal brotherhood.   Yet in the name of the author of the parable of the Good Samaritan, the Jews "have been hindered from pursuing agriculture and handicrafts; have been marked out as execrable figures by a peculiar dress; have been spat upon, pelted, and tortured; have been accused of killing and eating babies, poisoning wells, and taking pains to spread the plague; have been burnt because they refused to be baptised; and have been hounded by thousands and tens of thousands from their homes." —(George Eliot in 'Theophrastus Such.')

When we look back on the history of persecution among Christians, we must remember as a palliation that for centuries few could read the Bible; the knowledge of Christian mysteries was derived, not from the reading of the words of Christ, but from the ceremonies in the Churches. Moreover, the spirit of barbarism had as much influence on Christianity, as Christianity had on barbarism. When the barbarians adopted Christianity their savage spirits might be softened, but were not subdued. Jesus Himself had warned His disciples that the seed of Christianity would grow slowly, and that tares would be mingled with the wheat.

MARTHA AND MARY: DOING AND BEING.

The contrast between Martha and Mary is not a contrast between the life of action and contemplation, but between doing and being. The νομικός had asked what he should *do* to inherit eternal life; Jesus had replied by a parable which showed him that eternal life was a state, and that he who was in that state instinctively acted in accordance with it: if he had once possessed himself of the loving temper, he naturally acted in obedience to its dictates as the occasion arose. So Martha seeks to show her love to her Lord by *doing* something for Him; Mary, with a keener insight into His desires, by *being* what He would have her to be—and what this is she learns best by listening to His words. Activity is more likely to be well directed if based upon right principles derived from thought. It is really much harder to think than to do; and since doing gains readier credit than thinking, the latter usually involves more self-denial than the former, and therefore the noblest spirits combine both thought and action. The authoress of ' Jane Eyre ' was a skilled housekeeper on small means; Milton, who in his blindness could write, " they also serve that only stand and wait," though he was one of the most contemplative and studious men that ever lived, yet showed himself capable of exhibiting an active patriotism. The studious life may, however, from its isolation, degenerate into selfishness. Mary, it would seem, had combined active care for others with her thoughtfulness. She had already done her share of the serving, and her study was consecrated by her loving devotion to her Lord.

The schoolboy may check his studies from leading him into selfishness by taking some active share in the public work of his school, as in organising its games and its institutions. This active work, however, does not necessarily tend less to selfishness than solitary study. It brings more popularity, is stimulated by fellowship, and seems to have more immediate results than study, and for this very reason the latter may involve a higher virtue than the former, provided the motive be not selfish. Probably few boys reason about their motives, and their motives are mixed. They study for praise, for prizes, to please their parents or masters, and to ensure future success in life, as well as from a sense of duty or a love of knowledge. The story of Martha and Mary holds out a motive of a loftier and more permanent character. Mary at the feet of Jesus is the type of the schoolboy whom instinctive sense of duty and affection combined are preparing faithfully to perform the duties of life, whether he be successful or not, stimulated by the example of the character and self-sacrifice of Jesus and the love for His person. The noblest expression of the inward devotion to Jesus is to be found in the 'De Imitatione Christi'; but it is to be recollected in perusing it, that it is a book of a monastic character, dwelling too exclusively on the life of contemplation as opposed to the life of activity.

LESSON XXI.

St Matthew xx. 1-16.

THE PARABLE OF THE LABOURERS IN THE VINEYARD— THE REWARDS OF THE KINGDOM OF HEAVEN.

1 Ὁμοία γάρ ἐστιν ἡ βασιλεία τῶν οὐρανῶν ἀνθρώπῳ οἰκοδεσπότῃ ὅστις ἐξῆλθεν ἅμα πρωὶ μισθώσασθαι ἐργάτας εἰς τὸν ἀμπελῶνα αὐτοῦ· 2 συμφωνήσας δὲ μετὰ τῶν ἐργατῶν ἐκ δηναρίου τὴν ἡμέραν ἀπέστειλεν αὐτοὺς εἰς τὸν ἀμπελῶνα αὐτοῦ. 3 καὶ ἐξελθὼν περὶ τρίτην ὥραν εἶδεν ἄλλους ἑστῶτας ἐν τῇ ἀγορᾷ ἀργούς· 4 καὶ ἐκείνοις εἶπεν Ὑπάγετε καὶ ὑμεῖς εἰς τὸν ἀμπελῶνα, καὶ ὃ ἐὰν ᾖ δίκαιον δώσω ὑμῖν· 5 οἱ δὲ ἀπῆλθον. πάλιν [δὲ] ἐξελθὼν περὶ ἕκτην καὶ ἐνάτην ὥραν ἐποίησεν ὡσαύτως. 6 περὶ δὲ τὴν ἑνδεκάτην ἐξελθὼν εὗρεν ἄλλους ἑστῶτας, καὶ λέγει αὐτοῖς Τί ὧδε ἑστήκατε ὅλην τὴν ἡμέραν ἀργοί; 7 λέγουσιν αὐτῷ Ὅτι οὐδεὶς ἡμᾶς ἐμισθώσατο· λέγει αὐτοῖς Ὑπάγετε καὶ ὑμεῖς εἰς τὸν ἀμπελῶνα. 8 ὀψίας δὲ γενομένης λέγει ὁ κύριος τοῦ ἀμπελῶνος τῷ ἐπιτρόπῳ αὐτοῦ Κάλεσον τοὺς ἐργάτας καὶ ἀπόδος τὸν μισθὸν ἀρξάμενος ἀπὸ τῶν ἐσχάτων ἕως τῶν πρώτων. 9 ἐλθόντες δὲ οἱ περὶ τὴν ἑνδεκάτην ὥραν ἔλαβον ἀνὰ δηνάριον. 10 καὶ ἐλθόντες οἱ πρῶτοι ἐνόμισαν ὅτι πλεῖον λήμψονται· καὶ ἔλαβον [τὸ] ἀνὰ δηνάριον καὶ αὐτοί. 11 λαβόντες δὲ ἐγόγγυζον κατὰ τοῦ οἰκοδεσπότου 12 λέγον-

τες Οὗτοι οἱ ἔσχατοι μίαν ὥραν ἐποίησαν, καὶ ἴσους αὐτοὺς ἡμῖν ἐποίησας τοῖς βαστάσασι τὸ βάρος τῆς ἡμέρας καὶ τὸν καύσωνα. 13 ὁ δὲ ἀποκριθεὶς ἑνὶ αὐτῶν εἶπεν Ἑταῖρε, οὐκ ἀδικῶ σε· οὐχὶ δηναρίου συνεφώνησάς μοι; 14 ἆρον τὸ σὸν καὶ ὕπαγε· θέλω δὲ τούτῳ τῷ ἐσχάτῳ δοῦναι ὡς καὶ σοί· 15 οὐκ ἔξε- στίν μοι ὃ θέλω ποιῆσαι ἐν τοῖς ἐμοῖς; ἢ ὁ ὀφθαλμός σου πονηρός ἐστιν ὅτι ἐγὼ ἀγαθός εἰμι; 16 Οὕτως ἔσονται οἱ ἔσχατοι πρῶτοι καὶ οἱ πρῶτοι ἔσχατοι.

The interpretation of the denarius.—This parable is one of the most difficult in the New Testament, and has had very many interpretations.

It is difficult to determine what is implied by the $\mu\iota\sigma\theta\acute{o}\varsigma$ which the labourers all receive alike, whether they have worked early or late in the vineyard; difficult to determine what is meant by the hours of the day at which they are respectively called; and difficult not to feel with the labourers who had worked from the early morning that the scale of payment was unfair.

We shall put ourselves in a way to understand the parable if we fix our thoughts on the circumstances under which, and the audience to whom, it was uttered.

The rich young man (xix. 16) had sought the attain- ment of eternal life by offering to do some great thing, and on being challenged to devote himself to a life of poverty and attendance on Jesus, had gone gloomily away. Then Peter complacently contrasting the con- duct of the disciples with that of this young man, inquired what reward they should have who had left all to follow Jesus. To this the Master makes first an encouraging answer in figurative language, promising a hundredfold to His disciples for all that they had given up, and the inheritance of eternal life. But in the second place, it was necessary to teach Peter that his question betrayed a misunderstanding of the nature of

the kingdom in which he sought pre-eminence. It was
necessary also to prepare the little community of disciples for the difficulties that were sure to arise when
their Master was taken from them. Then disputes
about rank would be likely to occur, and those who had
been the companions of Jesus would be disposed to be
jealous of those who, like St Paul, joined the society
subsequent to His being taken from them.

Now Jesus understood Peter and the other disciples
too well to point out to them their mistake without any
figure, for He knew they could not at that time com-
prehend Him. They were always thinking of a material kingdom, with material thrones and material rewards.
It was no use for Him as yet to declare plainly that the
reward of being Christians was to be Christians, because
therein was the greatest happiness ; and that as patience,
humility, unselfishness, and self-sacrifice were among the
chief Christian virtues, the very expression of a desire
for a material reward above his fellows of itself deposed
a Christian from a post of eminence, and made him one
of a lower rank.

Jesus, therefore, in His usual manner, related a parable, at the end of which He reiterated the gnome or
saying with which He began—"The last shall be first,
and the first last,"—the other main point being apparently to rebuke the spirit of those who murmured at the
good fortune of their fellows. For it must be carefully
observed that the lord did no injustice to the labourers
who had worked longest in the vineyard ; what he did
was to show himself very liberal to those who had
worked but a short time.

The parable opens up the whole question of the relation of rewards to the system of Christ's teaching. Is
it not nobler to work without the expectation of a reward ? Is it not nobler to do what is right, without any
hope of our good conduct being recognised in any way,

even by a smile of approval? Take the case of a child who is falsely accused of a wrong action which has been done by his brother, and allows his brother to be petted while he is punished, and yet will not betray him, though he sees no prospect of his own innocence coming to light. Undoubtedly we look upon this child's conduct as nobler, because he has no hope of reward.

But we must bear in mind that he is cheered by the consciousness that his father would approve of his conduct if he knew of it; and this is the cheering confidence that the teaching of Jesus more firmly established in the world. The heavenly Father, He taught, does approve of self-denial and unselfishness in His children, though the outward manifestation of His approval seems remote.

In other words, we must think of the reward, of the payment given to the labourers, not as something external—not as a crown or a sceptre or a throne, or money or houses—but as a feeling of satisfaction in the soul of man, arising from the knowledge that the Lord of the universe approves of his conduct.

The work of the labourers in the vineyard of Jesus is a work of love, the fruits of the work are love, and its reward is love. Love is rewarded by appreciation, because appreciation is a loving act—is rewarded by being surrounded by an atmosphere of love, because this increases its power of loving.

Peter could not understand this yet; for he still thought of his Master as a Messiah who was to prove Himself, when He entered Jerusalem, conqueror over His enemies and an open distributor of rewards to His friends; but the time came when he thought more of his Lord's patience and suffering, as an incentive to well-doing, than of His power and glory, and looked upon giving pleasure to his Master as the highest reward (1 Pet. ii. 20)—"What glory is it, if, when ye be buffeted for your faults, ye shall take it patiently? but if, when ye do well, and suffer for it, ye take it patiently, this is acceptable with God. For even hereunto were ye called; because Christ also suffered for us, leaving us an example, that ye should follow His steps."

We are now in a position to understand how the μίσθος may be susceptible of all the interpretations that have been put upon it by various commentators. Thus one commentator regards it as " the promise of this life attached to godliness." Now this phrase may mean (1) a promise of worldly prosperity; but it is by no means true that prosperity always accompanies godliness. The wicked still " flourish like a green bay tree." There are, however, causes inherent in his character which make the godly man prosper, and which we may hope will gain greater strength in the coming ages as the race improves. His honesty makes him trusted, his freedom from distracting passion enables him to pursue his calling with regularity and stability of purpose; his unselfish and loving nature wins him friends; and the reciprocation of this love gives him daily fresh vigour for his work,—to which he is further strengthened by the consciousness of God's love for him. But (2) these last blessings are really the *promise* itself. For the treasure the labourer in the vineyard of Jesus cares for most is the love of God and man, which his unselfish loving character brings to him. So that wherever he is, he seems to radiate love, and move in an atmosphere of love. If, again, we think of prosperity in this life as consisting in honour rather than in wealth, by the godly man the pleasure derived from honour arises from the thought that his fellow-men trust him, and that his honourable position gives him greater opportunities of serving them.

Again, other commentators regard the μίσθος as eternal life. This idea is not very different from the other, if we regard eternal life as a state begun here and never ending. This state is defined by St John, in his First Epistle, chap. iii. 14—"We know that we have passed from death unto life, because we love the brethren. He that loveth not his brother abideth in death." And more mystically in chap. v. 2—" God hath given to us eternal life, and this life is in his Son. He that hath the Son hath life : and he that hath not the Son hath not life." The phrase, "having the Son," is full of mysterious meaning ; but whatever else it means, we cannot go wrong in taking it to imply being filled with the Spirit of the Son—that is, with the Spirit of Love. Now the connection of love with life is as obvious as the connection of hate with death.

Others regard the $\mu\iota\sigma\theta\sigma\varsigma$ as salvation; but this is synonymous with eternal life—for he who has the one has the other. Others as God Himself; but this corresponds to the "having the Son." Others to " a special reward of grace," consisting in the difference of place assigned to different individuals in the kingdom of God, in allusion to Matt. xix. 28—" Verily I say unto you, That ye which have followed me, in the regeneration, when the Son of man shall sit in the throne of His glory, ye also shall sit upon twelve thrones, judging the twelve tribes of Israel." But the language there is evidently metaphorical. A throne is the symbol of influence, and influence in the kingdom of God is attained only by love and unselfishness : position here or hereafter can only be looked upon by the members of the kingdom as involving duties, and giving enlarged opportunities of usefulness and the diffusion of love. We cannot regard such positions as assigned arbitrarily. Jesus Himself gives us a law respecting them in the latter part of this chapter, when He declares that His Father reserves them for His own disposition, and adds, as a warning to those who are ambitious for them (ver.

26), " Whosoever will be great among you, let him be your minister; and whosoever will be chief among you, let him be your servant" (or slave).

Again, a difficulty arises about ver. 14; there the lord of the vineyard appears to reprobate, if not to reject, the murmuring labourer. The word ὕπαγε, however, means no more than " withdraw," and does not necessarily imply dismissal from the service of the lord of the vineyard. Of course we cannot imagine murmurers as marring the peace of the kingdom of God in its final and perfected state. But no time is assigned for the scenery of the parable. We are not compelled to restrict the end of the day to the final judgment. A feeling of dissatisfaction with their lot, as compared with that of others, lurks at the bottom of the heart probably of the very best of men—even as ambition is " the last infirmity of noble minds." It may not present itself at all to the eyes of men, and yet may be known to God, who is " greater than our heart, and knoweth all things " (1 John iii. 20).

Jesus here declares that the very existence of such a feeling of itself assigns to that member who fosters it a lower place in the kingdom in this world, not without a hint that it may cut him off from membership altogether in the future.

The interpretation of the hours.—We have next to consider what is meant by the various times of the day at which the labourers were called. Here we shall probably make a mistake if we restrict our interpretation to one special application.

We may indeed fairly suppose that Jesus had in His mind Peter and the little inner circle of His disciples— their position and their ambition, which to Him, who foresaw for them a very different career to that they were anticipating, was pathetically ironical. Others, He foresaw, would become labourers in the vineyard, and

obtain greater fame and distinction before the world
than many, if not all, of those who had been with Him
from the first. This was notably true of St Paul, who
does indeed really seem to have been regarded at first
by the disciples with some envy as well as distrust.
The immediate object of the parable, therefore, was
probably to teach the disciples that their earlier calling
conferred on them no peculiar privilege, and that those
faithful labourers in the kingdom of God, who were
called at a later period, would be placed on an equal
footing with them. To put an extreme case, that even
if a St Peter or a St John were jealous of the penitent
brigand on the cross, they would be displaying a spirit
incompatible with the spirit and organisation of the
kingdom of Love.

But the teaching of the parable may also be extended
to apply to the relationship in which the heathen, as
being called at a later period into the kingdom of God,
stood to the Jews, as the first called. In this way it
conveyed to the future disciples of the kingdom the be-
quest of the Master's teaching on points that were afterwards raised, and did actually lead to jealousy, as we
find from Acts vi. 1—" There arose a murmuring of the
Grecians against the Hebrews, because their widows
were neglected in the daily ministration." Regarded
from this point of view, the parable is a complement of
that of " The Prodigal Son."

Again, its teaching may refer to the relation of individuals who are called late in life, with those who have
been called earlier. Experience tells us that its teaching is not inapplicable here. Jealousies do actually
arise among those engaged in Christian work with reference to the work and the offices connected with it.
Envy and uncharitableness do creep in among those
working together in Sunday-schools, in charitable organisations, in ministerial work—even in the highest offices

of the Church. In this parable we hear the Master's voice declaring that, in His sight, it is not the most successful, or the most energetic or prominent worker, that is first, but he or she who displays the most Christian temper, who is most loving and most unselfish, most free from envy and jealousy, and the least pushing— who, when posts of distinction are being competed for, can both say and feel, with the most sincerity, " Christianity has many worthier sons than I."

Again, since in the history of Christianity one age has had greater difficulties to contend with than another, the " hours " of the parable may fairly be applied to the ages of this history. So that Jesus seems to be cementing His disciples of all ages into one great brotherhood, in which invidious comparisons of their work done for Him and His community shall have no place. So that the saint who lives in an age when Christians are persecuted, tortured, and put to death, is encouraged not to envy his brother saint who lived in a preceding age, when Christians were honoured, and could live lives of comparative ease, but rather to rejoice that his brother was free from his sufferings. This spirit is illustrated by the eloquent passage of St Paul in 1 Cor. iv., in which he affectionately contrasts his sufferings with the pride in their ease displayed by the Corinthian converts. The saint who in one age lives a life of ease and distinction may be well known to God to have a spirit that could have endured unflinchingly all the horrors of martyrdom, if he had been called upon to do so. But in God's sight the only difference between one saint and another is the difference in their characters, and, above all, in their capacity for loving and diffusing love.

In the eloquent words of Archbishop Leighton, " Envy is a stranger to the company of heaven; there resides perfect love, in which each enjoys the happiness of his neighbour as much as his own, because he delights in it as his own; so that among those blessed beings is an infinite reflection and multiplication of happiness—like the splendour of a palatial chamber, full of kings and nobles, gleaming with gold and gems, whose walls are everywhere covered with most brilliant mirrors."

LESSON XXII.

St Luke xii. 13-21.

THE PARABLE OF THE RICH FOOL.

13 Εἶπεν δέ τις ἐκ τοῦ ὄχλου αὐτῷ Διδάσκαλε, εἰπὲ τῷ ἀδελφῷ μου μερίσασθαι μετ᾽ ἐμοῦ τὴν κληρονομίαν. 14 ὁ δὲ εἶπεν αὐτῷ Ἄνθρωπε, τίς με κατέστησεν κριτὴν ἢ μεριστὴν ἐφ᾽ ὑμᾶς; 15 εἶπεν δὲ πρὸς αὐτούς Ὁρᾶτε καὶ φυλάσσεσθε ἀπὸ πάσης πλεονεξίας, ὅτι οὐκ ἐν τῷ περισσεύειν τινὶ ἡ ζωὴ αὐτοῦ ἐστὶν ἐκ τῶν ὑπαρχόντων αὐτῷ. 16 Εἶπεν δὲ παραβολὴν πρὸς αὐτοὺς λέγων Ἀνθρώπου τινὸς πλουσίου εὐφόρησεν ἡ χώρα. 17 καὶ διελογίζετο ἐν αὐτῷ λέγων Τί ποιήσω, ὅτι οὐκ ἔχω ποῦ συνάξω τοὺς καρπούς μου; 18 καὶ εἶπεν Τοῦτο ποιήσω· καθελῶ μου τὰς ἀποθήκας καὶ μείζονας οἰκοδομήσω, καὶ συνάξω ἐκεῖ πάντα τὸν σῖτον καὶ τὰ ἀγαθά μου, 19 καὶ ἐρῶ τῇ ψυχῇ μου Ψυχή, ἔχεις πολλὰ ἀγαθὰ κείμενα εἰς ἔτη πολλά· ἀναπαύου, φάγε, πίε, εὐφραίνου. 20 εἶπεν δὲ αὐτῷ ὁ θεός Ἄφρων, ταύτῃ τῇ νυκτὶ τὴν ψυχήν σου αἰτοῦσιν ἀπὸ σοῦ· ἃ δὲ ἡτοίμασας, τίνι ἔσται; [21 Οὕτως ὁ θησαυρίζων αὐτῷ καὶ μὴ εἰς θεὸν πλουτῶν.]

LESSON XXIII.

St Luke xii. 14.

THE TEACHING OF JESUS AND MODERN CITIZENSHIP.

Jesus elsewhere declared that His kingdom was not of this world (John xviii. 36). He taught principles which, if adopted, would make disputes about inheritance impossible, or else transform them into rivalries in ἐπιεικεία, or " yieldingness," rather than in πλεονεξία. A fine illustration of this spirit in heathen times is found in the rivalry of Orestes and Pylades for the doom of death before Iphigenia in Tauris (Eur., Iph. Taur., 672-699).

Jesus' kingdom was one founded on spiritual disposition, not on outward law and jurisprudence. That this lawsuit should have been decided by the brothers themselves, in love, with mutual fairness, would have been much; that it should be determined by authoritative arbitration was, from a spiritual point of view, nothing. The right disposition of their hearts belonged to Christ's kingdom, and the right division of their goods would grow out of this right disposition. But with the apportionment of their property by the decision of a third person, His kingdom had nothing to do.

Suppose that both were wrong—one oppressive, the other covetous. Then, that the oppressor should become generous, and the covetous liberal, were a great spiritual gain. But there would be no spiritual gain in taking from one selfish brother to give to another selfish brother.

In a similar spirit, Jesus, on another occasion, lays down the great political principle—"Render unto Cæsar the things that are Cæsar's, and unto God the things that are God's" (Matt. xxii. 21). But He would not determine whether this particular tax was due to Cæsar or not.

He lays down general principles, out of which the best government may spring; but He does not determine what is the best government—whether monarchy or a republic, an aristocracy or a democracy. His religion was for all ages, and can be practised under all governments; it establishes a charity, a moderation, a sense of duty, and a love of right, which will modify human life according to any circumstances that can arise.

We shall understand this more clearly if we consider the relation the principles and precepts of Christianity bear to such subjects as slavery, rebellion against unjust government, and war.

I. SLAVERY.

Precepts.—St Peter (i. 18) bids slaves—whom he addresses by the milder term *domestics*—"to be subject to their masters with all fear; not only to the good and gentle, but also to the froward," — and exhorts them by the example of Christ to bear patiently even unjust buffeting. St Paul (Eph. vi. 5) exhorts them to obey their masters, as the slaves of Christ, expecting their reward from God, and to count their masters worthy of honour, that the name of God and His doctrine be not blasphemed (1 Tim. vi. 1). Cf. 1 Cor. vii. 21.

So far then from exhorting slaves to seek freedom, the apostles urge them to greater patience and zeal in their work because they are Christians. They have no thought of any political change with respect to their condition. This is still further exemplified by the history of the slave Onesimus. This man, after purloining money, fled from his master Philemon at Colossæ, and escaped to Rome, where he was converted to Christianity by St Paul. The great apostle sent him back to his master, begging not for his freedom, but that he might be forgiven his theft, and looked upon as a Christian brother (Philem. 16).

The time was not ripe for the abolition.—Suppose Jesus and His disciples had declaimed against slavery, and urged masters to give their slaves freedom, or slaves to rise, what would have been the consequence? The master would have turned a deaf ear to Christianity, the slave would have involved himself in a deadly and hopeless struggle, the propagation of Christianity would have been checked at the outset, for every Christian would have been regarded as an instigator of disorder, and the religion of peace and universal brotherhood would have lost a hearing, because it would have been associated in men's minds with rebellion and discord.

The hopelessness of the struggles of the slaves against their masters had been shown only seventy-one years before Christ, in the rising of the slaves of southern Italy under Spartacus. Though victorious for a time, and though they rebelled at a period when the government was memorably weak, and at one time even threatened Rome with a blockade, they were ultimately beaten; and as a token of the hopelessness of the contest, there might be seen along the road from Capua to Rome six thousand crosses bearing the figures of unhappy wretches who had been captured.

Moreover, so terrible was the poverty to which the citizens of the Roman Empire were subject, owing to bad government, bad finance, and civil war, that freedom to the slave would have been a doubtful boon. Again, the sudden abolition of slavery would have starved the ancient world, which only subsisted on the products of its labour : it would have thrown upon the soil whole populations without resources, and without the power of governing themselves.

Principles.—But though Jesus and His disciples uttered no words against the institution of slavery, they laid down principles which strike at its root, and have materially aided in its overthrow. Jesus, in such sentiments as "He that is greatest amongst you shall be your servant" (Matt. xxiii. 11), and the symbolic act of washing His disciples' feet (John xiii. 16); St Peter, in such sentiments as "Honour all men" (1 Pet. ii. 17); St John, in such as "He that loveth not his brother abideth in death" (1 John iii. 14); St James, in "If ye have respect to persons, ye commit sin, and are convinced of the law as transgressors" (James ii. 9); St Paul, in such phrases as "There is neither bond nor free : ye are all one in Christ" (Gal. iii. 28); "We, being many, are one body in Christ, and every one members one of another" (Romans xii. 5); "In honour preferring one another" (Romans xii. 10); and above all, in the passage already quoted from the Epistle to Philemon (verse 16), where he urges the master to receive his slave, now converted to Christianity, no longer as a slave, but as a brother beloved.

Historical influence of Christianity.—In the history of Christianity its influence on slavery was felt in three ways.

(1) **In the Church ceremonies and the penitential discipline the difference between the master and his slave was unknown.**—They were, as St Paul said, "one in Christ." Together they partook of the Supper of the Lord, side by side they sat at the love-feasts, and they

mingled together in the public prayers. In the penal system of the Church the distinction between wrongs done to a freeman and wrongs done to a slave was repudiated. Slaves, moreover, might enter the priesthood, and an emancipated slave often saw the greatest and most wealthy humbly kneeling at his feet imploring his absolution or his benediction. The Christian teachers and clergymen became known as " the brothers of the slave "; and the slaves themselves were called " the freedmen of Christ."

(2) **The Christian ideal of morality conferred a novel dignity on the slave.**—The Romans regarded slaves with profound contempt, not so much on account of their position, as of the character which that position had formed. Such virtues as humility, obedience, gentleness, patience, and resignation are all cardinal virtues in the Christian character: they were all neglected or underrated by the pagans, with the exception of a few Stoics; they can all expand or flourish in a servile condition. The monk St Benedict (born A.D. 480), by making manual labour the rule of the monasteries which he founded, raised it to new honour, and with it the slaves, by whom alone, for the most part, such labour had previously been carried on.

(3) **Christianity made unceasing efforts to procure the freedom of the slave.**—The emancipation of slaves was celebrated on Church festivals, and was always regarded as one of the most acceptable modes of expiating past sins. It became customary for masters to free their slaves on occasions of national or personal thanksgiving, on recovery from sickness, on the birth of a child, at the hour of death, and above all, in testamentary bequests. At last, in the ninth century, a Christian monk, St Theodore of Stude (Constantinople), put forth the command to the abbot of a monastery, " Thou shalt possess no slave, neither for domestic service nor for the

labour of the fields; for man was made in the image of God." Thirty-seven Church Councils are reported to have passed acts favourable to slaves. Other causes combined with Christianity in diminishing slavery. In the twelfth century it was very rare in Europe, and in the fourteenth century almost unknown. Unhappily, however, the practice was revived after the discovery of America; and the African slave trade commenced in the reign of Elizabeth, and even received the sanction of the Christian Church, both Roman Catholic and Protestant. In the seventeenth century, however, Christians, and notably the Society of Friends, began to protest against it. Wesley and Whitfield preached against it. It was not, however, till the year 1807 that, owing to the efforts of Clarkson and Wilberforce, instigated by feelings of Christian piety, a bill was passed in the House of Commons condemning the practice so far as England is concerned. In the year 1833 it was abolished throughout the British colonies, and is now extinct in almost every nation professing Christianity. In 1870 negro equality with the whites was completely recognised in the United States.

II. PASSIVE OBEDIENCE UNDER UNJUST RULE.

It has been asserted that the teaching of Christianity inculcates passive obedience to any ruler, however unjust.

Here again we must distinguish between the precept applicable to the time and to the persons to whom it was addressed, and the principle that may be applied to all circumstances at any time.

Precepts. — Jesus said, " Render unto Cæsar the things that are Cæsar's, and to God the things that are God's " (Matt. xxii. 21); " He that taketh the sword shall perish by the sword " (Matt. xxvi. 52). St Peter, " Submit yourselves to every ordinance of man for the

Lord's sake; whether it be to the king, as supreme; or unto governors, as unto them that are sent by him for the punishment of evil-doers, and for the praise of them that do well" (1 Pet. ii. 13). St Paul, "Let every soul be subject unto the higher powers. For there is no power but of God: the powers that be are ordained of God. Render therefore to all their dues: tribute to whom tribute is due; custom to whom custom; fear to whom fear; honour to whom honour" (Rom. xiii. 1, 7).

Now, in Matt. xxii. 21, Jesus was answering a question put to Him insidiously, as to whether it was in His eyes lawful to pay tribute to Cæsar or not. His answer implies nothing more than an assertion that His interrogators were bound to pay taxes to the government to whose authority they had submitted, and a refusal on His part to ally Himself to the hopeless cause of the zealots which, by a futile attempt at resistance against Rome, subsequently brought destruction on the country in the time of Titus, A.D. 70. St Peter and St Paul again were warning the early Christians, many of whom were Jews, against rebellious acts and feelings, which would at once have been useless, and brought destruction on the infant Church, and to which they were always liable under the influence of religious impulses. The danger of such conduct was so far real that the Roman Government, only a short time previously, had made it the pretext for expelling all Jews, and doubtless the Christians among them, from Rome. St Paul, to guard against this turbulent spirit, lays down the principle that civil government is a divine ordinance, and consequently civil obedience a duty which must be conscientiously rendered by the Christian. He then decides the question which the Jews were constantly raising as to the lawfulness of paying taxes to heathen Governments, and affirms that it is a Christian duty to do so, on the ground that the end of all government is the protection of the individual, and that this was the divine purpose in its institution. But He gives no precept as to what is the duty of Christians when governments fail to discharge their proper function. He was not writing a political treatise, but laying down rules for the guidance of a new and insignificant religious body, who, on account of the known rebellious spirit of the race to which many, if not most of them, belonged, were always liable to be looked upon with suspicion by the government.

Practice of Jesus.—In seeking from the life and teaching of Jesus for any principle on which resistance to a wicked and despotic government could be based, we must constantly bear in mind how very different the aspect of political affairs has become since the dissolution of the Roman Empire. In Jesus' own nation it was proved both immediately before and soon after His time how hopeless was any rising against the absolute power of Rome. Neither were the Jews in such a condition that there was any grave moral call for such a rising. There was no chance, in their condition of moral and political degradation, of their governing themselves better than the Romans governed them. There was no unity among them, and the Romans in His day were really making some efforts to govern justly. His own unjust death was due to the violence of the Jews and the weakness of Pilate, in spite of the evident reluctance to give judgment with which the latter was inspired by his Roman instinct for justice.

But both Jesus and His disciples *did* show by their lives that no political expediency would induce them to flatter the rulers where moral indignation or the cause of righteousness demanded a protest. When the crafty Herod Antipas sought by cunning to get rid of Him from his dominions, Jesus did not hesitate to express His indignation by using about him the epithet "fox"

(Luke xiii. 31) in the face of the rulers; and when He knew His doom was at hand, Jesus fearlessly reformed the popular abuse of the traffic in the Temple (Matt. xxi. 12); and it was His invectives against the Pharisees, who were at once the religious teachers and the misleaders of His countrymen, that roused them to contrive His death.

Practice of the disciples.—If we turn to the Acts of the Apostles, we never find the disciples submitting to any command that went against their conscience. In this sense they were always the champions of religious liberty against oppression.

Again, the early Christians, even young and tender women, faced death, preceded by fearful tortures, rather than conform to religious practices against which their consciences rebelled, especially to the divine honours paid to the emperor; and by so doing they prepared the way for the freedom of men's consciences from State interference, and uttered the earliest protest against the doctrine of the divine right of kings, which had its origin in this worship of the Roman emperors.

Historical influence of the precepts and practice of Christianity.—The precepts of Jesus and His disciples have, however, been used as arguments for passive obedience and the divine right of kings. If, it has been argued, the first Christians were to obey the heathen emperors, how can we ever be justified in shaking off the yoke of a Christian sovereign? If St Paul said this under Nero, how much more is it true of the subjects of King Charles I.?

It cannot be denied that arguments such as these have wrought evil in the world, by supporting the cause of tyranny against that of freedom; but it is always unfair to blame a religious teacher for the use made of his precepts by political partisans to serve their own purposes, and the impartial attitude of Jesus towards the political questions of His time gives Him a special claim to exemption from the reproach of a sinister influence on political relations. And if it be true that the cause of freedom has been injured by the application of His words to a totally different set of conditions from those under which they were uttered, it can be shown on the other hand that the friends of liberty have reaped advantage alike from His precepts and from the principles and practice of His disciples. For to struggle for freedom is to struggle for self-government. Now the mere aspiration after self-government does not fit men for it, and the bestowal of it on a people before they are fit for it, only subtracts from the sum of human happiness; and for men unprepared for self-government to be in constant rebellion leads to nothing but anarchy and misery. From this point of view, therefore, Jesus must be regarded as a good patriot when He refused to countenance a rising of His countrymen against the Romans; and His warning against "pouring new wine into old bottles" contains a valuable political lesson which, taken to heart, may have a large influence on the happiness of mankind.

But if, on the one hand, the principles and practice of Christianity contain warnings against premature and useless risings against rulers and dominant nations, on the other hand they have had an educating influence on mankind in preparing men for self-government. First, by substituting duty for fear as the motive for obedience, the new religion trained men at once to a distaste for force and to self-respect, both essential elements for good government. Secondly, the influence of the Popes, although sometimes itself tyrannical, was more often a restraint on tyranny, and as they frequently appealed to the people against their sovereigns, made the power of the people felt. For some centuries, indeed, the Popes represented the cause of moral restraint, of intelligence, and of humanity, in an age of physical force, ignorance, and barbarity.

Influence of Christian principles.—But it is by considering what is the real cause of rebellion that we shall discover how, apart from particular texts from either the Old or New Testament, it may be justified on Christian principles. For, first, with respect to kings and rulers, Christ regards them as stewards of God, and as responsible to Him for their stewardship and the use of their talents. This principle is enunciated especially in the parables of the Unjust Steward and of the Talents, and in such passages as Matt. xx. 25 and Mark x. 42—" Whosoever will be great among you let him be your minister;" and " Whosoever will be chief among you let him be your servant,"—which lays down the law for Christian princes and magistrates, that they are to regard kingship not as ownership or possession, but as a service or ministry to their people. Secondly, as regards subjects, Christianity conferred new dignity on individual men, and especially on the poor and humble. This recognition of the greatness of the individual soul tended naturally to the recognition of the claims of the poorer classes to exercise the rights of citizenship; for the religion that proclaims all men equal in the sight of God is in itself a protest against despotic government, whether exercised by one or many, whether a monarchy, an aristocracy, or a plutocracy. Thus St Peter, in the very passage quoted (1 Pet. ii. 16), bids Christians obey as " free " and " as the servants of God," and places the precept " Honour all men " before that of " Honour the king "; and shortly before had addressed the early Christians, to whom he is writing, and who, we have every reason to suppose, were in a very humble position (many of them even slaves), as " a royal priesthood " and " a holy nation " (1 Pet. ii. 9). Jesus also, Himself, had promised His disciples, in metaphorical language, that "they should sit on thrones, judging the twelve tribes of Israel;" and by associating with the poorest and most degraded of His countrymen, had practically asserted their rights against those of the privileged classes.

III. WAR.

Why has not Christianity done away with war? Even the prophets spoke of a time when nations should beat their swords into ploughshares, and their spears into pruning-hooks; when nation should not lift up sword against nation, neither should they learn war any more (Isa. ii. 4; Micah iv. 3). Jesus Himself bids His disciples "resist not evil: but whosoever shall smite thee on thy right check, turn to him the other also" (Matt. v. 39); St Peter, not to "render evil for evil" (1 Pet. iii. 9); St Paul, "Render to no man evil for evil. If it be possible, as much as lieth in you live peaceably with all men. Avenge not yourselves, but rather give place unto wrath. If thine enemy hunger, feed him; if he thirst, give him drink" (Rom. xii. 17, 18, 19). The earlier fathers were fond of repeating the phrase, "Jesus, in disarming Peter, disarmed all soldiers." Yet we see men professing to be Christians, contriving instruments of destruction against one another; declaring war against and slaying one another on the battle-field; praying to Jesus for victory over their fellow-Christians; dying with the name of Jesus on their lips, and solaced on the battle-field by the ministers of Jesus, who do not reproach them for the blood they have recently shed.

The principle on which war is permissible is contained in the text before us, and in such phrases as those of Jesus, "Render unto Cæsar the things that are Cæsar's, and to God the things that are God's" (Matt. xxii. 21); and in St Paul's reference to the civil governor, "He beareth not the sword in vain" (Rom. xiii. 4).

We do not find in the New Testament that soldiers are bidden, as Christians, to abandon their profession. John the Baptist, when the soldiers inquired of him what they should do to prepare for the kingdom of Christ, did not bid them give up serving in the armies, but required them to do no violence, and to be content with their wages (Luke iii. 14). When Jesus was brought into contact with a Roman centurion, He commended him for his faith, but did not bid him give up his vocation. Jesus and His disciples referred to the customs of war without expressing horror, or taking the opportunity to forbid it (Luke xiv. 31, 32; 2 Tim. ii. 4). When the Roman centurion Cornelius was converted, he was not ordered to give up his profession (Acts x). In the same hour in which Jesus said, "Put up again thy sword into his place: for all they that take the sword shall perish with the sword" (Matt. xxvi. 52), He had said, "He that hath no sword, let him sell his garment, and buy one (Luke xxii. 36). And though it is evident that in this latter clause He was speaking figuratively, and referring to the hostility His disciples were destined to meet, and at most warning them that they might have to defend themselves after the manner, for instance, St Paul defended himself, when he availed himself of an escort of soldiers (Acts xxiii. 23), yet the very use of the phrase shows that He did not shrink from reference to such means of defence.

But the words of our passage lay down the principle on which Christians not only may but sometimes ought to go to war. Christianity interferes in politics only so far as it changes the spirit of politicians and citizens. If all men were perfect Christians there would be no wars. For a Christian to say he will not go to war at all, is to give the world over to the violent and the wicked, and the weak to oppression and wrong.

The reason why Christians as members of nations must go to war is, that when disputes arise, there is no other means of settling them. Individual Christians need not fight duels, because their disputes can be settled by the law court or by a reference to public opinion. But there is no power to which nations can appeal in their disputes against one another. The influence of Christianity on war will be to check it at the outset by endeavouring to settle disputes by mutual concessions, through diplomacy or arbitration, and to soften its horrors by inducing generals and statesmen to show mercy to the captured and the wounded, and sending its missionaries, its Christian surgeons and priests, to soothe the sufferings of the wounded: and though it may not diminish the injuries inflicted in the contest, it may diminish the anger and the hate.

Sometimes, too, Christianity will, for the sake of peace, dictate a concession that is humble, almost humiliating. It is very difficult for a nation, however, to do this. A Christian statesman who did so without the well-ascertained consent of the nation, would be sacrificing not himself but the nation. Even if the majority of the nation consented, it might do so from selfish and not from Christian motives, because it preferred the immediate material welfare of its own generation to the permanent national good.

If, however, a nation should be so leavened with the Christian spirit as to make concessions for the sake of the world's peace affecting its own temporal welfare for a time, such conduct would no doubt come within the scope of Christ's precepts. Christian prudence as well as Christian humility would, however, enter into such counsels, and here Christians would be guided by the precept of their Master, " Give not that which is holy unto the dogs, neither cast ye your pearls before swine, lest they trample them under their feet, and turn again and rend you " (Matt. vii. 6). In other words, as only a part of each nation is Christian, and that not always the governing part, the ruling majority, or leading statesman, Christian prudence would forbid making concessions which, by encouraging the violent and grasping, might increase rather than diminish the misery and the hate in the world.

To conclude. It is evident that Christ nowhere forbids His followers to take their part in support and defence of the nation to which they belong, and that the most prominent teachers of Christianity, in bidding them submit to the civil governor, even enforce the duty of their doing so. But in addition to this, the morals of Christianity seem even to harmonise with the spirit of the soldier. The spirit of self-sacrifice is at once the spirit of Christianity and that of the patriot soldier. Therefore we may use the phrase Christian soldier, without hesitation, of the Christian who faces wounds and captivity and death for the sake of the nation to which he belongs, and accept as an ideal Christian character the " Happy Warrior " described by Wordsworth, the Christian poet.

At the same time, all true Christians must look forward to, and strive to hasten, a time when wars shall become as antiquated as duelling: and though wars waged for independence or freedom, or against injustice or apprehension, cannot be regarded as opposed to the spirit or teaching of Jesus, it is evident that wars of oppression or for aggrandisement, wars waged by stronger nations against weaker for selfish purposes, are anti-Christian, and opposed to the principles of the Founder of our religion.

LESSON XXIV.

St Luke xiv. 7-35.

THE PARABLE OF THE GREAT SUPPER.

Jesus had been invited by an eminent Pharisee to dine with him on the Sabbath-day. As the Scribes and Pharisees were watching all His actions, and listening to His words, with no friendly intentions, Jesus showed kindly feeling and courage in accepting the invitation.

7 Ἔλεγεν δὲ πρὸς τοὺς κεκλημένους παραβολήν, ἐπέχων πῶς τὰς πρωτοκλισίας ἐξελέγοντο, λέγων πρὸς αὐτούς 8 Ὅταν κληθῇς ὑπό τινος εἰς γάμους, μὴ κατακλιθῇς εἰς τὴν πρωτοκλισίαν, μή ποτε ἐντιμότερός σου ᾖ κεκλημένος ὑπ' αὐτοῦ, 9 καὶ ἐλθὼν ὁ σὲ καὶ αὐτὸν καλέσας ἐρεῖ σοι Δὸς τούτῳ τόπον, καὶ τότε ἄρξῃ μετὰ αἰσχύνης τὸν ἔσχατον τόπον κατέχειν. 10 ἀλλ' ὅταν κληθῇς πορευθεὶς ἀνάπεσε εἰς τὸν ἔσχατον τόπον, ἵνα ὅταν ἔλθῃ ὁ κεκληκώς σε ἐρεῖ σοι Φίλε, προσανάβηθι ἀνώτερον· τότε ἔσται σοι δόξα ἐνώπιον πάντων τῶν συνανακειμένων σοι. 11 ὅτι πᾶς ὁ ὑψῶν ἑαυτὸν ταπεινωθήσεται καὶ ὁ ταπεινῶν ἑαυτὸν ὑψωθήσεται. 12 Ἔλεγεν δὲ καὶ τῷ κεκληκότι αὐτόν Ὅταν ποιῇς ἄριστον ἢ δεῖπνον, μὴ φώνει τοὺς φίλους σου μηδὲ τοὺς ἀδελφούς σου μηδὲ τοὺς συγγενεῖς σου μηδὲ γείτονας πλουσίους, μή ποτε καὶ αὐτοὶ ἀντικαλέσωσίν σε καὶ γένηται ἀνταπόδομά σοι. 13 ἀλλ' ὅταν δοχὴν ποιῇς, κάλει πτωχούς, ἀναπήρους, χωλούς, τυφλούς· 14 καὶ

μακάριος ἔσῃ, ὅτι οὐκ ἔχουσιν ἀνταποδοῦναί σοι, ἀνταποδοθήσεται γάρ σοι ἐν τῇ ἀναστάσει τῶν δικαίων.   15 Ἀκούσας δέ τις τῶν συνανακειμένων ταῦτα εἶπεν αὐτῷ Μακάριος ὅστις φάγεται ἄρτον ἐν τῇ βασιλείᾳ τοῦ θεοῦ.   16 ὁ δὲ εἶπεν αὐτῷ Ἄνθρωπός τις ἐποίει δεῖπνον μέγα, καὶ ἐκάλεσεν πολλούς,   17 καὶ ἀπέστειλεν τὸν δοῦλον αὐτοῦ τῇ ὥρᾳ τοῦ δείπνου εἰπεῖν τοῖς κεκλημένοις Ἔρχεσθε ὅτι ἤδη ἕτοιμά ἐστιν.   18 καὶ ἤρξαντο ἀπὸ μιᾶς πάντες παραιτεῖσθαι. ὁ πρῶτος εἶπεν αὐτῷ Ἀγρὸν ἠγόρασα καὶ ἔχω ἀνάγκην ἐξελθὼν ἰδεῖν αὐτόν· ἐρωτῶ σε, ἔχε με παρῃτημένον.   19 καὶ ἕτερος εἶπεν Ζεύγη βοῶν ἠγόρασα πέντε καὶ πορεύομαι δοκιμάσαι αὐτά· ἐρωτῶ σε, ἔχε με παρῃτημένον.   20 καὶ ἕτερος εἶπε, Γυναῖκα ἔγημα, καὶ διὰ τοῦτο οὐ δύναμαι ἐλθεῖν·   21 καὶ παραγενόμενος ὁ δοῦλος ἀπήγγειλε τῷ κυρίῳ αὐτοῦ ταῦτα. τότε ὀργισθεὶς ὁ οἰκοδεσπότης εἶπε τῷ δούλῳ αὐτου, Ἔξελθε ταχέως εἰς τὰς πλατείας καὶ ῥύμας τῆς πόλεως, καὶ τοὺς πτωχοὺς καὶ ἀναπήρους, καὶ τυφλοὺς, καὶ χωλοὺς εἰσάγαγε ὧδε.   22 καὶ εἶπεν ὁ δοῦλος, Κύριε, γέγονεν ὃ ἐπέταξας καὶ ἔτι τόπος ἐστι·   23 καὶ εἶπεν ὁ κύριος πρὸς τὸν δοῦλον, Ἔξελθε εἰς τὰς ὁδοὺς καὶ φραγμοὺς, καὶ ἀνάγκασον εἰσελθεῖν, ἵνα γεμισθῇ ὁ οἶκός μου.   24 λέγω γὰρ ὑμῖν, ὅτι οὐδεὶς τῶν ἀνδρῶν ἐκείνων τῶν κεκλημένων γεύσεταί μου τοῦ δείπνου.

THE PARABLES OF THE BUILDER AND OF THE KING GOING TO WAR.

Jesus, on His way to Jerusalem, discourages those who are following Him out of political ambition.

25 Συνεπορεύοντο δὲ αὐτῷ ὄχλοι πολλοί· καὶ στραφεὶς εἶπε πρὸς αὐτούς,   26 Εἴ τις ἔρχεται πρός

με, καὶ οὐ μισεῖ τὸν πατέρα ἑαυτοῦ, καὶ τὴν μητέρα, καὶ τὴν γυναῖκα, καὶ τὰ τέκνα, καὶ τοὺς ἀδελφούς, καὶ τὰς ἀδελφάς, ἔτι τε καὶ τὴν ἑαυτοῦ ψυχὴν, οὐ δύναταί μου μαθητὴς εἶναι. 27 ὅστις οὐ βαστάζει τὸν σταυρὸν ἑαυτοῦ, καὶ ἔρχεται ὀπίσω μου, οὐ δύναταί μου εἶναι μαθητής. 28 τίς γὰρ ἐξ ὑμῶν, θέλων πύργον οἰκοδομῆσαι, οὐχὶ πρῶτον καθίσας ψηφίζει τὴν δαπάνην, εἰ ἔχει εἰς ἀπαρτισμόν; 29 ἵνα μήποτε, θέντος αὐτοῦ θεμέλιον, καὶ μὴ ἰσχύοντος ἐκτελέσαι, πάντες οἱ θεωροῦντες ἄρξωνται ἐμπαίζειν αὐτῷ 30 λέγοντες ὅτι Οὗτος ὁ ἄνθρωπος ἤρξατο οἰκοδομεῖν, καὶ οὐκ ἴσχυσεν ἐκτελέσαι. 31 ἢ τίς βασιλεύς, πορευόμενος συμβαλεῖν ἑτέρῳ βασιλεῖ εἰς πόλεμον, οὐχὶ καθίσας πρῶτον βουλεύσεται εἰ δυνατός ἐστιν ἐν δέκα χιλιάσιν ὑπαντῆσαι, τῷ μετὰ εἴκοσι χιλιάδων ἐρχομένῳ ἐπ᾽ αὐτόν; 32 εἰ δὲ μήγε, ἔτι αὐτοῦ πόρρω ὄντος πρεσβείαν ἀποστείλας, ἐρωτᾷ τὰ πρὸς εἰρήνην· 33 οὕτως οὖν, πᾶς ἐξ ὑμῶν, ὃς οὐκ ἀποτάσσεται πᾶσι τοῖς ἑαυτοῦ ὑπάρχουσιν, οὐ δύναταί μου εἶναι μαθητής· 34 καλὸν οὖν τὸ ἅλας· ἐὰν δὲ καὶ τὸ ἅλας μωρανθῇ, ἐν τίνι ἀρτυθήσεται· 35 οὔτε εἰς γῆν οὔτε εἰς κοπρίαν εὔθετόν ἐστιν· ἔξω βάλλουσιν αὐτό· ὁ ἔχων ὦτα ἀκούειν ἀκουέτω.

LESSON XXV.

St Luke xv. 1-10.

THE PARABLES OF THE LOST SHEEP AND THE LOST PIECE OF SILVER.

1 ᾿Ησαν δὲ αὐτῷ ἐγγίζοντες παντες οἱ τελῶναι καὶ οἱ ἁμαρτωλοὶ ἀκούειν αὐτοῦ. 2 καὶ διεγόγγυζον οἵ τε Φαρισαῖοι καὶ οἱ γραμματεῖς λέγοντες ὅτι Οὗτος ἁμαρτωλοὺς προσδέχεται καὶ συνεσθίει αὐτοῖς. 3 εἶπεν δὲ πρὸς αὐτοὺς τὴν παραβολὴν ταύτην λέγων 4 Τίς ἄνθρωπος ἐξ ὑμῶν ἔχων ἑκατὸν πρόβατα καὶ ἀπολέσας ἐξ αὐτῶν ἓν οὐ καταλείπει τὰ ἐνενήκοντα ἐννέα ἐν τῇ ἐρήμῳ καὶ πορεύεται ἐπὶ τὸ ἀπολωλὸς ἕως εὕρῃ αὐτό; 5 καὶ εὑρὼν ἐπιτίθησιν ἐπὶ τοὺς ὤμους αὐτοῦ χαίρων, 6 καὶ ἐλθὼν εἰς τὸν οἶκον συνκαλεῖ τοὺς φίλους καὶ τοὺς γείτονας, λέγων αὐτοῖς Συνχάρητέ μοι ὅτι εὗρον τὸ πρόβατόν μου τὸ ἀπολωλός. 7 λέγω ὑμῖν ὅτι οὕτως χαρὰ ἐν τῷ οὐρανῷ ἔσται ἐπὶ ἑνὶ ἁμαρτωλῷ μετανοοῦντι ἢ ἐπὶ ἐνενήκοντα ἐννέα δικαίοις οἵτινες οὐ χρείαν ἔχουσιν μετανοίας. 8 ῍Η τίς γυνὴ δραχμὰς ἔχουσα δέκα, ἐὰν ἀπολέσῃ δραχμὴν μίαν, οὐχὶ ἅπτει λύχνον καὶ σαροῖ τὴν οἰκίαν καὶ ζητεῖ ἐπιμελῶς ἕως οὗ εὕρῃ; 9 καὶ εὑροῦσα συνκαλεῖ τὰς φίλας καὶ γείτονας λέγουσα Συνχάρητέ μοι ὅτι εὗρον τὴν δραχμὴν ἣν ἀπώλεσα. 10 οὕτως, λέγω ὑμῖν, γίνεται χαρὰ ἐνώπιον τῶν ἀγγέλων τοῦ θεοῦ ἐπὶ ἑνὶ ἁμαρτωλῷ μετανοοῦντι.

THE PHARISEES.

The word Pharisee is derived from Perishîn, the Aramaic form of the Hebrew word Perushîm, and means "separated." The word does not occur either in the Old Testament or the Apocrypha. We read, however, in the books of Ezra and Nehemiah of men who separated themselves from the foreigners, and guarded carefully against all connection with them (Ezra vi. 21, x. 11, 16 ; Neh. ix. 2, x. 29). Such men, in the time of persecution under Antiochus, were called " Hasîdîm," or " pious "; and Judas Maccabeus is spoken of as their captain (2 Macc. xiv. 6): they are described as " voluntarily devoted to the Law " (1 Macc. ii. 42). The persecution intensified the hatred of the foreigner, and the scrupulous attention to the Law which distinguished the pious. But this attention required a separation on the part of the pious Jew—not only from the heathen, but even from those of his fellow - countrymen on whose obedience to the legal precepts he could not rely. Hence the term " pious " and the term " separatist " probably became interchangeable. To give an instance of the need of this separation on the part of the pious. Every pious Jew was expected to give tithes and gifts of his substance to the priest; but not only so—it was necessary also that he should see that, when he was in a friend's house, he never ate anything of which the priest had not received his share ; for by eating what really belonged to Jehovah, and therefore was holy, he would have sinned. Now, if any one wished to guard against this transgression, it was necessary for him to associate only with those whom he could thoroughly trust. Those who did this called themselves associates ("habérîm"). But we may easily imagine that others, who considered this scrupulousness exaggerated, called them Pharisees, or " the separated "; and such may have been the origin of the name.

The term Pharisee, then, was not the name of an office, but was the designation of a tendency or party. It may have been a term of reproach given to the party by their enemies: this we cannot tell for certain. Any one, whatever his rank or station, could join the Pharisees; whereas it depended on a man's birth or extraction whether he could be a Sadducee or not. In order to do this, he must belong to Aaron's descendants, or to the distinguished lay families.

The Scribes, as a rule, joined the Pharisees, though those who were less strict in their interpretation of the Law were sometimes Sadducees. But every Scribe was not a Pharisee, nor every Pharisee a Scribe. The Sadducees were an aristocratic and political party. They threw in their lot with that of the foreign rulers, and in religion they were conservative: they acknowledged the authority of the Law without any reservation, and accepted only so much of the oral tradition as was in existence when they constituted themselves a party.

The Pharisees, on the other hand, were a religious and national or democratic party. They desired home-rule and a riddance of the foreigner. In religion they were the advocates of progress, in the sense that they sought, by their interpretations and glosses, to add to and improve upon the Law; and they set no limit to these improvements. So far indeed did they carry them, that they not unfrequently, by means of them, annulled the Law itself. They were also democrats in religion, in so far that they sought to limit the privileges of the priests, and extend to every one the duties imposed on the priests alone.

In the time of Herod the Great there were more than 6000 Pharisees; and they distinguished themselves by refusing to take the oath of allegiance either to Herod or to the emperor. For this they were fined, and some of them put to death.

From all this it is evident that Pharisaism, in its origin, was far from ignoble. The historical party, with whom they were connected, had, under Ezra and Nehemiah, shown themselves zealous for the Law, though in a narrow and rigid manner—had, under the Maccabees, shed their blood to deliver their country from religious persecution, and had aided to secure its independence, and had always the appearance of siding with the cause of religion and of the people. How comes it, then, that Jesus singled them out from amongst His contemporaries for denunciation, preferring to them even the publican and sinner, and that their name is now a synonym for formalism and hypocrisy?

The answer is, that while the historic party in its beginnings had had the germs of vice mingled with its virtues, these germs had developed in the party of the time of Jesus, and were fatal to the moral improvement of the nation. Even in Jesus' time there were good Pharisees, such as Nicodemus and Gamaliel. But as a class they were distinguished for self-satisfaction, unreality, and an unloving temper.

Their self-satisfaction made it impossible that they should repent or improve: they would not have listened to the $\gamma\nu\hat{\omega}\theta\iota \ \sigma\epsilon\alpha\upsilon\tau\acute{o}\nu$ of Socrates, much less therefore to the teaching of Jesus, which demanded that before they entered the kingdom of heaven they should be "poor in spirit"—*i.e.*, should acknowledge that they had not attained, and could not attain, to the moral and spiritual standard of God's law. They believed they were in the kingdom of heaven, and that they set the standard.

Their unreality made them put custom, traditions, and forms, before morals and religious life, so that they thought more of the washing of hands than of a "clean heart"; more of the custom of devoting property to the priests, than of the moral duty of maintaining parents; more of keeping the Sabbath, than of doing an act of kindness. And "they had made a new discovery in the science of evil." [1] In the name of religion they served their own ambition and egotism. Their observance of outward ceremonies increased their importance in the society in which they lived. They made virtue instead of vice the servant of selfishness. They used their religious influence to destroy morality and aggrandise themselves. They were the chief religious teachers of their contemporaries, and their teaching tended to promote evil and to call it good, and to make it impossible for nobler teaching to gain a hearing.

Their unloving character promoted hatred and despair, instead of love and hope, among their countrymen, whom it was their function (or at least that of the Scribes among them) to teach. They taught that religion consisted in scrupulous attention to the precepts of the Law and their interpretations of it, and that holiness consisted in keeping one's self separated from the Gentile, and from all Jews who did not observe these ordinances. They prided themselves on their exclusive possession of this religion and holiness, and regarded those who had them not as no true Jews, and as aliens from the kingdom of heaven. But the political condition of their country was such, that they were the only class who could observe the Law and keep themselves separated from the Gentile. However much they might play at being independent of the Gentile, the Gentile was largely in possession of the land. The land was ruled by Romans, and populated by Greeks, Romans, and Syro-Phœnicians, as well as Jews. The Pharisees and Scribes might find it possible to observe the Law in all its details, and to keep themselves separated from "the unclean," because it was their profession to do so,— and they gained position directly, and money indirectly, by the exercise of their profession. But the "people,"

---

[1] Mozley's University Sermons.

who had to gain their living by agriculture and merchandise, were necessarily brought into contact with the Gentile, and so rendered unclean. For this inevitable uncleanness the Pharisees despised their fellow-countrymen, and said of them, with mingled contempt and spite, " This people, that knoweth not the Law, is accursed " (John vii. 49). Their idea of the kingdom of God was of an exclusive one, in which they themselves should figure most prominently, and all who did not conform to their ideas of " cleanness " should be excluded. Jesus' idea of the kingdom of God was that of a kingdom of love, which should include all loving hearts. The land in which Jesus taught was a land of hate. The Roman hated and despised the subject Jews, because he could not understand their customs, and resented their obstinate resistance to Roman rule and Roman thought; the Jew hated alike the Roman conqueror and the Samaritan schismatic; the Samaritan hated the Jew as a disdainful neighbour, while his relations with the Roman master were too insecure to be cordial;[1] the Pharisee hated Romans and Samaritans, and all Jews who did not agree with him. In this land of hate, the Scribe, who was usually a Pharisee, was the recognised religious teacher, and he, so far from being a softening influence, intensified the hatred and narrowness in his little country—a country about the size of Wales. No wonder that Jesus, who sought to make all men brothers, visited the teaching and persons of the Pharisees with burning indignation.

The Talmud speaks of seven classes of Pharisees: the " Heavy-footed," who were so exhausted by fasting that they could not walk like other people; the " Bleeding," who ran their heads against things, because, in mock modesty, they always walked with their eyes cast down;

[1] Josephus, Ant., xviii. 4. 1; B. J., iii. 7. 32.

the " Mortar Pharisees," who bent themselves till they resembled the handle of a mortar as they walked ; the " Hump-backed," who always hung the head ; the " Tell me another duty and I will do it "; the " Painted," whose pious manners can be seen from a distance ; and lastly, the " Pharisees from love," who obey God because they love Him from the heart.

So great a stress did they lay on the cleansing of the vessels used in the Temple, that the Sadducees cried out in mockery to a priest who was subjecting even the golden candlestick to a lustration after a feast, " Lo, the Pharisees will at last cleanse the sun for us !"

LESSON XXVI.

St Luke xv. 11-32.

THE PARABLE OF THE PRODIGAL SON.

11 Εἶπεν δέ Ἄνθρωπός τις εἶχεν δύο υἱούς. 12 καὶ
εἶπεν ὁ νεώτερος αὐτῶν τῷ πατρί Πάτερ, δός μοι τὸ
ἐπιβάλλον μέρος τῆς οὐσίας· ὁ δὲ διεῖλεν αὐτοῖς τὸν
βίον. 13 καὶ μετ' οὐ πολλὰς ἡμέρας συναγαγὼν
πάντα ὁ νεώτερος υἱὸς ἀπεδήμησεν εἰς χώραν μακράν,
καὶ ἐκεῖ διεσκόρπισεν τὴν οὐσίαν αὐτοῦ ζῶν ἀσώτως.
14 δαπανήσαντος δὲ αὐτοῦ πάντα ἐγένετο λιμὸς
ἰσχυρὰ κατὰ τὴν χώραν ἐκείνην, καὶ αὐτὸς ἤρξατο
ὑστερεῖσθαι. 15 καὶ πορευθεὶς ἐκολλήθη ἑνὶ τῶν
πολιτῶν τῆς χώρας ἐκείνης, καὶ ἔπεμψεν αὐτὸν εἰς
τοὺς ἀγροὺς αὐτοῦ βόσκειν χοίρους· 16 καὶ ἐπεθύμει χορτασθῆναι[1] ἐκ τῶν κερατίων ὧν ἤσθιον οἱ χοῖροι,
καὶ οὐδεὶς ἐδίδου αὐτῷ. 17 εἰς ἑαυτὸν δὲ ἐλθὼν ἔφη
Πόσοι μίσθιοι τοῦ πατρός μου περισσεύουσιν ἄρτων·
ἐγὼ δὲ λιμῷ ὧδε ἀπόλλυμαι. 18 ἀναστὰς πορεύσο-
μαι πρὸς τὸν πατέρα μου καὶ ἐρῶ αὐτῷ· Πάτερ,
ἥμαρτον εἰς τὸν οὐρανὸν καὶ ἐνώπιόν σου, 19 οὐκέτι
εἰμὶ ἄξιος κληθῆναι υἱός σου· ποίησόν με ὡς ἕνα τῶν
μισθίων σου. 20 καὶ ἀναστὰς ἦλθεν πρὸς τὸν πατέρα αὐτοῦ. ἔτι δὲ αὐτοῦ μακρὰν ἀπέχοντος εἶδεν
αὐτὸν ὁ πατὴρ αὐτοῦ καὶ ἐσπλαγχνίσθη, καὶ δραμὼν
ἐπέπεσεν ἐπὶ τὸν τράχηλον αὐτοῦ καὶ κατεφίλησεν

---

[1] *V. l.*, γεμίσαι τὴν κοιλίαν αὐτοῦ.

M

αὐτόν. 21 εἶπεν δὲ ὁ υἱὸς αὐτῷ Πάτερ, ἥμαρτον εἰς τὸν οὐρανὸν καὶ ἐνώπιόν σου, οὐκέτι εἰμὶ ἄξιος κληθῆναι υἱός σου· 22 [ποίησόν με ὡς ἕνα τῶν μισθίων σου]. εἶπεν δὲ ὁ πατὴρ πρὸς τοὺς δούλους αὐτοῦ Ταχὺ ἐξενέγκατε στολὴν τὴν πρώτην καὶ ἐνδύσατε αὐτόν, καὶ δότε δακτύλιον εἰς τὴν χεῖρα αὐτοῦ καὶ ὑποδήματα εἰς τοὺς πόδας, 23 καὶ φέρετε τὸν μόσχον τὸν σιτευτόν, θύσατε, καὶ φαγόντες εὐφραν- θῶμεν, 24 ὅτι οὗτος ὁ υἱός μου νεκρὸς ἦν καὶ ἀνέζη- σεν, ἦν ἀπολωλὼς καὶ εὑρέθη. καὶ ἤρξαντο εὐφραί- νεσθαι, 25 ἦν δὲ ὁ υἱὸς αὐτοῦ ὁ πρεσβύτερος ἐν ἀγρῷ· καὶ ὡς ἐρχόμενος ἤγγισεν τῇ οἰκίᾳ, ἤκουσεν συμφωνίας καὶ χορῶν, 26 καὶ προσκαλεσάμενος ἕνα τῶν παίδων ἐπυνθάνετο τί ἂν εἴη ταῦτα· 27 ὁ δὲ εἶπεν αὐτῷ ὅτι Ὁ ἀδελφός σου ἥκει, καὶ ἔθυσεν ὁ πατήρ σου τὸν μόσχον τὸν σιτευτόν, ὅτι ὑγιαίνοντα αὐτὸν ἀπέλαβεν. 28 ὠργίσθη δὲ καὶ οὐκ ἤθελεν εἰσελθεῖν· ὁ δὲ πατὴρ αὐτοῦ ἐξελθὼν παρεκάλει αὐτόν· 29 ὁ δὲ ἀποκριθεὶς εἶπεν τῷ πατρὶ αὐτοῦ Ἰδοὺ τοσαῦτα ἔτη δουλεύω σοι καὶ οὐδέποτε ἐντολήν σου παρῆλθον, καὶ ἐμοὶ οὐδέποτε ἔδωκας ἔριφον ἵνα μετὰ τῶν φίλων μου εὐφρανθῶ. 30 ὅτε δὲ ὁ υἱός οὗτος ὁ καταφαγών σου τὸν βίον μετὰ πορνῶν ἦλθεν, ἔθυσας αὐτῷ τὸν σιτευτὸν μόσχον· 31 ὁ δὲ εἶπεν αὐτῷ Τέκνον, σὺ πάντοτε μετ᾽ ἐμοῦ εἶ, καὶ πάντα τὰ ἐμὰ σά ἐστιν· 32 εὐφρανθῆναι δὲ καὶ χα- ρῆναι ἔδει, ὅτι ὁ ἀδελφός σου οὗτος νεκρὸς ἦν καὶ ἔζησεν, καὶ ἀπολωλὼς καὶ εὑρέθη.

LESSON XXVII.

St Luke xvi. 1-13.

THE PARABLE OF THE UNJUST STEWARD.

1 Ἔλεγεν δὲ καὶ πρὸς τοὺς μαθητάς Ἄνθρωπός τις ἦν πλούσιος ὃς εἶχεν οἰκονόμον, καὶ οὗτος διεβλήθη αὐτῷ ὡς διασκορπίζων τὰ ὑπάρχοντα αὐτοῦ. 2 καὶ φωνήσας αὐτὸν εἶπεν αὐτῷ Τί τοῦτο ἀκούω περὶ σοῦ; ἀπόδος τὸν λόγον τῆς οἰκονομίας σου, οὐ γὰρ δύνῃ ἔτι οἰκονομεῖν. 3 εἶπεν δὲ ἐν ἑαυτῷ ὁ οἰκονόμος Τί ποιήσω ὅτι ὁ κύριός μου ἀφαιρεῖται τὴν οἰκονομίαν ἀπ᾽ ἐμοῦ; σκάπτειν οὐκ ἰσχύω, ἐπαιτεῖν αἰσχύνομαι· 4 ἔγνων τί ποιήσω, ἵνα ὅταν μετασταθῶ ἐκ τῆς οἰκονομίας δέξωνταί με εἰς τοὺς οἴκους ἑαυτῶν. 5 καὶ προσκαλεσάμενος ἕνα ἕκαστον τῶν χρεοφιλετῶν τοῦ κυρίου ἑαυτοῦ ἔλεγεν τῷ πρώτῳ Πόσον ὀφείλεις τῷ κυρίῳ μου; ὁ δὲ εἶπεν Ἑκατὸν βάτους ἐλαίου· 6 ὁ δὲ εἶπεν αὐτῷ Δέξαι σου τὰ γράμματα καὶ καθίσας ταχέως γράψον πεντήκοντα. 7 ἔπειτα ἑτέρῳ εἶπεν Σὺ δὲ πόσον ὀφείλεις; ὁ δὲ εἶπεν Ἑκατὸν κόρους σίτου· λέγει αὐτῷ Δέξαι σου τὰ γράμματα καὶ γράψον ὀγδοήκοντα. 8 καὶ ἐπῄνεσεν ὁ κύριος τὸν οἰκονόμον τῆς ἀδικίας ὅτι φρονίμως ἐποίησεν· ὅτι οἱ υἱοὶ τοῦ αἰῶνος τούτου φρονιμώτεροι ὑπὲρ τοὺς υἱοὺς τοῦ φωτὸς εἰς τὴν γενεὰν τὴν ἑαυτῶν εἰσίν. 9 Καὶ ἐγὼ ὑμῖν λέγω, ἑαυτοῖς ποιήσατε φίλους ἐκ τοῦ μαμωνᾶ τῆς

ἀδικίας, ἵνα ὅταν ἐκλίπῃ[1] δέξωνται ὑμᾶς εἰς τὰς αἰω-
νίους σκηνάς. 10 ὁ πιστὸς ἐν ἐλαχίστῳ καὶ ἐν πολ-
γῷ πιστός ἐστιν, καὶ ὁ ἐν ἐλαχίστῳ ἄδικος καὶ ἐν
πολλῷ ἄδικός ἐστιν. 11 εἰ οὖν ἐν τῷ ἀδίκῳ μαμωνᾷ
πιστοὶ οὐκ ἐγένεσθε, τὸ ἀληθινὸν τίς ὑμῖν πιστεύσει;
12 καὶ εἰ ἐν τῷ ἀλλοτρίῳ πιστοὶ οὐκ ἐγένεσθε, τὸ
ὑμέτερον[2] τίς δώσει ὑμῖν; 13 οὐδεὶς οἰκέτης δύναται
δυσὶ κυρίοις δουλεύειν· ἢ γὰρ τὸν ἕνα μισήσει καὶ
τὸν ἕτερον ἀγαπήσει, ἢ ἑνὸς ἀνθέξεται καὶ τοῦ ἑτέρου
καταφρονήσει· οὐ δύνασθε θεῷ δουλεύειν καὶ μαμωνᾷ.

[1] *V. l.*, ἐκλίπητε.   [2] Westcott and Hort read ἡμέτερον.

LESSON XXVIII.

St Luke xvi. 19-31.

THE STORY OF THE RICH MAN AND LAZARUS.

19 Ἄνθρωπος δέ τις ἦν πλούσιος, καὶ ἐνεδιδύσκετο πορφύραν καὶ βύσσον εὐφραινόμενος καθ' ἡμέραν λαμπρῶς. 20 πτωχὸς δέ τις ὀνόματι Λάζαρος ἐβέβλητο πρὸς τὸν πυλῶνα αὐτοῦ εἱλκωμένος 21 καὶ ἐπιθυμῶν χορτασθῆναι ἀπὸ τῶν[1] πιπτόντων ἀπὸ τῆς τραπέζης τοῦ πλουσίου· ἀλλὰ καὶ οἱ κύνες ἐρχόμενοι ἐπέλειχον[2] τὰ ἕλκη αὐτοῦ. 22 ἐγένετο δὲ ἀποθανεῖν τὸν πτωχὸν καὶ ἀπενεχθῆναι αὐτὸν ὑπὸ τῶν ἀγγέλων εἰς τὸν κόλπον Ἀβραάμ· ἀπέθανεν δὲ καὶ ὁ πλούσιος καὶ ἐτάφη. 23 καὶ ἐν τῷ ᾅδῃ ἐπάρας τοὺς ὀφθαλμοὺς αὐτοῦ, ὑπάρχων ἐν βασάνοις, ὁρᾷ Ἀβραὰμ ἀπὸ μακρόθεν καὶ Λάζαρον ἐν τοῖς κόλποις αὐτοῦ. 24 καὶ αὐτὸς φωνήσας εἶπεν Πάτερ Ἀβραάμ, ἐλέησόν με καὶ πέμψον Λάζαρον ἵνα βάψῃ τὸ ἄκρον τοῦ δακτύλου αὐτοῦ ὕδατος καὶ καταψύξῃ τὴν γλῶσσάν μου, ὅτι ὀδυνῶμαι ἐν τῇ φλογὶ ταύτῃ. 25 εἶπεν δὲ Ἀβραάμ Τέκνον, μνήσθητι ὅτι ἀπέλαβες τὰ ἀγαθά σου ἐν τῇ ζωῇ σου, καὶ Λάζαρος ὁμοίως τὰ κακά· νῦν δὲ ὧδε[3] παρακαλεῖται, σὺ δὲ ὀδυνᾶσαι. 26 καὶ ἐν πᾶσι τούτοις μεταξὺ ἡμῶν καὶ ὑμῶν χάσμα μέγα ἐστήρικται, ὅπως οἱ θέλοντες διαβῆναι ἔνθεν πρὸς ὑμᾶς μὴ δύνωνται, μηδὲ ἐκεῖθεν πρὸς ἡμᾶς διαπερῶσιν·

[1] V. l., ψιχίων τῶν.   [2] V. l., ἀπέλειχον.   [3] V. l., ὅδε.

27 εἶπεν δέ Ἐρωτῶ σε οὖν, πάτερ, ἵνα πέμψῃς αὐτὸν εἰς τὸν οἶκον τοῦ πατρός μου, 28 ἔχω γὰρ πέντε ἀδελφούς, ὅπως διαμαρτύρηται αὐτοῖς, ἵνα μὴ καὶ αὐτοὶ ἔλθωσιν εἰς τὸν τόπον τοῦτον τῆς βασάνου. 29 λέγει δὲ Ἀβραάμ Ἔχουσι Μωυσέα καὶ τοὺς προφήτας· ἀκουσάτωσαν αὐτῶν. 30 ὁ δὲ εἶπεν Οὐχί, πάτερ Ἀβραάμ, ἀλλ' ἐάν τις ἀπὸ νεκρῶν πορευθῇ πρὸς αὐτοὺς μετανοήσουσιν. 31 εἶπεν δὲ αὐτῷ Εἰ Μωυσέως καὶ τῶν προφητῶν οὐκ ἀκούουσιν, οὐδ' ἐάν τις ἐκ νεκρῶν ἀναστῇ πεισθήσονται.

THE RICH MAN AND LAZARUS.

The story addressed to Pharisees.—This narrative was addressed to the Pharisees, who had been sneering at Jesus, as, in the parable of the dishonest steward, He gave instruction on the proper use of riches. That narrative had probably been addressed to the publicans, whose besetting sin was the love of money, which was so immediately connected with their occupation. But the Evangelist tells us that the Pharisees also were φιλάργυροι.[1] Now this seems strange at first, for the occupation of the Pharisees was to act as Rabbis, and no Rabbi could take money for any official duty. The great Rabbi Hillel said, "He who makes gain of the words of the Law, his life will be taken from the world." No teacher, preacher, judge, or other rabbinical official could receive money for his services. In practice the Law was somewhat modified, as a Rabbi might receive a moderate sum for his duties, to make good the loss of his time. The Rabbi earned enough money to satisfy his simple wants by the practice of a trade. But there were ways by which he could acquire wealth. He could become a partner in a prosperous commercial house, or marry into a rich family, for matri-

[1] Ver. 14.

monial alliance with him was eagerly sought after, and regarded as bringing with it a blessing. His scholars, also, would bring him presents. Rich and devout widows would maintain a Rabbi as an act of piety (Matt. xxiii. 14). We should, however, probably do wrong to think of the home of the rich man mentioned in the story as being typical of that of the Pharisee. Josephus even tells us of the Pharisees that they lived meanly and despised delicacies in diet; and this statement at first sight seems inconsistent with the character given them in this chapter. But we must bear in mind that we have really very little evidence to guide us in estimating their character, and that it is probable that both here and in Josephus a portion of them are described as if they were the whole class. It is quite intelligible, too, that a class of men who adopted a frugal fare at their own homes, and were courted by the rich for their reputation for piety, would display their love of money, and even of luxury, at the houses of their wealthy friends. Moreover, the story of Dives and Lazarus is directed not so much against luxurious living as against indifference to the poor. And though the exhibition of luxury before the eyes of the poor is one sign of this indifference, it is not the only one. The Pharisee showed at once a supercilious contempt for the poor, and, by his teaching, aggravated their condition. He himself lived by keeping the Law, and teaching men to keep it, and prided himself on his ceremonial cleanness, which gained him both honour and wealth. But this very teaching either hindered those who were not Rabbis from enriching themselves, and so kept them poor, or caused them to be regarded as unclean, and therefore outcasts in the sight of the godly.

And from a Pharisaic point of view. — In the parable of the Unjust Steward, addressed as it was to publicans accustomed to the views and maxims of men of the world, Jesus had pointed His lesson by the application of the maxims of men of the world to the conduct of His new converts in the new life on which they were entering. In this story, addressed to Pharisees, He uses warnings derived from the Pharisaic views of retribution, of the future state, and of the authority of Moses. The preceding parable was an *argumentum ad hominem* addressed to the publicans; this story seems to be an *argumentum ad hominem* addressed to the Pharisees. Thus the idea of retribution contained in ver. 25 was not only thoroughly Jewish, but a favourite one with the Pharisees. They had a saying, "With what measure a man metes, it will be measured to him again"; and, "In the same pot in which a man has cooked, others will cook him in return." Again, they spoke of "the bosom of Abraham" as the scene of future happiness, and the two parts of Hades as separated by a wall, as Jesus represents them as separated by a gulf. Abraham, on whom, as their father,[1] they rested their hopes, is brought forward in their condemnation, and the rich man's brethren are referred to Moses and the prophets.

The rich man not condemned because he is rich.—At first sight it would seem that the rich man was condemned merely because he was rich, and the poor man was saved because he was poor. But that this is not so we may learn both from the teaching of Jesus in other passages, and from the details of this story. For in Matt. xiii. 22, Jesus had spoken of "the cares of this world" as well as of "the deceitfulness of riches" as hindrances to the reception of the Word. And the very Abraham into whose presence the rich man's selfishness prevented him entering, and who is the presiding father of the poor man's joys, is described in Gen. xiii. 2 as "very rich in cattle, in silver, and in gold." The

---

[1] John viii. 39.

story must be taken in connection with what Jesus saw and experienced among the mixed population amidst whom His life was spent, where He found the religious teacher, if not luxurious, certainly proud and held in honour, and at the same time utterly selfish and callous to the misery around him, and unwilling to learn from His teaching or example the lesson of love and brotherly sympathy. On the other hand, He found the poor and oppressed eager to listen to Him, and susceptible to the new doctrine of brotherly love. "Listen then," He says to the former, "to your real condition in the sight of God, and compare it with that of these poor disciples of mine whom you despise."

And we know that Jesus showed no dislike to the rich as such. He was always ready to recognise their virtues and receive them as disciples, whether they were publicans as Zacchæus, or Pharisees as Nicodemus and Joseph of Arimathea.

Though, however, the parable was addressed primarily to the Pharisees, its lesson and warning extend to all time, and all societies. The selfish cannot enter the kingdom of love; the kingdom of love is the sphere for the active as well as for the passive virtues. Even piety may be selfish and indifferent to the sorrows of the world, and in the name of devotion to God, be negligent of the sufferings of the poor.

Rich and poor in Rome:—At the time when Jesus spoke, the contrast between riches and poverty throughout the world was a very terrible one. The wealth of civilisation was in the hands of a few; the majority lived in squalor and misery. In Rome itself half the population consisted of slaves, and a quarter of paupers. There was no middle class of moderate means. The wealthy minority lived for the most part in selfish luxury and reckless extravagance. To no other method of life had they been trained. Their riches, if not inherited, had been won by pillage in war, or by the still more demoralising pillage in peace of provincial cities and citizens. They knew nothing of the sobering influences of commercial or agricultural industry, nor had they been taught consideration towards the poor by the civilising relations between employers and employed. At that time all manual labour, as well in towns as in the country, was executed by slaves.

We may picture to ourselves the startling influence such a parable as this must have had when first read by a luxurious aristocrat of the Roman Empire, surrounded by Lazari in the persons of his poor clients and his slaves. To clothe and feed him, all the quarters of the world were ransacked; while to his clients he contemptuously doled out a miserable pittance, and his slaves were fed on sour wine, and on corn or even the olives that fell prematurely. Such a man may well have shuddered as the words of the great Master contrasted the burial of the rich and poor with their after condition. Before his mind would pass the pageant of his own funeral, the flute-players preceding the corpse, the female mourners following, the lictors in attendance to keep order; the strange figures representing his ancestors marching in front of the bier, wearing on their faces the waxen masks delineating their features, clad in the dress and wearing the insignia appropriate to each; the body on an ivory bier, which was covered with purple or gold embroidered coverlets. Then the solemn session of the mimic ancestors round the corpse, while the orator mounted the pulpit and extolled their deeds and those of the deceased; the odorous burning, and the loud lament; and, last of all, the stately tomb on the Via Appia or Latina, with the inscription that should keep the memory of the dead before the thoughts of men, and link him with the living.

Then he might well think of his slave, whom perhaps (such practices were common) he had turned out of doors, sick of an incurable disease, to die in the temple of Æsculapius on the island of the Tiber, or in whatever spot he could crawl to ; or if he had died in the narrow and perhaps subterranean cell in which his indoor life had been passed, his corpse had been hastily and summarily carried out by his comrades, placed on a rude bier, conveyed by night with as little noise as possible, and thrown naked into a hole, into which other corpses had been thrown before (Hor. Sat. I. viii. 8).

In so striking a form did the pageantry of death, the great leveller, maintain in the very centre of civilisation the glaring distinction between the lot of the rich and poor. The common portion of the grave made them no nearer kin. In death, as in life, there was a great gulf fixed between them.

Yet according to the great Teacher of the Christians, if the slave had been faithful and unselfish, his fate in the unseen future would contrast to his advantage with his master's, as greatly as in his life and in his burial it had contrasted to his disadvantage.

King Lear as Dives.—Shakespeare affords us a fine illustration of a Dives brought by his own sufferings to reflect on those of the poor, and on his own neglect of them, in " King Lear," iii. 4. 28 :—

> " Poor naked wretches, wheresoe'er you are,
> That bide the pelting of this pitiless storm,
> How shall your houseless heads, and unfed sides,
> Your loop'd and window'd raggedness, defend you
> From seasons such as these ? O, I have ta'en
> Too little care of this ! Take physic, pomp ;
> Expose thyself to feel what wretches feel ;
> That thou may'st shake the superflux to them,
> And show the heavens more just."

Influence of the story on the treatment of lepers.

—From the description of Lazarus as *εἱλκωμένος* in ver. 21, the word Lazar came to be used for a leper, and Lazaretto for a hospital for lepers. The Crusaders introduced the leprosy of the East into all the countries embracing the Mediterranean Sea. Perhaps it was partly on account of this parable that a sentiment of reverence towards the sufferers was widely diffused throughout the empire. In addition to this, however, the disease was invested with a sacred character, in consequence of its mysterious connection with the warfare of the Holy Sepulchre. Churchmen taught that Christ Himself had regarded lepers with peculiar tenderness. It was even inferred from Isa. liii. that Christ Himself had been a leper—"Nos putavimus eum leprosum, percussum a deo et humiliatum." Kings and princes visited, countesses ministered to them, saints (as it was believed) wrought miracles for their cure, and almost every considerable city erected hospitals for their reception and relief. We are told of St Francis d'Assisi, that on giving up his life of pleasure for a life of self-abnegation, he used to visit the lazar-houses which he had before held in horror, not only bestowing alms but personal service of the humblest description, and adding the kiss of human kindness to console the miserable, whose touch was dreaded by all the world. One of his followers, James surnamed the Simple, earned the title of steward and physician of the leprous.

LESSON XXIX.

St Luke xviii. 1-14.

THE PARABLES OF THE IMPORTUNATE WIDOW AND OF THE PHARISEE AND THE PUBLICAN.

1 Ἔλεγεν δὲ παραβολὴν αὐτοῖς πρὸς τὸ δεῖν πάντοτε προσεύχεσθαι αὐτοὺς καὶ μὴ ἐγκακεῖν,[1] 2 λέγων Κριτής τις ἦν ἔν τινι πόλει τὸν θεὸν μὴ φοβούμενος καὶ ἄνθρωπον μὴ ἐντρεπόμενος. 3 χήρα δὲ ἦν ἐν τῇ πόλει ἐκείνῃ καὶ ἤρχετο πρὸς αὐτὸν λέγουσα Ἐκδίκησόν με ἀπὸ τοῦ ἀντιδίκου μου. 4 καὶ οὐκ ἤθελεν ἐπὶ χρόνον, μετὰ ταῦτα δὲ εἶπεν ἐν ἑαυτῷ Εἰ καὶ τὸν θεὸν οὐ φοβοῦμαι οὐδὲ ἄνθρωπον ἐντρέπομαι, 5 διά γε τὸ παρέχειν μοι κόπον τὴν χήραν ταύτην ἐκδικήσω αὐτήν, ἵνα μὴ εἰς τέλος ἐρχομένη ὑπωπιάζῃ με. 6 Εἶπεν δὲ ὁ κύριος Ἀκούσατε τί ὁ κριτὴς τῆς ἀδικίας λέγει· 7 ὁ δὲ θεὸς οὐ μὴ ποιήσῃ τὴν ἐκδίκησιν τῶν ἐκλεκτῶν αὐτοῦ τῶν βοώντων αὐτῷ ἡμέρας καὶ νυκτός, καὶ μακροθυμεῖ[2] ἐπ᾽ αὐτοῖς; 8 λέγω ὑμῖν ὅτι ποιήσει τὴν ἐκδίκησιν αὐτῶν ἐν τάχει. πλὴν ὁ υἱὸς τοῦ ἀνθρώπου ἐλθὼν ἆρα εὑρήσει τὴν πίστιν ἐπὶ τῆς γῆς;

9 Εἶπεν δὲ καὶ πρός τινας τοὺς πεποιθότας ἐφ᾽ ἑαυτοῖς ὅτι εἰσὶν δίκαιοι καὶ ἐξουθενοῦντας τοὺς λοιποὺς τὴν παραβολὴν ταύτην. 10 Ἄνθρωποι δύο ἀνέβησαν εἰς τὸ ἱερὸν προσεύξασθαι, εἷς Φαρισαῖος

---

[1] *V. l.*, ἐκκακεῖν. [2] *V. l.*, μακροθυμῶν.

καὶ ὁ ἕτερος τελώνης. 11 ὁ Φαρισαῖος σταθεὶς ταῦτα
πρὸς ἑαυτὸν[1] προσηύχετο Ὁ θεός, εὐχαριστῶ σοι
ὅτι οὐκ εἰμὶ ὥσπερ οἱ λοιποὶ τῶν ἀνθρώπων, ἅρπαγες, ἄδικοι, μοιχοί, ἢ καὶ ὡς οὗτος ὁ τελώνης· 12 νηστεύω δὶς τοῦ σαββάτου, ἀποδεκατεύω πάντα ὅσα
κτῶμαι. 13 ὁ δὲ τελώνης μακρόθεν ἑστὼς οὐκ ἤθελεν
οὐδὲ τοὺς ὀφθαλμοὺς ἐπᾶραι εἰς τὸν οὐρανόν, ἀλλ᾽
ἔτυπτε τὸ στῆθος ἑαυτοῦ λέγων Ὁ θεός, ἱλάσθητί
μοι τῷ ἁμαρτωλῷ. 14 λέγω ὑμῖν, κατέβη οὗτος
δεδικαιωμένος εἰς τὸν οἶκον αὐτοῦ παρ᾽ ἐκεῖνον· ὅτι
πᾶς ὁ ὑψῶν ἑαυτὸν ταπεινωθήσεται, ὁ δὲ ταπεινῶν
ἑαυτὸν ὑψωθήσεται.

THE PARABLE OF THE IMPORTUNATE WIDOW: THE SUFFERINGS AND PATIENCE OF THE EARLY CHRISTIANS.

The parable contains a strong *a fortiori* argument, in
which the wicked character of the judge, his contempt
for the widow, and the brief period of her persistency,
are contrasted with the goodness of God, His care for
His elect, and their cry to Him day and night. If the
wicked judge could be induced to listen to the prayer of
the widow, whom he despised, after she had importuned
him for a time, how much more will the just and good
God hear the loud crying of His elect, who are precious
in His sight, when they cry to Him day and night?
The parable receives a striking illustration from Rev.
vi. 9-11 : " I saw underneath the altar the souls of
them that had been slain for the Word of God, and for
the testimony which they held: and they cried with a great
voice, saying, How long, O Master, the holy and true,
dost thou not judge and avenge (ἐκδικεῖς) our blood on
them that dwell on the earth? And there was given

---

[1] *V. l.*, πρὸς ἑαυτὸν ταῦτα.

them to each one a robe; and it was said unto them, that they should rest yet for a little while, until their fellow-servants also and their brethren, which should be killed even as they were, should be fulfilled" (or "should have fulfilled their course"). Here the martyred Christians are represented as crying for justice from under the symbolic altar where they lie, like slaughtered victims. In their voices we hear the early Church, widowed of her Lord, importuning for justice on her adversaries.

In John xvi. 12, we read how Jesus warned His disciples that they would have to undergo persecutions. "These things have I spoken unto you, that ye should not be offended. They shall put you out of the synagogues: yea, the time cometh, that whosoever killeth you will think that he doeth God service." He foresaw that the time would come when, in the days of darkness and persecution, they would be in danger of losing their trust and thinking that God was as indifferent to them as the wicked judge was to the widow. He Himself seems to have passed through some such dark hour when He cried on the cross, "My God, my God, why hast Thou forsaken me?" (Matt. xxvii. 46;) but was able, nevertheless, in calm confidence, with His last breath to say, "Father, into Thy hands I commend my spirit" (Luke xxiii. 46).[1]

His disciples were to be left in the world to struggle with the evil in sorrow and affliction, often almost in despair. They were not to spend lives of rapture and reverie and devotional idleness. In His dying intercessory prayer for them He said, "I pray not that Thou shouldest take them from the world, but that Thou shouldest keep them from the evil" (or "evil one") (John xvii. 15).

To the Jewish Christians the dark hour would seem to have come when Jerusalem was being besieged by

[1] Cf. p. 61.

Titus; yet the destruction of Jerusalem proved a boon to Christianity, by delivering it from its connection with Judaism. Darkest of all, in the early age, was the time of Nero, when the Christians were being persecuted on suspicion of being concerned in the burning of Rome. In the frightful horrors that accompanied that persecution, the sufferers must sometimes, amid all their heroism, have been tempted to regard God as careless and indifferent, and have importuned Him to right their cause, even as the widow called upon the judge. They were delivered to wild beasts, or burnt alive in the amphitheatre, after suffering and scourging. Their punishment was made part of a public festival, the spectacle of their butchery a public pastime. They were tortured and murdered amid the laughter and applause of the brutal populace. Well might they then cry unto God day and night. A great *fête* was held in Rome. In the morning numbers of condemned Christians, covered with the skins of wild beasts, were hurled into the arena of the amphitheatre to be torn to pieces by dogs. In the evening, a more hideous spectacle was prepared; clad in tunics steeped in oil, pitch, or rosin, the Christian martyrs, the ἐκλεκτοὶ τοῦ θεοῦ, were fastened to posts, and when the sun set were lighted as living flambeaus! For this spectacle Nero offered the magnificent gardens which he possessed on the other side of the Tiber. At this day the sufferings of the Christians seem to be avenged by the erection on that very site of the great Christian cathedral of St Peter. By the light of these hideous living torches Nero, who had instituted chariot-races for the evening, sometimes mingled with the people dressed as a jockey, sometimes drove his chariot, courting the plaudits of the mob (Tacitus, Annals, xv. 44). Even women, even young and modest maidens, were exhibited in tortures, and, to amuse the populace, were made to act the sufferings of legendary heroines, as of Dirce, who was tied to a bull, and dragged about by the savage beast till death put an end to her agonies.

It would not have been surprising if the Christian Church at that time, widowed of her Lord, neglected seemingly by God, and become the laughing-stock of men, had lost faith, and felt that God did not care to right the cause of His elect.

Yet, as a matter of fact, the Christians displayed the most noble fortitude, even tender women undaunted courage, amidst tortures worse than death.   And God did hear the cries of the elect, though He seemed to tarry long.   For " the blood of the martyrs became the seed of the Church."   The orgies of Nero proved the baptism of blood which set aside Rome, as the city of martyrs, to play a part in the history of Christianity, and to be the second Holy City.   Up to that hour the seed of Christianity had been growing secretly : the Christians consisted of slaves, of the poor in the low Jewish quarters by the Tiber, subsequently called the Ghetto.   But the seed was watered by the blood of the martyrs, and the blade began to appear.   Fifty thousand spectators had seen what was the true character of the Christians, had witnessed them put to the test in a way of which the world had never dreamt before.   Their high courage, their lowly resignation, their unflinching faith, were now known to all men, and could not fail to attract the attention of noble spirits to their religion.   The new ideal of virtue that hitherto had blushed unseen had now expanded its blossom before the eyes of the Roman world.   The fruit of the Spirit had publicly shamed the works of the flesh before the vastest audience that could be gathered for its display.   The adulterous and lascivious had seen the chaste and modest, beautiful even in a shameless and public death : the hating and murderous had witnessed love, joy, peace, long-suffering, and gentleness, amidst agonies never known before.[1] The virtues of the new religion so proclaimed did not fail to attract and to allure. In the bitterness of their hearts some Christians might look for the vengeance of God to fall on the guilty city, and, could they have foreseen it, might have regarded the havoc made of the empire by the barbarians in after-years as the punishment of its wickedness—as indeed it was. Not, however, the punishment wrought by an arbitrary act, but working by the natural law, expressed by Jesus in the words, "Wheresoever the carcass is, there will the vultures be gathered together" (Matt. xxiv. 28). For Rome fell through her own vices, when she had become a very carcass of corruption, and God avenged His elect when the barbarians were converted to Christianity. Then on the ruins of the Pagan rose the Holy Roman Empire, the new Civitas Dei, and the bond of Christian brotherhood supplied the place of the bond of Roman citizenship.

This last is the kind of ἐκδίκησις the Christian who prays always will look for,—such righting of his cause as converts his enemy sooner or later into his friend, and brings him into the Christian fold. For to pray always is to have our thoughts always in harmony with God, and this is to desire the welfare of all mankind: for God makes His sun to shine on the evil as well as on the good, and desires not the death of any man. This was the spirit of the prayer of Jesus on the cross, "Father, forgive them, for they know not what they do" (Luke xxiii. 34); and of His dying intercessory prayer, "Neither pray I for these alone, but for them also which shall believe on me through their word; that they all may be one; as Thou, Father, art in me, and I in Thee, that they also may be one in us" (John xvii. 20, 21).

[1] Renan.

LESSON XXX.

St Luke xix. 11-27.

THE PARABLE OF THE MINÆ.

11 Ἀκουόντων δὲ αὐτῶν ταῦτα προσθεὶς εἶπεν παραβολὴν διὰ τὸ ἐγγὺς εἶναι Ἰερουσαλὴμ αὐτὸν καὶ δοκεῖν αὐτοὺς ὅτι παραχρῆμα μέλλει ἡ βασιλεία τοῦ θεοῦ ἀναφαίνεσθαι· 12 εἶπεν οὖν Ἄνθρωπός τις εὐγενὴς ἐπορεύθη εἰς χώραν μακρὰν λαβεῖν ἑαυτῷ βασιλείαν καὶ ὑποστρέψαι. 13 καλέσας δὲ δέκα δούλους ἑαυτοῦ ἔδωκεν αὐτοῖς δέκα μνᾶς καὶ εἶπεν πρὸς αὐτοὺς πραγματεύσασθαι[1] ἐν ᾧ ἔρχομαι. 14 Οἱ δὲ πολῖται αὐτοῦ ἐμίσουν αὐτόν, καὶ ἀπέστειλαν πρεσβείαν ὀπίσω αὐτοῦ λέγοντες Οὐ θέλομεν τοῦτον βασιλεῦσαι ἐφ' ἡμᾶς. 15 Καὶ ἐγένετο ἐν τῷ ἐπανελθεῖν αὐτὸν λαβόντα τὴν βασιλείαν, καὶ εἶπεν φωνηθῆναι αὐτῷ τοὺς δούλους τούτους οἷς δεδώκει τὸ ἀργύριον, ἵνα γνοῖ τί διεπραγματεύσαντο. 16 παρεγένετο δὲ ὁ πρῶτος λέγων Κύριε, ἡ μνᾶ σου δέκα προσειργάσατο[2] μνᾶς. 17 καὶ εἶπεν αὐτῷ Εὖγε, ἀγαθὲ δοῦλε, ὅτι ἐν ἐλαχίστῳ πιστὸς ἐγένου, ἴσθι ἐξουσίαν ἔχων ἐπάνω δέκα πόλεων. 18 καὶ ἦλθεν ὁ δεύτερος λέγων Ἡ μνᾶ σου, κύριε, ἐποίησεν πέντε μνᾶς. 19 εἶπεν δὲ καὶ τούτῳ Καὶ σὺ ἐπάνω γίνου πέντε πόλεων. 20 καὶ ὁ ἕτερος ἦλθεν λέγων· Κύριε, ἰδοὺ ἡ μνᾶ σου, ἣν

---

[1] V. l., πραγματεύσασθε.
[2] Westcott and Hort read προσηργάσατο.

εἶχον ἀποκειμένην ἐν σουδαρίῳ· 21 ἐφοβούμην γάρ σε, ὅτι ἄνθρωπος αὐστηρὸς εἶ, αἴρεις ὃ οὐκ ἔθηκας, καὶ θερίζεις ὃ οὐκ ἔσπειρας 22 λέγει αὐτῷ· ἐκ τοῦ στόματός σου κρινῶ σε, πονηρὲ δοῦλε. ἤδεις ὅτι ἐγὼ ἄνθρωπος αὐστηρός εἰμι, αἴρων ὃ οὐκ ἔθηκα, καὶ θερίζων ὃ οὐκ ἔσπειρα; 23 καὶ δια τί οὐκ ἔδωκάς μου τὸ ἀργύριον ἐπὶ τράπεζαν; κἀγὼ ἐλθὼν σὺν τόκῳ ἂν αὐτὸ ἔπραξα. 24 καὶ τοῖς παρεστῶσιν εἶπεν· Ἄρατε ἀπ᾽ αὐτοῦ τὴν μνᾶν καὶ δότε τῷ τὰς δέκα μνᾶς ἔχοντι. 25 καὶ εἶπον αὐτῷ· Κύριε, ἔχει δέκα μνᾶς. 26 λέγω ὑμῖν ὅτι παντὶ τῷ ἔχοντι δοθήσεται, ἀπὸ δὲ τοῦ μὴ ἔχοντος καὶ ὃ ἔχει ἀρθήσεται. 27 Πλὴν τοὺς ἐχθρούς μου τούτους τοὺς μὴ θελήσαντάς με βασιλεῦσαι ἐπ᾽ αὐτοὺς ἀγάγετε ὧδε καὶ κατασφάξατε αὐτοὺς ἔμπροσθέν μου.

LESSON XXXI.

St Matthew xxi. 23-46.

THE PARABLES OF THE TWO SONS AND OF THE WICKED HUSBANDMEN.

23 Καὶ ἐλθόντος αὐτοῦ εἰς τὸ ἱερὸν προσῆλθον αὐτῷ διδάσκοντι οἱ ἀρχιερεῖς καὶ οἱ πρεσβύτεροι τοῦ λαοῦ λέγοντες Ἐν ποίᾳ ἐξουσίᾳ ταῦτα ποιεῖς; καὶ τίς σοι ἔδωκεν τὴν ἐξουσίαν ταύτην; 24 ἀποκριθεὶς [δὲ] ὁ Ἰησοῦς εἶπεν αὐτοῖς Ἐρωτήσω ὑμᾶς κἀγὼ λόγον ἕνα, ὃν ἐὰν εἴπητέ μοι κἀγὼ ὑμῖν ἐρῶ ἐν ποίᾳ ἐξουσίᾳ ταῦτα ποιῶ· 25 τὸ βάπτισμα τὸ Ἰωάνου πόθεν ἦν; ἐξ οὐρανοῦ ἢ ἐξ ἀνθρώπων; οἱ δὲ διελογίζοντο ἐν ἑαυτοῖς λέγοντες Ἐὰν εἴπωμεν Ἐξ οὐρανοῦ, ἐρεῖ ἡμῖν Διὰ τί οὖν οὐκ ἐπιστεύσατε αὐτῷ; ἐὰν δὲ εἴπωμεν 26 Ἐξ ἀνθρώπων, φοβούμεθα τὸν ὄχλον, πάντες γὰρ ὡς προφήτην ἔχουσιν τὸν Ἰωάνην· 27 καὶ ἀποκριθέντες τῷ Ἰησοῦ εἶπον Οὐκ οἴδαμεν. ἔφη αὐτοῖς καὶ αὐτός Οὐδὲ ἐγὼ λέγω ὑμῖν ἐν ποίᾳ ἐξουσίᾳ ταῦτα ποιῶ. 28 Τί δὲ ὑμῖν δοκεῖ; ἄνθρωπος εἶχεν τέκνα δύο. [1]προσελθὼν τῷ πρώτῳ εἶπεν Τέκνον, ὕπαγε σήμερον ἐργάζου ἐν τῷ ἀμπελῶνι·[2] 29 ὁ δὲ ἀποκριθεὶς εἶπεν Ἐγώ, κύριε· καὶ οὐκ ἀπῆλθεν. 30 προσελθὼν δὲ τῷ δευτέρῳ εἶπεν ὡσαύτως· ὁ δὲ ἀποκριθεὶς εἶπεν Οὐ θέλω· ὕστερον μεταμεληθεὶς ἀπῆλθεν. 31 τίς ἐκ τῶν δύο ἐποίησεν τὸ θέλημα

---

[1] *V. l.*, καί.　　　　[2] *V. l.*, ἀμπελῶνί μου.

τοῦ πατρός; λέγουσιν Ὁ ὕστερος. λέγει αὐτοῖς ὁ
Ἰησοῦς Ἀμὴν λέγω ὑμῖν ὅτι οἱ τελῶναι καὶ αἱ πόρναι προάγουσιν ὑμᾶς εἰς τὴν βασιλείαν τοῦ θεοῦ.
32 ἦλθεν γὰρ Ἰωάνης πρὸς ὑμᾶς ἐν ὁδῷ δικαιοσύνης,
καὶ οὐκ ἐπιστεύσατε αὐτῷ· οἱ δὲ τελῶναι καὶ αἱ
πόρναι ἐπίστευσαν αὐτῷ· ὑμεῖς δὲ ἰδόντες οὐδὲ μετε-
μελήθητε ὕστερον τοῦ πιστεῦσαι αὐτῷ.   33 Ἄλλην παραβολὴν ἀκούσατε. Ἄνθρωπος ἦν οἰκοδεσπότης ὅστις ἐφύτευσεν ἀμπελῶνα καὶ φραγμὸν αὐτῷ
περιέθηκεν καὶ ὤρυξεν ἐν αὐτῷ ληνὸν καὶ ᾠκοδόμησεν
πύργον, καὶ ἐξέδοτο αὐτὸν γεωργοῖς, καὶ ἀπεδήμησεν. 34 ὅτε δὲ ἤγγισεν ὁ καιρὸς τῶν καρπῶν, ἀπέστειλεν τοὺς δούλους αὐτοῦ πρὸς τοὺς γεωργοὺς
λαβεῖν τοὺς καρποὺς αὐτοῦ. 35 καὶ λαβόντες οἱ
γεωργοὶ τοὺς δούλους αὐτοῦ ὃν μὲν ἔδειραν, ὃν δὲ
ἀπέκτειναν, ὃν δὲ ἐλιθοβόλησαν. 36 πάλιν ἀπέστειλεν ἄλλους δούλους πλείονας τῶν πρώτων, καὶ ἐποίησαν αὐτοῖς ὡσαύτως. 37 ὕστερον δὲ ἀπέστειλεν
πρὸς αὐτοὺς τὸν υἱὸν αὐτοῦ λέγων Ἐντραπήσονται
τὸν υἱόν μου. 38 οἱ δὲ γεωργοὶ ἰδόντες τὸν υἱὸν
εἶπον ἐν ἑαυτοῖς· Οὗτός ἐστιν ὁ κληρονόμος· δεῦτε
ἀποκτείνωμεν αὐτὸν καὶ σχῶμεν τὴν κληρονομίαν
αὐτοῦ. 39 καὶ λαβόντες αὐτὸν ἐξέβαλον ἔξω τοῦ
ἀμπελῶνος καὶ ἀπέκτειναν. 40 ὅταν οὖν ἔλθῃ ὁ
κύριος τοῦ ἀμπελῶνος, τί ποιήσει τοῖς γεωργοῖς ἐκείνοις; 41 λέγουσιν αὐτῷ· Κακοὺς κακῶς ἀπολέσει
αὐτούς, καὶ τὸν ἀμπελῶνα ἐκδώσεται ἄλλοις γεωργοῖς οἵτινες ἀποδώσουσιν αὐτῷ τοὺς καρποὺς ἐν τοῖς
καιροῖς αὐτῶν. 42 λέγει αὐτοῖς ὁ Ἰησοῦς· Οὐδέποτε
ἀνέγνωτε ἐν ταῖς γραφαῖς·

λίθον ὃν ἀπεδοκίμασαν οἱ οἰκοδομοῦντες,
οὗτος ἐγενήθη εἰς κεφαλὴν γωνίας·
παρὰ Κυρίου ἐγένετο αὕτη,
καὶ ἔστιν θαυμαστὴ ἐν ὀφθαλμοῖς ἡμῶν;

43 διὰ τοῦτο λέγω ὑμῖν ὅτι ἀρθήσεται ἀφ᾽ ὑμῶν ἡ

βασιλεία τοῦ θεοῦ καὶ δοθήσεται ἔθνει ποιοῦντι τοὺς καρποὺς αὐτῆς. 44 [καὶ ὁ πεσὼν ἐπὶ τὸν λίθον τοῦτον συνθλασθήσεται, καὶ ἐφ᾽ ὃν δ᾽ ἂν πέσῃ λικμήσει αὐτόν.] 45 Καὶ ἀκούσαντες οἱ ἀρχιερεῖς καὶ οἱ Φαρισαῖοι τὰς παραβολὰς αὐτοῦ ἔγνωσαν ὅτι περὶ αὐτῶν λέγει· 46 καὶ ζητοῦντες αὐτὸν κρατῆσαι ἐφοβήθησαν τοὺς ὄχλους, ἐπεὶ εἰς προφητην αὐτὸν εἶχον.

LESSON XXXII.

St Matthew xxi. 23.

THE SANHEDRIN AND THE CHIEF PRIESTS.

The Sanhedrin.—The "chief priests and elders" here mentioned were a deputation from the Sanhedrin or chief council of the Jews. Officially it was their duty to inquire into the claims and conduct of Jesus; but they had an additional motive for doing so, as some of them had a personal interest in the banishment of the buyers and sellers from the Temple court. For some of the booths or bazaars belonged to the family of the high priest, who derived a large income from them, especially from the sale of pigeons, and it is said that they used their monopoly to raise the prices. Jesus was attacking both their authority and their interests.

The Jews traced the origin of the Sanhedrin to the seventy elders who assisted Moses (Exod. xviii. 25); but we find no written mention of it till B.C. 144, in 2 Macc. i. 10, in which the council ($\dot{\eta}$ $\gamma\epsilon\rho o\nu\sigma\acute{\iota}a$), with other authorities at Jerusalem, are represented as sending a letter to the Jews in Egypt congratulating them on the death of Antiochus. From this it seems probable that the Sanhedrin of the New Testament arose after the return from Babylon, in the time of the Seleucidæ or of the Maccabees.

Sanhedrin is an old poetic plural, which in later Hebrew took the place of the ordinary plural, Sanhedrim. It is not of Hebrew origin, but is formed from the Greek, συνέδριον. In Livy, xlv. 32, the senators of the Macedonians are called Synedri.

The council consisted of seventy, or, as some say, seventy-one members, at whose head stood the chief of the Sanhedrin, called Nasi, or a prince,—and a president — Ab-bet-din, "Father of the Judgment-house." The latter took the more active part in the deliberations, the former was the official representative of the assembly out of doors. The president at the time of the trial of Jesus was either Simon the son, or Gamaliel (Paul's teacher) the guardian, of the great Hillel.

The assembly was composed of the chief priests, the elders of the people, and ·the most renowned of the Rabbis. Their sittings were held in a basilica in the outer court of the Temple. They sat daily, excepting during the festivals, after the morning sacrifice.

They seem to have been the legitimate court for deciding questions of public worship, for the authentic interpretation of controverted passages of Scripture, for appointing the festivals, the new moons, and similar matters relating to religion. But since among the Jews all the details of life were connected with religion, the court was in the habit, when it chose, of judging nearly everything to be within its jurisdiction. Thus Josephus, in Ant. xiv. 9, 3, makes the Sanhedrin lay down the principle that without its assent no criminal may be executed. Peter and John are brought before it on a charge of promoting heresy (Acts iv. 1, v. 27), Stephen on a charge of blasphemy (Acts vi. 13), Paul on a charge of violating a Temple by-law (Acts xxi. 28).

The capital punishments were stoning, burning, beheading, and strangulation. But the council could only pass sentence,—they had no power to carry the penalty into execution. This was the reason why Jesus was taken before Pilate as well as the Sanhedrin. The Jews, however, maintained that the Roman procurator was bound to support the decree of the council, even where no offence had been committed against the Roman law.

The chief priests.—There were several men living at this time who had held the office of high priest. Annas was high priest at the commencement of John the Baptist's ministry, with Caiaphas as second priest, while the latter was high priest at our Lord's crucifixion. Herod made men of low birth high priests, deposed them at his will, and named others in their room. Josephus tells us of one Ananus and his five sons who all filled the office in turn.

Such changes had not been unknown in the earliest times. When Abiathar, the son of the high priest Ahimelech, fled to David, Saul seems to have appointed Zadok in his stead,[1] and David afterwards continued Abiathar and Zadok in a joint priesthood,[2] but Abiathar forfeited his place by taking part with Adonijah against Solomon, and Zadok became sole high priest.[3] This is the only instance recorded of the deposition of a high priest (a practice which became common in later times) until after the captivity.

The office of the high priest was hereditary under ordinary circumstances, but the kings seem to have occasionally interfered in the appointment.

After the loss of the ark to the Philistines and the rise of Samuel as a prophet, the power of the priests was greatly diminished. But the high priest gained fresh influence by the new organisation in the time of David, when for the performance of the principal Temple

---

[1] 1 Sam. xxii. 20.   [2] 1 Chron. xviii. 16.
[3] 1 Kings ii. 27.

duties there were formed out of the two ancient families immediately descended from Aaron twenty-four smaller families, each of which was to provide the service for a week (1 Chron. xxiv. 3-19).

The most remarkable high priests were Jehoiada, who overthrew Athaliah, the daughter of Ahab, and placed his kinsman Joash on the throne;[1] Azariah, who withstood the encroachments of King Uzziah upon the office and functions of the priesthood;[2] Hilkiah, who discovered the book of the Law and brought about a religious reformation in the time of Josiah.[3]   But in almost every reformation the civil power took the lead.   Thus David arranged the Temple service;[4] Solomon dictated the building and dedication of the Temple, the high priest being not so much as named;[5] Jehoshaphat sent the priests about to teach the people, and assigned to the high priest Amariah his share in the work;[6] Hezekiah took the lead in the reformation, and urged on Azariah and the priests and Levites;[7] Josiah encouraged the priests in the service of the house of the Lord.[8]   On the other hand, we read of no opposition by the high priest [9] to the idolatries of Manasseh; and when King Ahaz indulged in idolatrous practices, the high priest Urijah, so far from endeavouring to dissuade him, actually built an altar according to the pattern of one at Damascus to displace the brazen altar, and joined the king in his profane worship before it.[10]

After the captivity, the high-priesthood was restored in the person of Joshua, honourably distinguished for his co-operation with Zerubbabel in rebuilding the Temple, and restoring the fallen commonwealth.   A glow-

---

[1] 2 Kings xi. 4-27. [2] 2 Chron. xxvi. 17-21.
[3] 2 Kings xxii. 8-15. [4] 1 Chron. xxiii. 27-32.
[5] 1 Kings v. 13 ; viii. 12-66. [6] 2 Chron. xvii. 7-9 ; xix. 8-11.
[7] 2 Chron. xxix. 4. [8] 2 Chron. xxxiv. 29-33.
[9] 2 Kings xxi. 1-16. [10] 2 Kings xvi. 11-15.

ing description of the office of the high priest is found in Ecclus. l. 1-21 : " When Simon, the son of Onias, came forth from behind the curtain of the sanctuary, he was as the morning-star in the midst of a cloud, and as the moon at the full; and as the sun shining upon the temple of the Most High, and as the rainbow giving light in the bright clouds; as fire and incense in the censer, and as a vessel of beaten gold set with all manner of precious stones. When he put on the robe of honour, and was clothed with the perfection of glory, when he went up to the holy altar, he enlightened the whole sanctuary. When he took the portions out of the priest's hands, he himself stood by the hearth of the altar, compassed with his brethren round about, as a young cedar in Lebanon; and they as palm-trees compassed him round about. So were all the sons of Aaron in their glory, and had the oblations of the Lord in their hands, before all the congregation of Israel. And finishing the service at the altar, that he might adorn the offering of the Most High Almighty, he stretched out his hand to the cup, and poured of the blood of the grape; he poured it out at the foot of the altar, a sweet-smelling savour unto the Most High King of all. Then shouted the sons of Aaron, and sounded the silver trumpets, and made a great noise, to be heard for a remembrance before the Most High. Then all the people together hasted, and fell down to the earth upon their faces to worship their Lord God Almighty the Most High. The singers also sang praises with their voices; with great variety of sounds was there made sweet melody. And the people besought the Lord the Most High, by prayer before Him that is merciful, till the solemnity of the Lord was ended and they had finished the service. Then he went down, and lifted up his hands over the whole congregation of Israel, to give the blessing of the Lord with his lips, and to rejoice in His name.   And they bowed themselves down to worship the second time, that they might receive a blessing from the Most High."

The Syro-Greek kings introduced much uncertainty into the succession by deposing at their will obnoxious persons, and appointing whom they pleased, till the persecution of Antiochus Epiphanes roused the spirit of the Jews, and gave birth to a new and glorious succession of high priests in the Asmonean family, who united with the dignity of the high-priesthood that of civil rulers, and for a time of independent sovereigns. It is uncertain whether the great Judas Maccabeus himself was high priest, but his brother Jonathan was appointed to the office by Alexander, King of Syria. The Asmonean dynasty lasted from B.C. 153 till the family was damaged by intestine divisions, and then destroyed by Herod the Great.   He being an Idumean, could not unite the office of high priest with that of prince as the Maccabees had done: to lower, therefore, the dignity of the office, he appointed to it first a priest of common origin from Babylon; then Aristobulus, the youthful brother of his Maccabean wife Mariamne, whose descent, youth, and handsome person gained him extraordinary popularity.   This so excited the tyrant's jealousy, that he caused the ill-fated boy to be drowned while bathing.   After his death other high priests were appointed in rapid succession, and the office was no longer held for life.   Annas was deposed in the year A.D. 14 by Pilate's predecessor Valerius Gratus, who, it would seem, elected and deposed four high priests during four years.   Annas, however, still retained much of the prestige of the office in the eyes of the stricter Jews, and was perhaps the Nasi, or president of the Sanhedrin.   He was the father-in-law of Caiaphas.

LESSON XXXIII.

ST MATTHEW xxii. 1-14.

THE PARABLE OF THE MARRIAGE OF THE KING'S SON.

1 Καὶ ἀποκριθεὶς ὁ Ἰησοῦς πάλιν εἶπεν ἐν παραβολαῖς αὐτοῖς λέγων 2 Ὡμοιώθη ἡ βασιλεία τῶν οὐρανῶν ἀνθρώπῳ βασιλεῖ, ὅστις ἐποίησεν γάμους τῷ υἱῷ αὐτοῦ. 3 καὶ ἀπέστειλεν τοὺς δούλους αὐτοῦ καλέσαι τοὺς κεκλημένους εἰς τοὺς γαμους, καὶ οὐκ ἤθελον ἐλθεῖν. 4 πάλιν ἀπέστειλεν ἄλλους δούλους λέγων Εἴπατε τοῖς κεκλημένοις Ἰδοὺ τὸ ἄριστόν μου ἡτοίμακα, οἱ ταῦροί μου καὶ τὰ σιτιστὰ τεθυμένα, καὶ πάντα ἕτοιμα· δεῦτε εἰς τοὺς γάμους. 5 οἱ δὲ ἀμελήσαντες ἀπῆλθον, ὃς μὲν εἰς τὸν ἴδιον ἀγρόν, ὃς δὲ ἐπὶ τὴν ἐμπορίαν αὐτοῦ· 6 οἱ δὲ λοιποὶ κρατήσαντες τοὺς δούλους αὐτοῦ ὕβρισαν καὶ ἀπέκτειναν. 7 ὁ δὲ βασιλεὺς ὠργίσθη, καὶ πέμψας τὰ στρατεύματα αὐτοῦ ἀπώλεσεν τοὺς φονεῖς ἐκείνους καὶ τὴν πόλιν αὐτῶν ἐνέπρησεν. 8 τότε λέγει τοῖς δούλοις αὐτοῦ Ὁ μὲν γάμος ἕτοιμός ἐστιν, οἱ δὲ κεκλημένοι οὐκ ἦσαν ἄξιοι· 9 πορεύεσθε οὖν ἐπὶ τὰς διεξόδους τῶν ὁδῶν, καὶ ὅσους ἐὰν εὕρητε καλέσατε εἰς τοὺς γάμους. 10 καὶ ἐξελθόντες οἱ δοῦλοι ἐκεῖνοι εἰς τὰς ὁδοὺς συνήγαγον πάντας οὓς εὗρον, πονηρούς τε καὶ ἀγαθούς· καὶ ἐπλήσθη ὁ νυμφὼν ἀνακειμένων. 11 εἰσελθὼν δὲ ὁ βασιλεὺς θεάσασθαι τοὺς ἀνακειμένους

εἶδεν ἐκεῖ ἄνθρωπον οὐκ ἐνδεδυμένον ἔνδυμα γάμου·
12 καὶ λέγει αὐτῷ Ἑταῖρε, πῶς εἰσῆλθες ὧδε μὴ
ἔχων ἔνδυμα γάμου; ὁ δὲ ἐφιμώθη. 13 τότε ὁ βασιλεὺς εἶπεν τοῖς διακόνοις Δήσαντες αὐτοῦ πόδας καὶ
χεῖρας ἐκβάλετε αὐτὸν εἰς τὸ σκότος τὸ ἐξώτερον·
ἐκεῖ ἔσται ὁ κλαυθμὸς καὶ ὁ βρυγμὸς τῶν ὀδόντων.
14 πολλοὶ γὰρ εἰσιν κλητοὶ ὀλίγοι δὲ ἐκλεκτοί.

LESSON XXXIV.

St Matthew xxv. 1-13.

THE PARABLE OF THE TEN VIRGINS—"THE LORD IS AT HAND."

1 Τότε ὁμοιωθήσεται ἡ.βασιλεία τῶν οὐρανῶν δέκα παρθένοις αἵτινες λαβοῦσαι τὰς λαμπάδας αὐτῶν ἐξῆλθον εἰς ὑπάντησιν τοῦ νυμφίου. 2 πέντε δὲ ἐξ αὐτῶν ἦσαν μωραὶ καὶ πέντε φρόνιμοι. 3 αἱ γὰρ μωραὶ λαβοῦσαι τὰς λαμπάδας οὐκ ἔλαβον μεθ᾽ ἑαυτῶν ἔλαιον· 4 αἱ δὲ φρόνιμοι ἔλαβον ἔλαιον ἐν τοῖς ἀγγείοις μετὰ τῶν λαμπάδων ἑαυτῶν. 5 χρονί- ζοντος δὲ τοῦ νυμφίου ἐνύσταξαν πᾶσαι καὶ ἐκάθευ- δον. 6 μέσης δὲ νυκτὸς κραυγὴ γέγονεν· Ἰδοὺ ὁ νυμφίος, ἐξέρχεσθε εἰς ἀπάντησιν. 7 τότε ἠγέρθησαν πᾶσαι αἱ παρθένοι ἐκεῖναι καὶ ἐκόσμησαν τὰς λαμ- πάδας ἑαυτῶν. 8 αἱ δὲ μωραὶ ταῖς φρονίμοις εἶπον· Δότε ἡμῖν ἐκ τοῦ ἐλαίου ὑμῶν. ὅτι αἱ λαμπάδες ἡμῶν σβέννυνται. 9 ἀπεκρίθησαν δὲ αἱ φρόνιμοι λέγουσαι· Μήποτε οὐ μὴ ἀρκέσῃ ἡμῖν καὶ ὑμῖν· πορεύεσθε μᾶλ- λον πρὸς τοὺς πωλοῦντας καὶ ἀγοράσατε ἑαυταῖς. 10 ἀπερχομένων δὲ αὐτῶν ἀγοράσαι ἦλθεν ὁ νυμφίος καὶ αἱ ἕτοιμοι εἰσῆλθον μετ᾽ αὐτοῦ εἰς τοὺς γάμους, καὶ ἐκλείσθη ἡ θύρα. 11 ὕστερον δὲ ἔρχονται καὶ αἱ λοιπαὶ παρθένοι λέγουσαι· Κύριε κύριε, ἄνοιξον ἡμῖν. 12 ὁ δὲ ἀποκριθεὶς εἶπεν· ἀμὴν λέγω ὑμῖν, οὐκ οἶδα ὑμᾶς. 13 γρηγορεῖτε οὖν, ὅτι οὐκ οἴδατε τὴν ἡμέραν οὐδὲ τὴν ὥραν.

The thirteenth verse shows the lesson Jesus intended to teach by the parable. A difficulty, however, arises from the fact that the imagery of the parable dwells, not on the want of watchfulness, but on the improvidence, of the five virgins, who had not brought sufficient oil with them: the sleeping does not seem to be culpable, as both prudent and imprudent gave way to it; it is added to describe more graphically the long delay of the bridegroom. We must therefore connect the idea of want of vigilance with this improvidence in not providing sufficient oil; and we must bear in mind that all the virgins, both wise and foolish, were devoting themselves to the bridegroom's service—that is, they all represent persons professedly Christian, who, at the outset, had all prepared themselves to meet the bridegroom. The failure of the oil represents a failure of preparation for so long a delay. The early Christians lived in constant expectation of the speedy return of Jesus; and as the date of this return seemed protracted, this parable must to many of them have had an intensely real application. Many, no doubt, among the earliest believers, who had been converted from sin and misery, and were saved from relapsing by their belief in Jesus and their expectation of His return, *did* relax in their struggles against temptation when they found that return delayed. We know that grave sins were committed in the very midst of the Christian community, from such passages as 1 Cor. v. 1, where we read of a Corinthian convert living in adultery with his stepmother. We may judge of the demoralising effect this continual expectation and disappointment must have had upon the early converts, from the fact that even St Paul expresses his earnest dread lest in his absence his Corinthian converts should have relapsed into the sins from which they had been delivered by their belief in Jesus through his preaching (2 Cor. xii. 20, 21): " For

I fear, lest, when I come, I shall not find you such as I would, and that I shall be found unto you such as ye would not: lest there be debates, envyings, wraths, stripes, backbitings, whisperings, swellings, tumults; and lest, when I come again, my God will humble me among you, and that I shall bewail many which have sinned already, and have not repented of the uncleanness and fornication and lasciviousness which they have committed."

That this disappointed expectation caused the faith of many to grow cold, we learn from 2 Pet. iii. 3, where the author speaks of "scoffers who should come in the last days, walking after their own lusts, and saying, Where is the promise of His coming? for since the fathers fell asleep, all things continue as they were since the beginning of the creation."

We find St Paul in his earliest epistle expressing an expectation of being present in person at the return of Jesus (1 Thess. iv. 17). We find that the phrase, "The Lord is at hand," was a kind of watchword with him (Phil. iv. 5; 1 Cor. xvi. 22). In the last passage, Maran-atha is an Aramaic equivalent for it. It seems to have been a familiar form of recognition and warning in the early Church generally (1 Pet. iv. 7; Luke xxi. 31; James v. 8). St Paul recurs to the belief in the early return, though not in such unqualified terms, in 2 Thess. ii. 1-4; Rom. xiii. 11; 1 Cor. xv. 23-28, 50-57. But in the later epistles the expression becomes less frequent and less definite, till in that to the Philippians, which, if not his last, is one of his latest, the expectation of his being present in person to meet Jesus on His coming has vanished, and given place to a desire to depart and be with Him (Phil. i. 21-24).

Again, the expectation of the speedy return of Jesus is the key - note of the mysterious book of Revelation. It is the prologue, "Behold, He cometh with the clouds; and every eye shall see Him, and they which pierced Him" (Rev. i. 7). It is the epilogue, "He which testifieth these things saith, Surely I come quickly. Amen. Even so, come, Lord Jesus" (Rev. xxii. 20).

Since, then, the belief in the early and visible return of Jesus was so general, and yet met with continually renewed disappointment, we need not wonder that He foresaw danger of their faith and virtue breaking down under the strain, and dwelt on the need of intense and unremitting watchfulness throughout the whole of the lives of believers. In other words, He desires that His disciples should trust to habit rather than impulse, to characters formed on principles as well as on feelings. He Himself had prepared them for the uncertainty of His coming, when He said, "Of that hour knoweth no man; no, not the angels of God, nor the Son, but the Father" (Matt. xxiv. 36).

We may illustrate the parable thus. A mother leaves her child, with a promise to return, but without fixing the date. The child is passionately fond of its mother, but as she postpones her return from day to day, becomes impatient, and his love for her ceases to be a sufficient motive to keep him in obedience to her parting commands. Now, how would he retain a vivid impression of her? Plainly by taking pains to recall her to mind, by keeping her likeness before him, and by carefully marking and reproaching in himself every little deviation from her precepts. Similar efforts on the part of the believer to keep the thought of Christ before him may interpret to us the virgins' oil, if we regard the oil rather as the tone and spirit that result from those efforts than as the efforts themselves. To maintain the oil or Spirit of Christ, we must habitually think of Him, and "practise His presence," as the mental habit has been called, and so cultivate habits of

Christian thought and acts till they are as much a part of our being as the air we breathe. And for this purpose we must perseveringly seek the means to foster in ourselves this oil or spirit, whether by reading about Christ, or living in the society of others who believe in Him, or frequenting assemblies connected with His worship, or by meditating on what would please Him, and referring all our thoughts and acts to His pleasure.

We may also fairly adopt the later view of St Paul, and regard the day of our death as being to us the coming of Christ. And we may venture to go further than this, and regard any crisis in the history of the world or of our own lives as a symbolical coming of Christ. Thus the destruction of Jerusalem by Titus (A.D. 70) was regarded as a manifestation of Christ, for after that Christianity began to triumph, and Judaism to wane. Those believers who had remained faithful to Him, in spite of persecution and of the delay of their expected triumph, then found their recompense: for while other Jews regarded the destruction of the Holy City with despair, they were still able to look forward with confident hope to the future, while they found refuge from the scene of misery in their new home at Pella. Nor was their confidence misplaced. The dispersion of Jews and Christians that ensued, carried the principles of Jesus throughout the world.

The metaphorical, as opposed to the literal coming, is manifested whenever men are signally called upon to side for or against the principles of Christ's religion. Such crises are often sudden, and men then act with or against Christ according as they have or have not kept His Spirit alive in their hearts,—in the words of the parable, according to the sufficiency of the supply of oil in their lamps. Now one man may, at the risk of his life, infuse his blood into the veins of another; but none can suddenly imbue another with his own spirit,—

in the words of the parable, give another oil for his lamp. Men may, however, imbibe the spirit of those nobler than themselves by living and associating with them; and this, perhaps, is the meaning of going to "those that sell." But while men go to those that sell, the opportunity is gone—the door is shut. They have not declared for the Bridegroom, nor can they be recognised as among those He knows.

LESSON XXXV.

St Matthew xxv. 14-30.

THE PARABLE OF THE TALENTS—ON THE USE OF OUR TALENTS.

14 Ὥσπερ γὰρ ἄνθρωπος ἀποδημῶν ἐκάλεσεν τοὺς ἰδίους δούλους καὶ παρέδωκεν αὐτοῖς τὰ ὑπάρχοντα αὐτοῦ, 15 καὶ ᾧ μὲν ἔδωκεν πέντε τάλαντα ᾧ δὲ δύο ᾧ δὲ ἕν, ἑκάστῳ κατὰ τὴν ἰδίαν δύναμιν, καὶ ἀπεδήμησεν. 16 εὐθέως πορευθεὶς ὁ τὰ πέντε τάλαντα λαβὼν εἰργάσατο[1] ἐν αὐτοῖς καὶ ἐκέρδησεν ἄλλα πέντε· 17 ὡσαύτως ὁ τὰ δύο ἐκέρδησεν ἄλλα δύο· 18 ὁ δὲ τὸ ἓν λαβὼν ἀπελθὼν ὤρυξεν γῆν[2] καὶ ἔκρυψεν τὸ ἀργύριον τοῦ κυρίου αὐτοῦ. 19 μετὰ δὲ πολὺν χρόνον ἔρχεται ὁ κύριος τῶν δούλων ἐκείνων καὶ συναίρει λόγον μετ᾽ αὐτῶν. 20 καὶ προσελθὼν ὁ τὰ πέντε τάλαντα λαβὼν προσήνεγκεν ἄλλα πέντε τάλαντα λέγων Κύριε, πέντε τάλαντά μοι παρέδωκας· ἴδε ἄλλα πέντε τάλαντα ἐκέρδησα. 21 ἔφη αὐτῷ ὁ κύριος αὐτοῦ Εὖ, δοῦλε ἀγαθὲ καὶ πιστέ, ἐπὶ ὀλίγα ἦς πιστός, ἐπὶ πολλῶν σε καταστήσω· εἴσελθε εἰς τὴν χαρὰν τοῦ κυρίου σου. 22 προσελθὼν καὶ ὁ τὰ δύο τάλαντα εἶπεν Κύριε, δύο τάλαντά μοι παρέδωκας· ἴδε ἄλλα δύο τάλαντα ἐκέρδησα. 23 ἔφη αὐτῷ ὁ κύριος αὐτοῦ Εὖ, δοῦλε ἀγαθὲ καὶ πιστέ, ἐπὶ ὀλίγα ἦς πιστός, ἐπὶ πολλῶν σε καταστήσω·

[1] Westcott and Hort read ἠργάσατο.
[2] V. l., ἐν τῇ γῇ.

εἴσελθε εἰς τὴν χαρὰν τοῦ κυρίου σου. 24 προσελθὼν δὲ καὶ ὁ τὸ ἓν τάλαντον εἰληφὼς εἶπεν Κύριε, ἔγνων σε ὅτι σκληρὸς εἶ ἄνθρωπος, θερίζων ὅπου οὐκ ἔσπειρας καὶ συνάγων ὅθεν οὐ διεσκόρπισας· 25 καὶ φοβηθεὶς ἀπελθὼν ἔκρυψα τὸ τάλαντόν σου ἐν τῇ γῇ· ἴδε ἔχεις τὸ σόν. 26 ἀποκριθεὶς δὲ ὁ κύριος αὐτοῦ εἶπεν αὐτῷ Πονηρὲ δοῦλε καὶ ὀκνηρέ, ᾔδεις ὅτι θερίζω ὅπου οὐκ ἔσπειρα καὶ συνάγω ὅθεν οὐ διεσκόρπισα; 27 ἔδει σε οὖν βαλεῖν τὰ ἀργύριά[1] μου τοῖς τραπεζείταις, καὶ ἐλθὼν ἐγὼ ἐκομισάμην ἂν τὸ ἐμὸν σὺν τόκῳ. 28 ἄρατε οὖν ἀπ᾽ αὐτοῦ τὸ τάλαντον καὶ δότε τῷ ἔχοντι τὰ δέκα τάλαντα· 29 τῷ γὰρ ἔχοντι παντὶ δοθήσεται καὶ περισσευθήσεται· τοῦ δὲ μὴ ἔχοντος καὶ ὃ ἔχει ἀρθήσεται ἀπ᾽ αὐτοῦ. 30 καὶ τὸν ἀχρεῖον δοῦλον ἐκβάλετε εἰς τὸ σκότος τὸ ἐξώτερον· ἐκεῖ ἔσται ὁ κλαυθμὸς καὶ ὁ βρυγμὸς τῶν ὀδόντων.

This parable resembles that of the Minæ related in Luke xix. 12-27. The chief differences are: (1) In the value of the money intrusted; here a talent, worth probably about £243, there a μνᾶ, worth between £3 and £4 of our money,—roughly speaking, the talent being to the mina what a sovereign is to a threepenny-piece. This difference in value is probably due to the fact that this parable is addressed to those who were to be the preachers and founders of Christianity, whereas that in St Luke is addressed to the ordinary disciples. (2) In this parable different sums of money are assigned to the δοῦλοι, but they all receive the same reward; in that in St Luke, they all receive the same sum, but the rewards are different. This parable seems to teach that the Great Judge will estimate each man's work, not according to his abilities, but according to his devotion and faithfulness in the use of them,—the man who has

---

[1] V. l., τὸ ἀργύριόν.

faithfully served God on small means, in humble place, or with little ability, being regarded with the same favour as the man who has been faithful as a king or prime minister, a poet or an artist or a millionaire. In the ideal kingdom of love, these latter have no contempt for the former, but regard them with love in proportion to their zeal for the Master's cause. The parable in St Luke, on the other hand, is intended to represent different degrees of zeal in the management of one and the same thing granted to all alike.

One lesson of the parable is that uttered by the author of the Book of Ecclesiastes (chap. ix. 10): "Whatsoever thy hand findeth to do, do it with thy might." It teaches us to do with all our might the petty tasks that lie close at hand, not waiting for the chance of some great deed of heroism that may never present itself. Even the humblest in the kingdom of love has some work to do on which the Master looks with favour: the woodcutter as much as the artist who carves out of the wood a work that is to be the admiration of centuries; the mechanic who faithfully works all day at a piece of routine mechanism as much as the millionaire who profits by his labours and those of his fellow-workmen; the meanest clerk in the public office as much as the prime minister; the private soldier as much as the commander-in-chief,—that which makes the difference between His servants in the eyes of the Great Master being the intensity and purity of love they bear to Him and to their fellow-workers. It is obvious that this devotion will enable them to do better work, because it removes them from the distractions of passion and selfishness, and animates them with the sense of fellowship with the Great Human Brotherhood, the Great Elder Brother, and the Almighty Father Himself.

The doctrine that all that men possess is capital belonging to the Supreme King, and that He will exact the interest of it, was a new one in the history of the world. It soon had an influence on the condition of men's lives by promoting active beneficence in the name of Jesus. In His name were founded hospitals, asylums for the blind, the dumb, and the deaf; almshouses for the old and destitute, and schools for orphans. Before His time, in the old pagan world, the maniac and the idiot were at large; the blind and the dumb were on the public ways; the fevered and the fractured, who were not rich, were left to chance.

But in applying the lesson of the parable to ourselves, we must bear in mind we are in a different condition to the Christians of the apostolic times, and there is a corresponding difference in the claim on our talents. They were a despised community, who could not exercise, and did not think of exercising, any political influence; whose thoughts and habits were so different to those of the people among whom they lived, that they spoke of themselves as citizens of no earthly but of a heavenly state (Phil. iii. 20). They lived at a time when the whole civilised world was under the rule of one strong government, whose laws and institutions they could not hope to modify by bringing any political influence to bear upon them. But we are under no such disadvantage, and are bound to endeavour to use our influence as citizens that our country may be governed on Christian principles. Since, however, the cardinal principle of Christianity is, that we love our neighbour as ourselves, we shall not seek to attain this object by injustice, intrigue, or force. Again, the corruption of the society in which they lived, and their own powerlessness from sheer want of numbers to leaven it, would cause the first Christians to hold aloof from public duties; and perhaps they were further deterred from taking part in them by their expectation of the speedy return of Christ to reign upon earth. But it is evident that to act thus now would be cowardice and disloyalty to Christ; for it is by active and intelligent fulfilment of public duties that we can best fulfil His injunction to care for the hungry and thirsty, the stranger, the naked, and the prisoner. With our superior knowledge and power of influencing society, we can best alleviate misery by investigating the causes of physical evil, mastering the science of health, considering the questions of education, trade, and labour, with a view to health, and seeking to work out the rearrangement of human life in accordance with the results of our investigations. Since evil is often the result of ignorance, loyalty to Christ will urge us also to promote education; and this we shall do the more eagerly, because we regard every human being as our brother, and precious in the sight of our Master, and shall therefore desire to make him as perfect as possible. And that we may be able to serve Christ effectively, we shall seek to train ourselves, to develop our bodies, to take care of our health, to educate all our faculties, each according to his ability,—that is, each according to his special talent.

But this is far from all. It is not enough that in the name of Christ we use our talents to promote the physical wellbeing only of the community in which we live. Indeed physical comfort may lead to qualities, such as pride and self-indulgence, that are displeasing to the Master.

We may use our talents in His service by making Him known to those who are ignorant of Him either at home or abroad, either by serving personally as missionaries, or by rendering aid to missionary societies, by translating or aiding in the translation of the New Testament and other books that describe His life or enforce His teaching, and by helping personally or by our money in the distribution of them.

Nor is it enough that we support His cause by promoting knowledge about Him. We have also to strive to develop in the society around us a resemblance to His character. We cannot all do this by being preachers, nor perhaps is this always the most effectual way. Our characters rather than our words will have the greatest influence in this direction, whatever station in life we may occupy. We have to learn to combine the active and the passive virtues, the life of devotion and the life of activity; to be able to show moral indignation at wrong-doing without betraying pride in our own rectitude or a personal feeling against the wrong-doer; to seek truth by every method of investigation, and yet to be unassuming and simple before the ignorant and unlearned; to be resolute in will, and yet tender-hearted in our affections; to love all beautiful things that are in the world, and yet to be capable of showing sympathy with the unlovely and the deformed, and working, if necessary, amid squalor and misery; to combine heroism with refinement and saintliness with manliness; to be the light of the society in which we live, and yet to be so little conscious ourselves that we are so, that we shall create no jealousy in the minds of other men.

LESSON XXXVI.

St John x. 1-16.

THE GOOD SHEPHERD.

INTRODUCTION.

THE life of the shepherd in Palestine had many poetic associations. The patriarchs had all been shepherds; David, the ideal Hebrew warrior and poet, had been a shepherd, and the son of a shepherd, and when a mere stripling slew a lion and a bear in defence of his father's flock. The growth of civilisation had caused the nation to devote itself more to agriculture than to pasturage, and hence the life of the shepherd had not become too common to lose its poetry. The character of the country added at once to the romance and to the dangers of the shepherd's life. The long ranges of mountains, the wide grassy deserts, the ravines and rocky gorges, afforded to the poets pictures of the sheep wandering and the shepherd pursuing, of long journeys, adventurous climbs, of life endangered or even sacrificed by the faithful shepherd in search of his charge.

The loneliness of the shepherd's life, its perils and its hardships, drew the shepherd and the sheep closer together; they were often one another's sole companions, isolated from all other society, for weeks together. The literature of the Old Testament abounds in allusions to

this mode of life, and from these we can image to ourselves a vivid representation of it.

The shepherd had to defend his charge from the
attacks of wild beasts; he was consumed by the drought
in the day and the frost by night, and the sleep departed
from his eyes (Gen. xxxi. 39, 40); he sought out green
pastures for his flock, and led them by the side of re-
freshing streams, and through rugged and desolate
scenery, whose dreariness filled his spirit with gloom
(Ps. xxiii.); in cloudy and dark days, when they were
scattered, he went in search of them, and delivered them
from peril: if any were lost he sought them out, if any
driven away he brought them back to the fold; if the
limbs of any were broken he bound them up, if any were
sick he strove to strengthen them (Ezek. xxxiv. 12-16).
A bad shepherd was one who heeded not the drooping,
sought not the straying, healed not the wounded, tended
not the lean, and rent the hoofs of the fat by driving
them over hard and rugged ground (Zech. xi. 16);
whereas the good shepherd gathered the lambs with his
arm, and carried them in his bosom, and gently led those
that were with young (Isa. xl. 11).

The risks incidental to the shepherd-life are thus
described by the eminent preacher, Robertson of Brigh-
ton: "Beneath the burning skies and the clear starry
nights of Palestine there grows up between the shepherd
and his flock a union of attachment and tenderness. It
is the country where at any moment sheep are liable to
be swept away by some mountain-torrent, or carried off
by hill robbers, or torn by wolves. At any moment
their protector may have to save them by personal
hazard. Sometimes, for the sake of an armful of grass,
in the parched summer days, he must climb precipices
almost perpendicular, and stand on a narrow ledge of
rock, where the wild goat will scarcely venture. Pitiless showers, driving snows, long hours of thirst—

all this he must endure, if the flock is to be kept at all."

The affectionate and self-sacrificing rule of the shepherd over his sheep had, before the time of Jesus, been applied metaphorically. Thus Cyrus is spoken of as God's shepherd in Isa. xliv. 28; and in Jer. iii. 15, God is represented as saying, "I will give you pastors [*i.e.*, shepherds] according to mine heart, which shall feed you with knowledge and understanding." The teacher is compared to a shepherd in Eccles. xii. 11. The metaphor occurs as early as Gen. xlix. 24. God is termed the Shepherd of Israel in Ps. lxxx. 1, and is addressed as the Shepherd of the soul in Ps. xxiii.

But the contrast drawn between good and bad shepherds in the following allegory makes it probable that the passages whose associations Jesus was more especially recalling were Ezek. xxxiv. 22, "Woe to the shepherds of Israel that do feed themselves! Should not the shepherds feed the flocks?" and the eleventh chapter of Zechariah, which should be read through as an aid to the interpretation of this chapter. In that chapter the prophet, perhaps as a type of the Messiah, is represented as being called upon to feed the flock of slaughter—*i.e.*, the flock which was doomed to slaughter thorugh the misrule of bad shepherds (*i.e.*, princes), and their own misconduct. Three of the shepherds are cut off—*i.e.*, three kings are destroyed. The prophet succeeds so far as to win a hearing from the most miserable of the flock, but that only for a time. He controls them by the aid of two staves—the one called Beauty or Grace, and the other Binders or Concord. After a month's unsuccessful toil, in which the flock refuse obedience, he breaks his staff, and receives for wages thirty pieces of silver, as though he were a mere servant of the lowest class, and abandons the sheep to the bad shepherds, who were conducting them to the slaughter.

And such in great measure was the position of Jesus at this moment. By His staff Beauty,—by the beauty of His teaching, His character, and His actions; and by His staff Binders,—by His efforts to diffuse love in a land teeming with hate, He had essayed to unite the dwellers in Palestine into one flock. But the effort, as far as the main body of the nation was concerned, had been ineffectual. The Pharisees had just cast out from their presence the blind man whom Jesus' merciful interposition had won to a belief in Him. Jesus now describes in the following allegory how to such sheep the Pharisees had proved shepherds as false as the princes of the time of Zechariah were to their subjects, and how it was only through Himself, through His love and self-sacrifice, that admission to the new Christian flock could be gained,—a flock He was beginning to form, and which should comprise within its numbers Jews and Gentiles alike.

The picture that follows is an allegory rather than a parable. In the parable the thought takes a form which has its value independent of the moral application. The story is complete in itself, the interpretation is complete in itself. In allegory the application is felt immediately through each trait of the narrative; the image has not time to take a form independent of the thought. The parable is a picture, the allegory is a transparency (see pp. 34, 35).

1 Ἀμὴν ἀμὴν λέγω ὑμῖν, ὁ μὴ εἰσερχόμενος διὰ τῆς θύρας εἰς τὴν αὐλὴν τῶν προβάτων ἀλλὰ ἀναβαίνων ἀλλαχόθεν ἐκεῖνος κλέπτης ἐστὶν καὶ λῃστής· 2 ὁ δὲ εἰσερχόμενος διὰ τῆς θύρας ποιμήν ἐστιν τῶν προβάτων. 3 τούτῳ ὁ θυρωρὸς ἀνοίγει, καὶ τὰ πρόβατα τῆς φωνῆς αὐτοῦ ἀκούει, καὶ τὰ ἴδια πρόβατα φωνεῖ κατ' ὄνομα καὶ ἐξάγει αὐτά. 4 ὅταν τὰ ἴδια πάντα ἐκβάλῃ, ἔμπροσθεν αὐτῶν πορεύεται, καὶ

τὰ πρόβατα αὐτῷ ἀκολουθεῖ, ὅτι οἴδασιν τὴν φωνὴν αὐτοῦ· 5 ἀλλοτρίῳ δὲ οὐ μὴ ἀκολουθήσουσιν ἀλλὰ φεύξονται ἀπ' αὐτοῦ, ὅτι οὐκ οἴδασι τῶν ἀλλοτρίων τὴν φωνήν. 6 Ταύτην τὴν παροιμίαν εἶπεν αὐτοῖς ὁ Ἰησοῦς· ἐκεῖνοι δὲ οὐκ ἔγνωσαν τίνα ἦν ἃ ἐλάλει αὐτοῖς. 7 Εἶπεν οὖν πάλιν [ὁ] Ἰησοῦς Ἀμὴν ἀμὴν λέγω ὑμῖν, ἐγώ εἰμι ἡ θύρα τῶν προβάτων. 8 πάντες ὅσοι ἦλθον πρὸ ἐμοῦ[1] κλέπται εἰσὶν καὶ λῃσταί· ἀλλ' οὐκ ἤκουσαν αὐτῶν τὰ πρόβατα. 9 ἐγώ εἰμι ἡ θύρα· δι' ἐμοῦ ἐάν τις εἰσέλθῃ σωθήσεται καὶ εἰσελεύσεται καὶ ἐξελεύσεται καὶ νομὴν εὑρήσει. 10 ὁ κλέπτης οὐκ ἔρχεται εἰ μὴ ἵνα κλέψῃ καὶ θύσῃ καὶ ἀπολέσῃ· ἐγὼ ἦλθον ἵνα ζωὴν ἔχωσιν καὶ περισσὸν ἔχωσιν. 11 Ἐγώ εἰμι ὁ ποιμὴν ὁ καλός· ὁ ποιμὴν ὁ καλὸς τὴν ψυχὴν αὐτοῦ τίθησιν ὑπὲρ τῶν προβάτων· 12 ὁ μισθωτὸς καὶ οὐκ ὢν ποιμήν, οὗ οὐκ ἔστιν τὰ πρόβατα ἴδια, θεωρεῖ τὸν λύκον ἐρχόμενον καὶ ἀφίησιν τὰ πρόβατα καὶ φεύγει,—καὶ ὁ λύκος ἁρπάζει αὐτὰ καὶ σκορπίζει,— 13 ὅτι μισθωτός ἐστιν καὶ οὐ μέλει αὐτῷ περὶ τῶν προβάτων. 14 ἐγώ εἰμι ὁ ποιμὴν ὁ καλός, καὶ γινώσκω τὰ ἐμὰ καὶ γινώσκουσί με τὰ ἐμά, 15 καθὼς γινώσκει με ὁ πατὴρ κἀγὼ γινώσκω τὸν πατέρα, καὶ τὴν ψυχήν μου τίθημι ὑπὲρ τῶν προβάτων. 16 καὶ ἄλλα πρόβατα ἔχω ἃ οὐκ ἔστιν ἐκ τῆς αὐλῆς ταύτης· κἀκεῖνα δεῖ με ἀγαγεῖν, καὶ τῆς φωνῆς μου ἀκούσουσιν, καὶ γενήσονται μία ποίμνη, εἷς ποιμήν.

[1] *V. l.*, πρὸ ἐμοῦ ἦλθον.

LESSON XXXVII.

1 Corinthians xii. 12-31.

THE PARABLE OF THE BODY—THE USE OF CHRISTIAN GIFTS.

12 Καθάπερ γὰρ τὸ σῶμα ἕν ἐστιν καὶ μέλη πολλὰ ἔχει, πάντα δὲ τὰ μέλη τοῦ σώματος πολλὰ ὄντα ἕν ἐστιν σῶμα, οὕτως καὶ ὁ Χριστός· 13 καὶ γὰρ ἐν ἑνὶ πνεύματι ἡμεῖς πάντες εἰς ἓν σῶμα ἐβαπτίσθημεν, εἴτε Ἰουδαῖοι εἴτε Ἕλληνες, εἴτε δοῦλοι εἴτε ἐλεύθεροι, καὶ πάντες ἓν πνεῦμα ἐποτίσθημεν. 14 καὶ γὰρ τὸ σῶμα οὐκ ἔστιν ἓν μέλος ἀλλὰ πολλά. 15 ἐὰν εἴπῃ ὁ πούς Ὅτι οὐκ εἰμὶ χείρ, οὐκ εἰμὶ ἐκ τοῦ σώματος, οὐ παρὰ τοῦτο οὐκ ἔστιν ἐκ τοῦ σώματος· 16 καὶ ἐὰν εἴπῃ τὸ οὖς Ὅτι οὐκ εἰμί ὀφθαλμός, οὐκ εἰμὶ ἐκ τοῦ σώματος, οὐ παρὰ τοῦτο οὐκ ἔστιν ἐκ τοῦ σώματος· 17 εἰ ὅλον τὸ σῶμα ὀφθαλμός, ποῦ ἡ ἀκοή; εἰ ὅλον ἀκοή, ποῦ ἡ ὄσφρησις; 18 νῦν[1] δὲ ὁ θεὸς ἔθετο τὰ μέλη, ἓν ἕκαστον αὐτῶν, ἐν τῷ σώματι καθὼς ἠθέλησεν. 19 εἰ δὲ ἦν [τὰ] πάντα ἓν μέλος, ποῦ τὸ σῶμα; 20 νῦν δὲ πολλὰ μέλη, ἓν δὲ σῶμα. 21 οὐ δύναται [δὲ] ὁ ὀφθαλμὸς εἰπεῖν τῇ χειρί Χρείαν σου οὐκ ἔχω, ἢ πάλιν ἡ κεφαλὴ τοῖς ποσίν Χρείαν ὑμῶν οὐκ ἔχω· 22 ἀλλὰ πολλῷ μᾶλλον τὰ δοκοῦντα μέλη τοῦ σώματος ἀσθενέστερα ὑπάρχειν ἀναγκαῖά ἐστιν, 23 καὶ ἃ δοκοῦμεν ἀτιμότερα εἶναι τοῦ σώματος,

[1] *V. l.*, *νυνί.*

τούτοις τιμὴν περισσοτέραν περιτίθεμεν, καὶ τὰ
ἀσχήμονα ἡμῶν εὐσχημοσύνην περισσοτέραν ἔχει,
24 τὰ δὲ εὐσχήμονα ἡμῶν οὐ χρείαν ἔχει. ἀλλὰ ὁ
θεὸς σύνεκέρασεν τὸ σῶμα, τῷ ὑστερουμένῳ περισσοτέραν δοὺς τιμήν, 25 ἵνα μὴ ᾖ σχίσμα ἐν τῷ σώματι,
ἀλλὰ τὸ αὐτὸ ὑπὲρ ἀλλήλων μεριμνῶσι τὰ μέλη.
26 καὶ εἴτε πάσχει ἓν μέλος, συμπάσχει πάντα τὰ
μέλη· εἴτε δοξάζεται μέλος, συγχαίρει πάντα τὰ
μέλη. 27 ὑμεῖς δέ ἐστε σῶμα Χριστοῦ καὶ μέλη ἐκ
μέρους. 28 Καὶ οὓς μὲν ἔθετο ὁ θεὸς ἐν τῇ ἐκκλησίᾳ
πρῶτον ἀποστόλους, δεύτερον προφήτας, τρίτον
διδασκάλους, ἔπειτα δυνάμεις, ἔπειτα χαρίσματα
ἰαμάτων, ἀντιλήψεις, κυβερνήσεις, γένη γλωσσῶν.
29 μὴ πάντες ἀπόστολοι; μὴ πάντες προφῆται; μὴ
πάντες διδάσκαλοι; μὴ πάντες δυνάμεις; 30 μὴ
πάντες χαρίσματα ἔχουσιν ἰαμάτων; μὴ πάντες
γλώσσαις λαλοῦσιν; μὴ πάντες διερμηνεύουσιν;
31 ζηλοῦτε δὲ τὰ χαρίσματα τὰ μείζονα.

LESSON XXXVIII.

1 Corinthians xiii.

THE PRAISE OF LOVE.

1 Καὶ ἔτι καθ᾽ ὑπερβολὴν ὁδὸν ὑμῖν δείκνυμι. Ἐὰν ταῖς γλώσσαις τῶν ἀνθρώπων λαλῶ καὶ τῶν ἀγγέλων, ἀγάπην δὲ μὴ ἔχω, γέγονα χαλκὸς ἠχῶν ἢ κύμβαλον ἀλαλάζον. 2 κἂν ἔχω προφητείαν καὶ εἰδῶ τὰ μυστήρια πάντα καὶ πᾶσαν τὴν γνῶσιν, κἂν ἔχω πᾶσαν τὴν πίστιν ὥστε ὄρη μεθιστάνειν, ἀγάπην δὲ μὴ ἔχω, οὐθέν εἰμι. 3 κἂν ψωμίσω πάντα τὰ ὑπάρχοντά μου, κἂν παραδῶ τὸ σῶμά μου, ἵνα καυχήσωμαι,[1] ἀγάπην δὲ μὴ ἔχω, οὐδὲν ὠφελοῦμαι. 4 Ἡ ἀγάπη μακροθυμεῖ, χρηστεύεται, ἡ ἀγάπη οὐ ζηλοῖ, οὐ περπερεύεται, οὐ φυσιοῦται, 5 οὐκ ἀσχημονεῖ, οὐ ζητεῖ τὰ ἑαυτῆς, οὐ παροξύνεται, οὐ λογίζεται τὸ κακόν, 6 οὐ χαίρει ἐπὶ τῇ ἀδικίᾳ, συγχαίρει δὲ τῇ ἀληθείᾳ· 7 πάντα στέγει, πάντα πιστεύει, πάντα ἐλπίζει, πάντα ὑπομένει. 8 Ἡ ἀγάπη οὐδέποτε πίπτει. εἴτε δὲ προφητεῖαι, καταργηθήσονται· εἴτε γλῶσσαι, παύσονται· εἴτε γνῶσις, καταργηθήσεται. 9 ἐκ μέρους γὰρ γινώσκομεν καὶ ἐκ μέρους προφητεύομεν· 10 ὅταν δὲ ἔλθῃ τὸ τέλειον, τὸ ἐκ μέρους καταργηθήσεται. 11 ὅτε ἤμην νήπιος, ἐλάλουν ὡς νήπιος, ἐφρόνουν ὡς νήπιος, ἐλογιζόμην ὡς νήπιος· ὅτε γέγονα ἀνήρ, κατήργηκα τὰ τοῦ νηπίου. 12 βλέπομεν

[1] *V. l.*, καυθήσωμαι.

γὰρ ἄρτι δι' ἐσόπτρου ἐν αἰνίγματι, τότε δὲ πρόσωπον πρὸς πρόσωπον· ἄρτι γινώσκω ἐκ μέρους, τότε
δὲ ἐπιγνώσομαι καθὼς καὶ ἐπεγνώσθην. 13 νυνὶ δὲ
μένει πίστις, ἐλπίς, ἀγάπη· τὰ τρία ταῦτα, μείζων
δὲ τούτων ἡ ἀγάπη.

ON CHRISTIAN LOVE.

When we read the list of the various occupations
spoken of by St Paul in 1 Cor. xii. 28, we are
apt to think they have little interest for us but an
antiquarian one. "Apostles, prophets, teachers, miracles,
gifts of healings, helps, governments, diversities of
tongues," most of these have, as he foresaw, failed and
ceased (1 Cor. xiii. 8). Love remains, and may be
applied by the Christian to the new circumstances in
which he finds himself in modern times. He is no
longer as the primitive Christian was—a member of an
insignificant and struggling body, gifted with new enthusiasm, and possessed of strange powers. He finds himself
an important member of a great nation, able to carry
Christian principles and practice into active spheres of
life in a mixed community, some of whom do, and some
do not, recognise Jesus as their master. Even among
those who do, he finds grave differences of opinion, and
may even experience a difficulty among the conflicting
sects in finding the unity dwelt on by St Paul in this
chapter. For this, however, he may find a solace when
he considers the character of the Corinthian Church, in
whom St Paul hoped to promote this unity. They
were immoral, they were vain, they were split up into
sects, they looked on their Christian gifts as matter
rather for boast than spheres for usefulness ; yet he does
not despair of them, but calls on them to display that
love, the description of which has become as famous

in literature and in morals as in the history of Christianity.

Co-operation in love for the good of the community, that was St Paul's idea of a Christian Church at a time when Christians had little or no influence on social life or politics. Christians now have not the strange gifts he mentions, but they have far greater influence. They have greater gifts in natural talent, in education, in wealth, in position, and it is their privilege to seek to carry out the ideal of St Paul into the varied relations of modern life. As statesmen, as members of Parliament, as ministers of religion, as doctors, as lawyers, as schoolmasters, in the army, in the navy; as manufacturers, as merchants, as labourers, as artisans, they may display the qualities St Paul has classified under the name of love. In all these spheres there is room for patience, generosity, humility, dignity, peaceableness, good temper, unsuspiciousness, and love of realities.

Let us take examples from lives spent in the sphere of the intellect, of politics, and of industry.

The Christian student works not for himself but for the sake of Christ, and of Christ's community of which he is a member. He is patient over his own work and with the ignorant; he rejoices and is not envious when others are more successful than he is; he is willing to impart information, but shrinks from displaying his knowledge; he is humble because he thinks not of how much he knows in comparison with others, but of how little he knows in comparison with what is to be known; he is not angry at folly or at interruptions to his work; he is sorry when others make mistakes, and glad when they excel him; encourages those who are beginning, and works on steadily even when his work seems to meet with no recognition.

The Christian tradesmen or manufacturer is patient with the shortcomings of those under him, and seeks to take no mean advantage of his trade rivals; avoids lying and braggart advertisements, and for the good of the community strives to produce good work, and rejoices when others do so; "hastens not to be rich by dishonest means," is not suspicious that every one is seeking to cheat him, but promotes honesty by trustfulness, and for Christ's sake often endures poverty rather than be dishonest, even while his competitors are so; does not keep back the truth, or ungenerously turn another man's difficulties to his own account.

The Christian politician seeks to advance his views not by declamation, but by persuasion and argument; is diffident of his conclusions, and therefore conscientiously weighs his arguments; does not embitter political controversy by the introduction of rude personalities; easily forgets the personalities of his adversary; is conciliatory, dignified, and gentle in demeanour; willingly accepts a refutation, bears calumny with calmness, is never cynical, or bitter, or distrustful.

The words of St Paul, that we are "all members of one another," are especially applicable to the life of a public school.

The various members of a school have, like the primitive Christians, their various gifts: and first, there is the great division alluded to by St Paul of those who have the inferior and those who have the higher powers. The duty of the former he states to be twofold,—not to envy, and not to despond. The slow as well as the ready are members of Christ's kingdom, and their work is estimated by Him, not by its result, but by their willingness. The duty of the quick and clever is to be humble and to be sympathetic. Their readiness is a gift from God, and no merit of their own; and the first lesson they should learn from it is how much they have to learn, and the second, sympathy for those who are not so quick as they.

There is none of the attributes of love which may not find its sphere in school-work. School-life finds plenty of scope for suffering under injustice from masters or schoolfellows, for "graciousness" to lower or smaller boys, for the restraint of an excessive emulation bordering on envy, and of a love of praise leading to ostentation. There are temptations to be withstood that tend to vanity, to unseemly conduct, to bitterness, to vindictiveness. Schoolboys, like men, may feel themselves elated at the failings or depressed at the merits of others. There are wrongs to submit to, suspicions to keep down, cynicism to restrain, and bullying and persecution to endure without tale-bearing. All these things are a training to Christian manhood, and to the perfection of Christian love. The school is a little world, and resembles the Greek πόλις.

NOTES.

LESSON I.

The Visit of Jesus, when a Boy, to Jerusalem—
St Luke ii. 40-52.

40. Notice the imperfects.

41. According to the Law, which, however, the Dispersion would make it difficult to obey, men were bound to present themselves at the Temple at the three feasts of Passover, Pentecost, and Tabernacles (Exod. xxiii. 14-17). There was no such obligation for women; and by going with Joseph, Mary displays her piety, as Samuel's mother did in the olden days (1 Sam. i. 7, 21). The famous Rabbi Hillel had enjoined the duty on women.

42. **ἐτῶν δώδεκα.**—An Eastern boy of twelve would be much more precocious than an English boy of the same age. At that age a young Jew was called "grown-up," and "a son of the Law." He began to be responsible for legal observances, and to wear the phylacteries (from φυλάσσων), or cases of black leather containing strips of parchment, on which were written four passages of Scripture (Exod. xiii. 2-10, 11-16; Deut. vi. 4-9, 13-22): these were tied on the bend of the arm or the forehead. He was also presented by his father in the synagogue, and began to learn a trade.

ἀναβαινόντων.—The highest point of Jerusalem is 2600 feet above the sea: they had a distance of 80 miles to travel, and would go in a caravan composed of the inhabitants of the neighbourhood. From the Plain of Esdraelon, south of Nazareth, they would traverse the mountainous country rising gradually over the tract known as the mountains of Ephraim and Judah. Thousands flocked from all parts of the East to Jerusalem at the time of the Passover; many built themselves booths for shelter during the week. Jerusalem would be to Jesus far more than London to an English boy; because it was not only the capital of His country, but the great seat of His religion, full of the only literary and religious associations with which He was acquainted. It was to Him at once a London, a Canterbury, and an Oxford, but far more than these, because it was to Him the only cathedral and university town in the world, the only true religious centre. He would long to see "the hills that stand about Jerusalem," and above all, to see the Temple where God had promised that His eyes and heart should be perpetually (1 Kings ix. 3), where was His house (1 Kings viii. 13), His palace (1 Chron. xxix. 19), where especially He heard the prayers of His people (1 Kings viii. 30), and from which He sent His blessings (Ps. cxxxiv. 3).

43. **τὰς ἡμέρας.**—The seven days of the feast (Exod. xii. 15).

44. **συνοδία.**—"Caravan": the word occurs in that sense in Strabo.

ἦλθον.—Note the aorist, "they had gone."

ἡμέρας ὁδόν.—To Sichem or Shiloh. They would imagine Him to be with their friends in the caravan. His innocence and independence of character would lead them unhesitatingly to trust Him to Himself.

ἀνεζήτουν.—The prep. is intensive. "Began to seek Him earnestly" (cf. Acts xi. 25). The search would probably commence when at night they were assembled together.

45. **μή,** not **οὐ**—"as they did not find Him."

46. **μεθ' ἡμέρας τρεῖς**—i.e., dating from His staying behind. They would reach Jerusalem the second day, and at length on the third day find Him: the search would be attended with difficulty, on account of the narrowness of the streets and their crowded condition.

ἐν τῷ ἱερῷ.—There seems to have been a synagogue east of the Temple, in the precincts, where the Rabbis explained the Law. Eager for instruction, Jesus had gone thither, and become engrossed in the lesson. As the Rabbinical method consisted in teaching by means of question and answer,—in stating, e.g., a problem taken from the Law,—both master and pupil would have an opportunity

of displaying their sagacity.   Jesus no doubt had made some
remarkable answer, or put some original question ; and, as happens when a particularly intelligent pupil presents himself, He
had become for the moment the chief object of the instruction.
The scholars sat in a threefold ring.   Josephus says of himself,
somewhat boastfully, "At the age of fourteen I was commended
by all for the love I had for learning; on which account the high
priests and principal men of the city came then frequently to me
together, in order to know my opinion about the accurate understanding of points of Law."   We may imagine that the questions
of Jesus were directed rather to "principles" than points of Law,
and it was His originality and freshness rather than His accurate
knowledge that created amazement.

καθεζόμενον.—Sitting in the threefold ring of the scholars on
the ground.

47. συνέσει.—The faculty by which we understand the bearings
of things: cf. 2 Tim. ii. 7—νόει, ἅ λέγω, δώσει γάρ σοι ὁ Κύριος συνε-
σιν ἐν πᾶσιν.   Philo joins it with ἀγχίνοια, "quick-wittedness."

48. ἐξεπλάγησαν.—"They were awe-struck"—i. e., they were
amazed at finding Him calm and happy in that august presence
which filled their humble and pious souls with reverence.   But
Jesus was too simple-minded to be diffident, and too much in
earnest about learning to be afraid to ask questions: besides, the
free intercourse then customary between the teachers and the
taught would make it easy for Him to do so.   The schools were
free and open, and any one entering might propose or answer a
question.

ὀδυνώμενοι.—This word is translated "in anguish" in E.V.—
cf. xvi. 24.   It is used of the regret of the Ephesians at the
departure of St Paul in Acts xx. 38.   It may be rendered, "in
great distress," or (Dr Farrar) "with aching hearts."

49. τί ὅτι—condensed for τί γέγονεν ὅτι.

ἐν τοῖς.—We may understand either (1) δώμασιν, as in Joseph. c.
Ap. 2, τόν τε χρυσοῦν κίονα ἐν τοῖς τοῦ Διὸς ἀνέθηκε ; or (2) πράγμασι, and illustrate from John iv. 34, where Jesus says His meat
is to do the will of His Father.   Philo in a similar way under-
stands προστάγματα injunctions—οἱ τὸν πατέρα καὶ τὰ τοῦ πατρὸς
τιμῶντες, μητρὸς δὲ καὶ τῶν ἐκείνης ἥκιστα φροντίζοντες (De Temul.,
250 E.).   For πράγμασι cf. also Gen. xli. 51—ὅτι ἐπιλαθέσθαι με
ἐποίησεν ὁ θεὸς πάντων τῶν τοῦ πατρός μου.

For the construction of εἶναι with ἐν, cf. Ion, 638—θεῶν δ' ἐν εὐχαῖς ἢ λόγοισιν ἢ βροτῶν ; and 1 Tim. iv. 15—ταῦτα μελέτα, ἐν τούτοις ἴσθι.

51. διετήρει denotes careful consideration : cf. Gen. xxxvii. 11, "His brethren envied him, but his father διετήρησε τὸ ῥῆμα (of Joseph's dream).

52. προέκοπτε.—Probably derived from cutting down wood in advance of an army, pioneering ; hence, "making progress."

ἡλικίᾳ.—"Stature" or "age." St Luke seems to have had in his mind the description of Samuel in 1 Sam. ii. 21, 26. The latter passage runs thus in the LXX.: καὶ τὸ παιδάριον Σαμουὴλ ἐπορεύετο μεγαλυνόμενον καὶ ἦν ἀγαθὸν μετὰ Κυρίου καὶ μετὰ ἀνθρώπων, —which is translated in our version, "The child Samuel grew on, and was in favour both with the Lord, and also with men." This parallel indicates that ἡλικία refers to bodily growth, and σοφία to mental development.

LESSON III.

THE SERMON ON THE MOUNT—St Matt. v. 1-16.

THE CHARACTER, PRIVILEGES, AND RESPONSIBILITIES OF THE MEMBERS OF THE KINGDOM OF GOD.

1. τοὺς ὄχλους.—The plural seems used merely for the sake of emphasis, a usage not unknown in classic Greek and Latin. Capernaum, near which the sermon was delivered, was at that time the great halting-place and mart for the caravans on their way from Egypt to Damascus, and therefore a place of much resort— see p. 78.

τὸ ὄρος.—"The mountain which was near," or, "the mountain the readers of the Gospel had so often heard of, in discourses about Jesus." The Sea of Galilee, like most inland lakes, is almost surrounded by hills. It is impossible, therefore, to decide what particular eminence is referred to. The phrase may mean simply the highlands as opposed to the lowlands of the lake. We learn from Mark iii. 13 that Jesus went up into the mountain or mountain district before appointing His twelve disciples; and from Luke vi. 12, that He spent the previous night there in prayer. The district had a large population in Jesus' time; hence the need of retirement for prayer or preaching.

Tradition, dating probably from the Crusades, has chosen for "the mountain" a hill called the "Horns of Hattin." This is the only conspicuous hill on the western side of the lake, and its marked features might lead to its being called "the mountain," just as Helvellyn might be called "the mountain" at Ullswater, though that lake is surrounded by other less distinctive hills nearer to it. The "horns" are two eminences with a level place between them sixty feet below. This might be the spot alluded to in Luke vi. 17 as the scene of the sermon, which might thus be fairly described as a mountain or as a level place. It is doubtful, however, whether the latter is spacious enough for the multitudes alluded to. The hill is 1000 feet above the lake, from which it is easily accessible; and standing between the hills and the lake, it would be central both for the peasants and the fishermen.

καθίσαντος.—It was the custom for the scholars of a Rabbi to sit on the floor or benches, while the Rabbi himself sat a little above them on a raised platform: thus St Paul speaks of himself as brought up at the feet of Gamaliel (Acts xxii. 3): cf. Luke ii. 46.

2. **ἀνοίξας.**—The phrase here indicates solemnity: cf. Matt. xiii. 35; Job iii. 1.

3. **μακάριοι.**—In classic Greek μακάριος meant "one whose outward circumstances were free from trouble" —cf. Lat. *beatus*. It was applied more frequently to the dead than to the living. Hesiod says, μάκαρες θνητοὶ καλέονται. Homer opposes θεοὶ μάκαρες to θνητοὶ ἄνθρωποι. Christianity has ameliorated the use of the word with reference both to God and man. Of men, μακάριος is used of those who are happy, because at peace with God, even though they have external trouble; and the Christian's God is called μακάριος (1 Tim. i. 11), not because He is free from, and indifferent to, the cares which trouble men,—like the happy gods of the pagans, careless of mankind, that live above the thunderbolts,—but because He communicates His happiness to others. "That only is by nature happy of which everything which partakes becomes happy." The "blessed" God is the source and fountain of all blessings.

πτωχοὶ τῷ πνεύματι.—Cf. Isa. lvii. 15, where God is said to dwell with him that is of a contrite and humble spirit : Prov. xvi. 19, xxix. 23. The salvation which the Messiah should bring had already been especially promised to the poor, the captive, and the sorrowful, in Isa. lxi. 1, 2. In the Old Testament, poverty and piety are often almost synonymous, especially after the captivity. This arose from the contrast the Jews instituted between themselves, the worshippers of the true God oppressed and in poverty, and their idolatrous conquerors who seemed to them at once proud and successful. They never abandoned the idea that God would at some time bless them ; but while the grosser spirits regarded the poverty as consisting in the want, and the future blessedness in the restoration, of material prosperity, the nobler and more thoughtful regarded both from a spiritual point of view. In this paradox Jesus declares that the kingdom of heaven does indeed belong to the poor, but to those who are poor in spirit. He who feels his poverty will seek for riches. The treasury in this case is the grace of God : when Jesus spoke, it was His teaching. The poor in spirit would apply to that treasury, would drink in His words, and so win for themselves the kingdom of heaven,—not an outward possession, but a state. They who most feel their dependence on God seek His presence most constantly, and thus assimilate themselves to His likeness, and inherit the kingdom of heaven—that is, dwell with God and God with them, according to Isaiah's words (lvii. 15). This beatitude is appropriately put first : before His hearers could win the kingdom about which Jesus preached, they must feel a desire for it.

ἡ βασιλεία τῶν οὐρανῶν.—This is St Matthew's usual phrase for "kingdom of God." The plural arises from the popular idea among the Jews that there were seven heavens : cf. 2 Cor. xii. 2. The Rabbis very commonly substituted the term "heaven" for the name of God. In the Book of Wisdom (whose date lies probably between B.C. 217-165), the phrase "kingdom of God" is made parallel with "holy things," or "mysteries." "When the righteous (Jacob) fled from his brother's wrath, Wisdom showed him the kingdom of God, and gave him knowledge of holy things" (chap. x. 10). St Paul explains what these mysteries are (Rom. xiv. 17), "The kingdom of God is not eating and drinking ; but righteousness, and peace, and joy in the Holy Ghost."

Observe that the promise of the kingdom of heaven affixed to the first beatitude is repeated in the last, ver. 10. This indicates that the intermediate blessings are merely expansions or illustrations of this one. So the qualities to which the blessings are affixed may all meet in one and the same person : not different persons are implied, but various characteristics, as in Milton's " L'Allegro " and " Il Penseroso."

4. οἱ πενθοῦντες.—Among Jesus' hearers would be many Israelites who were mourning for the loss of their freedom and their lofty hopes, for the desecration of their holy land by the erection of heathen temples and palaces, and for the degradation of the people of God by their submission to a foreign ruler. Those of a lower nature would be full of rancour and hatred against the foreigner ; but the nobler spirits would see in the downfall of their nation the punishment for their sins, and would mourn for these rather than for their misfortunes. To them Jesus' words are addressed. They were destined to be comforted by the spiritual regeneration He was to bring about, and by the new hopes He was to inspire. This was the παράκλησις to which the most pious Jews of Jesus' time were looking forward, Luke ii. 25 : παρακαλεῖτε, παρακαλεῖτε, is the commencement and the key-note of the noblest passage in the Old Testament scriptures, Isa. xl. 1. But besides this, Jesus no doubt looked forward to the sorrows and persecutions His followers would have to endure in rejecting the popular idea of the Messiah. To this the author of the Apocalypse alludes, when speaking of those who had come out of the great tribulation, from whose eyes God should wipe away every tear (Rev. vii. 17),—an idea amplified in Rev. xxi. 4.

The Christian mourns for the sins of others as well as his own, because he loves the whole human race as his brothers, and sees in each man a noble ideal from which he falls short. This makes him always a mourner in the sense that he can give no time to levity, or frivolity, or pastime, excepting for the purpose of renewing his energies. The lofty teaching of Jesus, and the hopes He inspired, are his consolation amid the miseries he sees sin producing on all sides of him.

αὐτοί.—Not " they themselves," as in classic Greek. In modern Greek αὐτός = simply " he " ; in Hellenistic Greek it seems to have become the emphatic " he." " They are the people who shall be comforted": cf. Matt. i. 21, αὐτὸς σώσει, "He it is who shall save."

5. οἱ πραεῖς.—This occurs in Ps. xxxvii. 11. Like the preceding beatitude, it is a paradox. To man, the meek seem to be the class most easily banished from the earth. "Nay," says Jesus, "they shall inherit the earth." The phrase "inherit the earth" had been used of Canaan in Gen. xv. 7, Deut. iv. 1, where the nation is spoken of: it is referred to individual pious persons in Ps. xxv. 13, xxxvii. 9, 11, 22. This last psalm was written to encourage the good in patience while they saw the wicked flourishing. Many of Jesus' hearers would be looking to Him to gain the land for them by force of arms or by supernatural power, rather than by patience. Here He disclaims such measures, and reminds them of the teaching of their own scriptures on the subject.

But how were the meek to inherit the earth? Julius Cæsar, Alexander the Great, and Napoleon I. were not meek, yet they seem as conquerors to have inherited the earth in a greater degree than any other men.

It is easy to answer that the inheritance is promised in some future state of things. But it is perhaps quite as true that the meek inherit the earth now, though it is difficult to understand that it is so. There is as much real inheritance of the earth by a mind perfectly at rest in God, and at peace with man, enjoying the delights of nature for one hour, as in all the feverish joy of conquest for a lifetime. Real possession is internal, not external. We do not possess a daisy so much by holding it in our hands, as by enjoying its beauty and understanding its spirit. Napoleon had more daisies than Wordsworth, but the latter pre-eminently possessed them. Profound enjoyment of the gifts of the earth, of the beauties of nature and art, and the works of the human intellect, can only be attained by a serene mind—*i.e.*, a mind undisturbed by anger, or envy, or care, and therefore meek. Again, the only true conquest is that over the minds and wills of men. Men submit their minds and wills far more readily to those who are able and modest, than to those who are able and overbearing.

6. τὴν δικαιοσύνην.—In classic Greek, "righteousness in relation to our fellow-men." In Hellenistic Greek, "righteousness of which God is the standard." The figure of thirst to express the longing for this righteousness appears most forcibly in Ps. xlii. 1, 2: "As the hart panteth after the water brooks, so panteth my soul

after Thee, O God. My soul thirsteth for God, for the living God : when shall I come and appear before God ?"

Those who longed for righteousness in the sense of justice and a recognition of their claims, would have their longings satisfied by the new dignity Christianity was destined to give to the human race, and the fresh impulses it should afford to sympathy with the miserable and degraded : those who longed for nobler motives and feelings, by the loftier views with which it should inspire them about God and their fellow-men. The righteousness refers both to outward social arrangements and the inner thoughts of the soul.

χορτασθήσεται.—Cf. Ps. xvii. 15, " As for me, I will behold Thy face in righteousness : I shall be satisfied (χορτασθήσομαι), when I awake, with Thy likeness." Ps. cvii. 9, " The Lord satisfieth (ἐχόρτασε) the longing soul, and filleth the hungry soul with goodness." χόρτος means (1) an enclosed place, in which cattle are kept : with it are connected Lat. *hort-us*, Eng. *garth, yard, garden;* (2) a feeding-place ; (3) food for cattle. Cf. Alc., 495 : " θηρῶν ὀρείων χόρτον οὐχ ἵππων λέγεις." In Rev. xix. 21 the verb is used of bird's food. In classic Greek the word is rarely applied to men, and then only in a contemptuous sense ; but in later Greek, perhaps from the more colloquial nature of its vocabulary, this contemptuous sense has vanished.

7. ἐλεήμονες.—This follows naturally from the preceding verse, because in the Old Testament ἔλεος is closely connected in thought with δικ ᾿οσύνη. God manifests His own righteousness chiefly by showing mercy and pity : cf. 2 Cor. ix. 9 ; Ps. cxii. 9. In thirteen places in LXX. the translators have rendered the Hebrew word for righteousness by ἐλεημοσύνη. In English literature, the connection is beautifully illustrated by Portia's speech in the "Merchant of Venice," iv. 1, where "mercy" is said to be an attribute to God Himself; and "earthly power doth then show likest God's, when mercy seasons justice." In the land where, and at the time when, Jesus was speaking, "mercy" was little thought of. The Romans were iron in their rule over the provinces ; the Pharisees unbending in their exaction of obedience to ceremonial observances ; the Sadducees stiffened by their pride of intellect and place. Jesus twice quotes what seems to have been a favourite passage of His, from Hosea (ἔλεος θέλω καὶ οὐ θυσίαν—Matt. ix. 13, xii. 7 ; Hos. vi. 6), against the unmerciful disposition of His contemporaries.

He illustrated this pity especially by His conduct to Mar
dalene, to Zaccheus, and to the woman taken in adultery,
all sinners whose wrong-doing seemed to rise from weakn
stress of circumstances, rather than from pride and wil
He was severe in his standard of righteousness, but mer
His judgments on those who fell short of it, because H
that such show of love best enables the weak sinner to ris

ἐλεηθήσονται—*i.e.*, "both from God and man." Pity a
pathy beget pity and sympathy. The same principle is laid
the Lord's Prayer, Matt. vi. 12. Many of Jesus' hearers w
pecting Him to aid them in a merciless vengeance on the C

8. οἱ καθαροὶ τῇ καρδίᾳ.—Cf. Ps. xxiv. 3-6, "Who shall
into the hill of the Lord? and who shall stand in His hol
He that hath clean hands, and a pure heart. . . . Thi
generation of them that seek Him, that seek Thy face,
of Jacob." Jesus adds τῇ καρδίᾳ, to distinguish the pu
required from the ceremonial cleanness on which the F
insisted—cf. Ps. lxxiii. 1, li. 10. In these passages p
heart seems to be opposed to deceit and insincerity,
reference to God as well as to man ; so that here it seems to mean
that undivided love which regards God alone as the highest good,
and to be synonymous with the ἁπλοῦς ὀφθαλμός of chap. vi. 22.
The lusts that contend for the heart of man with this pure love
of God are summed up in 1 John ii. 16, as the lust of the flesh,
and the lust of the eyes, and the vainglory of life—*i. e.*, as it
seems, (1) the sensual appetites displayed to excess by gluttory,
drunkenness, and the irregular relations between the sexes ; (2) the
desires excited by what we see, which beget the vice of avarice ;
(3) and the love of power and of the praise of our fellow-men,
which produce ostentation and ambition. Against the motives of
pleasure, avarice, and ambition, Jesus sets as the principles of life
the love of God, and of man as God's representative.

ὄψονται.—This refers to the Eastern idea of the high privilege
of seeing the face of an earthly monarch—*i.e.*, of being constantly
in his presence, and enjoying his confidence—cf. Esther i. 14 ;
Exod. xxxiii. 18 ; Ps. xvii. 15.

The best commentary on the passage is contained in 1 John iii.
2 : "Beloved, now are we children of God, and it is not yet made
manifest what we shall be. We know that if He" (*or* "it")
"shall be made manifest, we shall be like Him ; for we shall see

Him even as He is. And every one that hath this hope set on Him purifieth himself, even as He is pure."

The organ of vision is the pure heart, not the bodily eye. With the latter God cannot be seen,—John i. 18 ; 1 Tim. vi. 16. Our knowledge of God's nature deepens with our capacity to understand it. Like only can understand like. The child who loves his father most, will understand his character best, and therefore see what is really his father, even though physical blindness hinder him from seeing his father's form. God is love, and undivided love for Him will best enable us to see Him.

"Purity of heart" was by some, however, narrowed to mean "chastity," and there is a most interesting token of the historical influence of this sentence of Jesus in a preamble to the Laws of Justinian, A.D. 528: "We enact, then, that all persons, so far as they can, should preserve chastity, which alone is able to present the souls of men with confidence before God."

υἱοὶ θεοῦ.—See note on xiii. 38. In Hosea i. 10, the children of Israel are to be called the sons of the living God. In Wisd. v. 5, the phrase is by parallelism equivalent to "saints." "How is he numbered among the children of God, and his lot is among the saints!" Cf. Wisd. ii. 13, 18. Many of Jesus' hearers would claim as Israelites to be the sons of God, while they regarded one of their chief prerogatives to be war to the knife with the foreigner. Jesus corrects their notion of sonship. God is a God of peace, and His sons are those who resemble him in this godlike quality.

9. κληθήσονται.—"Be called, because they are"—*i. e.*, they shall not only be, but enjoy the renown of being : cf. ver. 19 and xxi. 13 ; and Eur., Hec., 625—ὁ δ' ἐν πολίταις τίμιος κεκλημένος.

10. οἱ δεδιωγμένοι.—They who have been persecuted have shown their sincere attachment to δικαιοσύνη.

ἡ βασιλεία τῶν οὐρ.—This repeats verse 3, and serves as a kind of binding, so to speak, to the beatitudes. The repetition, too, implies that all the other promises are only various ways of regarding the kingdom of heaven.

13. ἅλας.—As preserving it from corruption. Salt is especially necessary in a hot climate.

μωρανθῇ.—"Sixty-five houses in Jûne" (Lady Stanhope's village) "were rented and filled with salt. These houses had merely earthen floors, and the salt next the ground in a few years entirely spoiled. I saw large quantities of it literally thrown into the street, to be trodden under foot of men and beasts. It was good for nothing. Similar magazines are common in this country, and the sweeping out of the spoiled salt and casting it into the street are actions common to all men " ('The Land and the Book'). The salt, too, of Syria contains much sulphate of lime, and this would be the insipid residuum when the chloride of sodium (which almost exclusively forms our salt) was dissolved by moisture (Nicholson on St Matthew).

The disciples of Jesus had shown themselves of all the men of their time the most willing to attach themselves to the Noblest and the Best. If now they lose their enthusiasm, whence is it to be rekindled ?

14. ἐπάνω ὄρους.—Towns and villages, crowning the summits of the surrounding eminences, might be seen from where they stood, especially the mountain city of Saphet, which is 3335 feet above the lake, and ten miles distant.

15. τὸν μόδιον.—The article denotes the particular grain measure that would be at hand in every Jewish house. High tables such as ours were not used ; and the lamp, which had no footpiece, and stood very low, had to be set on a tall candlestick or lampstand. If a person leaving the room wished to retain the light, he might cover it with some hollow vessel, such as the modius.

16. οὕτω—"in like manner." Contrast vi. 1-18. Observe, the good works are to be done that men may glorify God, not the doers of them,—e.g., a man may head a subscription-list in order to induce others to do so.

LESSON V.

THE SERMON ON THE MOUNT—St Matt. v. 17-32.

CHRISTIANITY A DEVELOPMENT OF THE MORALITY OF THE LAW.

*The General Principle. Special Instances—
Murder and Adultery.*

17-20. *The General Principle.*

17. τὸν νόμον ἢ τοὺς προφήτας.—A phrase equivalent to the Old Testament. The prophets are here regarded as uttering not prophecies but moral precepts. This is evident, as there is no ref-

erence to prophecies in what follows. The prophets expounded the Law, and gave it a deeper meaning as the nation progressed in civilisation and in the knowledge of God.

The Jews derived from Jer. xxxi. 31, 32, a notion that the Messiah was destined to abrogate the Law ; but it is not likely that many at this time regarded Jesus as the Messiah. It is probable that a rumour had arisen that He intended to abrogate the Law, because he slighted the legal traditions of the Scribes.

πληρῶσαι.—This means (1) "to confirm," so rendered in 1 Kings i. 14, and in this way opposed to καταλῦσαι ; or (2) to carry out or observe, as in chap. iii. 15—πρέπον ἐστὶν ἡμῖν πληρῶσαι πᾶσαν δικαιοσύνην. St Paul best describes this fulfilment of the Law by Jesus, when he says, Rom. xiii. 8, "He that loveth another hath fulfilled the Law." Jesus taught that Christian love, if allowed full play, would confirm the law against murder by abolishing hate, against adultery by introducing new grounds for respecting the body, and against oaths by breaking down the barriers of suspicion and distrust. He carried out the Law in the first sense by His profound teaching, and in the second by His stainless life.

18. ἀμήν—"firmly," "faithfully,"= ἀληθῶς (Luke ix. 27). The word is properly a verbal adjective = "firm, true": cf. Rev. iii. 14, "These things saith the Amen." It is used in the Gospels only by Christ.

ἕως ἄν, κ.τ.λ.—Both in the classics and the Old Testament the heaven and the stars are represented as remaining imperishable amid all earthly changes (cf. Hesiod's ἕδος ἀσφαλὲς ἀεί), so that the period may be regarded as one that will never come.

ἰῶτα.—The yod ( ), the smallest letter in the Hebrew alphabet.

κεραία.—"A horn," a little stroke or projection that distinguishes some Hebrew letters from others, as ב (Beth or b) is distinguished from כ (Caph or c).

πάντα.—"Until all that the Law requires shall be accomplished."

19. ἐλάχιστος.—Cf. Matt. xi. 11 ; and 1 Cor. xv. 9, "I am the least of the apostles."

λύσῃ does not mean to "abrogate officially," as princes and lawgivers do, but "to neglect" or "cause to fall into abeyance." Philo says that neither famine nor pestilence, or war, or king, or despot, or tumult in the soul or body, or from the passions or vices, or any other evil that Providence sends on man, has annulled (ἔλυσε) the Law of Moses—De Vit. Illus.

20. τῶν γραμματέων—i.e., τῆς δικαιοσύνης τῶν, κ.τ.λ. This verse is a climax on the preceding, "You shall not even enter the gate of the kingdom unless," &c.

περισ. πλεῖον.—A redundant expression : the verb is found with the genitive, and with ὑπέρ.

21-26. *Murder.*

Jesus confines Himself to the commandments of the second table, for the Pharisees in their pretended zeal for God had almost abrogated the love for man inculcated in the Law of Moses.

21. ἠκούσατε.—A frequentative aorist, "Ye are in the habit of hearing"—i.e., in the synagogue.

τοῖς ἀρχαίοις.—"To," not "by"; this is the usual construction of ἐρρέθη in the New Testament. The dative of the agent after a passive verb is scarcely ever found in the Greek of the New Testament; the antithesis, ἐγὼ δὲ λέγω ὑμῖν, seems to show that this passage is no exception. Jesus speaks of what their ancestors rather than of what they themselves had heard, because it was always the practice of Jewish teachers to refer to the tradition of the past. The reference is to the reading in the synagogues. If Jesus had meant "by," he would probably have used πρεσβύτεροι—cf. Matt. xv. 2, Mark vii. 3-5, τὴν παράδοσιν τῶν πρεσβυτέρων. In Diod. Sic., xii. 20, we have καλῶς εἴρηται τοῖς παλαίοις. The use of ἀρχαῖοι here, rather than παλαιοί, is significant. The former refers back to the beginning of the Jewish commonwealth, and implies venerability: cf. Luke ix. 8, προφήτης εἷς τῶν ἀρχαίων. Jesus is not scorning His hearers for what they knew and had heard, but showing them new depths of meaning in it. We are not necessarily better than our forefathers, because we know more than they did. It is our part to advance their knowledge.

οὐ φονεύσεις.—Exod. xx. 12.

ὅς δ' ἄν, κ.τ.λ., a traditional addition by the Scribes.

22. ὁ ὀργιζόμενος.—Cf. Prov. xvi. 32, "He that is slow to anger is better than the mighty." There is a reading εἰκῆ, "without a cause," after ὀργιζ., but this was probably a marginal comment.

Does Jesus, then, forbid all anger ? This can hardly be, for He Himself is said to have been angry—Mark iii. 5, and anger is attributed in the Scriptures to God. St Paul speaks of an anger that is without sin—Eph. iv. 26. Jesus is alluding to the anger that has no moral justification, but is grounded on selfishness ; but even anger against immorality ought not to be unloving or hostile : see the Essay on Forgiveness.

τῷ ἀδελφῷ.—" Brother," not by blood, but as a member of the Jewish nation : cf. Acts vii. 26, where Moses says to his fellow-countrymen, Ἄνδρες, ἀδελφοί ἐστε, and Rom. ix. 3. The term was subsequently transferred to members of the Christian community, Acts vi. 3 ; Phil. i. 14 ; 1 Cor. v. 11.

τῇ κρίσει.—The local court of the provincial towns referred to in Deut. xix. 12, xxi. 2, 3. These courts had the power of punishing murder by the sword, till the power of life and death was taken away by the Romans. According to the Rabbins, they consisted of twenty-three members each ; according to Josephus, of seven.

'Ρακά.—" Empty head " or "vain fellow,"—said to have been at that time a very common term of reproach. ἄνθρωπε κενέ is found in James ii. 20, addressed to a hypothetical person : cf. our " fool," from the Latin *follis*, wind-bag.

τῷ συνεδρίῳ.—The Sanhedrin (see Essay, page 200), or august Council at Jerusalem, which, before the Romans took away the power, could condemn to the more awful death by stoning, and inflict the bitterest disgrace by denying burial to the criminal, and causing his body to be cast into Hinnom to be burned.

Μωρέ.—" Fool," but in a moral sense, and therefore equivalent to " wicked," " infidel," " godless" : cf. Ps. xiv. 1, " The fool hath said in his heart, There is no God." The phrase, therefore, is stronger than Raca, implying a stigma on the moral character. Jesus Himself used the phrase, " Ye fools and blind " (Matt. xxiii. 17); but He was speaking in moral indignation, not in scorn,—there is no scorn in the Gospel. Cf. Tennyson's " Guinevere "—" No knight of Arthur's noblest dealt in scorn," and " Mockery is the fume of little hearts."

εἰς τὴν.—A condensed expression : sub. βληθῆναι, " to be cast."

γέενναν.—" The Gehenna of fire "—*i.e.*, " the fiery Gehenna " : Gehenna = " ravine of Hinnom." This valley stretches along the southern boundary of Jerusalem, and probably derived its name from some ancient owner or inhabitant. In it was a certain enclosure, walled off, and called " the Tophet," in which stood a number of altars and images. The meaning of the name is unknown. To this place children were brought for sacrifice (Jer. vii. 31, 32). They were first slaughtered, just like other victims, and their blood was poured on the sacred stones. Then the bodies were brought to the image of Moloch, which was probably in human form with an ox's head, and its arms stretched out before it, sloping downwards towards a hole filled with fire, into which the children rolled when laid upon the outstretched arms, while music was played in honour of the deity. The straits to which Judæa was reduced in the reign of Ahaz induced that monarch to offer one of these frightful sacrifices, and perhaps it was he who built the Tophet. Under Hezekiah the worship there was superseded, or at any rate languished ; but it flourished more than ever under Manasseh, who led the way himself by sacrificing his first-born. King Josiah afterwards expressed his abhorrence of these sacrifices by defiling the place with dead bodies. It then became the receptacle for the sewage and rubbish of the city, and into it the carcasses of animals and the dead bodies of criminals were cast, and perhaps all that was combustible burnt with fire. This last, however, is doubtful. From the hideous associations and actual horrors of the place, it came to be regarded as the symbol of the place of punishment for the wicked. We do not know at what date the word began to be so used, for the literature in which the metaphor first occurs is lost. Jesus described Gehenna (Mark ix. 48) as a place "where the worm dieth not, and the fire is not quenched"— words quoted from Isa. lxvi. 24, where the carcasses of those that had rebelled against God are a spectacle and abomination unto all flesh, because their worm should not die nor their fire be quenched. This passage is imitated in Judith xvi. 17, where we have the same combination of fire and worms : "Woe to the nations that rise up against my kindred ! the Lord Almighty will take vengeance on them in the day of judgment in putting fire and worms in their flesh, and they shall feel them and weep for ever ;" and in Ecclus. vii. 17. The phrase, therefore, had become proverbial before our Lord's time. It is probable that Isaiah had borrowed his image from the horrors of Hinnom.

It is uncertain whether Jesus is referring to the literal or metaphorical signification of the term : whether, *i. c.*, He would be understood by His hearers as declaring that he who used the term μωρέ was liable to be slain, and after death have his body flung as a criminal's on to that place of horrors, or that he was liable after death to be thrown into the place reserved for the punishment of the wicked.

There is a double climax in the verse. First, in the advance from the feeling of anger in the heart to an outburst in words, in which again a distinction is made between a mere hasty expression of contempt or anger and a deliberate stigma on the moral character. Secondly, in the advance from the simple lower court in the provincial towns, which had once had the power of inflicting death by the sword, to the high court at Jerusalem, which could once have condemned to the more awful death by stoning, and finally, to the horror of being flung, after death, into the valley of Hinnom, or suffering in the other world that punishment which those horrors symbolised.

Jesus is speaking figuratively and as an orator, and asserts in rhetorical language that the feeling or word that indicates a strength of passion which, under certain circumstances, would result in murder, is in His sight as guilty as murder.

To take an example: The stony-hearted husband of a wife who displays uninterrupted and self-denying affection for him may be more guilty than the loving husband of a dissolute, spendthrift, and wrangling wife, whose evil temper, after he has borne with it for years, drives him in a moment of anger to mar the patience of a lifetime by a hasty blow that results in her death. Human law, however, takes no cognisance of the conduct of the former.

23. δῶρον—*i.e.*, sacrifice: cf. ix. 13, "I will have mercy, and not sacrifice."

ἐπί.—"To," not "on": the priests put it on.

μνησθῇς.—Divine service is a time for reflection.

ἔχει τι—*i.e.*, ἔγκλημα: cf. Mark xi. 25.

24. Take πρῶτον with ὕπαγε: cf. vii. 5, xiii. 30. The devotee is represented as standing with his offering at the rails which separate the Court of the Israelites from that of the priests, into which it will presently be taken, there to be slain by the priest, and by him presented upon the altar of sacrifice. Jesus here teaches that ceremonialism without love to man is worthless: cf. 1 Tim. ii. 8. He is thinking primarily of the Jewish service, and we may transfer the idea to Christian public worship, especially to the Holy Communion: but we must not restrict it to public worship ; we approach God in private prayer as well as in church.

25. **ἀντίδικος.**—Perhaps it is best to regard this as the personification of the appeal of our injured brother to God : cf. Gen. iv. 10, "The voice of thy brother's blood crieth unto me from the ground."

ἴσθι εὐνοῶν.—For the construction cf. Luke xix. 17: εὐνοῶν is opposed to κακονοῶν, "bearing malice." The words imply an inward disposition, not a mere formal reconciliation to avoid punishment,—as of two schoolboys shaking hands because their master bids them, while they are only anxious to fight it out. The periphrastic form of the imperative implies, too, that the feeling is to be permanent.

ἐν τῇ ὁδῷ.—In the interpretation, "this life": cf. 1 Kings ii. 2, "I go the way of all the earth."

ὑπηρέτης.—In Luke xii. 58 called ὁ πράκτωρ: cf. Acts v. 22. He was the officer whose duty it was to enforce the execution of the sentence, and who could, if necessary, consign the condemned person to prison.

26. **ἕως ἂν ἀποδῷς.**—We can deduce nothing from this as to the duration of the punishment of the wicked. It seems to be a rhetorical way of saying, "It will go hard with thee." St Augustine says, "The punishments of sins are to be avoided, not to be known."

25. **κοδράντην.**—Quadrans ; the fourth part of an *as*, and the smallest Roman coin.

27-32. *Adultery.*

28. **πρὸς τό.**—*Eo ut*, not *ita ut*, implying intention.

29. **εἰ δὲ ὁ ὀφθαλμός.**—*I.e.*, we are, if necessary, to abstain from or limit the use of the eyes and the hands. St Paul talks of "beating his body under the eye" (ὑπωπιάζω, 1 Cor. ix. 27), and of crucifying the flesh (Gal. v. 24), referring to unsparing self-discipline.

Tennyson seems to be expressing the need that some have of physical discipline to escape from evil thoughts, in "The Sailor Boy"—

> "My mother clings about my neck,
>   My sisters crying 'Stay for shame!'
> My father raves of death and wreck—
>   They are all to blame, they are all to blame.
> God help me save I take my part
>   Of danger on the roving sea—
> A devil rises in my heart,
>   Far worse than any death to me."

One of the old Fathers referring to the entertaining evil thoughts, says: "I cannot prevent a bird flying over my head, but I can prevent it nestling in my hair or biting off my nose."

σκανδαλίζει, from σκάνδαλον, a Biblical and ecclesiastical word for the classic σκανδάληθρον, "the crooked stick forming the part of the trap on which the bait is placed." Here it means, "is alluring thee to destruction." The present implies that the cutting off is not to be postponed till the mischief is done.

συμφέρει σοι.—"It is of importance to thee."

30. ἔκκοψον.—Josephus tells of his ordering a young man who had been ungrateful to him to be his own executioner and cut off one of his own hands, threatening him with the loss of both if he refused. We may illustrate Jesus' meaning by His words to Peter. That apostle was His right hand; yet when he was a σκάνδαλον to Him, He was ready to put him away from Him: Matt. xvi. 23, "Get thee behind me, Satan." Seneca says, "Cast out whatsoever rends thy heart: nay, if they could not be extracted otherwise, thou shouldst have plucked out thy heart itself with them."

31. ἐρρέθη.—Deut. xxiv. 1. The object of Moses was not to encourage divorces, but to throw impediments in their way by this formality. The Scribe only could write the bill, and would have an opportunity of suggesting a removal of misunderstanding. The legislation of Moses, therefore, was in the same direction with that of Jesus.

The reason allowed for a divorce was "some uncleanness." This the disciples of Rabbi Shammai interpreted of adultery, those of Hillel of anything that amounted to adultery in the eyes of the husband. Hillel is even thought to have maintained that a man might dismiss his wife for not cooking his dinner properly.

32. ποιεῖ αὐτήν.—I.e., if she marry again: the object of the ἀποστάσιον was to allow her to do this.

These words of Jesus had a slow but certain influence in sanctifying the marriage tie, which was slighted to a frightful extent among the Romans of His age. The Emperor Augustus vainly endeavoured to struggle against the licence exercised in divorces. Separation could be legally caused by either the husband or the wife, by a desire to divorce expressed in writing (*libellum repudii*). The Julian law deprived of this right women who provoked divorce, but without effect. Juvenal speaks of a woman who had eight husbands in five years, Seneca of daily divorces, and of illustrious and noble-born women who reckon their years not by the number of the consuls, but by that of their husbands. Cicero divorced Terentia in order to escape his creditors, by giving up to them the dowry of his new wife Publilia, whom again he afterwards repudiated. Seneca speaks of Mæcenas as having "married a thousand times." The Emperor Tiberius divorced his wife Vipsania in order to marry Julia, the daughter of Augustus. Messalina, the wife of the Emperor Claudius, compelled Caius Silius to divorce his wife, and then married him in her husband's absence. Nero divorced Octavia, who was afterwards murdered.

With such views of marriage, and with the practice of exposing children, there could be little of the beauty of family life such as we enjoy, and such indeed as was common among the Jews in Jesus' time and in earlier ages. Jesus, by His views here uttered about divorce, and by enrolling women among His disciples, and giving them tasks to perform and a dignity of character to maintain, and by the tender respect He showed towards them, brought about a revolution in the treatment of woman throughout the world.

The great saying of St Paul (1 Cor. vi. 19), that men's bodies are the temple of the Holy Ghost, and that any connection other than marriage defiles that temple, added further sanctity to the marriage tie, and therefore to the respect in which women were held.

Marriage was the only institution existing in His time to which Jesus ever referred in His words: in all other cases His words apply to principles.

LESSON VI.

THE SERMON ON THE MOUNT—St Matt. v. 33-48.

ON THE LOVE OF OUR NEIGHBOURS AND OF OUR ENEMIES.

33-37. *Oaths.*

33. ἐπιορκήσεις.—This refers to the Third Commandment, Exod. xx. 7; and to Lev. xix. 12, "Ye shall not swear by my name falsely, neither shalt thou profane the name of thy God;" and Deut. xxiii. 21.

The Pharisees seem to have held that an oath was not binding unless the name of God directly occurred in it, taking the passages from the Old Testament so literally as practically to add, "and whatsoever thou shalt swear not to the Lord may be transgressed." Cf. xxiii. 16.

In what follows, Jesus rests every oath on God, whether His name occurs or not, thus condemning all *frivolous* swearing by anything which could save men from taking God's name in vain. It appears that the Jews were much given to idle swearing—cf. Matt. xxvi. 74, where Peter, after the manner of a Galilean fisherman, heaps curses and imprecations on himself if he did not speak the truth. Dr Thomson, in the ' Land and the Book,' says they are so still. "No people that I have ever known can compare with these Orientals for profaneness in the use of the name and attributes of God. They swear by the head, by their life, by heaven, and by the temple, or, what is in its place, the church." We know, however, from the language in our streets, that Western nations have no right to look down with Pharisaic complacency on Orientals in this matter.

34. ὅλως.—Does this imply that oaths are under no circumstances to be taken ? Some of the greatest of the Fathers thought so, as do many Christians now. But (1) in the grammar of ver. 34 nothing more is necessarily implied than that oaths are not to be taken in the form mentioned ; (2) these forms were never employed in the Jewish law courts ; (3) solemn oaths were enjoined in the Old Testament ; (4) God is represented as putting Himself on oath, Gen. xxii. 16 ; Num. xiv. 28 ; Ps. cx. 4 ; (5) Jesus Himself accepted an oath, Matt. xxvi. 63, 64 ; (6) Paul makes frequent appeals to God after the manner of an oath, 2 Cor. i. 23 ; Rom. i. 9 ; 1 Cor. xv. 31 ; Gal. i. 20 ; (7) a godly man naturally looks up to God and appeals to Him as witness of his truthfulness. Cicero defines a *jusjurandum* as an *affirmatio religiosa.*

We must not, however, weaken the words of Jesus. Though His own practice and that of His disciples seem to show that He does not forbid oaths to be taken by His followers in their relations with those who are not Christians, or in solemn adjurations with one another, as children might appeal to a common father to attest their assertions, yet there can be no doubt that the letter as well as the spirit of His commands are best obeyed by a total abstinence from oaths. He seems to say that every man ought so to live that he does not need an oath to bring him back into the presence of God, his absence from God being the evil out of which oaths spring. Where evil is, there must oaths be, but Christians should be able to carry on their intercourse without them. Even oaths taken in solemn causes are below the Christian ideal, because they must spring from distrust. Liars are given to asseveration, and asseveration begets distrust.

The Stoics and the Essenes rejected oaths as inconsistent with self-respect ; Plato, Philo, Epictetus, and Maimonides allowed them to be used rarely.

θρόνος.—Cf. Isa. lxvi. 1, "The heaven is my throne, and the earth is my footstool."

35. **εἰs** is etymologically connected with *ἐν*, its original form being *ἐν s*. The *ἐν* implies that the oath cleaves to the object appealed to, the *εἰs* that the thought is directed towards it. In late Greek, the meanings of *ἐν* and *εἰs* were interchanged. The modern Greeks, in their popular speech, use *εἰs* only. Both *ἐν* and *εἰs* with *ὀμνύειν* are Hebraisms. The classical usage is *κατά τινος* or the acc. (James v. 12).

τοῦ μεγάλου βασιλέως—*i.e.*, of God. Ps. xlviii. 2.

37. **τοῦ πονηροῦ.**—Either *neut.* or *mas.*, "the evil one." See note on vi. 13.

38-42. *The law of retaliation.*

38. The statute, as it stands in Exod. xxi. 24, was addressed to judges—"Thou shalt give [*i.e.*, award] an eye for an eye, and a tooth for a tooth ;" but the Scribes seem to have quoted the words as if they ran thus, "Thou shalt rigidly exact for thyself an eye for an eye, and a tooth for a tooth "—*i.e.*, " be satisfied with nothing less."

As a law, it is common to the legislation of Moses and of Solon, and of the Twelve Tables, and of other ancient nations beside the Jews and Romans. It would make masters and rich men careful how they injured slaves and the poor : the prospect of losing a member would have a much more deterrent effect than that of paying a sum of money ; moreover, the law at all events limited the vengeance taken. There is, however, no record in Jewish history of the law having been literally carried out, and it is probable that in all nations a proportionate money fine was very early substituted as a rule for the bodily punishment,—the principle being observed by the judge inflicting a fine of a sum of money, whose worth represented as nearly as possible the value of the members lost by the injured person.

That the best of the Israelites understood the principle of forgiveness, is clear from David's conduct to Saul—1 Sam. xxiv., xxvi. 5-25 ; and from Ps. vii. 4 ; Lev. xix. 18 ; Prov. xxiv. 29, "Say not, I will do to him as he has done to me ; I will render to the man according to his work."

39. ἀντιστῆναι τῷ πονηρῷ.—The evil man, him who injures thee. See pp. 124-126.

ῥαπίζει.—This verb means primarily "to beat with a stick "; secondarily, "to strike with the hand": cf. John xviii. 22, 23 ; Acts xxiii. 3.

σιαγόνα.—Cf. Lamentations iii. 30 — δώσει τῷ παίοντι αὐτὸν σιαγόνα. Striking on the cheek was regarded as a great indignity. Seneca says, a slave would rather be scourged than so treated : but he also says, "What will the wise man do when he is buffeted [*colaphis percussus*] ? He will do as Cato did, when he was smitten on the mouth. He did not burst into a passion, did not avenge himself, did not even forgive it, but denied its having been done."

40. τῷ θέλοντι.—" Who is bent on."

κριθῆναι.—" To be brought before the judge," "to go to law": cf. 1 Cor. vi. 1.

χιτῶνα.—The narrow under garment: ἱμάτιον, the more expansive upper garment, a large square woollen robe, which was also used by the poor as a coverlet by night: hence the command, Exod. xxii. 26, not to detain it in pawn over night.

41. ἀγγαρεύσει. — Originally a Persian word. The Persian arrangements respecting post messages, instituted by Cyrus, justified the couriers (ἄγγαροι) in making requisitions from station to station of men, or cattle, or carriages for the carrying on of their journey—Herod., viii. 98. The Roman government exercised the same right over the provincials—cf. xxvii. 32, where Simon of Cyrene is pressed to carry Jesus' cross. The verb is found once in Menander. Epictetus (Discourses, iv. 1) says, "If there be a press (ἀγγαρεία), and a soldier should lay hold of your ass, let it go ; do not resist nor murmur."

μίλιον.—Distance is usually reckoned in the New Testament by furlongs : here only, in connection with the Roman military service, is the Roman measure (1680 yards) given. The word is late, found in Strabo.

42. **δανίσασθαι**—late Gr. for δανεισ. Jesus refers to lending for charity, not for trading. The injunction was a very necessary one in a primitive state of society, when articles of convenience were scarce, employment for the poor precarious, and there were no public institutions to make provision for them, and when, therefore, small sums of money would often be needed, either in gift or loan, to prevent actual starvation or immediate and utter destitution. In modern times, a loan is often truer charity than a gift, because it does not tend to destroy a man's independence and self-respect. The best gift to an idle beggar is a lecture on the sin of idleness. To one who asked Jesus to make his brother divide his inheritance with him, He answered by a lecture on the sin of covetousness—Luke xii. 14. The spirit of the precept seems to be, "Give that which will make the recipient truly richer." See note on Matt. xxv. 27, and cf. 1 Tim. v. 8.

ἀποστραφῇς.—The pass. has the force of the mid. The verb signifies, "to turn away from in dislike or disgust": cf. Heb. xii. 25.

43. The former clause is from Lev. xix. 18, where, however, the conception of neighbour is limited to the national frontier. The latter clause was an inference of the Scribes, who taught that the Gentile must be hated as the enemy of God. But though the Jews as a rule hated public enemies, and even extended their hatred to all foreigners, yet in the Old Testament magnanimous conduct towards the enemy is inculcated by example, 2 Kings vi. 22, where Elisha forbids the King of Israel to slay the Syrians, whom the prophet had led into the midst of Samaria. Kindness towards private enemies is enjoined by the Law—Lev. xix. 17, 18 ; and Exod. xxiii. 5, " If thou see the ass of him that hateth thee lying under his burden, and wouldest forbear to help him ; thou shalt surely help him."

44. **ἀγαπᾶτε.**—Hesiod inculcates the opposite view, ' Works and Days '—"Bid to thy feast a friend : a foe forbear." Socrates condemns the hatred of enemies, because of the reflexive evil on our own souls ; Plato, because our judgment as to who is our enemy may be wrong ; the Stoics, because a wise man ought not to be moved by any passion.

45. Cf. Seneca, De Benef., iv. 2-6, "If thou wouldest imitate the gods, do good even to the unthankful; for the sun rises on the wicked, and the seas are open to pirates:" and contrast Tobit iv. 15-17, "Do that to no man which thou hatest, and give nothing to the wicked;"—where the precept in the former clause is negative only, whereas that of Jesus is positive.

βρέχει.—Before the time of Alexander this was a poetic word for ὕει.

46. τελῶναι—i. e., men absolutely worldly. Some of these tax-gatherers were Romans, and some native Jews who were either in the service of Roman farmers of taxes as sub-farmers, or else (as seems to have been the case in Palestine at that time) were appointed directly by the government. They were detested, both on account of their unpatriotic occupation, and also because of the various unjust and oppressive means which they employed in order to obtain what was due to them. The Talmud classes publicans with thieves and assassins.

47. ἀσπάσησθε.—Salute lovingly as a symbol of the feeling of love. Tyndale translates, "If ye be friendly to." In Eur., Ion, 1363—ἴσον σ' ὡς τεκοῦσ' ἀσπάζομαι—it seems to mean, "cling fondly to." Plato couples it with φιλεῖν, as here it is used co-ordinately with ἀγαπήσατε, but in the New Testament it always means "saluting," and is never used of loving a person in Philo, though he uses the phrase ὁ νοῦς μόνωσιν ἀσπασάμενος, "the mind that delights in solitude."

περισσόν.—"Excellent deed more than they do": cf. xi. 9—περισσότερον προφήτου.

48. ἔσεσθε.—Equivalent to an imperative.

τέλειοι.—Full-grown—used in the New Testament of moral perfection: cf. Wisd. iv. 13, "He being made perfect in a short time, fulfilled a long time" (of Enoch): here, perfection as regards the comprehensiveness of our ἀγάπη—cf. Lev. xi. 44, xix. 2; Eph. v. 1. In Luke vi. 36 the phrase is οἰκτίρμονες.

Perfection is to be our aim; there is no assertion that it is attainable.

LESSON VII.

The Sermon on the Mount—St Matt. vi. 1-18.

A CRITICISM OF THE THREE FAVOURITE WAYS OF EXPRESSING PIETY
WHICH PREVAILED AT THE TIME—VIZ., ALMSGIVING, PRAYER,
AND FASTING.   HITHERTO JESUS HAD BEEN TEACHING HIS DIS-
CIPLES WHAT TO DO : HE NOW TELLS THEM HOW TO DO IT.

1-4. *Almsgiving.*

1. δικαιοσύνην.—This is here synonymous with ἐλεημοσύνην in
ver. 2. In several passages the LXX. renders the Hebrew word for
"righteousness" by "alms," and the latter is called "righteousness" in the Talmud.   In the later Hebrew usage δικαιοσύνη
came to mean "doing good" in the sense of kind actions : cf.
δίκαιος, chap. i. 19, which Chrysostom explains by χρηστός (kind).
Prov. xi. 4, "Riches profit not in the day of death, but righteousness delivereth from death."   Ps. cxii. 9, "He hath dispersed, He
hath given to the poor ; His righteousness endureth for ever."
Tobit xiv. 11, "Wherefore now, my son, consider what alms
doth, and how righteousness doth deliver."

πρός.—Cf. v. 17.

εἰ δὲ μήγε.—"But if you do not do what I say."

μισθόν.—This is an allusion to the Pharisaic teaching.

2. σαλπίσῃς. —The classic form would be σαλπίγξῃς.   The
phrase probably is metaphorical, as we say " trumpet forth," and
" blow your own trumpet."   Cf. Cic., Ad Div., xvi. 21, " te bucci-
natorem fore existimationis meæ."   The offertory chests in the
court of the women in the Temple are known to have been called
trumpets, from the shape of their mouths, and some have supposed that there is a reference to the money being ostentatiously
thrown into them, perhaps in such a way as to make them ring ;
but this would not apply to the synagogues or the streets.

ὑποκρίνομαι, " to answer," then " to take part in a dialogue,"
then " to act a part in a play."   The noun = an actor.   In LXX.
only in Job xxxvi. 13.

συναγωγή in classic Greek has an abstract meaning, " bringing
together of men or of the harvest," " a wrinkling of the face."   In
LXX. and the New Testament " assembly," then " synagogue."
In the synagogues alms were collected before prayers.

ῥύμη, from ῥέω, in classic Greek = a rushing, then "a going," then "a narrow street": cf. "alley," from Fr. *aller*, which is connected with *adnare*, "to swim to." In the East the streets are narrow, so that people can be better observed than with us.

ἀπέχουσι, "have in full": cf. ἀπέλαβες, Luke xvi. 25, and Phil. iv. 18, ἀπέχω πάντα καὶ περισσεύω.

3. ἀριστερά.—Seneca says, "One ought so to give that another may receive. It is not giving or receiving, to transfer to the right hand from the left;" and, again, "This is the law of a good deed between two: the one ought at once to forget that it was conferred, the other never to forget that it was received."

5-15. *Prayer.*

5. ἑστῶτες.—There is no emphasis on the word. The Eastern practice in the synagogues, and for a time in the early Christian churches, was to stand with uplifted hands.

6. ταμεῖον—classic ταμιεῖον—the upper room, used as a store-house, or for lodging strangers, or for religious duties or discussions, as greater privacy could be ensured in it. Cf. Isa. xxvi. 20, εἴσελθε εἰς τὰ ταμεῖα σου, ἀπόκλεισον τὴν θύραν σου. Ps. iv. 4, "Commune with your own heart upon your bed, and be still."

7. βατταλογέω.—The allusion is to the repeated attempts of the stammerer: the word is derived by onomatopœia. It is explained afterwards by πολυλογία. "Battalos" was a nickname of Demosthenes.

δοκοῦσι.—There was a Rabbinical saying, "He who prays long is certain to receive something."

πολυλογία.—Elsewhere we are told that Jesus taught that men ought always to pray, and not to faint—Luke xviii. 1; and He is said Himself to have spent all night in prayer. His protest here is not against hearty prayers, but against unmeaning wordiness in prayer. Prayer is to be the heartfelt communion with a Being we love, not a wordy attempt to prevail over the will of a Being we dread. οὕτως introduces an example of the manner.

9. πάτερ.—God is termed the Father of the nation of Israel in Isa. lxiii. 16: "Thou, O Lord, art our Father, our Redeemer." He is compared to a father in Ps. ciii. 13: "Like as a father pitieth his children, so the Lord pitieth them that fear Him." He is addressed as Father in Wisd. xiv. 3: "Thy providence, O Father, governeth it" (the ship); and in ii. 16, the righteous is

represented as making his boast that God is his Father; and in Ecclus. xxiii. 1, "O Lord, Father and Governor of all my whole life." Jesus Himself used the phrase as the name of God, Mark xiv. 36; and by His life and teaching has influenced man so to regard God. He uses the term to the disciples only, never to the multitude.

ἡμῶν.—The Christian in his prayers is to think of all his brothers.

οὐρανοῖς.—In the Old Testament "heaven and earth" is (1) a phrase implying the universal presence of God. Gen. xiv. 22, "The Lord, the most high God, the possessor of heaven and earth." Deut. iv. 39, "The Lord He is God in heaven above, and upon the earth beneath." (2) Subsequently the heaven denoted the idea of distance from God,—Eccles. v. 2, "God is in heaven, and thou upon earth, therefore let thy words be few." (3) Then the idea of space being dropt, the word came to mean the invisible, infinite, and absolute. The religious spirit of all nations has by an unconscious symbolism regarded the ether in its depth and repose, in its boundlessness and unchangeableness, as the dwelling-place of Deity. Aristotle, De Cœlo, πάντες ἄνθρωποι τὸν ἀνωτάτω τῷ θείῳ τόπον ἀποδιδόασι. Job xxii. 14, "He walketh in the circuit of heaven."

. ἁγιασθήτω.—Holiness is an attribute of God's name throughout the Bible: cf. Lev. xxii. 32, "Neither shall ye profane my holy name; but I will be hallowed among the children of Israel: I am the Lord which hallow you." Isa. xxix. 23, "They shall sanctify my name." Ezek. xxxvi. 23, "I will sanctify my great name."

ὄνομα.—The "name" was used by the Jews as a substitute for God. Traces of this usage are found in Acts v. 41, ὑπὲρ τοῦ ὀνόματος ἀτιμασθῆναι; and 3 John, 7.

The "name" of God sums up all our thoughts of God. To hallow God's name, therefore, is to have holy and noble thoughts about God.

10. ἡ βασιλεία.—The coming of the kingdom and the sanctification of the name are brought together in Zech. xiv. 9: "And the Lord shall be King over all the earth: in that day shall there be one Lord, and His name one." The Rabbis said, "Any benediction which is without mention of God as King is no benediction at all."

The ideal kingdom had been described in Isa. xi. 1-6, xlii. 1-7; Dan. vii. 14.

The coarser-minded Jews, as Judas the Galilean, looked upon

the "kingdom" as the establishment of a material rule of their nation in Palestine, to be brought about by the sword. But Jesus never had recourse to force of any kind, never hinted a threat against the Roman rule, and never even predicted its end. St Paul defines the kingdom of God as being "not eating and drinking ; but righteousness, and peace, and joy in the Holy Spirit" —Rom. xiv. 17. This kingdom is progressive, and its progress is dependent on the influence of the Spirit of God on the spirit of man.

We may perhaps find a point of distinction between this clause and the next in this way. The "kingdom" would have come if all men everywhere acknowledged God as King by resolving to do His will and earnestly endeavouring to do so. Then men would have no hindrance to doing the will from one another's wilfulness or selfishness : they would still, however, need to pray for strength against their own passions and impulses. Thus the first clause refers rather to social arrangements, the latter to our own souls.

τὸ θέλημα.—Cf. Ps. cxxxv. 6, "Whatsoever the Lord pleased, that did He in heaven and in earth."

11. τὸν ἄρτον.—Jesus' hearers would think of the description of the giving of the manna in Exod. xvi. 4: "Behold, I will rain bread from heaven for you" (the petition in the prayer is addressed to "our Father in heaven "); "and the people shall go out and gather τὸ τῆς ἡμέρας εἰς ἡμέραν, a certain rate every day." Cf. 2 Kings xxv. 30, λόγον ἡμέρας ἐν τῇ ἡμέρᾳ αὐτοῦ. Jer. lii. 34, ἐξ ἡμέρας εἰς ἡμέραν. Dan. i. 5, τὸ τῆς ἡμέρας εἰς ἡμέραν. In the parallel passage in St Luke (xi. 3), we have τὸ καθ' ἡμέραν. The manna is frequently spoken of as "the bread from heaven," —Ps. lxxviii. 24, cv. 40 ; Neh. ix. 15 ; Wisd. xvi. 20.

ἐπιούσιον.—This word is nowhere else found in all literature excepting in the parallel passage in Luke xi. 3, and was perhaps coined to express some Aramaic word used by Jesus, who may have been referring to 2 Kings xxv. 30, "A daily rate for every day all the days of his life": cf. Jer. lii. 34.

Two derivations have been suggested for the word: I. From ἐπί and οὐσία. In this case it will mean "food necessary for our subsistence." Cf. Prov. xxx. 8, "Give me neither poverty nor riches : feed me with food convenient for me." James ii. 16, "Things which are needful for the body." The objections to this are (1) that the form would be ἐπούσιος, not ἐπιούσιος; (2) that οὐσία does not mean *subsistence*, but essence, reality, and possessions; (3) that there was no need to coin a word to express this idea for which other words, as ἐπιτήδειος, existed.

II. From ἐπί, ἰέναι, either from (1) mas. part., ὁ ἐπιών, sc. χρόνος, or (2) fem. part., ἡ ἐπιοῦσα, sc. ἡμέρα.

(1) In the former case it will mean " of the future," either (α) the remote future in the sense of " eternal, heavenly, or spiritual "; but this would have been expressed rather by ἐπουράνιος, αἰώνιος, or μέλλων; or simply (β) of the immediate future = " bread which is successive or continual," and we may illustrate the idea from John vi. 34, " πάντοτε δὸς ἡμῖν τὸν ἄρτον τοῦτον " ; and Ps. xl. 11, " Let Thy loving-kindness and Thy truth *continually* preserve me "; and the combination with σήμερον—*i.e.*, the prayer that in each day so much only may be given as is needful for that day, from 2 Kings xxv. 29, 30, " And he did eat bread *continually* before him all the days of his life.   And his allowance was a *continual* allowance given him of the king, *a daily rate for every day all the days of his life*."   Cf. also Exod. xxix. 38, " day by day continually "; Num. xxviii. 3, " day by day for a continual offering "; Isa. lii. 5, " My name continually every day is blasphemed."

(2) If it come from ἡ ἐπιοῦσα it will mean " to-morrow's "; and this explanation is supported historically by the fact that Jerome found the Hebrew for " morrow's " in the lost Gospel of St Matthew to the Hebrews, and that it would be necessary to coin a Greek word to translate it, as there is no adjective in Greek to express it.   Moreover, " to-morrow " is expressed by ἡ ἐπιοῦσα in Prov. xxvii. 1, and τῇ ἐπιούσῃ ἡμέρᾳ in Acts vii. 26.   If it be objected that we are taught in verse 34 " to take no thought for the morrow," it may be answered that this prayer obeys the precept, since in it we cast all our care upon God (1 Pet. v. 7) —see the note on that verse.   We may paraphrase the clause, " Enable us to earn to-day sufficient for our morrow's wants." Thus rendered, the petition becomes peculiarly appropriate in the lips of the poor, who are the great majority in all communities, whose earnings, like those of the fishermen apostles, are precarious, and who of necessity live from hand to mouth.   To have put into the lips of such men a prayer for a more distant provision, would have been to bid them ask for an alteration of the conditions of society.

σήμερον.—This seems to assume that the prayer is offered in the early morning. The word is beautifully illustrated by Wisd. xvi. 27, 28, "That [of the manna] which was not destroyed by fire, being warmed with a little sunbeam, soon melted away: that it might be known that we must prevent the sun to give Thee thanks, and at the day-spring pray unto Thee"—where the Israelites are taught the lesson of early prayer, from their being compelled to gather the manna before the sun grew hot and melted it. Cf. Ps. v. 3, "In the morning will I direct my prayer unto Thee"; lxiii. 1, "Early will I seek Thee"; lxxxviii. 13, "In the morning shall my prayer prevent [anticipate] Thee." Josephus tells us of the Essenes that they lifted up their hands and prayed as soon as they saw the sun beginning to rise.

12. ὡς καὶ ἡμεῖς ἀφήκαμεν.—The aorist implies that the petitioner has already forgiven those who are indebted to him: cf. the πρῶτον in chap. v. 24 ; and Ecclus. xxviii. 2-4, "Forgive thy neighbour the hurt that he hath done unto thee, so shall thy sins also be forgiven when thou prayest. One man beareth hatred against another, and doth he seek pardon of the Lord? He showeth no mercy to a man which is like himself: and doth he ask forgiveness of his own sins?"

13. πειρασμόν.—From πειράζω, the usual meaning of which is to *test* or *try:* in this sense God "tempted" Abraham; and πειρασμός is used to express this "testing" in 1 Macc. ii. 52; Ecclus. xliv. 20. So the author of Ecclus. (vi. 7) advises, "If thou wouldst get a friend prove him first, and be not hasty to credit him"; and Jesus (John vi. 6) "tempts" Philip. This putting to the proof may have a good or a bad motive. In the former sense our whole lives are a probation or πειρασμός,—we are daily undergoing πειρασμοί, or being tested whether we prefer duty to pleasure. In the latter sense Satan is said to tempt (as he did Job), and men and boys tempt one another with the view to lead into sin. In the former sense temptation develops and displays nobility of character, as tests of skill or strength do physical prowess, and it is difficult to conceive of virtue without such tests. In the latter sense temptation is intended to ruin and mar the character, just as the temptation to a break-neck physical feat is intended to slay the body. From such tests men are taught to pray that they may be freed. They result either from the circumstances by which we are surrounded, or

from the desires and passions within us. There can be no exact limit placed between the test or temptation that strengthens and that which ruins the character. What each man can bear depends on his own spiritual condition and nearness to God. When St James (i. 13) says, God " tempteth not any man, but every man is tempted when he is drawn away of his own lust and enticed," he seems to be referring to temptation with hostile intent, and warning his hearers against laying the blame of their sins on the circumstances which God has placed them in, and therefore on God. In the latter sense of testing, all the circumstances of life tempt—*i.e.*, are part of our probation. St Paul seeks to console the Corinthians under the difficulties connected with the subject when he says (1 Cor. x. 13), "There hath no temptation taken you but such as is common to man " (or "as is measured to man's strength "): "but God is faithful, who will not suffer you to be tempted above that ye are able ; but will with the temptation also make a way to escape, that ye may be able to bear it."

Jesus seems to refer to this clause of the prayer in the Garden of Gethsemane, when He says to the disciples (Matt. xxvi. 41), "Watch and pray that ye enter not into temptation"; and Himself recognised that His Father was tempting Him, and yet prayed against the temptation when He cried (ver. 42), "O my Father, if this cup may not pass from me except I drink it, Thy will be done."

We may paraphrase the clause thus: "If the occasion of sinning present itself, grant that the desire may not be found in us; if the desire is there, grant that the occasion may not present itself."

ῥῦσαι.—This is a Homeric and military term, meaning primarily "to draw to one's self," then "to rescue." It occurs in Ps. vii. 1, "O Lord my God, in Thee do I put my trust: save me from all them that persecute me, and deliver me " (ῥῦσαι). In Wisd. xvi. 8, God is said to be ὁ ῥυόμενος ἐκ παντὸς κακοῦ. In 2 Tim. iv. 18, there is a reminiscence of this passage: ῥύσεταί με ὁ Κύριος ἀπὸ παντὸς ἔργου πονηροῦ, καὶ σώσει εἰς τὴν βασιλείαν αὐτοῦ τὴν ἐπουράνιον· ᾧ ἡ δόξα εἰς τοὺς αἰῶνας τῶν αἰώνων. ἀμήν.

πονηροῦ. This may be either mas. or neut. The passages above quoted seem to favour the neut. In Gen. xlviii. 16, Jacob speaks of ὁ ἄγγελος ὁ ῥυόμενός με ἐκ πάντων τῶν κακῶν. On the other hand, in Ps. cxxxix. 1, we read ἀπὸ ἀνδρὸς ἀδίκου ῥῦσαί με. We have πονηρός mas. in chap. xiii. 19 and 1 John ii. 13, v. 18. We have the neut. in Eccles. viii. 11, 12. If the word be mas., it does not necessarily follow that the allusion is to Satan alone; cf. v. 39, μὴ ἀντιστῆναι τῷ πονηρῷ. The following clause in a Talmudic prayer illustrates the phrase: "May it be Thy will, O Lord our God, and the God of our fathers, to deliver us from the shameless and from shamelessness: from evil man and from evil hap: from evil companion, from evil neighbour, and from Satan the destroyer."

We may safely paraphrase thus: "Rescue us from all the evil influences in the universe, whether they be known to us or unknown."

St Clement of Rome gives us a very ancient paraphrase in the words, "that we should be rescued from every sin, and from those that hate us unjustly."

14. Cf. Lev. xix. 18; Prov. xx. 22; Ecclus. xxviii. 1, "He that revengeth shall find vengeance from the Lord, and He will surely keep his sins in remembrance."

16-18.—*Fasting.*

16. σκυθρωποί.—This word seems to imply sadness combined with squalor in dress and appearance. Cf. Philo, De Leg. ad Cai., μεθέμενοι τόν ἀβροδίαιτον βίον ἐσκυθρώπαζον: and, σκυθρωπάζων μὲν τῷ προσώπῳ, μειδιῶν δὲ τῇ διανοίᾳ.

ἀφανίζουσι probably means to make unseen—i. c., partly by sprinkling themselves with ashes, and by the dirt on the unwashed face and beard, and partly by actually veiling themselves. Cf. 2 Sam. xv. 30, where David in his grief covers his head, as does Haman in Esth. vi. 12. In Ælian we read, ἀφανίζειν τρίχα βαφῇ, "disguising the hair by dyeing." Some have thought that there was a play of words with φανῶσι which follows; but this could hardly be, as Jesus would not speak Greek.

φανῶσι.—"May be seen." The warning is against ostentation, not hypocrisy.

νηστεύοντες.—The Pharisees fasted on Thursday, when Moses was supposed to have ascended Mount Sinai, and on Monday, when he was believed to have come down again. Mourning attire was worn during the fasting. See note on Luke xviii. 12.

17. ἄλειψαι.—Cf. Luke vii. 46. Anointing was a sign of joy. Other signs may be adopted now.

ADDITIONAL NOTE ON THE LORD'S PRAYER.

The Lord's Prayer consists of seven clauses, the first three of which bear upon God's relation to man, and the last four on man's relation to God. In the first three the pronoun σου occurs in an emphatic position; in the last four, the first person plural. The prayer may be thus arranged,—it may be entitled

THE DESIRE FOR THE KINGDOM OF GOD.

PART I.—GOD'S RELATION TO MAN.

God's Kingdom advancing to Completion: Man's Will working with God's.

Thy Name be hallowed:—Prayer for right ideas about God.

Thy kingdom come to us:—Prayer for the carrying out of God's will in the external arrangements of the world.

Thy will be done:—Prayer for the carrying out of God's will in our own hearts.

PART II.—MAN'S RELATION TO GOD.

Removal of the Impediments to the Kingdom.

To us give to-morrow's bread:—Removal of the fear of earthly want.

To us forgive sins:—Removal of the fear of God.

Us lead not into temptation:—Removal of the danger of doing wrong arising from our own passions.

Us deliver from evil:—Removal of the danger of doing wrong arising from external influences.

PARAPHRASE OF THE LORD'S PRAYER.

My Father, and Father of my brother men, listen from Thy pure home in heaven to Thy child who cries to Thee from the sinful earth for his brothers and himself. Fill our souls with holy and noble thoughts of Thee, that we may know Thy will, and so obey Thee more and more every day, till we shall all so love Thee, and be so holy, that we shall find it easy to do Thy will, having no hindrance from one another's selfishness or unholiness.

And that we may have less temptation to be selfish, teach us to look to Thee to supply our daily wants, and grant that we may neither by poverty be led to despair of Thy care for us, nor by riches be led to forgetfulness of Thee. Make our love for one another so perfect that we may continue to love even those who injure us; and do not Thou cast us out from Thy love when we do wrong, that so our love for Thee may be without fear. And that we may not do wrong, if the occasion of sinning presents itself, grant that the desire may not be found in us; if the desire is there, grant that the occasion may not present itself. Rescue us from all the evil influences in the universe, whether they be known to us or unknown.

LESSON VIII.

The Sermon on the Mount—St Matt. vi. 19-34.

THE KINGDOM IS TO BE THE DISCIPLES' FIRST CARE.

19. **θησαυρίζετε.**—Cf. the phrase πλουτεῖν εἰς θεόν in Luke xii. 21; and Seneca, Ep. Mir., cx. 18, "Apply thyself rather to the true riches; it is shameful to depend for a happy life on silver and gold." That this precept was not understood absolutely, and does not imply improvidence, is evident from St Paul's words in 1 Cor. vii. 30, 31—οἱ ἀγοράζοντες ὡς μὴ κατέχοντες καὶ οἱ χρώμενοι τὸν κόσμον ὡς μὴ καταχρώμενοι: "Those that buy as though they possessed not, and those that use the world as not using it to the full"; and 2 Cor. xii. 14, "The children ought not to lay up (θησαυρίζειν) for the parents, but the parents for the children."

σής.—Jewish wealth consisted in a great measure of apparel: cf. 2 Kings v. 22.

βρῶσις.—"Eating, corroding," hence "rust;" in classic Greek = (1) eating, (2) food. Cf. James v. 2, 3, "Your riches are corrupted, and your garments are moth-eaten (σητόβρωτα). Your gold and silver is cankered; and the rust of them shall be a witness against you."

ἀφανίζει.—"Causes to disappear, annihilates." Cf. Ar. Nub., 971—ὡς τὰς Μούσας ἀφανίζων. Cf. v. 17.

διορύσσουσι.—Cf. Job xxv. 16, "In the dark they dig through houses which they had marked for themselves in' the day-time." Houses in the East were for the most part built of soft unbaked bricks or of clay. The Greek for a burglar is τοιχωρύχος. For the sense cf. Seneca, De Vit. Beat., "Let thy good deeds be invested like a treasure deep buried in the ground, which thou canst not bring to light unless it be necessary."

22. ὁ λύχνος.—"The lamp which holds the light." This clause is a proverb; what follows is the inference: cf. Arist., Top., i. 14— ὡς ὄψις ἐν ὀφθαλμῷ, νοῦς ἐν ψυχῇ.

ὁ ὀφθαλμός.—The eye in the Scriptures is used metaphorically as the organ of inward knowledge: cf. Ps. cxix. 18, "Open Thou mine eyes, that I may behold wondrous things out of Thy law." Eph. i. 18, "The eyes of your understanding being opened."

It seems necessary to take the word here in the metaphorical sense, because ἁπλοῦς never refers to physical, but always to moral integrity. ἁπλότης καρδίας occurs in 1 Chron. xxix. 17; Eph. vi. 5; Wisd. i. 1. On the other hand, the occurrence of σῶμα immediately afterwards seems either to blend the metaphor with literalism, or to point to ἁπλοῦς having a literal signification. There is a similar blending in Prov. xx. 27, to which this passage seems to refer—"The spirit of man is the candle of the Lord, searching all the inward parts (or chambers) of the belly." This seems decisive in favour of taking ἁπλοῦς in a moral signification. In this case, the passage will mean, "If your spiritual eye is sound, it will give light to all your spiritual members"—i.e., if your conscience or power of discriminating between good and evil is unimpaired, then it will afford you light to judge all your motives, and decide on all the details of your conduct. A man's conscience may be perverted, so that he may cease to have the power of discerning between good and evil—may put "light for darkness," and "darkness for light."

24. ἀνθέξεται.—Cf. Pindar, N. I., 20—ἀντέχεσθαι Ἡρακλέους, " to worship Hercules above all "; and Tit. i. 9.

μαμωνᾷ.—A Chaldee word, meaning "riches." It seems here to be personified, and taken as an idol.

25. μὴ μεριμνᾶτε.—See the following Essay.

26.—τὰ πετεινά.—We may here think of Jesus pointing to birds flying overhead.

τοῦ οὐρανοῦ.—This phrase points to the careless freedom of

the birds: cf. Ps. viii. 9, civ. 12. μᾶλλον is redundant, and strengthens the verb.

27. ἡλικίαν means first "age," then "stature" as indicating age. Here it is more likely to be the former than the latter, because men are more likely to want to add to their years than to their height; besides, a cubit would be an extraordinary addition to height, whereas the rhetoric of the passage requires a very small amount. On the other hand, the word in the New Testament quite as often means "stature" as age—cf. Luke ii. 52; and a man by care may lengthen his days, but cannot add to his height.

28. κρίνα are lilies of any kind, λείρια are white lilies: the former word is invariably used in the LXX. The flower alluded to is probably the *Lilium chalcedonicum*, or Scarlet Martagon, which abounds in Galilee during April or May; an illustration of this is given under "Lily" in the 'Dictionary of the Bible.' Lips are compared to lilies in the Song of Solomon, v. 13, but we cannot tell whether the comparison there is to the colour or the fragrance.

αὐξάνουσι.—After a neut. plural we should expect the singular: the reason for the plural here seems to be that the lilies are almost personified.

30. σήμερον ὄντα.—The south wind will parch the lily in twenty - four hours: cf. Horace's "breve lilium" — Odes, I. xxxvi. 16.

τὸν χόρτον.—"Grass," under which head lilies which grow in grass are included.

κλίβανον, Att. κρίβανον—Dried grass was used as fuel for heating ovens. Philo uses κλίβανον.

βαλλόμενον.—The present (instead of the future) brings the action done on the morrow more vividly before the eyes.

34. ἡ κακία.—"Trouble," a Hellenistic use of the word: cf. Eccles. xii. 1, Remember now thy Creator in the days of thy youth, while the evil days (αἱ ἡμέραι τῆς κακίας) come not. Amos iii. 6: cf. Epictet., Enchirid., 14 — θέλεις τὴν κακίαν μὴ εἶναι κακίαν ἀλλ' ἄλλο τι, "You wish trouble not to be trouble, but something else"—the allusion being to the loss of relatives.

LESSON IX.

THE SERMON ON THE MOUNT—St Matt. vii. 1-14.

ON JUDGMENT ON OTHERS, ON PRAYER, AND THE ENTRANCE INTO THE KINGDOM.

1-5. *On judgment on others.*

1. μὴ κρίνετε.—It is clear that this precept is not to be taken without qualification, for Jesus bids us "know men by their fruits," and "judge righteous judgment" (John vii. 24) ; and St Paul says, "there are some sins which are manifest, going before unto judgment"—1 Tim. v. 24. It is a warning against judgments that are prejudiced, uncalled for, one-sided, and unmerciful. It is directed against those who are always ready to attribute lower rather than higher motives to men's actions, against the cynics and the censorious, the malevolent and the idle: cf. the proverb, "Ill doers are ill deemers." The precept is not directed against the spirit of honest criticism, which is the attempt to judge right, and as such, is the result of the spirit of truth working within us.

2. κριθήσεσθε.—Cf. Ps. xviii. 26, "With the froward Thou wilt show Thyself froward." Not that God will judge us unfairly because we judge others unfairly, but that we shall suffer from our imperfect love in the future state.

ἐν ᾧ μέτρῳ.—Love and generosity beget love and generosity.

3. κάρφος.—A minute fragment of twig, wood, or straw, the figurative representation of a slight moral fault, as δοκός of a serious fault: transient anger may illustrate the former, hatred the latter. Cf. Seneca, De Vit. Beat., 27, "Do ye mark the pimples of others, being covered with countless ulcers? This is as if a person should mock at the moles or warts on the most beautiful persons, when he himself is devoured by a fierce scab." It must be remembered, however, that one man may rebuke his Christian brother in love, while another may refrain from rebuking him out of cold indifference.

6. τὸ ἅγιον.—The meat which had been offered in sacrifice: cf. Lev. xxii. 10, "There shall no stranger eat of the holy thing (τὰ ἅγια): a sojourner of the priest, or an hired servant, shall not eat of the holy thing."

κυσί—χοίρων.—Dogs and swine were traditional names for the Gentiles, and also for impure and vulgar-minded men generally: cf. 2 Pet. ii. 22, "The dog is turned to his own vomit again ; and the sow that was washed to her wallowing in the mire." Phil. iii. 2, "Beware of dogs"—*i.e.*, of impure men.

Those men are meant to whom, on account of their impurity and selfishness, it is useless to talk on the subject of religion, unless, indeed, something softens them. The Christian must use discretion. Jesus Himself declined to answer when His answer would have been misunderstood—chap. xxvii. 12-14.

ἐν τοῖς ποσίν.—With their feet. Probably this verse is an example of Chiasmus — the fourth line, the turning about and rending, referring to the dogs in the first ; the third, to the swine in the second : cf. "Macbeth," ii. 2 :

> "O horror ! horror ! horror !
> Tongue nor heart cannot conceive nor name thee ;"

—*i.e.*, tongue cannot name nor heart conceive. See p. 37.

7-14. *On Prayer.*

7. The figure here is explained by its context in the parallel passage in Luke xi. 5-10, where it follows the parable of the man who knocks at his friend's door at midnight asking the loan of three loaves, which is granted to his importunity. Of Jesus Himself it is said, that while He was praying, He saw the heaven opened (Luke iii. 21), though, of course, we need not regard this literally. The figure of knocking occurs in Luke xiii. 25, where κρούειν is followed by τὴν θύραν, as usual in the classics.

ζητεῖτε is illustrated from Jer. xxix. 12, 13, "Then shall ye call upon me, and ye shall go and pray unto me, and I will hearken unto you. And ye shall seek me and find me, when ye shall search for me with all your heart."

The three words do not seem to refer to different objects of prayer, but contain three different figures exhorting to urgency.

8. Jesus here speaks absolutely, giving no limitations. He was speaking as an orator to the multitude, and seeking to inspire them with hope and confidence in their heavenly Father : subsequently He and His disciples taught the limitations to the subjects of prayer. He Himself did not obtain the answer to His prayer in the way He asked for it—Matt. xxvi. 39 ; St James

(iv. 3) declares that unworthy prayers will not be answered—
"Ye ask and receive not, because ye ask amiss, that ye may consume it upon your lusts." In this passage, the word ἀγαθά—cf.
ver. 11—suggests a limitation. Men cannot tell what are ἀγαθά
to them. See the Essay on Prayer, p. 63.

9. Here is a change of construction, or anacolouthon. The interrogative sentence beginning with τίς is interrupted by μή,
which is redundant. Translate, "Or what man is there among
you of whom his son shall ask a loaf, he will not give him a
stone, will he?"

A stone in size and shape might be like the thin and flat
loaves of the East: Satan tempts Jesus to turn stones into
loaves, iv. 3.

10. A serpent, which resembles some fish, as eels. Loaves, hard
eggs, and dried fish are the traveller's fare in the East.

11. ὄντες.—"Although ye are.'

ἀγαθά.—In Luke xi. 13, "the Holy Spirit" is substituted.

12. οὖν.—This may sum up the whole sermon, and refer back
to v. 17, as the clause, "for this is the law and the prophets," seems
to hint. We may compare with it the οὖν of v. 48. It may
refer, however, to vii. 1-5.

οὕτως καί.—According to the Talmud, the great Rabbi Hillel, who
died when Jesus was a boy, was asked by a heathen to make him a
convert by teaching him the entire Law while he stood on one foot,
and answered, "That which is hateful to thyself, do it not to thy
neighbour; for this is the entire Law—the rest is commentary."
And in Tobit iv. 15 we have the negative form of the precept,
"That which thou hatest, do to no man." The Greek orator
Isocrates had said in the same negative way, "What stirs your
anger, when done to you by others, that do not to others. Seneca the Stoic philosopher, again, "Expect from others what you
do to others," "Let us so give as we would wish to receive." Confucius, the religious reformer of China, who flourished from 550-
478 B.C., said, "What you do not like when done to yourself, do
not to others." The precept of Jesus differs from these in being
positive.

13. There is probably an allusion here to the smaller gates
which were to be found at intervals in the wall of an Eastern city,
or to the doors sometimes made in the larger gates to admit
people one by one when the gate itself was closed. The gates are

not entrances to the ways, but the ways lead to the gates. The wide gate and the broad way represent the entrance to the life of pleasure, "the primrose path of dalliance," which is not fenced in by any consideration for the feelings of others or the laws of God: the strait gate and narrow way, the effort and self-denial which Christian duty imposes. Cf. Philo, De Vict., ἐντραπόμενος τῆς ἐπ' ἀρετὴν καὶ καλοκαγαθίαν ἀγούσης ὁδοῦ. and the remarkable parallel in the Tabula Cebetis, where the πύλη stands at the end of the ὁδός—οὐκοῦν ὁρᾷς θύραν τινα μικράν, καὶ ὁδόν τινα πρὸ τῆς θύρας ἥτις οὐ πολὺ ὀχλεῖται, ἀλλ' ὀλίγοι πάνυ πορεύονται· αὕτη ἐστὶν ἡ ὁδὸς ἡ ἄγουσα πρὸς τὴν ἀληθινὴν παιδείαν.

14. τεθλιμμένη (θλίβω). — "Confined." Cf. Theoc., xxi. 18, θλιβομένα καλύβα, " a small, close hut," or as some take it, "a hut confined in a bay between two headlands," a meaning which would better illustrate our passage. Plutarch uses the verb of a man's shoe pinching him.

LESSON X.

The Sermon on the Mount—St Matt. vii. 15-29.

15-23.—*The Guides to the Way.*

15. ἐν ἐνδύμασι προβάτων.—Not literally, but "with a guileless appearance." It is explained by 2 Cor. xi. 13—ἐργάται δόλιοι, μετασχηματιζόμενοι εἰς ἀποστόλους Χριστοῦ. For the use of ἐν cf. Æn. v. 37, "Horridus in jaculis et pelle Libystidis ursæ."

λύκοι ἅρπαγες.—Cf. John x. 12 and Acts xx. 29, where St Paul seems to be referring to this passage.

16. ἀπὸ τῶν, κ.τ.λ.—This is repeated in ver. 20, after a manner common in Jesus' teaching.

τριβόλων.—This is first an adjective, meaning "three-pointed," then a substantive, "a three-spiked instrument"; and so "a burr or thistle." The buckthorn and a species of cactus simulating the grape and the fig remain to point the proverb. Cf. Seneca, Ep. Mor., xxxvii. 24, 25, "Good things cannot spring of evil; . . . good does not grow of evil, any more than a fig of an olive-tree. The fruits correspond to the seed."

17. **ἀγαθόν.**—Sound.

18. **οὐ δύναται.**—A climax on the preceding verse.

19. **μὴ ποιοῦν.**—If it does not produce.

21-29.—Conclusion ;—on the Hearers.

22. **ἐκείνῃ τῇ ἡμέρᾳ.**—Probably a reference to Isa. ii. 2, 11, 12, 20, in which chapter the phrase "that day" recurs like a refrain.

ἐπροφητεύσαμεν.—The augment comes before the preposition, as the verb is not a compound, but from subst. προφήτης, as βασιλεύω, δουλεύω. Prophecy does not here mean "foretelling." The word is derived from πρό in the sense of "instead of," and means "one who speaks for God," and interprets His will to man. In classic Greek it was applied to the interpreters of the pagan oracles, who expounded the unintelligible answers of the Pythoness of Delphi, or of the rustling of the leaves at Dodona. In a metaphorical sense it is used of poets as interpreters of the gods or muses. It was then adopted by the LXX. as the best equivalent of the "nabi" or "seer" of the Old Testament. The office of the prophet of the New Testament is defined in 1 Cor. xiv. 3, 24, 25, to be "building up, exhorting, and comforting," and "convincing, judging, and making manifest the secrets of the heart." The title of Jeremy Taylor's book on "The Liberty of Prophesying" means "the Liberty of Preaching." The word here is best rendered "preached" = prædicare, not prædicere.

23. **ἔγνων.**—Cf. John x. 14 : "I am the good shepherd, and know my sheep, and am known of mine." It is love that creates this knowledge.

οἱ ἐργαζόμενοι.—Cf. Ps. vi. 8 : ἀπόστητε ἀπ' ἐμοῦ πάντες οἱ ἐργαζόμενοι τὴν ἀνομίαν.

24. **φρονίμῳ.**—"Prudent." Cf. xxv. 2.

25. Notice the Hebraistic form of the narrative in the sentences co-ordinated by καί. "Down came the rain, and on rushed the torrents, and blew the winds," &c. Contrast the form in Luke vi. 48 : see p. 37.

τεθεμελίωτο.—The New Testament has usually no augment in the plup.

26 **τὴν ἄμμον.**—Dean Stanley, in 'Sinai and Palestine,' illustrates this from the rising of the Kishon described in Judges v. 21, 22, and says the locality best fitted for the scene is the long sandy strip of land which bounds the eastern plain of Acre, and

through which the Kishon flows into the sea. In Palestine the dry beds of the torrents are rapidly and suddenly filled by the streams that flow down the mountains after rain.

27. **προσέκοψαν.**—"Assailed," more vigorous than *προσέπεσον* in ver. 25.

29. **οἱ γραμματεῖς**—who always quoted the authority of their predecessors for everything they said, with some such formula as "Shemaiah and Abtalion received from Jehuda ben Tabai and Shimeon ben Shatach" (their predecessors in the office of Scribes: see p. 44).

LESSON XII.

THE PARABLE OF THE SOWER—St Matt. xiii. 1-23.

THE RISE OF THE KINGDOM.

1. **τῆς οἰκίας.**—In Capernaum: St Mark (iii. 20) mentions His entering it. *ἐκάθητο*, the usual position of a Jewish teacher: *τὴν θάλασσαν*—i.e., of Galilee.

2. **πλοῖον.**—This would form a pulpit from which He could watch the expression of the people's faces, and where He could be free from the press.

ἐπὶ τὸν αἰγιαλόν.—"Had ranged themselves over the shore."

ἐπὶ with acc. always implies motion. Cf. xviii. 12.

3. **παραβολαῖς.**—Comparisons: a putting side by side. *βάλλω*, *mitto*, and *mettre* lose their stronger force of "throwing," and get the simpler meaning of "setting." See p. 34.

By this parable Jesus (1) showed His hearers that His kingdom was a spiritual one. In founding it He uses spiritual *means*,—not force, nor authority, nor miracle, but the word of preaching, the acceptance of which depended on the will and disposition of the hearer. His *aim* is spiritual, to produce in men's hearts and lives the fruit of knowledge, consolation, and good works. (2) He showed that He was not deceived by the sight of the crowds, and their apparent attention, into the expectation of large or immediate results, and sobered the sanguine hopes of his more intimate disciples.   (3) He warned His hearers of the perils which threatened the holy impressions they were experiencing.

Amongst the multitude He would distinguish four kinds of expression: (1) thoughtlessness and indifference; (2) enthusiasm and delight ; (3) careworn preoccupation; (4) serene joy, indicating a full acceptance of the truth that was being taught.   These are the various characters alluded to in the parable.

Dean Stanley thus describes (in his 'Sinai and Palestine') a scene he saw, which best illustrates this parable: "There was the undulating corn-field descending to the water's edge.   There was the trodden pathway running through the midst of it, with no fence or hedge to prevent the seed falling here and there on either side of it, or upon it,—itself hard with the constant tramp of horse and mule and human feet.   There was the 'good' rich soil which distinguishes the whole of the plain of Gennesaret and its neighbourhood from the bare hills elsewhere descending into the lake, and which, when there is no interruption, produces one vast mass of corn.   There was the rocky ground of the hillside protruding here and there through the corn-fields, as elsewhere through the grassy slopes.   There were the large bushes of thorn, —*Nalk*, that kind of which tradition says the crown of thorns was woven,—springing up like the fruit-trees of the more inland parts in the very midst of the waving wheat."

3. ὁ σπείρων.—The sower whom I have in view.

ἐξῆλθεν.—From the village.

4. τὴν ὁδόν.—The path which went round the edge of the field.

5. τὰ πετρώδη.—*I.e.*, the places where the rocky soil was covered only by a thin layer of earth.

6. ἐκαυματίσθη.—Scorched by the sun.

ῥίζαν.—Owing to the shallowness of the earth, the seed sent up shoots before the root was duly formed.

7. τὰς ἀκάνθας.—*I.e.*, which were about to spring up there.

8. ἐδίδου.—"Began to render."

ἑκατόν—sup. καρπούς.

In Gen. xxvi. 12, we read that Isaac received a hundred measures for each measure sown.   Palestine (especially Galilee) was very fertile, and the plain of Jezreel at the present day bears corn without cultivation.

11. δέδοται.—"By God :" "it is," as we should say, "your gift."   Their hearts were more susceptible to religious feeling,

and therefore their intellect quicker to understand religious truths, than those of the multitude.

γνῶναι.—*I.e.*, without the help of illustration from parables.

12. This is a proverbial saying derived from the experience of ordinary life. The richer a man, the better he will be able to increase his riches by the influence of superior capital. The more he has cultivated his powers of observation, or memory, or reason, the more and the more rapidly will he see, the greater will be the power and treasures of his memory, the larger the number, and the more certain the quality, of his conclusions.

So in language and thought : the more we have studied, the more rapidly shall we take in new ideas. So in morality and religion : the more we have accustomed ourselves to good habits, the more readily shall we adopt fresh ones, the less easily be inured to bad ones. The majority of Jesus' hearers were commonplace and sensual. They required stories to attract their attention, and even then had not their interest sufficiently aroused to make them desire to know the meaning of the stories. Jesus is not deceived about them. He knows that not many will be influenced, but foresees that the few will ultimately extend the influence of His teaching, and become the leaven of the world. But He does not seek to influence them by other than quiet means, which alone are likely to have lasting effect.

περισσευθήσεται = have more than enough : cf. Luke xv. 17.

ὅστις οὐκ ἔχει.—Perhaps the best illustration of this is the condition of the plebeians at Rome in the early period of its history : they, as a rule, had no capital, and when summoned to go to war, left their lands untilled,—on their return were obliged to borrow money from the patricians at exorbitant interest,—and frequently, at last, were sold to pay their debts.

13. διὰ τοῦτο—*i.e.*, lest they, like the poor, should lose the little they have. διά τ. refers to what has preceded ; ὅτι introduces an additional explanation.

βλέποντες.—This is a common proverbial expression : cf. Isa. xxxii. 3, xxxv. 5 ; Jer. v. 21.

14. καί still dependent on ὅτι, and part of the reason for speaking in parables.

ἀναπληροῦται.—Both its position and the preposition add emphasis to the verb, "full well is being fulfilled."

αὐτοῖς.—Dat. of reference, "in their case."

'Hσαίου—Isa. vi. 9, 10 : the quotation is taken from the LXX., not from the Hebrew, for the sake of Greek readers.

15. ἐπαχύνθη.—Cf. " Well-liking wits they have—gross, gross —fat, fat ; " " Love's Labour's Lost," v. 2. 268.   But Shakespeare refers to dulness of understanding, Isaiah to bluntness of feeling : the heart is represented as covered over with fat, so that it cannot heed the words of the prophet. Cf. "callous," from *callum*, " thick skin," and πεπωρωμένη in Mark vi. 52, and the expression, " fatty degeneration of the conscience."

βαρέως.—" Sluggishly," not a classical expression.

ἐκάμμυσαν, for κατέμυσαν.

ἰάσομαι (*v. l.*, ἰάσωμαι).—Probably dependent on μήποτε with a change of construction : for the sequence of a subj. and fut. ind. co-ordinated after a final particle, see Rev. xxii. 14.   In classic Greek the fut. ind. in pure final clauses is found after ὅπως and ὄφρα, never after ἵνα or ὡς, and very seldom after the simple μή. —(Goodwin, quoted by Carr.)

16. ὑμῶν here, and ὑμεῖς in ver. 18, are both emphatic by position.

βλέπουσι.—" Are capable of seeing." In the next verse the word =" see."

18. οὖν.—" So then "—*i.e.*, since your eyes are sufficiently open to make you desire to know the explanation.

19. παντός.—An anacolouthon : cf. Shakes., " Tempest," iv. 1. 186 : " The trumpery in my house, go bring *it* hither."

μὴ συνιέντος.—In Thuc., i. 138, οἰκείᾳ συνέσει, " mother wit," is opposed to μαθήσει, " learning"; and in Thuc. i. 84, συνετός is opposed to μαθών (see the note on Luke ii. 47). So the point seems to be that they have no aptitude for understanding : they have exposed their hearts as common roads to every evil influence of the world, till they have become hard as pavement.

τὸ ἐσπαρμένον, κ.τ.λ.—*Constructio prægnans* = " that which has been sown into and is placed in it."

οὗτός ἐστιν.—As a matter of fact, it is the truth taught, not the man, that is ὁ σπαρείς : but we can say σπείρειν γῆν, as well as σπείρειν σπέρμα.   The phrase is an Eastern way of saying, "This is he in whose case the seed was sown upon the road." Luke (viii. 14) explains the phrase. This character we should call *hard*, and may illustrate it from Tennyson's first " Northern Far- mer."   The next is *superficial*, shallow : cf. " Still waters run deep," and its opposite, "Noisy waters run shallow." Contrast him who sold all for the sake of this treasure (ver. 44).

20. εὐθύς.—*I.e.*, he does not count the cost; thinks only of the sensation of having a new ideal and new hopes—nothing of the difficulties.

21. πρόσκαιρος.—Temporary, not enduring.

σκάνδαλον.—See note on chap. v. 29. In N. T. σκάνδαλον includes anything which can hinder the development of spiritual life, or deter man from faith in the divine.

22. μέριμνα, the burdens of life; ἀπάτη, the pleasures.

ἀκάνθας.—Fields were often divided by hedges of thorns: cf. Exod. xxii. 6; Jer. iv. 3; Job v. 5. Here it is rather seeds and roots of thorns that are alluded to. For the thought, cf. Prov. xxx. 8, 9: "Give me neither poverty nor riches; feed me with food convenient for me: lest I be full, and deny Thee, and say, Who is the Lord? or lest I be poor, and steal, and take the name of my God in vain."

23. δή emphasises ὅς = "and now this is he who."

LESSON XIII.

THE PARABLES OF THE TARES, OF THE MUSTARD-SEED, AND OF THE LEAVEN.—St Matt. xiii. 24-43.

THE PARABLE OF THE TARES—vers. 24-30.

The Obstacles to the Growth of the Kingdom.

24. ὡμοιώθη.—"Has become like"—*i.e.*, since I (the speaker) have begun to establish the kingdom.

25. ζιζάνια.—This is a word for which it is difficult to find an equivalent; the nearest approach to it is darnel. The plant is one so like wheat, that in the early stages of its growth the two can scarcely be distinguished; so like, that it could even be imagined that the stalks of it, which appeared in fields sown with wheat, sprang not from separate seed, but from wheat-grains that had suffered degeneracy through unfavourable influences of soil or season. This opinion was actually entertained by the inhabit-

ants of Palestine in our Lord's time, as it is still. The opinion, however, is probably a mistaken one, and the theory is not put forth in the parable, which represents the tares as springing from separate seed, sown after the wheat-seed had been cast into the ground. This darnel is poisonous, and is not uncommonly known as bastard wheat.

ἐν τῷ καθεύδειν.—The τοὺς ἀνθρώπους has no special force: the phrase means simply, "in the night": cf. Job xxxiii. 15, "In a dream, in a vision of the night, when deep sleep falleth upon man." Cf. Hdtus., ix. 44, ὡς δὲ πρόσω τῆς νυκτὸς προελήλατο, καὶ ἡσυχίη ἐδόκεε εἶναι ἀνὰ τὰ στρατόπεδα, καί μάλιστα οἱ ἄνθρωποι εἶναι ἐν ὕπνῳ.

The "sowing in the night" refers to the secrecy with which evil deeds are done, and to their dark nature. Wickedness and goodness are constantly contrasted as light and darkness in the New Testament: cf. John iii. 20, "Every one that doeth evil hateth the light, neither cometh to the light, lest his deeds should be reproved."

ἐπέσπειρεν.—"Sowed over the first seed."

26. τότε.—Thomson, 'The Land and the Book,' says: "In those parts where the grain has *headed out*, a child cannot mistake the ζιζάνια for wheat or barley ; but where both are less developed, the closest scrutiny will often fail to detect them. I cannot do it at all with any confidence."

28. συλλέξωμεν.—Deliberative subjunctive. This was, and is, the usual practice, when the tares are merely stray stalks growing accidentally in the field. But owing to the malignity of the enemy, the case here mentioned is a special one : there was a crop of tares growing over the whole field.

30. κατακαῦσαι.—Cf. 2 Sam. xxiii. 7.

THE PARABLES OF THE MUSTARD-SEED AND THE LEAVEN—
vers. 31-33.

The Growth of the Kingdom.

31.—ἄλλην.—Jesus seems to be thinking of the paucity and insignificance of His disciples. In a similar spirit He called them a little flock, Luke xii. 32, and "babes," Matt. xi. 25.

32.—μικρότερον. — For the comparative cf. xviii. 1. "As small as a grain of mustard-seed," was a proverbial phrase current at that time. Jesus employed it, when He said, "If ye have faith as a grain of mustard-seed, ye shall say unto this mountain, Remove hence to yonder place, and it shall remove,"—Matt. xvii. 20. Like other proverbs, however, it was not based on strict scientific truth. Smaller seeds do exist, such as those of the poppy and rye. The mustard-seed is not even perhaps the smallest of all seeds in proportion to the plant which springs from it; for it may be questioned, for example, whether the disproportion between the mustard-seed and the mustard-tree be greater than that between the acorn and the oak. Jesus as an orator is adopting the popular language of the day, in which the mustard-seed was regarded as an emblem of the superlatively little. For the sentiment we may compare Seneca, Ep. Mor., xxxvii. 1, 2—"Words must be sown like seed, which, though it be small, yet when it has found a suitable place unfolds its strength, and from being the least spreads into the largest growth."

τῶν λαχάνων.—"Than the (other) vegetables."

δένδρον.—A tree in comparison with the other plants. Stories are told of mustard-trees so tall, that a man could climb up into their branches, or ride beneath them on horseback ; and Thomson ('The Land and the Book') tells us, that in the plain of Akhar, where the soil is rich, he has seen samples of the tree "as tall as the horse and his rider." All which, if true, proves that in Palestine the mustard-plant attains to a remarkable height for a garden herb, and especially for a herb growing from so small a seed. The aptness of the emblem here arises from the smallness of the seed as compared with the greatness of the result. It is surprising that the oak should come from the acorn, but the mustard-seed is microscopic as compared with the acorn, and hence the size of the plant that springs from it creates more surprise, for ordinary people are not accurate in calculating dimensions ; so that the growth of the mustard-tree from the mustard-seed is more sensational, so to speak, than the growth of the oak from the acorn.

κατασκηνοῦν.—"Dwell," not necessarily "build nests"; "settle upon"—i.e., for the sake of the seed. The word comes from σκηνή, a tent or tabernacle, which, as being easily removed, came to mean a temporary habitation, and the verb to imply, "dwell in a temporary habitation." Cf. viii. 20.

33. σάτα τρία.—An ephah, the usual amount in baking. Cf. Gen. xviii. 6 ; Judges vi. 19 ; 1 Sam. i. 24.

JESUS' PARABLES FORESHADOWED IN THE SAYING OF ASAPH—
vers. 34, 35.

34. **οὐδὲν ἐλάλει.**—*I.e.*, at that time.

35. **προφήτου.**—*I.e.*, Asaph. The passage referred to is Ps. lxxviii. 2.

ἐρεύξομαι.—A word whose meaning has been ameliorated. It occurs in Ps. xviii. 2. It is derived by onomatop. from the sound in the throat. It is used (1) of spitting or spewing out ; (2) of the sea surging or foaming against the land ; (3) in aor. ἤρυγον, of roaring, in Homer, of oxen, in Thucyd., of men.

In Ps. lxxviii. Asaph the prophet (so called 2 Chron. xxix. 30) shows from history that the laws of God's providence are eternal, and that the history of the Jews is a parable of the government of the world. St Matthew here applies the phraseology of Asaph to the discourses of Jesus, in which He shows how the operations of nature in their most ordinary course are illustrations of the same providence.

INTERPRETATION OF THE PARABLE OF THE TARES.—vers. 36-43.

36. **φράσον** occurs in the New Testament only here and in xv. 15, and means "speaking in the way of explaining."

37. **ὁ υἱὸς τοῦ ἀνθρώπου.**—See note at the end of the chapter.

38. **υἱοὶ τῆς βασιλείας.** — *I.e.*, those whose moral nature is derived from the kingdom—*i.e.*, from the king, and who are the subjects of the king. So we have υἱοὶ τοῦ νυμφῶνος, υἱοὶ τοῦ αἰῶνος τούτου, "the sons of Eli were sons of Belial," Matt. ix. 15, Luke xvi. 8, 1 Sam. ii. 12 ; in Ezek. xxx. 5, "the children of the land"; and in 1 Macc. iv. 2, υἱοὶ τῆς ἄκρας for "the men who were in the fortress." See note on v. 9.

40. **συντελείᾳ τοῦ αἰῶνος.**—"The close of the current age"—*i.e.*, of the epoch that precedes the second coming of Christ. The word συντέλεια is found in Dan. ix. 26, 27, xii. 4, 13.

41. **ἐκ τῆς βασιλ.**—*I.e.*, the ἄγρος, which in ver. 38 is defined by κόσμος, "the world," as the sphere of the kingdom.

σκάνδαλα.—Abstract for concrete = "those who by their conduct put stumbling-blocks in the way of others." Cf. xvi. 23.

42. **τὴν κάμινον.** — The phrase occurs in Dan. iii. 6, of Nebuchadnezzar's fiery furnace. Here it seems to refer to Gehenna. Cf. Rev. xx. 15: τὴν λίμνην τοῦ πυρός.

ὁ κλαυθμός.—The article is emphatic: "the ideal wailing and gnashing," such that all other misery sinks into insignificance beside it.

43. ἐκλάμψουσιν.—This is from Dan. xii. 3. Cf. Rev. i. 16; Wisd. iii. 7: ἐν καιρῷ ἐπισκοπῆς αὐτῶν ἀναλάμψουσιν. They shall shine forth clearly from the mists which the sins of others have thrown around them.

ADDITIONAL NOTE ON ὁ υἱὸς τοῦ ἀνθρώπου (ver. 37).

This title is found outside the Gospels only in Acts vii. 56; Rev. i. 13, xiv. 14.

The phrase is used in the Old Testament to express the weakness and frailty of human nature, as in Job xxv. 6, "The stars are not pure in His sight: how much less man, that is a worm? and the son of man, that is a worm?" Ps. cxlvi. 3, "Put not your trust in princes, nor in the son of man, in whom is no help."

About the time of the captivity the title received new prominence from its use in Ezekiel's prophecies, where it occurs eighty-seven times as addressed by Jehovah to the prophet, apparently to keep him in remembrance of his frailty amidst the high honours of the revelations he was receiving.

The passages, however, which seem to throw most light on its usage in the New Testament are—

(1) Ps. viii. 4-8, "What is man, that Thou art mindful of him? and the son of man, that Thou visitest him? For Thou hast made him a little lower than the angels, and hast crowned him with glory and honour. Thou madest him to have dominion over the works of Thy hands; Thou hast put all things under his feet: all sheep and oxen, yea, and the beasts of the field; the fowls of the air, and the fish of the sea, and whatever passeth through the paths of the seas."

Here the sacred writer is glorying in the sovereignty that man, in spite of his frailty, possesses over the works of the Creator.

(2) Dan. vii. 13, 14, "I saw in the night-visions, and, behold, one like a [not "the" as in E. V.] son of man came with the clouds of heaven, and came to the Ancient of days, and they brought him near before Him. And there was given him dominion, and glory, and a kingdom, that all people, nations, and languages, should serve him: his dominion is an everlasting dominion, which

shall not pass away, and his kingdom that which shall not be destroyed."

The prophet had previously described four secular or profane kingdoms of the earth under the image of four beasts which were powerful for a time, but whose dominion was taken away, whereas the being like a son of man is invested with a dominion that is universal and everlasting.

It is not impossible that the thought of the Psalmist had suggested the imagery of the prophet. In both passages we have the notion of the son of man triumphant over the beasts.

The date of the book of Daniel is not certainly known, but we know that the struggles of the Maccabees against Antiochus Epiphanes (B.C. 175-164) had made it a popular book, because it gave a scheme of universal history, from which the Jews derived fresh stimulus for their aspirations after freedom and empire. Jesus, Stephen (Acts vii. 56), and the author of the Apocalypse (Rev. i. 13, xiv. 14), all refer to it.

It is probable that the Jews regarded this "son of man" as representing the holy people, and the dominion with which he was invested as symbolical of the future theocratic kingdom they were to enjoy, in contrast to the perishable earthly monarchies symbolised by the four overthrown beasts. Such indeed is the explanation given by the prophet himself in vers. 17, 18: "These great beasts, which are four, are four kings, which shall arise out of the earth. But the saints of the Most High shall take the kingdom, and possess the kingdom for ever, even for ever and ever."

We have no certain proof that "son of man" ever became a title of the Messiah; indeed, the question put to Jesus by the Jews in John xii. 34, "Who is this Son of man?" seems to prove the contrary. The title "the Son of man" adopted by Jesus was new. He constantly used it of Himself as a periphrasis for "I," primarily, as it would seem, in connection with His proclamation of the approaching establishment of the kingdom of God.

The title was, first of all, an assertion on His part that in Him and through Him were to be fulfilled the aspirations of His countrymen to which the popular prophet had given expression,—that He was *the* Son of man who was invested with universal and everlasting dominion by God Himself. What that kingdom was, however, and how it differed from the ordinary conceptions of His countrymen, He took pains to define not only by His teaching in the Sermon on the Mount and in the parables bearing on the subject, but by the phrases and sentences in which He employed the title.

If we confine our attention to those passages in which all the three synoptic Gospels represent Him as using the title, we find that it has invariably an official or Messianic significance, insomuch that we might almost venture to form a creed from the clauses in which it occurs. Thus the Son of man has power on earth to forgive sins—Mark ii. 10, Matt. ix. 6, Luke v. 24 ; is Lord of the Sabbath—Mark ii. 28, Matt. xii. 8, Luke vi. 5 ; is destined to suffer and to be slain, and to rise again the third day—Mark viii. 31, Matt. xvi. 21, Luke ix. 22 ; and to return in the glory of His Father with the angels—Mark viii. 38, Matt. xvi. 27, Luke ix. 26 ; to be delivered up to the chief priests and Scribes, and by them to the Gentiles, and to be mocked and scourged and slain, and to rise again the third day—Mark x. 33, 34, Matt. xx. 18, 19, Luke xviii. 32, 33; to be a minister or servant—Mark x. 45, Matt. xx. 28, Luke xxii. 27 ; to come on or in the clouds, or a cloud, with great power and glory—Mark xiii. 26, Matt. xxiv. 30, Luke xxi. 27; goes to fulfil His destiny, betrayed by one of His followers—Mark xiv. 21, Matt. xxvi. 24, Luke xxii. 22.

The last quotation but one seems to refer especially to Dan. vii. 13, as does Matt. xvi. 27, 28, xix. 28, xxv. 31 ; Luke xxii. 69

In one passage Jesus may have been referring to Ps. viii.—viz., in Matt. viii. 20 ; Luke ix. 58 : " Foxes have holes, and the fowls of the air have nests, but the Son of man [under whose feet they are all put] hath not where to lay His head." This psalm is interpreted of the Messiah in 1 Cor. xv. 27, " For He hath put all things under His feet,"—Eph. i. 22, Heb. ii. 8; and Jesus uses it in answer to His enemies in Matt. xxi. 16.

If, then, we connect the words of the psalmist and the prophet with the words of Jesus, we may fairly infer what it was that Jesus implied by the title " Son of man." He claimed to be the mysterious Being mentioned in Daniel in whom the aspirations of the nation were to be fulfilled, and who was to be invested with everlasting dominion. But on His lips the words lose their narrow reference to Israel, and assert His relationship to the whole of humanity; they declare His kingdom to be no mere aggrandisement of Judaism, but a dominion over the hearts of men, won by seeking and saving the lost, maintained by serving and self-sacrifice.

By adopting the title Jesus asserted His Messiahship, and yet guarded against the errors into which the assertion of it might lead His countrymen, and even His disciples. In taking such a " modest and lovable " name as His ordinary appellation, rather than that of Prophet, or King, or Christ, or Son of God, He expressed His ardent desire to embrace all men in His Messianic kingdom, whether they were publicans and sinners, or Pharisees and Sadducees ; whether philosophers and theologians, or the veriest outcasts in the most squalid habitations in any quarter of the globe. *Nihil humani a se alienum putat.* By the complete humanity of His life, His privations, His loneliness, His love and sympathy for all that bears the image of man, He has given new hopes to the human race, and brought them nearer to His Father, with whom He seeks to unite them in trust and love.

LESSON XIV.

THE PARABLES OF THE HID TREASURE, OF THE PEARL, AND OF THE NET—St Matt. xiii. 44-52, with St Mark iv. 26-29.

44-46.—The Parables of the Hid Treasure and of the Pearl. The appropriation of the kingdom by mankind.

44. In an unsettled country like Palestine it would be quite common to conceal money, as men would never feel secure from the extortions of the oppressor : cf. Jer. xli. 8 ; Job. iii. 21 ; Prov. ii. 4. " The present population of Palestine has a passion for treasure-seeking. There are at this hour hundreds of persons thus engaged all over the country. Not a few spend their last farthing in these ruinous efforts."—' The Land and the Book.' Cf. xxv. 18.

Readers of Scott will remember the scene in the 'Antiquary.'

τῷ ἀγρῷ.—" *The* field of the estate on which he was working." Cf. Luke xv. 15.

ἔκρυψε.—His conduct would be in accordance with Jewish law. If a man had found a treasure in loose coins among the corn, it would certainly be his if he bought the corn. If he had found it on the ground, or in the soil, it would be his if he could claim

ownership of the soil; and even if the field were not his own, unless others could *prove* their right to it (Edersheim). But this is
an unessential detail: the point of the parable is the man's earnestness, which leads him to sell all he has that he may buy the field
containing the treasure.

τῆς χαρᾶς αὐτοῦ.—" His joy," *not* " joy over it."

ὑπάγει.—The present, more animated than the aorist, expresses
the speed with which the finder resolves and carries his resolution
into execution.

45. ἐμπόρῳ. — One who *travels* for mercantile purposes: from
πόρος, opp. to κάπηλος, a small trader.

46. μαργαρίτας.—The pearl would probably be found in the
pearl-oyster, of which there would be an abundance in the Persian
Gulf. The simile is the more appropriate, as " wise sayings " are in
Arabic called " pearls " : cf. vii. 6. The ἕνα πολύτιμον might
be rendered into Latin by the word "*unio*," a unique pearl, of
which we are told two were never found together. The ancients
had a very beautiful though unscientific theory about the origin
of the pearl. They believed that it was formed by the dew of
heaven entering into the shell in which it was found, the quality
and form of the pearl depending on the purity of the dew, the
state of the atmosphere, and even the hour of the day at the time
of its conception. An ancient pearl was valued by Pliny at
£80,000 sterling. A pearl is mentioned as being in the possession
of the Emperor of Persia which was bought of an Arab in 1633,
and valued at a sum equal to £110,400.

In our time we should probably prefer to use the diamond as an
emblem of the highest good. Shakespeare uses " pearl " for " the
élite" — " I see thee compassed with thy kingdom's pearl," —
" Macbeth," v. 7. 56.

πέπρακε.—" Sells at once." The perfect marks the rapidity of
the transaction.

47-50.—*The Parable of the Net—The separation at the judgment.*

47. σαγήνη—from which probably comes our word *seine*—was a
large drag-net, which was leaded and buoyed, and then drawn
in a circle. " Some row the boat, some cast out the net, some on
shore pull the rope with all their strength ; others throw stones
and beat the waters at the ends of the net, to frighten the fish
from escaping there."—' The Land and the Book.'

48. **τὰ σαπρά.**—This may have a reference to the distinction between the clean and unclean fish. The word literally means "putrid," then, more generally, "worthless, useless for food"; so that it may here mean those fish which were not worth preserving.

This parable is a complement to that of the tares; it refers to missionary labours. Not all the converts will display Christian virtues. The missionaries are prepared for disappointment, and for patience and tolerance.

49. **ἀφοριοῦσι.**—The contracted Attic future. Cf. xxv. 32.

51, 52.—*The Scribes of the kingdom of heaven.*

52. **διὰ τοῦτο.**—An expression of consequence, but not a strong one: "well then."

γραμματεύς.—This word, which to the Jew presented the idea of an exponent of the Jewish law, is here ameliorated and referred to the exponent of the religion of Jesus; but in order to distinguish the new Scribes from the old, the clause μαθητευθεὶς τῇ βασιλ. is added.

μαθητεύειν τινι properly means, "to be a disciple of any one." Here the verb is used transitively—"made a disciple of the kingdom of heaven."

ἐκβάλλει.—Cf. Luke x. 35.

θησαυροῦ.—In the illustration this means *the chest* (ii. 11, xii. 35) in which the householder keeps his money and jewels; in the interpretation it means the stores of knowledge which the teacher has at his disposal for purposes of instruction.

καινὰ καὶ παλαιά.—Thoughts and principles hitherto unknown, and those which had been taught in former ages. The Jewish Scribe taught the old only, and always quoted authority for what he said, and hence in his teaching there could be no progress. The Christian teacher is to find fresh thoughts and illustrations for and from the various countries and ages in which he lives. Jesus had taken His illustrations from the scenery and life of Galilee ; St Paul, after Christianity had spread over the Roman Empire, took his from the Roman soldiers, the Greek πόλις, the Ephesian temple, the Olympian games. The words of Jesus grant liberty to Christian teachers to seek new meanings from the spirit of His teaching : His great sayings will furnish them with new thoughts, as they and their successors in all ages of the world gain new experiences. They are, so to speak, to work out deductions as well as to learn their book work. New problems will constantly be presenting themselves, to solve which, wisdom, and judgment, and knowledge will be necessary, and the illumination of their Master's spirit.

THE PARABLE OF THE SEED GROWING SECRETLY AND SLOWLY—Mark iv. 26-29.

26. βάλῃ.—The aorist expressing the single act completed once for all, while the presents, καθ. and ἐγείρ., express continually repeated acts. Cf. Matt. xxv. 5, ἐνύσταξαν καὶ ἐκάθευδον.

The construction seems to be, "the kingdom of God is thus, that a man shall have cast"—*i.e.*, shall be as though he have cast: it appears to be a combination of ὡς ἄνθ. βαλών and ὡς ἐὰν ἄνθ. βάλῃ.

ὡς may be either "when," as in Luke iv. 25, or "how." Observe the emphatic position of αὐτός, and translate, "how knoweth not he:" cf. John iii. 8,—"The wind bloweth where it listeth, and thou hearest the sound thereof, but canst not tell whence it cometh, and whither it goeth: so is every one that is born of the Spirit." Both in that passage and in ours, Jesus seems to have had in His thoughts Eccles. xi. 4, 6: "He that observeth the wind shall not sow; and he that regardeth the clouds shall not reap. In the morning sow thy seed, and in the evening withhold not thine hand; for thou knowest not whether shall prosper, either this or that, or whether they both shall be alike good." Cf. Ps. cxxvi. 5, 6.

Thomson ('The Land and the Book') says: "The idea of the passage in Ecclesiastes is, sow early and sow late as opportunity offers or circumstances require: and the wise farmer in Palestine must act thus; for no human sagacity, no length of experience, will enable him to determine, in any given year, that what is sown early will prosper best. If the spring be late, wet, and cold, the early grain grows too rank, lodges, and is blasted; while the late sown yields a large harvest.

28. πλήρη σῖτον—*v. l.*, πλήρης σῖτος—*i.e.*, ἐστι, which emphasises the fulness. There is another *v. l.*, πλήρης σῖτον, as in Acts vi. 5, πλήρης being indeclinable in the sing. For this usage there is

good authority in the LXX.: cf. (perhaps) John i. 14. But the acc. πλήρη occurs in 2 John 8.

The ear may be defined as holy feeling, lofty ideals; the fruit as virtue that can withstand temptation: the first is a good impulse, the second a good habit.

29. παραδοῖ.—Either (1) intrans., "deliver itself over"—*i.e.*, by its ripeness in the harvesting; but it is doubtful whether any other instance of this meaning can be found: cf., however, Virg., Georg., i. 287, "Multa adeo gelidâ melius se nocte dederunt." The modern Greek version, ὡριμάσῃ, seems to favour this rendering. Or (2) = "allow": cf. Polyb., xxii. 24. 9, τῆς ὥρας παραδιδούσης. The tense is the 2d aor. conj., as if from a pres. verb, δόω; cf. Mark xiv. 11 : cf. γνοῖ, as if from γνόω, in Luke xix. 15.

ἀποστ. τὸ δρέπ.—Cf. Joel iii. 13, ἐξαποστείλατε τὸ δρέπανον ὅτι παρέστηκεν ὁ τρυγητός: Rev. xiv. 15, 16.

LESSON XV.

THE PARABLE OF THE LITTLE CHILD—St Matt. xviii. 1-14.

THE LITTLE ONES OF THE KINGDOM.

1. τίς ἄρα.—"Who under these circumstances?" with a reference to something that had preceded, but what that was cannot now be determined. Jesus and His disciples were about to leave Galilee, and proceed on their way to Jerusalem. The disciples dreamt that Jesus would, on reaching the capital, assume the sovereignty, and already began to apportion the honours among them. Peter, too, had recently been told he was to have the keys of the kingdom of heaven (Matt. xvi. 19), and there were occasions when Peter, James, and John were specially selected by their Master to be His companions.

μείζων—*i.e.*, τῶν ἄλλων. Cf. Matt. xiii. 32.

2. Jesus acts a parable : teaching by such parabolic actions was common among the prophets—cf. 1 Kings xxii. 11.

3. στραφῆτε.—"Turn back ;" ambition is the wrong road : they

must retrace their steps, and seek the road of childlike humility, or they will not even enter the kingdom, far less attain eminence in it.

4. ταπεινώσει, coming before ἑαυτόν, is emphatic.

τὸ παιδίον τοῦτο.—The child was probably at that moment displaying its natural modesty by shrinking from the attention drawn to it.

5. δέξηται contains the notion of " cherish and take thought for."

τοιοῦτο—*i.e.*, one who had become like the child in simplicity and humility, and, being unassuming and unselfish, would especially need protection, and be exposed to wrong from the pushing and self-asserting.

ἕν.—Emphatic—*i.e.*, a single one.

6. μικρῶν.—Cf. x. 42. The passage occurs also in Mark x. 42 and Luke xvii. 2, without any reference to children. Jesus seems to be passing away from the metaphor : perhaps a motion of the hand towards His most recent converts indicated that He meant the young in faith. He speaks with fatherly tenderness of them : cf. the phrase, μικρὸν ποίμνιον in Luke xii. 32, where Jesus is seeking to encourage His disciples against fear and anxiety. Here He is probably answering a thought rising in the minds of the disciples —" If the members of the kingdom are to be like little children, how shall they defend themselves and its dominions in this rough world ? " Solomon, in succeeding to the kingdom, had spoken of himself as "a little child" in experience and knowledge (1 Kings iii. 7).

σκανδαλίσῃ.—Lit., " trip up with a σκανδάληθρον " (the touch-twig in a trap), and so " be the cause of his fall."

συμφέρει ἵνα.—In classic Greek we should have the inf.

μύλος ὀνικός.—The larger kind of millstone, as opposed to that worked by a woman (xxiv. 41).

καταποντισθῇ. — A punishment not spoken of in the Jewish law ; but Josephus (Ant., xiv. 15. 10) records that the Galileans, revolting from their commanders, drowned the partisans of Herod. Among the Romans, a parricide, after being scourged, was sewn up with a dog, a cock, a snake, and a monkey, and thrown into the sea. What is meant is, that such men would subject themselves to a destruction equal to that of the most infamous criminals.

πέλαγος.—Curtius says this word means the sea especially in

its dangerous character, and connects it with the root πλαγ. Cf.
πλήσσω, to beat; and the Lat. *plango*: cf. Od., v. 335, ἁλὸς ἐν
πελάγεσσι ; Hec., 938, ἅλιον ἐπὶ πέλαγος.   Others derive it from
πλάξ, a flat surface, plain : cf. *æquor*.

7-10 contains a parenthetic lament over the inevitable σκάνδαλα.

7.—οὐαί.—Not a curse, but a lamentation.

τῷ κόσμῳ.—Here = humanity.

ἀπό.—"Resulting from," not "because of."   Cf. vii. 16 ; Luke
xix. 4.

8. The hand and the foot are symbolical of the energies exercised
by them.   Cf. v. 29, 30.

καλὸν . . . ἤ.—In later Greek the particle ἤ appears to have gained
an independent comparative force, so as occasionally to dispense
with a comparative degree : cf. Luke xv. 7, xviii. 14.   The usage is
very common in the LXX., and was perhaps derived from the
Hebrew usage, by which the comparative idea is expressed by the
positive adjective, followed by the preposition *min* (from).   There
are, however, instances in the classics, as Thuc., vi. 21—αἰσχρὸν
βιασθέντας ἀπελθεῖν ἢ ὕστερον ἐπιμεταπέμπεσθαι (Carr).

πῦρ αἰώνιον.—See note on v. 22.

αἰώνιον.—See note on Luke x. 25.

*10.—Jesus resumes the reference to the "little ones" interrupted
at ver. 7.*

λέγω ὑμῖν.—This is one of those expressions of solemn certainty
which caused His hearers to say that Jesus taught as one having
authority, and not as the Scribes (vii. 29).

οἱ ἄγγελοι.—There are other indications of the belief in guardian angels, in Acts xii. 15 ; Heb. i. 14.

βλέπουσι—*i.e.*, "have free access to His presence, are in high
honour with Him :" the simile is taken from an oriental court.
Cf. 2 Kings xxv. 19 ; Esth. i. 14 ; 1 Kings x. 8—οἱ παῖδές σου οὗτοι
οἱ παρεστηκότες ἐνώπιόν σου διόλου ; Matt. v. 8 ; Heb. xii. 14 ;
Tobit xii. 15 : " I am Raphael, one of the holy angels which present the prayers of the saints, and which go in and out before the
glory of the Holy One."

12. **ἐπὶ τὰ ὄρη.**—To be taken with ἀφείς—"having let them
range over the mountains."   Cf. Matt. xiii. 2, ἐπὶ τὸν αἰγιαλὸν
εἱστήκει ; and for ἀφείς, the use of ἄφετος in Æsch., Pr., 666, and

Eur., Ion, 822., where it is used of an animal allowed to range at will.

13.—See Luke xv. 4, where the parable is further expanded.

14. ἔμπροσθεν.—Hellenistic for ἐνώπιον, "in the presence of.'

Not only are the μικροί not to be despised, but if they go astray those that are stronger in the faith are to seek to amend them.

There is an irony in the use of the word μικροί, for the great ones of the earth may be μικροί in the faith. Thus the Emperor Theodosius did public penance, at the bidding of St Ambrose, for the massacre of the people of Thessalonica (A.D. 390).

LESSON XVII.

ON DISPUTES WITHIN THE KINGDOM—St Matt. xviii. 15-35.

15-20.—*The method of dealing with an offending brother.*

15. ὕπαγε.—Do not wait for him to come : it is easier for the offended person to make the first advances.

ἔλεγξον.—Convict him of his fault by reasoning : cf. John viii. 9, where the sin of the Pharisees is brought home to them by their own conscience. The precept appears to be an adaptation of Lev. xix. 17 : "Thou shalt not hate thy brother in thine heart: thou shalt in any wise rebuke thy neighbour, and not suffer sin upon him" (*i.e.*, bear not secret ill-will). Cf. James v. 19.

ἐκέρδησας.—Instead of gaining an advantage in money or otherwise over thy brother in a law-court, and so embittering him more than ever, thou hast gained thy brother for thyself and for God. κερδέω is used in this sense in 1 Cor. ix. 19; 1 Pet. iii. 1.

A beautiful illustration of this method is found in the 'Meditations' of the Stoic emperor, Marcus Aurelius (xi. 10) : "What will the most violent man do to thee if thou continuest to be of a kind disposition towards him, and if, as opportunity offers, thou gently admonishest him and calmly correctest his errors at the very time when he is trying to do thee harm, saying, 'Not so, my child ; we are constituted by nature for something else : I shall certainly not be injured, but thou art injuring thyself, my child ' ?

And show him with gentle tact and by general principles that this is so, and that even bees do not as he does, nor any animals that are formed by nature to be gregarious. And thou must do this neither with any double meaning nor in the way of reproach, but affectionately and without any rancour in thy soul ; and not as if thou wert lecturing him, nor yet that any bystander may admire, but when he is alone."

16. ἐπὶ στόματος.—These words are partly taken from the Law. Cf. Deut. xix. 15 ; 1 Tim. v. 19 ; 2 Cor. xiii. 1.

ῥῆμα.—Hebraistically used for " the fact spoken of." Cf. Luke ii. 15, τὸ ῥῆμα τοῦτο τὸ γεγονός (the birth of Christ as told by the shepherds).

17. ἐκκλησία.—In classical Greek this word signified the assembly of the free burghers of a Greek state, called together by a κῆρυξ, the word being derived from ἐκ and καλέω, because the citizens were summoned from among the mass of the population. In this signification it occurs in Acts xix. 32 of the assembly at Ephesus ; but its use in the New Testament must be traced to the LXX., in which it frequently appears as a translation of the Hebrew *Kahal, the congregation* of Israel summoned or met for a definite purpose, or the *community* or *house* of Israel (for the assembly mustered by houses, and on the house the Hebrew polity was based), viewed in the light of a congregation. Thus the word expresses the idea of the Greek πολιτεία, except that the Hebrew nation was a "holy people," held together by religious rather than political bonds.

It was in the latter sense that the word was adopted by the writers of the New Testament, and applied by them to the new Christian society. . ἐκκλησία occurs only twice in the Gospels (here and in Matt. xvi. 18)—both times in a speech uttered by Jesus. It is applied in Acts ii. 47 for the first time to an actually existing institution. It is often found in the writings of St Paul in the sense of "a society" or "community" of Christ, whether belonging to a single locality (1 Cor. i. 2), or the whole body of Christ's followers, viewed as a *house*, like Israel,—a community bound together by bonds of religion (Eph. v. 25).

It was customary to denounce obstinate offenders in the synagogue. The medieval Jewish commentator Maimonides says : " If any refuse to feed his children they reprove him, they shame him, they urge him ; if he still refuse, they make proclamation against him in the synagogue, saying, 'He is a cruel man, and will not nourish his children,—more cruel than the unclean birds themselves, for they feed their young ones.'"

ὁ ἐθνικός.—The article is generic, as we say, "the historian," "the poet." The Jews had no communion of worship with the Gentiles and publicans,—these were cut off from the holy nation: so Jesus means here that such an obstinate transgressor cannot be associated with as a Christian. We see practical illustrations of the working of this precept in 1 Cor. v. 1-5 ; 1 Cor. vi. 1-6 ; 2 Cor. ii. 6, 7.

18. **ὅσα ἐὰν δήσητε, κ.τ.λ.**—Binding and loosing, in Jewish religious phraseology, meant forbidding and allowing. Many things that the school of Shammai "bound," the school of Hillel "loosed."

In xvi. 19 this power had been adjudged to Peter ; here it is given to all the disciples, representing the Church. In that passage the reference seems to be to the external organisation of the kingdom ; in this, especially to the power of forgiveness of sins. Jesus brought a new power of forgiveness into the world, and has infused it into His disciples—*i.e.*, into those who are filled with His spirit. But besides this, He introduced new moral powers and a deeper code of morals, so that those who are loyal to Him "bind," that is, "forbid," vindictiveness and lustful thoughts, and pride and selfishness—sins of the thought as well as of the act. Historically, as Christianity has been the religion accepted by the most civilised nations in the world, the precepts of Peter and the other disciples of Jesus have been those which have "bound" and "loosed"—*i.e.*, "forbidden" or "allowed" thoughts, words, and acts in the civilised world.

19. **παντός.**—The construction is a case of attraction : πᾶν should have been the subject of the principal clause of the sentence, but was attracted to the subordinate clause and joined to πράγματος, so that without the attraction the clause would run thus : ἐὰν δύο συμφ. περὶ πράγματος, πᾶν ὅ ἐὰν αἰτ. γεν. αὐτοῖς.

20. **δύο.**—The trustworthiness of the Christian judgment does not depend on numbers, but on the fulfilment of the true conditions of the Christian life.

συνηγμένοι.—σύναξις was subsequently used of assemblies of the Church for religious services, and especially for the Holy Communion.

εἰς τὸ ἐμὸν ὄνομα.—For Christian objects and in a Christian temper, having in view what my name implies.

ἐκεῖ εἰμί.—The Rabbis also spoke of the Shechinah being present where two or three elders sat together in judgment.

21-35.—*The limits of forgiveness : the parable of the Unforgiving Debtor.*

21. ποσάκις. — There must, thought the disciples, be some limit to the forgiveness just implied ; so Peter, anxious for a rule, suggests the sacred number seven. Even this was more than twice the number of times declared by the Rabbis to be requisite : they said three times, not four.

καὶ ἀφήσω. — A Hellenistic construction ; in classic Greek ἀμαρτήσει would be in a participial form.

22. The answer of Jesus has found expression in modern times in the words of the poet Wordsworth, when speaking of self-sacrifice—

> "Give all thou canst ; high heaven rejects the lore
> Of nicely calculated less or more."

It finds apt illustration in the words of Euripides (Bacchæ, 209), when speaking of the worship due to a god, δι' ἀριθμῶν δ'οὐδὲν αὔξε-σθαι θέλει—"The god desires not to be glorified by certain fixed numbers."

So Jesus, in His answer to Peter, implies forgiveness is not a matter of arithmetic : it is to be measured out in quality, not in quantity.

ἑβδ. ἑπτά perhaps should be rendered 77 times : cf. Gen. iv. 24 (LXX.), of Lamech's seventy and seven-fold. The use of the symbolical number intensified was doubtless intended to lead Peter away from any numerical standard,—from the letter to the spirit.

23. διὰ τοῦτο.—Because I have enjoined such unlimited forgiveness.

ὡμοιώθη.—Past tense, because the kingdom of heaven was already established with Jesus as King, and His disciples as subjects.

συνᾶραι λόγον.—An unclassical expression for διαλογίζεσθαι πρός τινα : cf. chap. xxv. 19. "To take up along with another," and so "to cast up accounts with another." The δοῦλοι are the king's ministers, who are indebted to him through having received money on loan, or as treasurers, land stewards, or the like. In an Eastern monarchy all the subjects are slaves. Probably an Eastern satrap would be thought of here.

24. μυρίων ταλάντων.—The Attic talent of silver was equivalent to about £243, 15s. of English money, so that the sum would not fall far short of two millions and a half English. This immense sum represents the falling short on the part of man of the standard of the perfections of God.

25. μὴ ἔχοντος.—μὴ states reasons or conditions, οὐ states facts ; but this distinction is not maintained in Hellenistic Greek : hence μὴ ἔχοντος may = (1) when he had not ; or (2) because he had not.

πραθῆναι.—The Mosaic law allowed the sale of an insolvent debtor, apparently with his family, but he might be redeemed at the year of jubilee—Lev. xxv. 39, 47. The king was therefore acting simply in accordance with the laws, with no unusual cruelty. Such indeed was the universal code of antiquity : cf. 2 Kings iv. 1.

26. πάντα ἀποδώσω σοι.—He has not a very high standard. He thinks the future can make up for the past. The severity of God, as represented in the parable, is like Joseph's harshness with his brethren, love in disguise.

In Wisd. iv. 20 there is a picture of the sinner before the tribunal of God that contains a similar figure to that in the parable— " When they cast up the accounts of their sins, they shall come with fear : and their own iniquities shall convince them to their face."

27. σπλαγχνισθείς. — "Touched to the heart," or simply "touched."

28. ἐξελθών.—As soon as he leaves his lord's presence, he is changed from a humble suppliant to a hard-hearted tyrant. So it has been said no one can abide in the presence of God and be without sympathy. The finest illustration in all literature, perhaps, of callousness connected with departure from the divine presence, is found in the terribly brief and telling words about Judas when he left the presence of Jesus in order to betray Him, as recorded in John xiii. 30—λαβὼν οὖν τὸ ψωμίον ἐκεῖνος, εὐθέως ἐξῆλθεν · ἦν δὲ νύξ. So in the parable, as he leaves the presence of his lord, the night of hatred and selfishness seems to settle down on the soul of the debtor.

ἑκατόν δηνάρια.—The denarius was the standard Roman coin.

It was worth considerably less than one shilling, and may perhaps best be rendered *franc*. A hundred denarii would be much less than £5. The proportion Jesus wishes to enforce on Peter's mind is, that the offences of one man against another are to the trespasses of man against the standard of the perfection of God what five pounds are to two millions.

ἔπνιγε (imperf.)—As the Roman law allowed creditors to drag their debtors before the judge, holding them by the throat. Cf. Plautus, "Obtorto collo ad prætorem trahor."

εἴ τι ὀφείλεις.—The ind. with εἰ implies, "if you owe me, as you do,"—*i.e.*, "you owe me; therefore pay." He employs the phrase εἴ τι in preference to the more definite ὅτι, because from shame he uses the vaguest expressions he can find in alluding to the sum, so small in comparison with what he owed himself. This conditional form was originally, though not here, a sign of courtesy. Cf. Luke xix. 8·—εἴ τινός τι ἐσυκοφάντησα.

29. The phraseology of ver. 26 is dramatically repeated, except that for προσεκύνει is substituted παρεκάλει, a more appropriate word to express the entreaty of an equal. This very posture of his fellow-servant should have reminded him of his Lord's mercy when he was entreating Him in a similar attitude. Cf. Hecuba's appeal to Ulysses—Eur., Hec., 273-278.

31. ἐλυπήθησαν.—A very beautiful word : they were pained, rather than angry. The same phrase is used to express the pain of the disciples when Jesus told them one of them was destined to betray Him—Matt. xxvi. 22.

διεσάφησαν.—A strong word, vividly depicting the animation of the indignant narrators. "Told him plainly all that had happened." So in the Geneva version. The word = *declaraverunt*.

32. πᾶσαν τὴν ὀφειλήν.—A very emphatic expression. We can estimate the value of the debt if we bear in mind that 10,000 talents of silver is the sum at which Haman reckons the revenue derivable from the destruction of the whole Jewish people—Esth. iii. 9.

34. τοῖς βασανισταῖς.—This is a detail from the practice in the East, where torturing to discover hidden money was common ; and cf. Livy, ii. 23 : "Ductum se ab creditore non in servitutem sed in ergastulum et carnificinam esse : inde ostentans tergum fœdum recentibus vestigiis vulnerum." There is no mention of torturing in the Old Testament ; it was introduced into Palestine by Herod :

cf. Jos., B. J., i. 30. 2; Ant., xvi. 1.   Here the word does not, probably, imply that the debtor was to be tortured, but that he was to be given into the custody of the roughest kind of jailers, who had the power of torturing in certain cases.

ἕως ἀποδῷ.—This is too vague to be interpreted as throwing any light on the duration of future punishment.

The object of the parable is to teach us there is no moral fitness for the kingdom of heaven in the heart of him who is unsympathising, unforgiving, and unkind.

35. ἀπὸ τῶν καρδιῶν. — To the exclusion of all μνησικακία, "remembrance of the injury."

Cf. Ecclus. xxviii. 3, 4: "One man beareth hatred against another, and doth he seek pardon from the Lord? he showeth no mercy to a man who is like himself, and doth he ask forgiveness of his own sins?"

The favourite expression for the mercy and forgiving disposition of God in the Old Testament is that found in Ps. xxxvi. 6, lvii. 10: "Thy mercy is great unto the heavens, and thy truth unto the clouds;" which is expanded in Ps. ciii. 11, 12: "As the heaven is high above the earth, so great is His mercy toward them that fear Him: as far as the east is from the west, so far hath He removed our transgressions from us."

The finest expression of the purity of God, as contrasted with the impurity of man, is perhaps that in Job xv. 15, 16: "Behold, He putteth no trust in His saints; yea, the heavens are not clean in His sight.   How much more abominable and filthy is man, which drinketh iniquity like water?" and cf. Job iv. 18, 19, xxv. 5: "Behold even to the moon, and it shineth not; yea, the stars are not pure in His sight: how much less man, that is a worm; and the son of man, which is a worm?"

Cf. Isa. lxiv. 6: "We are all as an unclean thing, and all our righteousnesses are as filthy rags."

In the Book of Job, however, God is regarded as the great and unapproachable Creator; in the Book of Isaiah, as the King of His people Israel.   In the one case man is regarded as puny and unclean beside the vastness and purity of the Creator, as imperfectly represented by His works; in the other God's people are regarded and punished as rebellious subjects, because they have failed to keep His laws: therefore they are sent away into captivity out of His presence.

But, in the thought of Jesus, God is a Father, and men are brothers in the same family. The profounder the knowledge the children have of the character of their Father, the profounder is their consciousness of their own deficiencies as compared with His perfections. The infinite greatness and purity of the character of the Father is made a ground not for their fear of Him, but for their love and forbearance toward one another. Such a thought the disciples, men of a race the general stability of whose character made it very difficult for them to uproot the feeling of vindictiveness from their hearts, were naturally slow to learn. Neither could Jesus teach them at once the full meaning of the new Christian idea of forgiveness. We find it learnt and taught in the Epistle of St John, i. 11, "He that hateth his brother is in darkness;" iii. 14, "He that loveth not his brother abideth in death;" iv. 8, "He that loveth not knoweth not God;" 20, "He that loveth not his brother whom he hath seen, how can he love God whom he hath not seen?"

LESSON XIX.

On Doing and Being—St Luke x. 25-42.

25-37.—*The Good Samaritan.*

25.—νομικός.—An interpreter of the Mosaic law. St Mark (xii. 28) uses γραμματεύς in this passage; St Matt. (xxii. 35) νομικός. νομικός seems to be more specific = *jurisconsultus;* γραμματεύς more general = *literatus.* Luke probably prefers νομικός, as more intelligible to Gentiles.

ἀνέστη.—Jesus and those with Him being seated. Cf. Mark xiv. 57; Acts vi. 9.

ἐκπειράζων.—The preposition strengthens the word; we may perhaps translate, "putting Him to a strong and carefully chosen test." Cf. iv. 12; Deut. vi. 16; Matt. iv. 7; 1 Cor. x. 9.

τί ποιήσας.—He was thinking of some isolated act: Jesus directs him to a habitual state of the soul—that of love, which does not "nicely calculate less or more." He was thinking of eternal life as a prize to be gained ; Jesus teaches him that he who loves lives, and he who loves not lives not.

ζωήν.—In Hellenistic Greek ζωή has been ameliorated in usage ; βίος has deteriorated. The classic usage is seen in the derivation of zoology as opposed to biography ; the Hellenistic in such phrases as ἡδοναὶ τοῦ βίου, in Luke viii. 14, contrasted with αἰώνιος in this passage, and ζωὴ τοῦ θεοῦ in Eph. iv. 18. With the Hebrew, ζωή meant life worth living : cf. Ps. xxx. 5, "In His favour is ζωή : weeping may endure for a night, but joy cometh in the morning." Jesus (Luke xii. 15) says, "A man's ζωή consisteth not in the abundance of things he possesses." And when Moses (Deut. xxx. 19) solemnly lays before all Israel the consequences of obedience and disobedience to God, and continues, in ver. 20, to speak of God as their "life," it is obvious that neither life nor death is used in a barely literal sense, but as identical with good and evil respectively. Consequently the Hebrews had no further term than "life" by which to express the enjoyment of the perfect blessings of Messiah's reign, when ὁ αἰὼν οὗτος with all its evils should have passed away, and ὁ αἰὼν ὁ ἐρχόμενος at last have come. Hence what the young man means is, "What shall I do to inherit the blessings of the Messianic reign ?" To these blessings the Psalmist alludes (Ps. xvi. 10, 11) in the words, "Thou wilt not leave my soul in the place of the dead : Thou wilt show me the path of *life :* at [*or* in] Thy right hand there are pleasures for evermore."

αἰώνιον.—This adjective means sometimes "without beginning or end," as of God, Rom. xvi. 26 (ὁ μόνος αἰώνιος, 2 Macc. i. 25) ; sometimes "without beginning, *or* ascertainable beginning," as in χρόνοις αἰωνίοις, Rom. xvi. 25 ; or "without end, *or* ascertainable end," as 2 Cor. iv. 18, "The things which are seen are for a time (πρόσκαιρα), but the things which are not seen are eternal" (αἰώνια).

It does not necessarily mean imperishable ; for in Habak. iii. 6, the everlasting hills (βούνοι αἰώνιοι) are said to be scattered (*or* fall) to dust.

κληρονομήσω.—An idea consecrated to the Hebrew mind by the promise to Abraham (Gen. xv. 7, 8, and xvii. 8), that his seed should inherit the land of Canaan, and by the actual possession of the land subsequently. κληρονομεῖν τὴν γῆν was the constant Old Testament phrase for the Israelites "going in and possessing the land" (Lev. xx. 24). The phrase supplied them with a description of what should happen when the kingdom should be restored to Israel (Acts i. 6), and Messiah should reign in a "new Jerusalem" over a renewed and glorified nation.

26. **πῶς ἀναγινώσκεις.**—A customary Rabbinical formula, such as the *νομικός* probably often used himself : thus the teacher is made to teach himself.

27. **ἀγαπήσεις, κ.τ.λ.**—These words are from Deut. vi. 5 and Lev. xix. 18. The Jews had to repeat daily, morning and evening, the former passage, together with Deut. xi. 13 *et seq.:* it appears also on the phylacteries, but not Lev. xix. 18. Jesus may have pointed to one of these, for the Scribe would wear them on his forehead and wrist : they were little leather boxes, containing four texts in their compartments.

28. **ζήσῃ.**—Cf. 1 John iii. 15 : "Whosoever hateth his brother is a murderer ; and ye know that no murderer hath eternal life abiding in him ;" and 1 John iv. 20, 21 : "If a man say, I love God, and hateth his brother, he is a liar ; for he that loveth not his brother whom he hath seen, how can he love God whom he hath not seen ? And this commandment have we from Him, that he who loveth God love his brother also."

29. **δικαιῶσαι**—*i.e.*, to prove that he had put the question with reason and justice.

καὶ τίς.—The *καί* is abrupt, and almost rude, implying peevishness at being put to a rebuke, or the arrogant presumption of expected victory in the testing.

πλησίον.—Without an article = "Who is neighbour to me?" The Rabbinical answer to this question would be that the Jew's nearest neighbour is his fellow-Jew. The lawyer expects Jesus to give some heterodox reply.

30. **ὑπολαβών.**—A good classic word, only found here in the New Testament = "taking up by way of reply." Cf. Lat. *excipio,* Æn., iv. 114, ix. 258.

ἄνθρωπος.—There is no word about his rank, descent, or religion ; he was a human being—that is his only claim to compassion. That he was a Jew we may assume, because it is the hatred that existed between Jews and Samaritans that gives point to the parable.

ἀπὸ 'Ιερουσ.—As the next incident related took place at Bethany (v. 38-42), the first village the traveller reaches on leaving Jerusalem for Jericho, it is probable that Jesus was on the very road to which the parable refers. The road descends 600 feet from Jerusalem to the Jordan valley : according to St Jerome, it was called the "Pass of the Red," Adummim (Josh. xv. 17), from the blood shed in it by robbers.   It runs through gorges, and is overhung by mountains ; numerous caverns afford concealment to the Bedouin robbers, while the sharp turns of the road and projecting spurs of rock facilitate their attack and escape.   The distance is about 21 miles.

καί—καί.—The repeated conjunction gives a pathetic emphasis to the tale : they not only stripped him to rob him ; but as he resisted, they beat him too.   As the sun in the neighbourhood of Jericho is almost tropically hot, and reflected from the limestone mountains, the agony to a wounded man from this exposure would be very great.

ἡμιθανῆ.—Lat. *semincx*, Æn., v. 275.

31. κατὰ συγκυρίαν.—A rare post-classical word, "by a coincidence."   It was unlikely that four such personages should meet at such a crisis, though not impossible.   There is perhaps a tinge of irony in the phrase, which prepares the hearers for something of interest to follow.

ἱερεύς.—The road would be frequented by priests and Levites, if, as there is reason to suppose, Jericho was a priestly city.   The priest and the Levite were probably both fresh from their duties at the Temple services, the object of which was to give outward expression to the love of God, so fully set forth in ver. 27.   In thus introducing the official sacrificers displaying indifference to the claims of mercy, Jesus is illustrating the saying from Hosea, which seems to have been a favourite with Him : " I will have mercy, and not [*i.e.*, rather than] sacrifice," Matt. ix. 13, xii. 7. In a similar spirit, Isaiah, at the commencement of his prophecies, had denounced the futility of the Temple sacrifices when unaccompanied by morality—Isa. i. 11, 17 : " I delight not in the blood of bullocks, or of lambs, or of he-goats. . . . Cease to do evil, learn to do well : seek judgment, relieve the oppressed," &c.   The words "sacrifice" and "devotion" have both a narrow and a wide meaning. The Jewish worshipper gave his sacrifice in the Temple through the priest ; but prophets and psalmists alike taught him that that sacrifice was only a symbol of the sacrifice of himself, heart, soul, strength, and mind, to the service of God—that is, of love to his fellow-men (for "God is love").   The Christian worshipper "pays his devotions" to God in church or chapel ;

these, however, are intended only as aids to the perfect devotion of himself to Christ.

The repetition by the priests and Levites of the symbolic acts of sacrifice and devotion in a perfunctory manner, without any thought of the meaning of them, would tend to make them less devoted and self-sacrificing even than others in whom the familiarity with holy things had not wrought such indifference to their true meaning.

τῇ ὁδῷ ἐκείνῃ.—There was another road to Jericho which was safer, and therefore more frequently used.

ἰδών.—The Jews were, as a rule, singularly familiar with their sacred books, and the sight of the naked traveller could scarcely fail to bring to the mind of the priest Isa. lviii. 7, "When thou seest the naked, that thou cover him."

ἀντιπαρ.—"Passed by in the face of (ἀντι-) that sight." Cf. Xen., Anab., iv. 3. 17 : αἱ τάξεις τῶν ἱππέων ἀντιπαρῇεσαν—"The line of cavalry moved on parallel with them on the opposite side of the river."

32. κατὰ τὸν τόπον.—The spot where he lay. A little more detail is thus given to the conduct of the Levite than to that of the priest. The words perhaps indicate that the Levite, being less refined than the priest, did not, as the latter did, feign to himself that he did not see him : he is curious, though not compassionate.

33. Σαμαρείτης.—See the following Essay, and cf. John iv. 9, "Now the Jews have no dealings with the Samaritans." We may perhaps illustrate the tale for ourselves by supposing that, during the feuds between England and Scotland, an English Protestant had been left by robbers. half dead on some wild Highland road, and a Protestant clergyman and layman had passed him by, while a wild Roman Catholic Highlander had befriended him.

In the case before us, all three men had great temptations to leave the traveller to his fate : the road was very dangerous, and the traveller might be past help,—and his misfortune was so common ! The Samaritan, in addition to this, had his national and religious prejudices to overcome.

34. ἐπιχέων.—"While pouring in."

ἔλαιον καὶ οἶνον.—Oil would be used to soothe, and wine to cleanse the wound. Oil was highly esteemed for its medicinal properties : cf. Mark vi. 13. In the last illness of Herod the Great, he was bathed in warm oil. Travellers were seldom without oil and wine—Gen. xxviii. 18.   In an invasion of Arabia by Ælius Gallus, in B.C. 24, when his army suffered severely from heat and want of water, oil and wine were applied as remedies, both internally and externally.

κτῆνος.—Rarely found in the sing. in the classics.   Probably an ass is meant here.   It is so rendered in the Syriac version.   The word literally means cattle; but in Acts xxiii. 24, it means "beasts of burden."

πανδοχεῖον—*i.e.*, a caravanserai.   The ruins of one are still seen on the mountain-side, about half-way between Jerusalem and Jericho.

35. **ἐπί**—"towards."   Cf. Acts. iii. 1, ἐπὶ τὴν ὥραν τὴν ἐννάτην.

ἐκβαλών.—Out of his girdle or purse.   Cf. Matt. xiii. 52.

δύο δηνάρια.—A little less than two francs; equal in purchasing value to six or seven shillings of our money.   It was the amount of two days' wages.   Cf. Matt. xx. 2; Tobit v. 14.   But what is the point of this detail?   The smallness of the sum indicates that he purposed an early return; his method and thrift, that it was his habit to be charitable.   He was not indulging in a mere impulse of generosity.

πανδοχεῖ.—The Attic forms are πανδοκεύς and πανδοκεῖον. This is the only place in the New Testament where a host is mentioned in connection with a caravanserai.   As a rule they were empty, and travellers had to bring their own provisions. The addition of a host may have come in with other Greek customs.

ἐγώ.—Emphatic : the wounded man was not to be asked.

36. **γεγονέναι.**—"To have shown himself."   Cf. Xen., Anab., i. 7. 4, εὐτόλμων γενομένων.

37. **ὁ ποιήσας.**—The νομικός, though subdued and softened by the beauty and appropriateness of the tale, cannot bring himself to use the hateful term Samaritan.

ποιεῖν ἔλεος is a Hebraism.   Cf. i. 72; Gen. xxiv. 12; and ποιεῖν μεγαλεῖα, i. 49; κράτος, i. 51; τὴν δικαιοσύνην (kindness), Gen. xx. 13.

τὸ ἔλεος.—The compassion related.

μετά.—The prep. with gen. is Hebraistic for the simple dat. Cf. Acts xiv. 27, xv. 4; Gen. xxvi. 29, μὴ ποιῆσαι μεθ' ἡμῶν κακόν.

καὶ σύ.—This belongs to ποίει.

U

38-42.—*Martha and Mary.*

38. ἐν τῷ πορ—*i.e.*, on the way to Jerusalem. Mary and Martha lived at Bethany. St Luke appears to have had before him some λόγιον which mentions the fact and the names of the persons, but not the time and place of the incident.

αὐτός.—He Himself, without the disciples.

οἰκίαν.—Probably the open leafy booth in which they would live during the Feast of Tabernacles, which was then being celebrated. As the booth probably stood in the court, we can picture to ourselves Martha moving backwards and forwards between it and the house on her busy errands, and seeing, as she passed again and again, Mary still sitting, a rapt listener, not heeding what passed around.—(Edersheim.)

39. παρακαθεσθεῖσα.—A late Greek form of the 1st aor. pass. found in Josephus: the usual word would be παρακαθίσασα. Mary sat as a learner, not at the meal, which had not begun.

40. περιεσπᾶτο.—Also a late Greek word = "distracted"; lit., "was being dragged in different directions." The adverb ἀπερισπάστως occurs in 1 Cor. vii. 35 (εὐπάρεδρον τῷ Κυρίῳ ἀπερισπάστως), where the metaphor in εὐπάρεδρον, and the occurrence of μεριμνᾷ in ver. 34, show that St Paul had this passage in his mind. With the metaphor cf. Hor., Sat., ii. 8. 67, "Tene, ut ego accipiar laute, torquerier omni sollicitudine districtum," and our expression, "to be put about." In Ecclus. xli. 1, we find ἀνδρὶ ἀπερισπάστῳ, and in Epictetus (Diss., iii. 22. 29), ἀπερίσπαστον εἶναι δεῖ ὅλον πρὸς τῇ διακονίᾳ τοῦ θεοῦ.

ἐπιστᾶσα.—Probably "suddenly coming up"—*i.e.,* from the house into the booth. Cf. xx. 1; Acts xxiii. 27. In Philo the word generally implies unexpectedness. The verb is a favourite one with St Luke, who is also fond of these participles, which add vividness to his narrative.

κατέλειπε.—This implies that she had been helping Martha.

εἰπὲ οὖν αὐτῇ.—"For it is no use my telling her."

συναντιλάβ. — The middle implies "taking on one's self a burden"; ἀντί, "for another"; σύν, "sharing it with him." The metaphor is of taking hold of along with another.

41. Μαρθά. — The repetition implies tenderness. Cf. Σίμων, Σίμων, in xxii. 31.

μεριμνᾷς.—See note on Matt. vi. 25.

θορυβάζῃ.—Translate "anxious and bustling," or even "fretting and fuming." This word occurs nowhere else in Greek. There is a *v. l.*, τυρβάζῃ.

ὀλίγων, κ.τ.λ.—*v. l.*, ἑνὸς δέ ἐστι χρεία.—Jesus seems to imply that Martha's preparations were excessive, but He passes from the consideration of bodily to spiritual nourishment, as He did when He spoke to the Samaritan woman of the "living water" (John iv. 10), and to His disciples of His having bread to eat that they knew not of, which He explains of the doing the will of Him that sent Him (John iv. 32, 34).

ἑνός, then, will refer to the spiritual nourishment derived from hearing the divine word, the desire for which will naturally lead to simplicity in living, as "plain living and high thinking" go together. The "stuffed body cannot see hidden things."

42. τὴν ἀγαθὴν μερίδα.—The article is emphatic = "that part which alone deserves the name of good."

μερίς is the word translated in Gen. xliii. 34 by "mess"; and Ps. lxxiii. 26, "God is my *portion* for ever." It occurs also in 1 Sam. ix. 23, where Samuel set before Saul the best or "kingly" portion, as Josephus calls it. Mary had chosen the royal mess of the banquet, the listening to Jesus. In Plutarch, μερίς is the share contributed to a common feast, the ἔρανος. Philo joins μερίδα καὶ κλῆρον.

ἥτις—*quippe quæ*, "which is of such a nature that."

οὐκ ἀφαιρεθήσεται—*i.e.*, primarily by Martha's requirements, but it was also true absolutely. The terrestrial banquet, the social intercourse of the table, is for this earth only; but the celestial banquet, the intercourse of spirits, is part of the ζωὴ αἰώνιος, and lasts for ever.

LESSON XXI.

The Parable of the Labourers in the Vineyard—
St Matt. xx. 1-16.

1. γάρ refers to the verse immediately preceding.

ἅμα πρωΐ.—πρωΐ is properly an adverb. In classic Greek we should have ἅμα ἕῳ. For the thought, cf. Jer. xxxv. 14, "I have spoken unto you, rising early and speaking; but ye hearkened not unto me." The Jewish working day is reckoned from sunrise to sunset.

μισθώσασθαι εἰς.—*Constructio prægnans.* "To hire labourers (to send) into his vineyard."

With **ἀμπελῶνα** cf. the parable in Isa. v., and the note on Matt. xx. 33.

2. **ἐκ** expresses the source or foundation of the *συμφωνία.* Cf. ποιήσατε ἑαυτοῖς φίλους ἐκ τοῦ μαμωνᾶ τῆς ἀδικίας—Luke xvi. 9. The bargain resulted from the money paid. Cf. xxvii. 7—ἠγόρασαν ἐξ αὐτῶν (ἀργυρίων) τὸν ἀγρόν.

δηναρίου.—A Roman silver coin which passed current as equal to the Greek drachma, though, in fact, some few grains lighter. At the end of the Roman Commonwealth it was equal to 8½d. of our money, afterwards something less. It was the pay of a Roman soldier for a day in Tiberius's time, a few years before this parable was uttered—Tac., Ann., i. 17, " Denis in diem assibus animam et corpus æstimari." It is mentioned as the usual wages for a day's work in Tobit v. 14. It was translated "penny" in the old Anglo-Saxon versions, and by Wycliffe and almost all succeeding trans-lators down to the time of our authorised version. The principal piece of money current among our Anglo-Saxon forefathers was a small silver coin called successively *pending, pening, penig,* and *peni.* The word means "a pledge," and comes from the Latin *pannus,* a rag = French *pan,* English *pawn,* because a piece of clothing is the readiest article to leave in pledge. Our copper coinage dates from A.D. 1665. δηνάριον would now be more suit-ably rendered "shilling" or "franc"; or, having regard to the purchasing value of money, "half-a-crown." The coin con-tained more than twice as much silver as the English penny at its heaviest and purest,—more than six times as much as that currrent in the time of our translators. See notes on Luke x. 35 and xv. 8.

τὴν ἡμέραν.—Acc. of respect, not of time.

3. **τρίτην ὥραν.**—About nine o'clock in the morning, called some-times πληθώρη ἀγορᾶς, when the market-place was full.

5. **ἕκτην καὶ ἐνάτην.**—About mid-day, and at three in the afternoon.

7. **ὅτι οὐδείς, κ.τ.λ.**—In the story they are not blameworthy, and therefore in the interpretation of the parable they were not

so. They represent men not living in a Christian land, or, if so, such as have never heard of Christianity,—which may easily be in a place with such a large heathen population as London, for instance; or, if they have heard of Christianity, have not yet been fired with any enthusiasm for the cause. Their labour has been for themselves only, and not for others; but when the good influence of Christianity is brought to bear upon them, they yield to it at once.

8. ὀψίας.—By the Mosaic law the hirer was bound to pay the labourer before night—Deut. xxiv. 15, "At his day (αὐθημερόν) thou shalt give him his hire, neither shall the sun go down upon it; for he is poor, and setteth his heart upon it."

ἐπιτρόπῳ.—In Luke viii. 3, the word is used of Herod's steward. The word for the unjust steward is οἰκονόμος. Both words occur in Gal. iv. 2, where the ἐπίτροπος looks after the education and bringing up of the heir, and the οἰκονόμος after his property. οἰκονόμος appears to have a narrower meaning than ἐπίτροπος. The latter means a viceroy, a guardian, one's man of business.

9. οἱ περὶ, κ.τ.λ—Sub. ἀπεσταλμένοι εἰς τὸν ἀμπελῶνα.

ἀνά.—At the rate of.

10. τὸ ἀνὰ δηνάριον.—The sum amounting in each case to a denarius.

λήμψονται.—Hellenistic for λήψονται.

11. γογγύζω.—Ionic and late Greek for the Attic τονθορύζω. γογγύζω is used constantly in the LXX. of the Israelites murmuring in the wilderness.

12. οὗτοι.—"These men," with a disdainful emphasis.

ἐποίησαν.—"Spent." Cf. the phrase ποιεῖν χρόνον, "to spend some time," in Acts xv. 33 and xviii. 23. So Demosthenes uses the phrase ποιεῖν οὐδένα χρόνον, "to make no long time"—i.e., "not to delay."

τὸν καύσωνα.—The searching wind of the desert at sunrise. Cf. Matt. xiii. 6, ἡλίου δὲ ἀνατείλαντος ἐκαυματίσθη; James i. 11, ἀνέτειλε γὰρ ὁ ἥλιος σὺν τῷ καύσωνι; Jonah iv. 8, ἅμα τῷ ἀνατεῖλαι τὸν ἥλιον προσέταξεν ὁ θεὸς πνεύματι καύσωνι συγκαίοντι: cf. Luke xii. 55. In Gen. xxxi. 40, Jacob describes his work as a shepherd by saying that he was consumed by the καύσων by day and the frost by night.

The word may be illustrated by the French chômer, "to be out of work," or "to keep holiday," which comes from the medieval *cauma*, the time of day when it is too hot to work, from which again comes French *calme*, Eng. *calm*.

13. ἑταῖρε.—Lit., " comrade,"—a mild way of introducing a rebuke, similar to "good friend" among ourselves. It is used to Judas, and to the guest without the wedding garment, chap. xxii. 12, xxvi. 50.

δηναρίου.—Gen. of price.

14. ἆρον.—Cf. ἆρον τὸ κράββατόν σου, Mark ii. 11. The word suggests that the wages of the labourer had been laid down for his acceptance, and had been left lying while he was giving vent to his grumbling.

τὸ σόν. — "Your property," with a slightly contemptuous accent. "Since you take this purely commercial view of our relations."

15. πονηρός—*i. e.*, "envious." Cf. Mark vii. 22. ἐγώ, "emphatic."

LESSON XXII.

The Parable of the Rich Fool—St Luke xii. 13-21.

13. It was the custom to refer questions of all kinds to the Rabbis for their counsel and decision, which carried great weight, even when informal and extrajudicial. It was almost criminal to dispute or oppose their words. The man, therefore, who asked the question that follows, was in good hopes that, if Jesus would decide for him, he would gain his point. The severity of Jesus' answer is due to the man's selfishness, and the unworthy use to which he sought to put Jesus' influence. He was in a far worse degree acting as Martha did (chap. x. 40). She neglected His teaching to care for His bodily comfort; but this man neglects it for his own personal interests, and acts as though the great Teacher existed only to gain him an inheritance!

ἐκ τοῦ ὄχλου goes with εἶπε.

κληρονομίαν.—The eldest son had a double portion of the inheritance, and the charge of maintaining his mother and unmarried sisters (Deut. xxi. 17). We learn from the parable of the Prodigal Son (chap. xv. 12) that the younger son might have his inheritance paid to him at once in money. This man was perhaps one of those younger members who was not satisfied with the sum allotted to him, or who, after having spent it, still claimed, under some pretext or other, a part of the patrimony. "The Jewish law of inheritance was so clearly defined and so just, that if this person had had any good cause there would have been no need to appeal to Jesus."—(Edersheim.)

14. ἄνθρωπε implies disapproval; it is used in Plato in addressing slaves. Cf. Rom. ii. 1, ix. 20.

μεριστήν (v. l., δικαστήν).—This word occurs nowhere else but in this passage, and seems to have been coined to express the Aramaic word used by Jesus to correspond with the verb expressed by μερίσασθαι. Jesus, in His answer, was perhaps referring to Exod. ii. 14, the words of the Hebrew to Moses: τίς σε κατέστησεν ἄρχοντα καὶ δικαστὴν ἐφ᾽ ἡμῶν. The v. l. δικαστήν for κριτήν may have arisen from that passage. Cf. Acts vii. 35.

15. πάσης.—"Every kind of." The πλεονέκτης is one who claims more than his share, one who grasps.

Construe, "Not [οὐκ being emphatic by position] because a man has a superfluity of riches is his life derived from his possessions" —i.e., "even a superfluity of riches will not constitute a man's possessions the source of his life."

τινί is the dative of possession after περισσεύειν.

ἐστιν ἐκ = "proceeds from," "has its source in." Cf. John xviii. 36, ἡ βασιλεία ἡ ἐμὴ οὐκ ἔστιν ἐκ τοῦ κόσμου τούτου; Acts xix. 25, ἐκ ταύτης τῆς ἐργασίας ἡ εὐπορία ἡμῖν ἐστιν.

"Riches," says Jesus, "do not really increase the *quantity* of a man's life." Quantity may be regarded either as *extensive* or *intensive*. The rich man has not more life than the poor in *extension*, because, as Jesus shows in the following parable, His life is as uncertain as that of the poor: he has not more life in *intensity*, because ζωή is independent of great riches. What is life but the full development of all our faculties, and the perfect exercise of all our energies, physical, intellectual, and spiritual? The poor may be as active in body and as vigorous as the rich, may have greater intellectual faculties, and may display more love to God and man. Extreme riches and extreme poverty both have a tendency to paralyse men's faculties, and therefore to destroy their life. Riches make men indolent in body, because there are many to minister to their wants ; inactive in mind, because, as they seem to have all they desire, there is nothing to stimulate them ; unloving, because the ease with which their desires are gratified makes them feel independent of God and of their fellow-men. On the other hand, the extremely poor have neither time nor leisure to develop their physical and intellectual $\zeta\omega\eta$, and through depression and misery are apt to become callous and indifferent to others.

The words of the text may be illustrated by the following picture in 'Daniel Deronda,' contrasting two married couples—the one rich in possessions but poor in love, the other poor in possessions but rich in love : " While Gwendolen, throned on her cushions at evening [on a yacht in the Mediterranean], and beholding the glory of sea and sky softening as if with boundless love around her, was hoping that Grandcourt [her husband] was not going to pause near her, not going to look at or speak to her, some woman under a smoky sky, obliged to consider the price of eggs in arranging her dinner, was listening for the music of a foot-step that would remove all risk from her foretaste of joy,—some couple bending, cheek by cheek, over a bit of work done by the one and delighted in by the other, were reckoning the earnings that would make them rich enough for a holiday among the furze and heath."

These two brothers quarrelling about their inheritance were losing the more precious possession of one another's love.

Perhaps the most striking examples of men having many possessions but little $\zeta\omega\eta$ are exhibited in the lives of some of the tyrannical Roman emperors, such as Nero, Domitian, and Caligula, to supply whom with luxuries every city and district of the civilised world was ransacked, yet who in the midst of splendour led indolent and isolated lives, with but little enjoyment from refined intellectual tastes, and often had their lives cut short by assassination.

Far more real $\zeta\omega\eta$ had the Athenian citizen, however poor, whose body had been fully and harmoniously developed by exercise in the gymnasium, whose mind and taste were cultivated by listening to the finest oratory and looking upon the noblest statues the world has ever known. But since the spirit is higher than the intellect, still greater abundance of $\zeta\omega\eta$ had the poor Galilean peasants as they hung on the lips of Jesus, and learnt the new laws of love which were to give them new powers of loving God and man more intensely, and more extensively too, since from their minds the barriers of national prejudice, which limited their love to the love of the men of their own nation, were to be swept away.

16. This parable seems to refer to Ecclus. xi. 18, 19 : "There is that waxeth rich by his wariness and pinching, and this is the portion of his reward ; whereas he saith, I have found rest (ἀνάπαυσιν), and now will eat continually of my goods : and yet he knoweth not what time shall come upon him, and that he must leave those things to others and die."

For βίος and ζωή, see note on Luke x. 25.

The difference between the two—between the life that consists in external possession and the life of thought—is beautifully and forcibly illustrated in the following stanzas by Mr Matthew Arnold :—

> "In his cool bath with haggard eyes
>   The Roman noble lay :
> He drove abroad in furious guise
>   Along the Appian Way.
> He made a feast, drank fierce and fast,
>   And crowned his head with flowers :
> No easier and no quicker past
>   The impracticable hours.
>
> The brooding East with awe beheld
>   Her impious younger world :
> The Roman tempest swelled and swelled,
>   And on her head was hurled.
> The East bowed low before the blast,
>   In patient deep disdain :
> She let the legions thunder past,
>   And plunged in thought again."

ἡ χώρα—The estate.

18. ἀποθήκας.—"Storehouses." It is not implied that he was wrong in doing this : his sin consisted in his utter selfishness. He might have learnt differently from Ecclus. xxix. 9-12 : "Help the poor for the commandment's sake, and turn him not away because of his poverty. Love thy money for thy brother and thy friend, and let it not rust a stone to be lost. Lay up thy treasure according to the commandment of the Most High, and it shall bring thee more profit than gold. Shut up thy alms in thy *store-houses*, and it shall deliver thee from all affliction."

19. **ἀγαθά.**—Cf. xvi. 25, where the word is opp. to κακά. It is used of produce in Gen. xlv. 18, δώσω ὑμῖν πάντων τῶν ἀγαθῶν Αἰγύπτου. There is a *v. l.* γεννήματα, which is a late Greek word for produce.

Observe the egotistic repetition of μου in this verse. The history of Nabal seems to have been in Jesus' mind : cf. 1 Sam. xxv. 11, "Shall I then take *my* bread, and *my* water, and *my* flesh that I have killed for *my* shearers." Both men forget that property has duties as well as privileges.

ψυχή.—For this periphrasis for the person, cf. Eur., Hipp., 174, τί ποτ' ἔστιν μαθεῖν ἔραται ψυχά — "I long to know what it is about." *Animus* is used in a similar way.

ἀναπαύου.—Notice the asyndeton (absence of conjunctions).

εὐφραίνου.—Cf. xvi. 19.

20. **ἄφρων.**—"Insensate," nom. for voc. Cf. μὴ φοβοῦ τὸ μικρόν ποίμνιον, ver. 32, and 1 Cor. xv. 36. The same usage occurs in English,—as in "King Lear," i. 4. 271, "The jewels of our father, with washed eyes, Cordelia leaves you ; " "Julius Cæsar," v. 3. 99, "The last of all the Romans, fare thee well." For the word cf. 1 Sam. xxv. 25, Νάβαλ (fool) ὄνομα αὐτῷ, καὶ ἀφροσύνη μετ' αὐτοῦ.

ταύτῃ τῇ νυκτί.—Opp. to the πολλὰ ἔτη of which he had been dreaming.

αἰτοῦσιν.—There is a *v. l.* ἀπαιτοῦσιν. The construction is probably impersonal, as in ver. 48—ᾧ παρέθεντο πολύ, περισσότερον αἰτήσουσιν αὐτόν : and Matt. ii. 20, "They are dead which sought the young child's life." Cf. the death of Nabal, 1 Sam. xxv. 36.

21. **μὴ πλουτῶν.**—"*If* he is not also rich toward God." This is explained by the θησαυρὸν ἐν τοῖς οὐρανοῖς of ver. 33, and by the phrase, "He that hath pity on the poor, lendeth to the Lord," Prov. xix. 17. Cf. Matt. vi. 19-21.

That, however, it is the loving temper and loving will, rather than the giving of much riches, that stores up the greatest treasure in heaven, is evident from Jesus' commendation of the poor widow who cast into the treasury of the Temple out of her penury two mites only, which were all her βίος—Luke xxi. 4.

A beautiful illustration of this parable is found in Adams's allegory of "The King's Messengers." The messengers are the poor who carry the alms to the king's treasury. In that allegory the importance of the motive is insisted on. To give alms for ostentation, or the sake of the reward, is not a way of "being rich toward God." It is the loving temper that swells, and draws from, the treasury of love.

Covetousness displays itself (1) in the love of gold for its own sake. This is the narrowest form of covetousness, and the English language, as well as the Italian and Spanish, has uttered the popular verdict on it by stigmatising those who exhibit it as "misers" —"miseri"—"wretched beings." This term, however, does not, probably, imply any moral feeling: it is a reproach on their folly for relinquishing for the gold itself the pleasures that gold can buy. (2) In the love of other possessions, as land, houses, pictures, &c., for their own sake, for the sake of ostentation, or for the sake of the pleasure they afford; and these grounds are here arranged in the order of merit.

Jesus elsewhere, as in the parables of the Talents and of the Dishonest Agent, lays down the principle that all property is held in trust for God, and is to be spent in the interests of the community. He does not enter into details as to how this should be done : hence His principles hold good for all ages, civilisations, and polities. In His time and country almsgiving would be good, because there were no organisations for the dispensation of charity. In our day indiscriminate charity is an evil, and charitable work is, as a rule, best done through organisations, provided these organisations do not destroy the intercourse between the donor and the recipient. Nor is charity now confined to the providing merely for animal existence, as food and shelter : but a man may do more good by providing flowers, pictures, and music for public use. But the principle is the same in whatever way it be applied. The selfish man diminishes his faculties for living, because he diminishes his powers of sympathy and love, and receives less of these from others.

The temptation of our own age is not, however, solely to the pursuit of the mere animal pleasures to which the man in the parable is represented as devoting himself. Men may give themselves up to intellectual pleasures, forgetting or neglecting all the sorrows that are in the world. In his poem, "The Palace of Art," Tennyson has depicted a soul so doing, and the despair that ensued ultimately from the unnatural absence of human affection. At first—

> " Singing and murmuring in her feastful mirth,
>   Joying to feel herself alive ;
> Lord over Nature, Lord of the visible earth,
>   Lord of the senses five :
> Communing with herself, ' All these are mine,
> And let the world have peace or wars,
>   'Tis one to me.' "

At last—

> " Shut up as in a crumbling tomb, girt round
>   With blackness as a solid wall ;
> Far off she seemed to hear the dully sound
>   Of human footsteps fall."

Then she resolves to retire to a cottage and pray till she has purged her guilt—to return, perhaps *with others*, to her palace.

Even our studies may make us selfish, and the safest corrective to this for a schoolboy is to take part in the games and other institutions of his school, that he may not become absorbed in himself.

LESSON XXIV.

The Parable of the Great Supper—St Luke xiv. 7-35.

7-12.—The choosing of the lowest place.

7. παραβολήν.—The word is a translation of the Hebrew *má-shâl*, as it is constantly in the LXX. That word meant "similitude," and had a very wide application, sometimes referring to short proverbs, as 1 Sam. x. 12, "Is Saul also among the prophets?" sometimes to dark prophetic utterances, as of Balaam in Num. xxiii. 7; sometimes to enigmatic sayings, as in Prov. i. 6, "To understand a proverb, and the interpretation; the words of the wise, and their dark sayings." It is applied in Luke iv. 23 to the phrase, " Physician, heal thyself." The French *parole* comes from it. Here it seems, from ver. 11, to mean a lesson in humility generally, based upon the practice of it in a particular instance.

ἐπέχων—*i.e.*, τὸν νοῦν.

πρωτοκλισίας.—The Jews in Jesus' time had adopted the Roman fashion of reclining at meals. They sat on three divans round the table which was brought in to them, and which was low: there would be several tables in a large feast such as this. The most honourable couch was the *medius*, then the *summus*, then the *imus*. At one end was a railing, on which lay a cushion ; the rest of the places were separated by pillows. The most

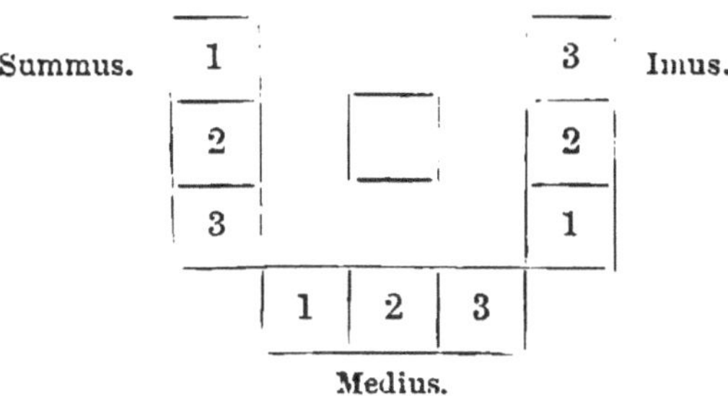

honourable place was that next the railing, which in the *imus* would be 1 and in the *summus* 1, but in the *medius* 3, and this was the seat of honour of the whole triclinium, and was left for the most distinguished person. Sometimes more than three would recline on each divan, the table being, in that case, oval or elongated. Such, probably, was the arrangement at the Last Supper.

ἐξελέγοντο.—" Were picking out for themselves."

8. γάμους.—This word is translated "*feast*" in Esth. ii. 18, but there it may mean "a wedding-feast." But in Esth. ix. 22 it seems certainly used of any feast, so that the meaning of the word seems to have been expanded. The feast at which Jesus was now present could not be a marriage-feast, for marriages were not solemnised on the Sabbath-day. He may, however, have spoken of a marriage-feast to avoid personality, or because he used " marriage-feast " on other occasions as a type of the kingdom of God.

Jesus, in thus speaking, was only acting as acknowledged Rabbis were in the habit of doing. It is said of one Rabbi, that to produce gravity at a marriage-feast, he broke a vase worth £25; of another, that at his son's wedding he broke a costly glass ; and of a third, that being asked to sing, he exclaimed, " Woe to us, for we must all die !"

As an illustration of the anxiety of the Rabbis to secure for themselves the best couch, we are told that at a banquet given by

King Alexander Jannæus, at which several Persian satraps were present, Rabbi Simeon Ben Shatach seated himself between the king and queen; and on being asked his reason, replied that it was written in the book of Jesus Ben Sirach, "Exalt wisdom and she shall exalt thee, and shall make thee sit among princes."

9. ἄρξῃ expresses the reluctance with which he will move. The intervening places would by this time be taken. The host or a friend (the master of the feast: cf. John ii. 8, ἀρχιτρικλίνῳ) would arrange who should take them. For the arrangement of guests according to their rank, we may compare Gen. xliii. 33, where Joseph's brethren are so arranged, and 1 Sam. ix. 22 (the chiefest place—τόπον ἐν πρώτοις τῶν κεκλημένων). We know from the Talmud that the Rabbis occupied the uppermost seats.

10. προσανάβηθι.—"Come up hither towards me." Cf. Prov. xxv. 7, "Better is it that it be said unto thee, Come up hither, than that thou shouldest be put lower in the presence of the prince."

ἵνα must be interpreted as introducing a sentence co-ordinate to that introduced by μή ποτε in ver. 8, and almost equivalent to "the result will be that." To take a lower seat *for the purpose of* being invited to a higher, is not a spirit Jesus would inculcate. He is pointing out to the worldly Pharisees, whom He elsewhere rebukes for loving the uppermost seats in the synagogues (Matt. xxiii. 6), that even from a worldly point of view their pushing conduct is a mistake. But from this He leads on the conversation to the general principle of ver. 11.

The arrangements of modern dinner-parties do not usually admit of this pushing eagerness, but it sometimes—too often—finds its way into our places of worship.

δόξα.—A stronger word than τιμή—honour accompanied with recognition.

11. Men who overestimate themselves constantly suffer chagrin, and since we are all prone to do so, we are safe in taking up inferior positions to those we think our due. Yet men must not shrink from their official positions, in which they are representatives of the dignity of others. This saying of Jesus occurs also in Matt. xxiii. 12; Luke xviii. 14, where see note. Cf. Prov. xxix. 23. Men are always very ready to detect presumption, even in those who take chief seats with a justification for doing so.

12-14.—*Who are our best guests.*

It was an old custom in Israel to invite the poorer neighbours to the special meals on the consecrated flesh of offerings not used at the altar, and to similar religious feasts. Cf. Neh. viii. 10; Deut. xiv. 28, 29. But in the time of Jesus this usage was a thing of the past, for the priests and Rabbis of His day shrank from contact with the people. It is possible that, in accordance with the freedom of intercourse in the East, many poor neighbours had crowded into the courts of the house, some even into the rooms, to look on and listen to the Rabbis, especially to the famous new Teacher. On these the Rabbis, while they pushed for pre-eminence among themselves, would look askance and with contempt. It is probable that this was a feast to which many distinguished persons were invited.

12. ἄριστον ἢ δεῖπνον.—A breakfast or a dinner. Cf. John xxi. 12, where early in the morning Jesus is represented as saying, "δεῦτε ἀριστήσατε." It is probable that breakfast took place immediately after the return from morning prayers in the synagogue, about 9 or 10 A.M., and dinner towards evening.

ἄρ-ιστον is probably connected with our ear-ly. Cf. the Homeric ἠέριος ἠριγένεια.

φώνει.—In ver. 13 we have the more classic καλεῖ. The former refers to the calling by the voice, the latter rather to the invitation, so that the former implies more ostentation, the latter more feeling. Since φωνέω always in the Greek Testament refers to calling aloud, there may be a reference to the holding of banquets in the open air, to which passers-by were invited. Cf. Gen. xviii. 1-3.

In what follows Jesus is speaking rhetorically, not logically, in accordance with the Rabbinical practice, and would be so understood by his hearers. The negative μὴ φώνει, followed by ἀλλά, would be regarded as implying that the practice of inviting the poor, &c., as expressed in the latter clause, was to be preferred to that of inviting the rich, &c., as expressed in the former. Cf. Matt. ix. 13, ἔλεον θέλω καὶ οὐ θυσίαν—i.e., "I prefer a compassionate temper to sacrifice." The negative is actually explained by parallelism in Prov. viii. 10: "Receive my instruction and *not* silver; and knowledge *rather than* choice gold." See also ver. 26 of this chap. Here, too, as elsewhere in His teaching, He is thinking of the motive, and the scene to His eyes is a painful one. The distinguished guests are thinking each of his own dignity and advancement. They are filled with mean motives, and displaying their customary contempt for the poor and oppressed. Jesus bids them look for the rewards of the pious rather than of the worldly. That it is unworthy to be hospitable for the sake of a return, that we should spend our sustenance in acts of beneficence rather than of ostentatious entertainments,—such is the instruction Jesus seems here to be giving. It is not likely that His hearers would understand Him as forbidding them to entertain their relations, who, indeed, would often be the poor, nor to abstain from showing hospitality to their neighbours because they were rich. He is reprobating heartless hospitality for the sake of mutual advantage. It is obvious that in our time and country it would not always be a kindness to invite the poor to dinner-parties. But in the time of Jesus there were no poor-laws, workhouses, hospitals, or other organisations for relieving poverty. It is very much due to the influence of His teaching that these have sprung up. The teaching of the Pharisees about pollution had bred a feeling of extreme hardness towards the poor, that does not exist to anything like the same extent in our day. One of the best practical illustrations of carrying out the injunction in detail is perhaps the custom of entertaining the poor and old in the Birmingham Town Hall at Christmas time ; one of the most painful illustrations of the social feeling that led to the instruction, the struggle for social eminence and good matrimonial alliances in London society which Thackeray has satirised, especially in the life and conversation of Major Pendennis. The Christian who has the spirit of love in him will naturally shrink from such feasts ; and all his feasts, whether given to the poor or to the rich, will tend to promote Christian love and unity.

Seneca recommended masters to sit down to table with their slaves; and Epictetus says, " It would be best if, while making your preparations, and while feasting at your banquets, you distribute among the attendants some of the provisions." We are told of Pope Gregory (A.D. 590) that he was in the habit of sending dishes from his own table to persons whom he knew to be ashamed to ask relief; that he entertained strangers and wanderers as his guests ; and that, when a poor man had been found dead in the street, he abstained from the celebration of the Eucharist for some days, considering himself the cause of his death.

It was in harmony with these words of Jesus that the Council of Nicæa (A.D. 325) issued an edict that Xenodochia (ξενο-δοχεῖα), or refuges for strangers, should be erected in every city.

13. δοχήν.—Only found here and in St Luke v. 28, in the New Testament. Cf. Gen. xxi. 8, καὶ ἐποίησε ᾽Αβράαμ δοχὴν μεγάλην.

14. ἐν τῇ ἀναστάσει τῶν δικαίων.—According to the Rabbis, only the perfectly just enter at once into Paradise; all the rest pass through a period of purification and perfection, of various duration, up to one year. The first mention of a resurrection of the body in the Old Testament is in Dan. xii. 3, where a partial resurrection is alluded to. But it takes a more explicit form in the Second Book of Maccabees, chap. vii., where the hope of a resurrection of the body, followed by eternal happiness, sustains, in the midst of torments, a Jewish family, composed of a mother and her seven sons, who, during the persecution of Antiochus Epiphanes, refused to sacrifice to idols, and died heroically for their faith. The second of the children cries out before expiring: "Thou, like a fury, takest us out of this present life; but the King of the world shall raise us up, who have died for His laws, unto everlasting life." The general tone of this remarkable seventh chapter tends to prove that the resurrection of the dead was regarded as reserved only for the children of Israel who were faithful to the law of God. The time of the resurrection is defined, in ver. 29, by ἐν τῷ ἐλέει (in the mercy), as the commencement of the reign of the Messiah. The Jews, first of all, conceived of a partial resurrection at the beginning of the Messiah's reign, and then, later on, of a general resurrection at the end of it. Jesus seems to allude to this first resurrection in chap. xx. 35. Josephus speaks of the Pharisees as restricting the transmigration of souls (writing to Greeks, he prefers this phrase to *resurrection*) to the righteous; and this view St Paul seems to combat in Acts xxiv. 15, where he speaks of a resurrection both of the just and the unjust. There is probably a distinction in the New Testament between ἡ ἀνάστασις νεκρῶν, which refers to the resurrection of the just and the unjust, and ἀνάστασις ἐκ νεκρῶν, which refers to the resurrection of the just only.

15-24.—*The parable of the Great Supper.*

15. The Rabbis believed that the resurrection of the just was to be followed by a great festival. It is possible that the speaker

here was one whose life did not warrant him in the complacent assurance that he should take part in this festival. Jesus, on other occasions, protested against the theory that none but Jews should do so. Cf. Matt. viii. 11, " Many shall come from the east, and from the west, and shall recline with Abraham, Isaac, and Jacob in the kingdom of heaven." Jesus, in the parable, shows how the Jews, by the treatment of God's messages through the prophets, through John the Baptist, and finally, through Himself, had rejected the invitation to the great banquet, which was a banquet of the soul—of love and holiness.

φάγεται.—Fut. for the classic **ἔδομαι.** Cf. Luke xvii. 8, **φάγεσαι.** The phrase "eat bread," both in the Old Testament and among the Rabbis, = "partake of a meal." Cf. Exod. ii. 20.

16. **ἐκάλεσε.**—The technical term for inviting ; Lat., *voco.*

πολλούς here refers to the Jews.

δεῖπνον μέγα.—The mas. form is rare and late.

17.—**ἀπέστειλεν τὸν δοῦλον.**—It is still the custom in the East to repeat the invitation when all is prepared. Cf. Esth. vi. 14, where the king's chamberlains haste to bring in Haman to the banquet Esther had prepared, and to which she had previously invited him. It was a Roman custom also. Cf. Ter., Heaut., i. 1. 117, "Monere oportet me hunc vicinum Phaniam, ad cœnam ut veniat"; and Martial, Epig., viii. 67. 1—

> " Horas quinque puer nondum tibi nuntiat, et tu
> Jam conviva mihi Cœciliane venis."

Thomson, in 'The Land and the Book,' describes the servant of a sheikh as inviting his guests at the proper time, in the very formula used in the parable—"Come, for the supper is ready."

τὸν δοῦλον αὐτοῦ.—Jesus is probably referring here to Himself.

ἔρχεσθε.—This corresponds to the preaching by John the Baptist and by Jesus—" the kingdom of heaven is at hand."

18. **ἀπὸ μιᾶς**—*i.e.,* **γνώμης,** "consent," or **φωνῆς,** "voice." Philo, in Flacc., has **ὡς ἄπαντας ὁμοθυμαδὸν μιᾷ φωνῇ κεκραγέναι.**

ἔχε με παρῃτημένον.—" Have me as one begged off." Cf. chap. xix. 20, **ἡ μνᾶ σου ἦν εἶχον ἀποκειμένην ἐν σουδαρίῳ.** Xen., Cyr., iii. 1. 35, **οὐ θαρροῦντά με ἕξεις.**

19. **ζεύγη πέντε.**—So Elisha was found ploughing with twelve yoke of oxen before him—1 Kings xix. 19.

δοκιμάσαι.—A bullock unaccustomed to the yoke would be nearly useless.

The excuses include the three motives of wealth, business, and pleasure. As their engagement had been made previously with the host, they were uncourteous, however apparently reasonable. There is a climax of rudeness in their answers : the first says, "ἔχω ἀνάγκην"; the second, "πορεύομαι"; the third, flatly, "οὐ δύναμαι." It is related of Sir T. More, that on being sent for by the king, when he was at his prayers in public, he returned answer he would attend him when he had first performed his service to the King of kings. So all men have a prior engagement with God. Hardly any of the spiritual chiefs of the Jewish nation attached themselves openly to Christ, His messenger. Cf. John vii. 48, " Have any of the rulers or Pharisees believed on Him ?"

21. **πλατείας καὶ ῥύμας**—*i.e.*, broad streets and narrow lanes ; but πλατείας, in modern Greek, would mean squares, as in French *place* (*platea*). In Isa. xv. 3, some translate " broad places." The word was originally an adjective, with ὁδός understood, which is supplied in Xen., Cyr., i. 6. 43. Cf. τραχεῖαι, chap. iii. 5.

τῆς πόλεως.—In the interpretation, " the theocracy "—*i.e.*, the holy nation of Israel.

ῥύμη, from **ῥέω** = a violent movement, then a " going " ; then like " alley," from French *aller*, a narrow lane. Roma is probably connected with the same word, and means " impetuous strength," ῥώμη, or perhaps " the stream town."

πτωχούς, κ.τ.λ.—The repetition of these words from ver. 13 is a great guide to us in interpreting the parable. We must recollect that the feast at which Jesus was present commenced with His healing a 'man who had the dropsy. For him the Pharisees showed no sympathy. Then, probably, there were looking on, but not partaking of the feast, many of the classes here spoken of, whom, on account of their pollution, the spiritual rulers regarded as outcasts. Yet these had shown themselves willing to enter into the kingdom of God, to hear the message of John the Baptist and of Jesus, which the Pharisees would not hear.

23. This call probably refers to the Gentiles outside Palestine.

φραγμούς.—Hedges beside which wanderers and beggars and the homeless have encamped. Cf. Mark xii. 1.

ἀνάγκασον—*i.e.*, in spite of their timidity. Cf. Matt. xiv. 22. Good clothes should not be necessary in Christian churches : the shy, the morose, the surly, are all to be won to Christ. Cf. the saying of the Rabbis, "Let the poor be the sons of thy house;" and the invitation of Wisdom in Prov. ix. 2, 3.

24. The spiritual rulers of the Jews had voluntarily excluded themselves. The banquet of brotherly love and unselfishness was not for those who were wilfully narrow and selfish. They had put religious form in place of morality, and therefore the Gentile whom they hated, and their own countrymen, polluted by the Gentile, whom they despised, came to the banquet in their place.

THE PARABLES OF THE BUILDER AND OF THE KING GOING TO WAR.

25-35.—*Jesus, on His way to Jerusalem, discourages those who are following Him from political motives.*

25. συνεπορεύοντο.—Notice the imperf.

στραφείς.—This is a favourite word with St Luke. Reverence would keep the ὄχλοι from going on in front.

26. The same principle of interpretation applies here as in ver. 12. Cf. Gen. xxix. 30 with 31, "Jacob *loved* Rachel *more* than Leah;" "and when the Lord saw that Leah *was hated.*"

There is a softer form of the saying in Matt. x. 37, "He that loveth son or daughter more than me is not worthy of me;" in that passage it is addressed to missionaries, in this to the disciples generally.

Jesus had left the house of the Pharisee, and was on His journey, surrounded by multitudes from the villages and cities, many of whom He knew were unprepared to sacrifice anything in His cause, and only followed Him from curiosity or self-interest. They were looking forward to His showing Himself in Jerusalem as the political Messiah, and thought to gain advancement or fame. It was necessary they should be undeceived. He knew that He was going to Jerusalem to win neither renown nor position, but death. Cf. chap. xiii. 33, "It cannot be that a prophet perish out of Jerusalem." The idea of utter devotion He was setting before His followers was familiar to them from the description of Levi in Deut. xxxiii. 9, "Who said unto his father and to his mother, I have not seen him; neither did he acknowledge his brethren, nor his own children." The claims of morality over natural affection had been asserted in the stern precept contained in Deut. xxi. 18-21, that if a son showed himself determinately vicious or impious, his father or mother was to bring him before the magistrates that he might be stoned. So the claims of public duty over natural affection were taught to the Romans in the story of Brutus on the tribunal condemning his treasonous sons to death.

In His paradoxical saying, and in the parables that follow, Jesus sought to separate from His society followers whose motives and conduct were likely to be a hindrance and embarrassment to Him, and at the same time to prepare those who were sincerely "hungering and thirsting after righteousness," for the difficulties and trials that awaited them. The kingdom of heaven was neither to be a field for the ambitious nor a rest for the meditative ; neither the mere statesman and soldier, nor the dreaming mystic and sentimentalist, would find his ideal there. The followers of Jesus were to be at war with the world, and yet to carry on this war with no pomp or circumstance, fired by nothing of the soldier's combativeness, and cheered by none of his honours : they were to be peaceful devotees, and yet to forego the rest and solitude of the philosopher or of the Essene. It was their destiny to do battle with Roman vices, not with Roman legions ; and they were to be soldiers under no visible commander, for an invisible country, without the stimulus of patriotism or of pay. In the burning language of St Paul (1 Cor. iv. 9-13), the apostles, at least, resembled the condemned in the Roman theatre. God seemed to have given orders for their sufferings in the arena of the world, even as the Roman emperor gave orders for the contests of prisoners with wild beasts in the more confined arena of the amphitheatre. On the degradation and sufferings of the apostles, angels and men seemed to be looking without sympathy ; they were regarded as fools ; they were weak and dishonoured ; they suffered hunger and thirst, and nakedness and buffeting, and had no certain dwelling-place — neither home nor fatherland ; they had to preach, and yet had no pay, nor position, nor leisure, but supported themselves by the labour of their own hands ; when reviled, they neither retaliated in words, nor satisfied their outraged human feelings with the calm contempt of the Stoic, but answered with blessings ; persecution they met with endurance, defamation with mild exhortations ;

they had become as the filth of the world, and the offscouring
of all things.

But perhaps the worst of all the evils the converts to Christianity would have to face would be the anger, or, what was far more
terrible, the grief of their parents. The home feeling among the
Jews was very strong, and among the Romans obedience to parents
was one of the first principles of religion ; yet the Jew who became a convert must renounce all his home ties, and the Roman
go counter to one of his first instincts, and become not only a
traitor to his country but a rebel to his father ! And we must
bear in mind parents and relatives, both Jewish and Roman, would
quite conscientiously look on Christianity as a pernicious superstition calculated to bring down the vengeance of heaven, and to
ruin the country or the empire ; nay, they would often regard it
as their duty to give up their renegade children to death.

Yet if the disciples of Jesus did not set their love for Him above
their love of their parents and their home, how was His religion to
be propagated ? Nay, if children always thought as their parents,
how would the world progress ? Jesus in these words emancipated
children, at least when they have arrived at years of discretion,
from the tyranny of parents over their minds and thoughts ; and
St Paul laid down the limits of obedience when he said, " Children,
obey your parents *in the Lord* "—Eph. vi. 1.

27. τὸν σταυρόν.—This figure is used only on this occasion, and
at the announcement of the passion in Matt. xvi. 24. We cannot
determine whether Jesus had His own death in His mind, or if
He were referring to the spectacle, only too common in Palestine since the Roman subjugation, of the criminal on his way to
crucifixion carrying his own cross. The custom is alluded to in a
lost play of Plautus, " The Carbonaria ": " Patibulum ferat per
urbem, deinde affigatur cruci." In Latin we never have " ferre
crucem," but always " ferre furcam " or " ferre patibulum." It
is probable that the criminal carried not the whole cross, but only
the transverse beam. Plutarch uses the phrase of a guilty conscience : καὶ τῷ μὲν σώματι τῶν κολαζομένων ἕκαστος κακούργων
ἐκφέρει τὸν αὑτοῦ σταυρόν.

To the multitudes who were following Jesus at this time—
whether to those who were following Him in the expectation of
His leading a revolt from the rule of Rome, or to those who
were looking to Him to guide them in their aspirations after a life

of tranquil piety—the words must have sounded appalling, and have produced the result He desired, of thinning the numbers of His followers by repelling the merely political or curious. The figure He set before them was not that of the heroic patriot or the peaceful meditative Essene, but of the degraded criminal bending under the yoke of his own cross—a figure that can only be represented to our minds by the image of the murderer carrying his own gallows, his sufferings unrelieved by any of the religious sympathy Christianity now affords to such wretches.

St Paul uses the verb σταυρόω metaphorically, speaking of "crucifying the flesh," and of "being crucified to the world," Gal. v. 24, vi. 14. We use the weaker word "mortify," as St Paul used the weaker phrase "being dead to sin," Rom. vi. 2. Cf. Col. iii. 5, νεκρώσατε τὰ μέλη ὑμῶν. Cf. Plautus, Cistell., iii. 1. 16, "Nil mecum tibi, mortuus tibi sum."

πύργον.—Towers would be built for the protection of vineyards (Matt. xxi. 33), of wells, of flocks, and of villages. The Herodian family had a passion for building. The word here may mean a turreted mansion. Cf. Hor., Od., i. 4. 14, "Pauperum tabernas regumque turres."

28. καθίσας.—The participle emphasises the carefulness of the computation. Cf. chap. xvi. 6, and see note on xv. 18.

ἀπαρτισμόν.—This word only occurs here and in Dion., Hal. The adverb ἄπαρτι, in the sense of "completely," occurs in Herodotus, 5. 53.

30. οὗτος is used contemptuously.

31. ἐν δέκα may mean "surrounded by" or "with."

32. εἰ δὲ μήγε—i.e., δυνατὸς εἴη. Cf. Matt. vi. 1.

τὰ πρὸς εἰρήνην.—"Things which tend to peace"—i.e., "arrangements for peace," "terms of peace."

33. ἀποτάσσεται.—Lit., "to set apart"; then in later Greek (1) "to bid farewell to," as in Mark vi. 46; Luke ix. 61: (2) to "abandon" or "renounce," as here: Vulg., renunciare. Philo speaks of ἀποτάσσεσθαι τῇ γαστρί and ταῖς αἰσθήσεσι, "renouncing the belly" and "the senses." Notice the solemn repetition of the refrain, οὐ δύναταί μου εἶναι μαθητής.

34. ἐὰν δὲ καί.—"But if even the salt."

35. ἔξω.—Emphatic by position, "out they cast it."

Salt is good to preserve some substances from corruption, and to give to others a taste: so Jesus expects His followers to preserve the society in which they live from moral corruption, and to give a tone to it. But should they lose their own moral tone, how can they who have known the Highest Example, and felt it, recover their tone from any other influence? They are likely to be of no further use. Their unfaithfulness causes men to be disgusted with Christianity.

Again, inferior kinds of salt were used as manure to the soil, and to hasten the decomposition of dung; but savourless salt would be useless even for these purposes. The Christian who has proved unfaithful to his calling will neither fertilise what is good in society nor put an end to what is evil. He is more useless than if he had never been a Christian at all, because he has become a scandal.

Travellers tell us of the finding of salt in the East that had lost its flavour, through the earth and other impurities being mixed with it: so may Christians lose their influence by adopting a worldly tone and worldly motives.

The saying occurs in the Talmud, and seems to have been a Jewish proverb. The Jews compared the soul, as also the Scriptures, to salt. Jesus employs the gnome also in Matt. v. 13; Mark ix. 50. Cf. Job vi. 6 and Col. iv. 6. In this passage it seems to mean, "It will be better that you should not become my disciples, than that you should do so without counting the cost, and so incur the risk of afterwards falling away and being a scandal to my teaching."

Jesus does not say that it is impossible for such of His disciples as fall away to rise again. He points out the great and obvious difficulties of their doing so.

ὁ ἔχων ὦτα, κ.τ.λ.—Philo, De Charit., completes the phrase thus: τοῖς ὦτα ἔχουσιν ἐν ψυχῇ.

LESSON XXV.

The Parables of the Lost Sheep and the Lost Piece of Silver—St Luke xv. 1-10.

1. ἦσαν ἐγγίζοντες.—This periphrastic form of the imperfect is not unusual in classic Greek, though more common in poetry than prose. Cf. Eur., Hec., 122, ἦν δὲ τὸ μὲν σὸν σπεύδων ἀγαθόν. In Hellenistic Greek it is frequent in prose, partly perhaps because it was frequent in Aramaic, the language of natives of Palestine, partly because it is the tendency of language to resolve condensed expressions for the sake of clearness and force. An illustration of this in English is the Elizabethan use of the simple preterite where we should now use the past participle with the auxiliary verb, as in the "Tempest," v. 1. 114—

> "And since I *saw* thee,
> The affliction of my mind amends,"—

where we should now say, "have seen."

In this passage the circumlocution seems to imply custom. Cf. Mark ii. 18, ἦσαν οἱ μαθηταὶ Ἰωάννου νηστεύοντες.

πάντες presents a difficulty from which Luther in his translation endeavoured to extricate himself by rendering "all kinds of publicans and sinners." The word cannot be taken literally, but is a rhetorical way of expressing that on His last journey to Jerusalem Jesus drew to Himself publicans and sinners from every town and village on His route. Cf. the ὄχλοι in xiv. 25 and Matt. iii. 5, τότε ἐξεπορεύετο πρὸς αὐτὸν Ἱεροσόλυμα καὶ πᾶσα ἡ Ἰουδαία, καὶ πᾶσα ἡ περίχωρος τοῦ Ἰορδάνου. .

τελῶναι.—"Tax-gatherers." The word "publicans" is a literal translation of the Latin *publicani*, adopted by Wycliffe in his version. During the reign of Richard II., when that version was made, it would have been particularly dangerous to give the plain English rendering (Nicholson). The persons here meant were the middle-men between the Roman farmers of taxes—the real *publicani*—and those who were commonly called "publicans," the ordinary collectors of taxes.

See note on Matt. v. 46, and cf. Luke iii. 13, xix. 8, where their extortionate practices are alluded to.

Tax-gatherers are never a popular class, but these men were especially detested as collecting from their own countrymen and co-religionists for the unpopular Roman government; above all, hated and despised by the advanced national party, the Pharisees and Scribes, who regarded all contact with the Gentiles as pollution, and all breakers of even the details of the Law as accursed. With them to sin was not necessarily to be immoral, but to break the ceremonial law, and hence to be unclean. It is probable, however, that none but the debased and degraded would undertake so odious an office as tax-gathering, and that such men might fairly be classed with " the sinners." In the state of religious ferment Palestine was in at that time, even they, however, would have their religious aspirations, and many of them who had succeeded perhaps to a hereditary office, or been driven into it by sheer want, would deeply feel their degradation. To such the loving and sympathetic spirit of Jesus, the new Teacher, presented a great contrast to the chilling and supercilious contempt of the Pharisees and Scribes, the professional religionists. Not only did He attract them as a class, but the names of two who attached themselves to Him are especially mentioned,—Matthew (St Matt. ix. 9), the author of the gospel that bears his name, and Zacchæus (Luke xix. 2).

In the trilogy of parables that follow, Jesus seeks to induce the Pharisees to think less of the sins and shortcomings, and more of the aspirations after holiness, of their erring brethren. But though they seem to refer primarily to the relations of Pharisees and publicans, the parables may fairly be regarded as having a wider application to those of Jews and Gentiles generally, and point to the time spoken of by St Paul, when there should be " neither Jew nor Greek, but all should be one in Christ Jesus " —Gal. iii. 28.

The parables, however, contain a lesson for " the sinners " as well as for the Pharisees, leading them to think of God as a loving and forgiving father, rather than as a stern, hard taskmaster.

2. διεγόγγυζον.—The preposition intensifies the meaning,—" kept angrily muttering to one another." Cf. " curses not loud but deep." St Luke is fond of verbs compounded with διά and ἐπί. Cf. διασκορ-

πίζω, ver. 13; διατηρέω, ii. 51; διαφυλάσσω, "to guard carefully," iv. 10; διαμαρτύρομαι, "to bear solemn attestation," xvi. 28.

Φαρισαῖοι καὶ γραμματεῖς.—See the Essays, pages 41 and 171.

οὗτος.—Contemptuous.

προσδέχεται.—Intensive prep., "receives with welcome." Cf. Thuc. ii. 12; Phil. ii. 29, προσδέχεσθε αὐτὸν ἐν Κυρίῳ μετὰ πάσης χαρᾶς.

3. τὴν παραβολήν.—Of the three parables that follow, the first sets forth the compassion of the Father for sinners, the second the value He sets on them, the third illustrates both. Again, the lost sheep represents the sinner who is altogether ignorant that there is a God and a heavenly home; the piece of coin, the sinner who knows God as a King but not as a Father (for the coin bears the King's image); the prodigal son, the sinner who, having known the Father's love and the joys of His home, wilfully and knowingly banishes himself from both. Again, the first two parables dwell solely on God's feeling towards the sinner; the last treats also of the feelings of the sinner towards God. See note on ver. 9.

4. ἐνενήκοντα ἐννέα.—The Jews often used the expression "ninety-nine."

ἐρήμῳ.—Not a sandy desert, but a wide grassy place, without habitations of men, where the rest of the flock would be quite safe.

6. οἶκον.—His heavenly home, whence He had come forth to earth to seek the lost sheep—the publicans and sinners, or perhaps we may take it as the kingdom of God, the new order of things introduced by Christianity, as opposed to ἔρημος, the Jewish Church. Jesus makes all men one family, into which the outcasts from the theocracy may be admitted, though the Pharisee refuse to join it.

7. οἵτινες.—"Of the class who."

Contrast with this saying of Jesus that of the Pharisees, "There is joy before God when those who provoke Him perish from the world" (Edersheim).

With the parable cf. 1 Kings xxii. 17; Num. xxvii. 17.

A parable similar to this is ascribed to Rabbi Simeon, the chief of the Ascetics, the great teacher of the Essenes. He is reported to have said that a certain man had a flock of sheep which were daily led to pasture. Here they were joined by a gazelle, who regularly fed with them, and returned with them to the fold.

The owner of the flock bade his shepherd take the greatest care of the stranger; and when he was asked why he showed it such favour, answered: "This creature has left the wilderness, and, in spite of its own untamed and timid nature, has joined the flock. It is well that I should welcome it more affectionately than I do those who have been fed by me, and tended by my care; for that which is customary with them, is strange to the gazelle." And thus the Rabbi draws the moral: God will welcome the stranger who joins himself to the chosen people, more than He will those who have always had the blessing of His covenant, because they are born to Israel.

8. δραχμή.—From δράσσομαι, "what one can grasp in the hand." Cf. δράγμα, a sheaf. The Greeks generally reckoned by drachmas, as the Romans reckoned by sesterces. Roman coinage owed the origin of the weights of its gold and silver money to Greece, and the denarius, the chief silver coin, was under the early emperors equivalent to the Attic drachma, then greatly depreciated. The currency in Palestine was mainly of copper, though gold and silver Roman money was also in use. The word δραχμή here is probably another name for the denarius, the coin mentioned in the passage respecting the tribute to Cæsar (Matt. xxii. 19). It would bear the head of Tiberius, with the title of Cæsar. A denarius appears to have been the ordinary pay for a day's labour, Tobit v. 14. It was the principal silver coin in circulation in the Roman Empire. On one side of it would be the head of Tiberius, with the inscription, "TI. CÆSAR DIVI AUG. F. AUGUSTUS"; on the other side "PONTIF. MAX.," with a seated female figure. It was called denarius, because it was originally equal to 10 *asses;* but on the reduction of the weight of the *as,* it was made equal to 16 *asses.* The denarius of this period would be worth about 8½d.; it was subsequently reduced to 7½d. See note on Matt. xx. 2.

λύχνον.—Necessary, because in the East the room would have no other light than that admitted by the door.

ἕως οὗ.—The relative attracted into the case of its antecedent τοῦ χρόνου understood.

9. τὰς φίλας καὶ γείτονας. — To be distinguished from the τούς of ver 5. In Old English we might say "friendesses and neighbouresses" (Trench).

ἣν ἀπώλεσα.—Contrasted with τὸ ἀπολωλός of ver. 4, because

the woman's search for the coin arises from the value she herself sets on it.

It has been suggested that the δραχμαὶ δέκα may have been part of the woman's head-dress—her most cherished ornament. "The women of Bethlehem and of other parts of the Holy Land still wear a row of coins sewn upon their head-dress, and pendent over their brows; and the number of the coins is very commonly *ten*, as I, in common with other travellers, have ascertained by counting. The custom reaches far beyond the Christian era."—(A. G. Weld, in 'The Expositor,' No. xxxvii.) This interpretation throws additional light on the progress of thought in the three parables. Great is the grief of the shepherd for his one sheep lost out of a hundred; still greater that of the woman for the loss of one of her ten constant and valued ornaments; but how much greater that of the father for the loss of one of his two sons?

LESSON XXVI.

The Parable of the Prodigal Son—St Luke xv. 11-32.

THE DRAMATIS PERSONÆ: THE PRODIGAL (11-19)—THE FATHER (20-24)—THE ELDER BROTHER (25-32).

11-19.—*The Prodigal.*

12. ὁ νεώτερος.—The younger is represented as the sinner, rather than the elder, as being more likely to be thoughtless, and more easily led astray. Jesus is depicting the follies of inexperience, and the miseries resulting from them—not the deliberate wickedness of mature age. The former is a subject for compassion as well as reprobation. The parable lovingly invites all who have, through thoughtlessness, wasted their youth, to return to God, who will gladly receive the service of their lives, however late, provided their repentance be sincere. Cf. Ps. ciii. 3-5, where the forgiveness of God and its healing power are said to renew the sinner's youth like the eagle's; and ver. 13, "Like as a father pitieth his children, so the Lord pitieth them that fear Him."

τὸ ἐπιβάλλον μέρος.—A quite classical expression.   Cf. Hdtus., iv. 115, ἀπολαχόντες τῶν κτημάτων τὸ ἐπιβάλλον.   The verb occurs several times in this sense in the Apocrypha.   Cf. 1 Macc. x. 30, τοῦ κάρπου τοῦ ἐπιβάλλοντός μοι.

The elder received as his inheritance a double share of the patrimonial lands, the younger members a single share (Deut. xxi. 17). This explains the petition of Elisha to Elijah (2 Kings ii. 9), that a double portion of his spirit should rest upon him—*i.e.*, twice as much as on any other of the sons of the prophets, Elijah's spiritual children.   As in this case the father, anticipating the division of the lands, gives the younger son an equivalent in money, the entire domain, on the father's death, would come to the elder.

διεῖλεν αὐτοῖς.—To both his sons,—reserving to himself, however, the right of *usufruct* over the portion of the eldest, who remained in his service.

τὸν βίον.—"That whereon the family lived—their means."   Cf. viii. 43 and Mark xii. 44.

13. **εἰς χώραν μακράν.**—The pleasures of sin carry men farther away from the presence of God.   Cf. Ps. lxxiii. 26-28, "God is the strength of my heart, and my portion for ever.   For, lo, they that are far from Thee shall perish. . . . But it is good for me to draw near to God."   Between an earthly father and son there may be estrangement without separation.   A father and son, corresponding weekly, while living in different countries, are really nearer one another than a father and son in the same house, rarely speaking, and having no thoughts in common.

διεσκόρπισε.—Note the prep., "scattered wastefully."   Cf. ver. 2.

ἀσώτως.—ἀσωτία occurs in Eph. v. 18 ; 1 Pet. iv. 4.   Philo opposes ἀσωτία to φειδωλία ; Cebes connects it with ἀκρασία and ἀπληστία—"incontinence" and "greediness."   From the adverb comes the title of the parable, which might be rendered by the old Spenserian word, "a scatterling," or by "wastrel," the opposite to which is "niggard."   "The waster of his goods will very often be a waster of everything besides—will lay waste himself, his time, his faculties, his powers ; and so, the active and passive meanings of the word being united, will be himself laid waste—he loses himself and is lost."—Abp. Trench.   In the English version the word is translated "riotously"—a word that implies disorderly excess, an ill-regulated indulgence of the passions.   Cf. Chaucer's Wife of Bath's Prologue—

> " Mercury loveth wisdom and science,
> And Venus loveth riot and dispence."

14. **λιμὸς ἰσχυρά.**—In classic Greek λιμόs is usually mas. The interpretation of this famine is supplied in Amos viii. 11, " Behold, the days come, saith the Lord God, that I will send a famine in the land ; not a famine of bread, nor a thirst for water, but of hearing the words of the Lord."

The prodigal craves for the spiritual food of his heavenly Father's home.

κατά.—" Throughout."

αὐτός is used in later Greek for the emphatic " he," and often does no more than distinguish the new subject,—as here " he " from " the famine " of the previous sentence. In modern Greek it means simply " he," without emphasis.

15. **ἐκολλήθη.**—" He clave to, attached himself to "—a favourite word with St Luke. That it is a very strong word is evident from St Paul's use of it in Rom. xii. 9, ἀποστυγοῦντες (loathing utterly) τὸ πονηρόν, κολλώμενοι τῷ ἀγαθῷ. Here the word seems to imply that the citizen of the country to whom he applied was unwilling at first to receive him, and only after persistent entreaties took him into his service. It paints more forcibly, therefore, the picture of his degradation. Contrast 2 Kings xviii. 6, where it is said of Hezekiah, ἐκολλήθη τῷ Κυρίῳ—" he clave to the Lord" ; and cf. 2 Sam. xx. 2, " But the men of Judah clave (ἐκολλήθησαν) unto their king." Cf. Acts x. 28.

χοίρους.—An abomination to the Jews, being the type of uncleanness and unwholesome food. Jesus may have been referring to the occupation of the publicans, who would seem, in the eyes of strict and patriotic Jews, to be doing nothing better than keeping swine for foreigners when they collected taxes for the Romans.

16. **ἐπεθύμει.**—Cf. xvi. 21.

χορτασθῆναι—v. l., γεμίσαι τὴν κοιλίαν αὐτοῦ—" to fill his belly." " This may be a periphrastic exposition of the supposed meaning of χορτασθῆναι. It misses the true point, however ; for the prodigal son could easily ' fill his belly ' with the ' husks,' though he could not ' be satisfied ' with them."—(Westcott and Hort.)

ἐκ.—Perhaps there is no instance in classic Greek of ἐκ or ἀπὸ being used with a verb of eating ; but ἀπολαύειν ἀπό τινος (to enjoy one's self) occurs in Plato, Rep., x. 605.

κερατίων.—The fruit of the carob-tree, which flourishes in South

Italy, in Spain, in the northern coasts of Africa, and in the Levant—being sometimes eaten by the very poor, but oftener used for the foddering of cattle. Cf. Hor., Ep., ii. 1, 123, "Vivit siliquis et pane secundo." The beans were used for weights, and hence probably the word "carat," the botanical name of the tree being *Ceratonia siliqua.* "There was a Jewish saying, 'When Israel is reduced to the carob-tree they become repentant'" (Edersheim).

ὧν.—Relative attracted into the case of its antecedent.

ἐδίδου.—Notice the imperf., "ever gave him."

17. ἑαυτόν.—His higher or better self, which brought to his mind the memory of the influence his father's love and training had had upon it.

μίσθιοι.—Men doing his father's will, with no filial love for him, but yet better off than himself in his banishment. The word δοῦλοι is understood. Cf. πλατεῖαι, xiv. 21.

18. ἀναστάς may express nothing more than the rousing himself from apathy : "I will up and go to my father." Cf. Exod. xxxii. 1, "Up, make us gods"—ἀνάστηθι καὶ ποίησον ἡμῖν θεούς. In classic Greek the verb sometimes means "to rise and go," as in Thuc., i. 87, ἀναστήτω εἰς ἐκεῖνο τὸ χωρίον

St Luke is fond of using participles to give vividness to his narrative. Cf. ἐπιστᾶσα, in x. 40 ; καθίσας, xiv. 28, 31, and xvi. 6 ; σταθείς, in xviii. 11 ; σπεύσας, xix. 6.

εἰς τὸν οὐρανόν.—A Hebraism for "God," used for reverence. Cf. Pharaoh's speech in Exod. x. 16, "I have sinned against the Lord your God, and against you ;" and 2 Sam. xii. 13, the words of David's repentance, "I have sinned against the Lord."

19. ποίησον, κ.τ.λ.—This he does not say when he meets his father, for his father's ready welcome interrupts his speech. The premeditated confession was the confession of fear ; the actual confession is the confession of love.—(Godet.) Cf. Rom. viii. 15.

20-24. *The Father.*

20. ἐσπλαγχνίσθη.—Cf. chap. x. 33. The verb seems not to be classical, and was perhaps a coinage of the Jewish dispersion, the metaphor being more common in Hebrew than in Greek. The σπλάγχνα are properly the nobler *viscera,* the heart, lungs, liver, &c., as distinguished from the ἔντερα, the lower viscera,

the intestines. Cf. Æsch., Agam., 1221, σὺν ἐντέροις τε σπλάγχνα. The Greeks regarded the σπλάγχνα, but not the ἔντερα, as the seat of the affections, whether love, anger, pity, or jealousy. With the Hebrews ἔντερα as well had this meaning. Hence the common occurrence of the metaphor in the Old Testament. Both "lung" and "spleen" are etymologically connected with σπλάγχνα. In Eph. iv. 32, 1 Pet. iii. 8, εὔσπλαγχνοι means "having a good heart," in the sense of "pitiful"; in Eur., Rhes., 132, εὐσπλαγχνία means "the having a good heart," in the sense of "courage." "Bowels" is used for "the heart" in the sense of "the affections" in Shakespeare. Cf. Troil., ii. 1. 54, "Thou thing of no bowels, thou." Cf. Ps. xvii. 10, "They have enclosed their heart in fat,"—i.e., "shut it up against pity." Cf. Ps. lxxiii. 7, cxix. 70.

κατεφίλησεν.—"Kissed him again and again." The word is used of the kiss of Judas—Matt. xxvi. 49. Cf. Luke vii. 38, 45; Gen. xxxiii. 4 (the meeting of Jacob and Esau), προσέδραμεν Ἡσαῦ εἰς συνάντησιν αὐτῷ· καὶ περιλαβὼν αὐτὸν, προσέπεσεν ἐπὶ τὸν τράχηλον αὐτοῦ, καὶ κατεφίλησεν αὐτόν.

21. **ἥμαρτον**—"I sinned."

ἐνώπιόν σου—Hellenistic. The classic form would be παρά σοι.

22. In Gen. xli. 42, Pharaoh puts a ring upon Joseph's hand, and clothes him in στολὴ βυσσίνη: so Daniel (Dan. v. 29) is clothed in scarlet.

The στολή is the long and wide robe of people of distinction, such as the Pharisees love to walk in—Mark xii. 38.

πρώτην.—Probably "best," though it might mean "former" —i.e., which he wore before his wanderings. There is a similar ambiguity in Hor., Odes, ii. 7. 5, "Pompei meorum prime sodalium." πρῶτος means "chief" in 1 Tim. i. 15. In John i. 30 there may be an ambiguity. Cf. Luke xiv. 7, πρωτοκλισίας, and 1 Sam. ix. 22. So Soph., Philoctet., 1425, ἀρετῇ τε πρῶτος ἐκκριθεὶς στρατεύματος.

δακτύλιον.—Among the Romans the sign of freedom; among the Jews, of honour and distinction.

ὑποδήματα—which the slave might not wear.

Observe, the father makes no reply to his son : the sight of his misery and nakedness urges him at once to remedy them ; deeds, not words, express the depth of his pity and his love. When the sinner shows genuine repentance, which implies self-abasement, the first and most urgent necessity is to restore to him his self-respect. We may compare the swift answer of Nathan when David repented (2 Sam. xii. 13), and Isa. lxv. 24, "While they are yet speaking I will hear." Cf. also James iv. 8, "Draw nigh to God, and He will draw nigh unto you."

τὸν μόσχον τὸν σιτευτόν.—The repeated article adds a rhetorical emphasis: the father in his joy uses it again in ver. 27. But in ver. 30 the elder son has no such emphasis. Cf. Judges vi. 25, τὸν μόσχον τὸν ταῦρον, or (according to another reading) τὸν σιτευτόν. Cf. also ὁ ποιμὴν ὁ καλός, John x. 11. As the herds were part of an oriental's capital, he would only kill on special occasions, but on every farm there would be a calf fattening for festivities. Cf. Gen. xviii. 8.

23. θύσατε.—This word seems here to have the extended meaning of "slay" generally, instead of "slay for sacrifice." Cf. Matt. xxii. 4; John x. 10; and Hdtus., i. 126.

24. νεκρός.—*I.e.*, in a moral sense, through his sins. Cf. Matt. viii. 22, "Let the dead bury their dead," and Rev. iii. 1, "Thou hast a name that thou livest, and art dead." Musonius the Stoic, the teacher of Epictetus, used to say, "When any man is cowardly or mean, one ought to speak of him as a corpse and say, 'Favour us with the corpse and blood of so-and-so'"—(Farrar's 'Seekers after God'). Aristophanes, Ranæ, 491, calls the Athenians dead on account of their misgovernment,—νυνὶ δὲ δημαγωγεῖ ἐν τοῖς ἄνω νεκροῖσι. Notice the joyous rhythm of the verse, and cf. ver. 32.

The younger son would hereafter love his father much, since to him much had been forgiven (Luke vii. 4). His elder brother knows not forgiveness, because he has no sense of sin ; knows not love, because he has no sense of forgiveness. The prodigal has learnt to value his father's presence through his experience of the want of it, and to value his father's love through the knowledge he has gained of its depth and tenderness. He will hereafter need all the help this presence and love can afford him in his struggle against the evil habits which indulgence in them has strengthened, and which the tears of penitence alone are not sufficient to resist or break. The years of his life which the locusts of his sins and indulged passions have eaten can be restored (Joel ii. 25) only by the greater intensity of purpose given to his thoughts and actions through the energising influence of this full assurance of his father's perfect love for him, and of his watchful sympathy in his efforts "to cleave to what is good, and abhor what is evil" (Rom. xii. 9). On "the sowing of wild oats," cf. 'The Christian Year,' "The Second Sunday after Trinity," and Tennyson's 'In Memoriam,' liii. (old edition, lii.)

25-32. *The Elder Brother.*

25. The morose character of the elder brother, and his spiritual estrangement from his father in spite of his nearness to him, is brought out, first, by the fact that the father does not send for him to share his joy, and secondly, that he puts his questions to a servant, not to his father.

συμφωνίας.—The musicians and dancers would both be hired to do him honour. Cf. Eur., Ion, 1177, where, speaking of the incidents of a feast made by a father in honour of a newly found son, the messenger says, ἐπεὶ δ' ἐς αὐλοὺς ἧκον.—(Carr.)

26. **τί ἂν εἴη.**—Cf. Acts x. 17, the optative signifying remote possibility, "what this could possibly be."

27. **ὑγιαίνοντα.**—The servant, as compared with the father, is prosaic and matter-of-fact.

28. **παρεκάλει.**—Imperf., "kept urging him."

29. **δουλεύω.**—The present here signifies service past and still continued,—quite a classical usage. Notice he does not say πατέρ, as his younger brother did (ver. 21).

In the eyes of Pharisaism virtue is a task, sin a pleasure; hence there ought to be a payment for the first, an equivalent of pain for the second.

The Scribe Antigonus of Socho, however, expressed a different view in the saying, "Be not as slaves that minister to the lord with a view to receive recompense, but be as slaves that minister to the lord without a view to receive recompense; and let the fear of heaven be upon you."

ἐμοί coming first has the emphasis of wounded selfish feeling.

ἔριφον.—Contrasted with the μόσχος. There is a *v. l.*, ἐρίφιον, "a little kid," which would still further enhance the contrast. Similarly the μετὰ πορνῶν of ver. 30 is contrasted with the μετὰ τῶν φίλων of this verse.

30. **ὁ υἱός σου.**—He will not say, "my brother." His father corrects him by the ἀδελφός of ver. 31, and further rebukes him by addressing him as τέκνον in ver. 32,—a term of stronger feeling than the υἱός he had used himself.

οὗτος—contemptuous.

31. τέκνον.—A loving word ; σύ emphatic.

πάντα, κ.τ.λ.—Cf. 1 Cor. iii. 21, 22, "All things are yours ; whether Paul, or Apollos, or Cephas, or the world, or life, or death, or things present, or things to come; all are yours."

32. εὐφρανθῆναι.—"To be jovial." Cf. xvi. 19.

The goodness with which the father bore the surly peevishness of the elder brother is little inferior to the mercy shown in pardoning the younger.

Though he had been living so many years with his father, the elder brother had known as little of his spirit as the younger: so in spite of his privileges as a member of the holy people, the unloving Pharisee could not know the Spirit of the heavenly Father, for, " If we love one another, God dwelleth in us, and His love is perfected in us." " God is love ; and he that dwelleth in love, dwelleth in God, and God in him."—1 John iv. 12, 16. To be unloving is to be in a far country away from God.

We are not told whether the elder brother went in. It is left for the Pharisees, by their own after conduct, to finish the narrative.

The sacred books might have trained the Pharisees out of this slavish spirit. Cf. Prov. iii. 17, " Her ways are ways of pleasant-ness, and all her paths are peace : " Ps. xix. 8-11, " The statutes of the Lord are right, rejoicing the heart : the commandment of the Lord is pure, enlightening the eyes : the fear of the Lord is clean, enduring for ever : the judgments of the Lord are true and righteous altogether. More to be desired are they than gold, yea, than much fine gold : sweeter also than honey and the honeycomb. Moreover by them is thy servant warned : and in keeping of them there is great reward : " cxix. 54, " Thy statutes have been my songs in the house of my pilgrimage.

So they might have found the key to Jesus' association with publicans and sinners in Isa. lvii. 15, " I [the Eternal] dwell with him that is of a contrite and humble spirit;" and Ps. li. 17, " The sacrifices of God are á broken spirit: a broken and a contrite heart, O God, Thou wilt not despise."

LESSON XXVII.

THE PARABLE OF THE UNJUST STEWARD—St Luke xvi. 1-13.

MAMMON, LOVE'S KEY THAT *UNLOCKS* THE GATE OF THE KINGDOM OF LOVE.

1. **δὲ καί.**—This may mean simply, "Here is another specimen of Jesus' teaching," or, as the imperfect seems to imply, the conjunctions may be intended to connect the parables of this with those of the preceding chapter. As the latter exhibit the tender compassion of the heavenly Father, so the former teach the sons to imitate that example by showing love to their brother men. There is a similar relation in the Old Testament between Psalms cxi. and cxii., in which the attributes of God and of the godly man are made to correspond almost verse by verse. Cf. especially cxi. 5, "He [the Lord] hath given meat unto them that fear Him: He will ever be mindful of His covenant;" with cxii. 5, "A good man showeth favour, and lendeth: he will guide his affairs with discretion;" and cxi. 9, "He sent redemption unto His people; He hath commanded His covenant for ever: holy and reverend is His name;" and cxii. 9, "He hath dispersed, he hath given to the poor; his righteousness endureth for ever; his horn shall be exalted with honour."

οἰκονόμον. — The word might be rendered "bailiff" (as in Wycliffe and the Rheims version), "agent," or "factor." From this parable the word *steward* has gained a sacred meaning, as the word *talent* has from the parable recorded in Matt. xxv. 14-30.

From the Greek word *οἰκονόμος* comes our word "economy," which, though often deteriorated to mean "thrift" or "parsimony," properly signifies "management of a house." The true economist is not he who saves, but he who manages discreetly, gets the most for his money in the best sense, makes his expenses in all directions bear a due proportion to one another, and adjusts his means to his ends. The Christian economist manages his household with a view to charity and his brother's need, dispensing not merely alms but hospitality, refinement, kindliness, always in a thoughtful manner, with a view to the good of those around him.

Jesus may have had in his mind the great Italian estates, the owners of which were usually absentees, and left the management of them to bailiffs who were either slaves or freedmen (*villici*), such as the οἰκονόμος mentioned in Luke xii. 42, or, where the estates were very large, freemen (*procuratores*), such as the οἰκονόμος here. On account of the difficulty of obtaining a lease, tenant-farmers were very rare in the Roman empire, and the estates were usually worked by slaves superintended by the bailiff. Whether there were any such estates in Palestine we cannot tell.

διεβλήθη, in classic Greek, means "slandered"; Wycliffe translated it here "defamed"; the Rheims version "was ill reported." The word occurs nowhere else in the New Testament. It implies a hostile denunciation—evidently, however, founded on fact, for the steward does not attempt to defend himself. In Dan. iii. 8, it is used of an accusation that is true. It has followed the law of amelioration.

διασκορπίζων.—This word occurs in chap. xv. 13, and some have thought it a connecting link between the two parables. The prodigal wastes his own substance, the steward his master's. σκορπίζω is used in a good sense in Ps. cxi. 9, ἐσκόρπισεν, ἔδωκε τοῖς πένησιν—"He hath dispersed, he hath given to the poor." Cf. 2 Cor. ix. 9, where the psalm is quoted.

2. φωνήσας.—Stronger than καλέσας, "calling him with the master's tone." Cf. xix. 15.

τί τοῦτο, κ.τ.λ.—"Why do I hear this of thee?" or, a condensed sentence, "What is this I hear of thee?"

τὸν λόγον.—"The account." Cf. Matt. xii. 36, where the phrase is used of giving account to God.

δύνῃ here hovers in meaning between "may" and "can"; "it is out of the question that you should." Cf. Matt. ix. 15. In the interpretation the dismissal is a summons to die.

3. ἐν ἑαυτῷ.—Cf. xv. 17; xviii. 11. Such soliloquies are common in St Luke.

σκάπτειν. — Such agricultural labour his position had made him best acquainted with.

οὐκ ἰσχύω.—"I am not strong enough." His luxurious life had unfitted him for manly labour.

αἰσχύνομαι.—Cf. Ecclus. xl. 28, 30, "Better it is to die than to beg: begging is sweet in the mouth of the shameless, but in his belly there shall burn a fire."

4. **ἔγνων.**—"An idea has struck me." Cf. Eur., Ion, 1115. The form of a statement regarding one's self is less obtrusive when made in a purely past tense, like the aorist, than when made by the perfect, which in Greek is always a present past.

δέξωνται.—The subject is his master's debtors.

τοὺς οἴκους.—The author of Ecclesiasticus (xxix. 22-28) enlarges on the disagreeable character of this mode of living: " Better is the life of a poor man in a mean cottage, than delicate fare in another man's house : for it is a miserable life to go from house to house ; for where thou art a stranger thou darest not open thy mouth."

5. **χρεωφειλετῶν.**—Either (1) merchants who used to get their supplies from him on credit, paying him after they had made their own sales ; or (2) tenants, rent in the East being often paid in kind—a system which gave the steward ample scope for cheating, since the produce would vary from year to year. Though, however, the steward exhibits a low moral tone, there was no necessary criminality in his conduct, as he had absolute control over his master's affairs until he left his service.

The **βάτος**, or bath, seems to have contained about 60 (Josephus says 70) pints.

Wycliffe translates "barrels," Tyndale and Cranmer " tuns," the Rheims version "pipes." These are far too large. We might better translate "firkins." A firkin = fourth-kin = the fourth of a barrel (30 galls.) The value of these ten firkins would probably be about £10 of our money. The value of money in Palestine would be about five times as great as in our country.—(Edersheim.)

6. **τὰ γράμματα.**—The Vulgate translates " *cautio*," which was a form of release a debtor obtained from his creditor on satisfying his demand. Wycliffe rendered "caution," the Geneva Bible "obligation." We may render "invoice" or "voucher." *γράμματα* is used of one document (like *literæ*) in Acts xxviii. 21.

καθίσας.—A pictorial touch. Cf. chap. xiv. 28.

ταχέως.—Either furtively, or because he has but little time to lose.

πεντήκοντα.—The Hebrew letters (by which numerals are represented) very nearly resemble one another ; hence a very slight forgery might represent a large difference. The bonds would be written on wax, and figures readily erased by the blotter end of the stylus, which was flat and thick.—(Edersheim.)

7. **κόρους.**—Probably = 10 Attic *medimni* = 15 bushels; so that 100 *κόροι* = 1500 bushels. *κόρους* might be translated "quarters," as Tyndale, Cranmer, and the Rheims version render it.

The *ἑκατὸν κόροι* would be ten times the value of the oil. The steward made a difference in his bribes, knowing perhaps that one man would require a heavier bribe than another

By making them commit the forgery with their own hands, he makes them partners in his cheat, if cheat it were.

If they were tenants, he thus returns them the produce they had brought as rent.

8. **ὁ κύριος.**—The steward's master.

τῆς ἀδικίας.—Gen. of quality. Cf. ver. 9, *μαμωνᾶ τῆς ἀδικίας*, and xviii. 6, *κριτὴς τῆς ἀδικίας*. Cf. also iv. 22, *τοῖς λόγοις τῆς χάριτος*.

φρονίμως.—"Prudently,"—*i.e.*, adapting skilfully his means to his ends: Wycliffe so renders the word. Cf. Matt. xxv. 2. *φρόνησις* is the practical wisdom by which a man manages the affairs of his life well. Jesus bids His disciples be *φρόνιμοι* as serpents, and at the same time innocent as doves—Matt. x. 16.

τοῦ αἰῶνος τούτου.—Cf. xx. 34-36, where *οἱ υἱοὶ τοῦ αἰῶνος τούτου* are opposed to *οἱ καταξιωθέντες τοῦ αἰῶνος ἐκείνου τυχεῖν καὶ τῆς ἀναστάσεως τῆς ἐκ νεκρῶν*, who are further defined as *υἱοὶ Θεοῦ* and *υἱοὶ τῆς ἀναστάσεως*.

So that the *αἰών* here means this world as opposed to eternity, but with a reference to the *spirit* of the world rather than its external form or the men living in it. It may sometimes almost be rendered "spirit of the age," as in Eph. ii. 2, *κατὰ τὸν αἰῶνα τοῦ κόσμου τούτου*.

οἱ υἱοί.—Cf. the phrase, "son of valour," and 1 Sam. ii. 12, "the sons of Eli were sons of Belial"—*i.e.*, "wicked men."

The *υἱοί* implies that they belong to the light in the same intimate way as a child to its mother.

We might render *οἱ υἱοὶ τοῦ αἰῶνος τούτου*—"men of the world."

υἱοὺς τοῦ φωτός.—Jesus had termed His disciples "the light of the world" in the Sermon on the Mount—Matt. v. 14. St Paul terms Christians *υἱοὶ φωτός* and *υἱοὶ ἡμέρας*, in contrast to *νυκτός* and *σκότους* (1 Thess. v. 5); and still more emphatically, in Eph. v. 8, he says of them that they were once "darkness, but now light in the Lord," and bids them "walk *ὡς τέκνα φωτός*," and continues, by a bold confusion of metaphors, "the fruit of the light is in all goodness, and righteousness, and truth" (the good, the right, and the true).

In 1 John i. 5, 6, God is defined as light, and "the walking in darkness" as incompatible with fellowship with Him.

The same idea had been already beautifully expressed in Ps. xxxvi. 9, "With Thee is the fountain of life: in Thy light shall we see light."

As the highest revelation of divinity, Jesus is spoken of in John i. 5, viii. 12, ix. 5, as "the light of the world"; and He says, "He that followeth me shall not walk in darkness, but shall have the light of life."

In the classics $\phi\hat{\omega}s$ is used metaphorically of one who brings joy and victory, as of Agamemnon in Hec., 841, $\mathring{\omega}$ $\mu\acute{\epsilon}\gamma\iota\sigma\tau\sigma\nu$ $^{"}E\lambda\lambda\eta\sigma\iota\nu$ $\phi\acute{a}os$, and Il., xvi. 39, $\mathring{\eta}\nu$ $\pi o\acute{v}$ $\tau\iota$ $\phi\acute{o}\omega s$ $\Delta a\nu ao\hat{\iota}\sigma\iota$ $\gamma\acute{\epsilon}\nu\omega\mu a\iota$. On the other hand, $\sigma\kappa\acute{o}\tau\iota os$ is used of secret and immoral acts.

In Gen. i. 3, God is said to have created light immediately after the creation of the heaven and the earth. In Exod. xiii. 21, the presence of God among the Israelites on their march out of Egypt is symbolised by night by "a pillar of fire." In Isa. x. 17, God is termed the "light of Israel." In Isa. xlii. 6, the ideal Israel is described as appointed "for a light of the nations." In Isa. lx. 19-21, the prophet has a vision of a time when, instead of the sun and the moon which set and wane, God shall be to His people "an everlasting light," and immediately connects this metaphor with righteousness,—"Thy people shall be all righteous:" and this connection between light and righteousness is expressed with fine terseness in the last of the prophets, Mal. iv. 2, "But unto you that fear my name shall the Sun of righteousness arise with healing in His wings."

While He was on earth, Jesus was to His disciples in the wilderness of the world what the pillar of fire had been to the Israelites in the wilderness of their wanderings; and in John xii. 35, He exhorts them to make progress in holiness while He is still with them: "Walk while ye have the light, lest darkness come upon you." In Philip. ii. 15, St Paul speaks of Christians as $\tau\acute{\epsilon}\kappa\nu a$ $\Theta\epsilon o\hat{v}$ and $\phi\omega\sigma\tau\hat{\eta}\rho\epsilon s$ $\acute{\epsilon}\nu$ $\kappa\acute{o}\sigma\mu\wp$, "luminaries in the world." In 1 John ii. 9, 10, light and love are connected: "He that saith he is in the light, and hateth his brother, is in darkness even until now. He that loveth his brother abideth in the light."

So that, in fine, men become "sons of light" by believing in

Jesus—John xii. 36 ; the same process by which they become children of God—John i. 12. They are even said to become light in the Lord—Eph. v. 8 ; and the result of this is the renunciation of all immorality—1 Thess. v. 5-8 ; and the test of their being "sons of light" is the love of their brother man—1 John ii. 9.

υἱοὶ φωτός might be rendered "Christians" as opp. to "men of the world." In Heb. vi. 4, φωτισθέντας means converted to Christianity, and in ecclesiastical Greek φωτισμός is almost equivalent to baptism.

φρονιμώτεροι ὑπέρ.— The prep. strengthens the comparative. Cf. Heb. iv. 12, τομώτερος ὑπέρ.

εἰς = "towards" *or* "as regards."

γενέαν, which usually distinguishes one age from another, or the men of one age from those of another, is here used to distinguish contemporaries who base the actions of their lives on different principles. Cf. Ps. xxiv. 6, lxxiii. 15 ; Prov. xxx. 11-14.

9. **καὶ ἐγὼ ὑμῖν.**—A solemn introduction to the application of the parable. ἐγώ is in an emphatic place. Jesus is comparing His teaching with that of the steward's master; and the ὑμῖν is also emphatic, corresponding to the steward in the parable. "As the lord praised the steward for his providence in dealing with his wealth, so do *I* recommend to you foresight in the use of your worldly goods ere you be dismissed from your stewardship,"—*i. e.*, by death.

ἐκ implies either the *material* or the *means.*

μαμωνᾶ.—An Aramaic word for riches. The original seems to be retained rather than translated into Greek, partly, perhaps, because of the peculiar solemnity of the passage (cf. Matt. vi. 24, and the use of the word ἐπιούσιος in the Lord's Prayer, Matt. vi. 11), partly because μαμωνᾶ, by its popular usage, represented wealth in a wider aspect than any Greek equivalent would have done.

τῆς ἀδικίας.—Cf. οἰκονόμος τῆς ἀδικίας above. The mammon is called unrighteous as an instrument of unrighteous dealing. Conversely, Philo (De Judic., § 5) speaks of the ψυχικὸς πλοῦτος, ὃς μόνος ἀληθείᾳ πλοῦτός ἐστιν, meaning wisdom and knowledge. St Paul (1 Tim. vi. 10) speaks of the love of money as the root of all evil.

Never, perhaps, could wealth with more justice be called ἄδικος than at the time when Jesus spoke, when the wealthy among the

Romans had for the most part obtained their money by misrule and extortion in the provinces. Most fitly, too, did He speak thus to His disciples, many of whom, as we learn from xv. 1, were tax-gatherers, a class addicted to injustice and extortion.

Seneca, Ep. Mor., xxxi. 11, says : " What is a Roman knight, or a freedman, or a slave ? Names which had their origin in ambi-tion or injustice."

It is only the imperfection of human nature that causes any difference between *meum* and *tuum*. In a perfect state of society all things would be in common. Cf. Barrow : " That distinction which thou standest upon, and which seemeth so vast between thy poor neighbour and thee, what is it ? whence did it come ? whither tends it ? It is not anywise natural or according to primitive design. Inequality and private interest in things (to-gether with sicknesses and pains, together with all other infeli-cities and inconveniences) were the by-blows of our guilt : sin introduced these degrees and distances ; it devised the names of rich and poor ; it forged those two small pestilent words, *meum* and *tuum*, which have engendered so much strife among men, and created so much mischief in the world."

ἐκλίπῃ.—Sub. μαμωνᾶ, which fails by the event of death ; and cf. Heb. i. 12, τὰ ἔτη σου οὐκ ἐκλείψουσιν ; and Xen., Hell., i. 5. 2, ἔχων δὲ ἥκειν τάλαντα πεντακόσια, ἐάν δὲ ταῦτα ἐκλίπῃ.

δέξωνται—*i.e.*, the φίλοι. It may, however, be impersonal, like αἰτοῦσι in chap. xii. 20.

σκηνάς.—Jesus probably uses this word on account of its association with the wanderings in the wilderness and the Feast of Tabernacles. That feast was a symbol of the presence of God among the holy people, reminding them of the time when their forefathers pitched their tents in the wilderness round the Taber-nacle or Holy Tent, where the Shechinah or sacred light was a symbol of the presence of God in their midst.

The αἰώνιοι σκηναί are opposed to these temporary tents. So in Heb. xi. 9, 10, " The city which hath *the* (immovable) foundations, whose builder and maker is God," is opposed to the tents in which dwelt the patriarchs Abraham, Isaac, and Jacob. The yearly dwelling in tents at the Feast of Tabernacles was a constant memorial to the Israelites of the transitoriness of this life ;— that their houses were not their own ; that in God's sight no man had any claim to a better habitation than another; that

"Pallida Mors æquo pulsat pede pauperum tabernas regumque turres" (Hor., i. 4. 13); that the time must come when all would be dismissed from their stewardship, when "the earthly house of their tabernacle would be dissolved" (2 Cor. v. 1).

The phrase "everlasting tabernacles" occurs in 2 Esdras ii. 11, "the everlasting tabernacles which I had prepared for them" (*i.e.*, Israel); and the Talmud has a saying, "When the wicked are burnt up, God makes a tent in which He hides the just." In Ps. xlviii. 11, the graves of the wicked are termed their σκηνώματα εἰς γενεὰν καὶ γενεάν.

We may compare the saying of Jesus (John xiv. 2), "In my Father's house are many mansions" (or abiding-places); and Ps. xv. 1, "Lord, who shall dwell in Thy tabernacle?" xxvii. 5, "In the secret of His tabernacle shall He hide me;" where the reference is probably to the Temple as the successor of the Tabernacle.

But how do the friends whom men make by their money (*i.e.*, by doing kindnesses with their money) receive them into æonian tents (*i.e.*, into future happiness)? The best answer to this question is perhaps found in Matt. xxv. 39, 40. All men in Jesus have become one brotherhood, and through Him those benefited will admit their benefactors into everlasting habitations. Men prove themselves "sons of light"—followers of Jesus—by loving their brothers (1 John ii. 10). The means or test of showing this love is their disposition of the mammon of unrighteousness, of which they have regarded themselves stewards, not lords. It is characteristic of the gracious condescension of Jesus that instead of saying, "*I* may receive you," He says "*they* may." The poor whom loving Christians have befriended are pictured, as it were, introducing their benefactors into the æonian tents, and making themselves witnesses that by loving deeds to them they have proved themselves "sons of light." To this picture we may find a contrast in Isa. xiv. 9, where the dead rise up to salute the fallen King of Babylon as he enters the halls of Hades.

Virgil (Æn., vi. 664) places among others in the Elysian plains, "Quique sui memores alios fecere merendo."

10. πιστός.—"Trusty." Lest any misunderstanding should arise out of the term ἀδικία, Jesus proceeds to supplement the recommendation to prudence by a recommendation to faithfulness. Cf. xix. 17, "Well done, thou good servant: because thou

wast found faithful in a very little, have thou authority over ten cities."

11. **ἀληθινόν.**—This word—a favourite one in the fourth Gospel—occurs nowhere else in the Synoptics. St Paul, after being with St Luke, uses it once, in 1 Thess. i. 9, where the living and ἀληθινός (real) God is opposed to idols. It occurs three times in the Epistle to the Hebrews (viii. 2, ix. 24, x. 22). Adjectives in -ινος express the material out of which anything is made, as λίθ-ινος, made of stone; ξύλ-ινος, made of wood: so ἀληθ-ινός, made of truth (real). The word means "that which is genuine." We may compare St Paul's phrase, "the unsearchable riches of Christ" (Eph. iii. 8). It is better, perhaps, not to make it agree with μαμωνᾶ, a word of bad signification. The antithesis is not quite perfect. We should expect either τὸ δίκαιον here (opp. to τῷ ἀδίκῳ), or ψευδές with μαμωνᾶ: but τῷ ἀδίκῳ μαμωνᾷ seems to be used as a logical noun.

Philo speaks of the ἀληθινὸς πλοῦτος ἐν οὐράνῳ; Seneca says, "Turn thyself to the true riches, learn to be content with a little." So Jesus speaks of "laying up treasure in heaven" (Matt. vi. 20). Socrates (at the end of the "Phædrus") prays that he may regard the wise man as rich—πλούσιον δὲ νομίζοιμι τὸν σόφον.

12. **τῷ ἀλλοτρίῳ.**—All external goods are lent to us by God, and we leave them when we die; but our characters, our virtues, and graces are given us by God, and remain our own for ever, because they are genuine parts of ourselves; whereas the μαμωνᾶ τῆς ἀδικίας is only lent us to train us in the management of the heavenly riches of the future.

ὑμέτερον.—Epictetus says (i. 25), "Keep by every means what is your own: do not desire what belongs to others. Fidelity is your own; virtuous shame is your own: who then can take these things from you? who else than yourself can hinder you from using them?" If ἡμέτερον be read, we must regard Jesus as associating the inner circle of His disciples with Himself, as in John iii. 11, ix. 4. . Cf. also Matt. xvii. 25, 26.

δώσει.—How does God give us τὸ ἀλλότριον? Because He is the source of all good; because χάρις καὶ ἀλήθεια, "grace and truth" (or "reality," τὸ ἀληθινόν), came by Jesus Christ; and because, in a future state, we believe all obstacles to the perfection of these "goods" will be removed, whereas the μαμωνᾶ τῆς ἀδικίας will have ceased to exist. This verse is a warning at once to the publicans and to the Pharisees : to the publicans, because they were outwardly involved in the world as stewards to their Roman masters, while they were inwardly longing to attach themselves to the teaching and principles of Jesus ; to the Pharisees, because, though outwardly linked with the divine, as being the representatives of the theocracy, their inward life was attached to the world. See Matt. vi. 24.

REMARKS ON THE PARABLE GENERALLY.

The parable, which was addressed to the disciples (ver. 1), is intended to teach Christians that they ought to be as careful about using their money for good and charitable purposes, as men of the world are about using it for worldly purposes. The motive proposed is at first sight a low one, that of self-interest— the hope of being received into everlasting habitations. But we must remember that Jesus was addressing a homely lesson to homely men, to disciples who were yet children in understanding spiritual truths, and it was not in accordance with His method to "pour new wine into old bottles." After His death His disciples would come to understand, as we can do now, that it is *He* who will receive us into the everlasting habitations, which is His own presence, and therefore the feeling of self-interest may be merged into a desire to please, and to be with, Him. The parable, therefore, viewed in this light, becomes a warning against regarding religion as a sentiment of love for Jesus, unaccompanied by any active charity towards the poor and afflicted with whom He has graciously chosen to identify Himself (Matt. xxv. 36). Put briefly, then, the parable teaches us that they who do not use their money and all that it can buy with a perpetual reference to Christian love, cannot enter the kingdom of love ; while they who do so shall be welcomed by the Lord of love, and all who love and whom they have loved.

In interpreting the parable, we must regard the lord of the unjust steward—a mere man of the world—as representing God the Father, under whom all men are stewards of all they possess. We shall then have an *a fortiori* argument similar to that in which God the Father is compared, or rather contrasted, with the unjust judge. "If the man of the world praised his steward for his shrewdness and foresight in making worldly friends out of his money (even after he had been cheated by him), how much more will your heavenly Father be pleased with you, if you use your money, all that you possess, to increase the happiness and numbers of those who are to enter into the kingdom of heaven ?" See note on chap. xviii. 8.

LESSON XXVIII.

THE RICH MAN AND LAZARUS—St Luke xvi. 19-31.

MAMMON, SELF-LOVE'S KEY THAT *LOCKS* THE GATE OF THE KINGDOM OF LOVE.

This story is connected with the preceding parable in the following manner: The rich man might have made a friend of Lazarus out of the money which hardened his heart into selfishness: as God's steward he showed himself faithless by using for selfish purposes the money with which he had been intrusted (τὸ ἀλλότριον) ; therefore the genuine good (τὸ ἀληθινόν) was not intrusted to him, and he never won for himself the gift of a loving temper, which might have been his for ever. Love cannot be exercised without an object, and for its full and open display requires an external medium : the poor are the objects, and money, which Jesus calls the mammon of unrighteousness, the medium of its display. To display loving-kindness to the poor by means of money is called by Jesus making friends out of the mammon of unrighteousness, and these friends are depicted in the preceding parable as welcoming their benefactor into the æonian tents. In this story we are shown the other side of the picture. Instead of the welcome we have the rejection : we have the rich man turned away from Abraham's bosom because he had been unloving and cold-hearted towards Lazarus, of whom by his mammon he might have made a friend.

19. καὶ ἐνεδιδύσκετο.—In classic Greek we should expect ὅς. The construction indicates that St Luke is here translating from some Aramaic document.

πορφύραν = (1) the colour obtained from a sea-shell ; (2) that which is dyed with it. We learn from Prov. xxxi. 22 that wealthy Jews clothed themselves in purple. This would be used for the woollen outer robe brought from Tyre.

βύσσον.—An Aramaic word, used of the clothing of kings (1 Chron. xv. 27), of priests (2 Chron. v. 12), and of those who were very rich (Esth. i. 6, viii. 15). In the last two passages the adjectives βύσσινον and πορφυροῦν occur together. The βύσσος would be used for the inner garment. It consisted of white cotton brought from Egypt.

The rich man's garments are brought from the north and the south, and are warm without and delicate within, combining comfort with ostentation. Of the garments of Lazarus we hear nothing.

εὐφραινόμενος λαμπρῶς.—Cf. xii. 19 and xv. 32 — "Making merry in splendour." The combination seems to imply that the rich man made mirth and jollity the object of his life, and mingled with them no thought of the misery of the poor, squandering on useless and ostentatious splendour wealth which might have been used to alleviate their sufferings. Cf. the passage in the first chapter of Carlyle's ' History of the French Revolution,' describing, on the one hand, the thoughtless extravagance of the Court of Louis XV. : " Beautiful Armida - Palace, where the inmates live enchanted lives ; lapped in soft music of adulation ; waited on by the splendours of the world ; " and the condition of the poor at the same epoch,—" Those lank scarecrows, that prowl hunger-stricken through all highways and by-ways of French existence." And again, in the second chapter, of the nobles,— " Their industry and function is that of dressing gracefully and eating sumptuously ; " of the people,—" Untaught, uncomforted, unfed ; to pine stagnantly in thick obscuration, in squalid destitution and obstruction : this is the lot of the millions."

John Ball, at the time of the peasant's revolt in 1377-1381, said : "The great folk are clothed in velvet and warm in their furs and their ermines, while we are covered with rags : they have wine and spices and fair bread, and we oat-cake and straw, and water to drink : they have leisure and fine hours ; we have pain and labour, the rain and the wind in the fields." Piers Ploughman says of the poor man to the knights,—" Though he be thine underling here, well may hap in heaven that he be worthier set and with more bliss than thou." Cf. George Eliot on ." good society" and "the poor." "Good society has its claret and its velvet carpets, its dinner engagements six weeks deep, its opera and its faëry ball-rooms ; rides off its *ennui* on thorough-bred horses, lounges at the club. . . . But good society . . . is of very expensive production ; requiring nothing less than a wide and arduous national life condensed in unfragrant deafening factories, cramping itself in mines, sweating at furnaces, grinding, hammering, weaving, under more or less oppression of carbonic acid; or else, spread over sheep-walks, and scattered in lonely houses and huts on the clayey or chalky corn-lands, where the rainy days look dreary."—('The Mill on the Floss,' Book IV. chap. iii.)

In the time of Jesus, among the Romans, the miseries of the poor were aggravated by the absence of a middle class. Nearly all manual work was done by slaves, who in Rome constituted half the population. Of the remainder, a proportion of six and a half to one were more or less paupers—a proportion very far above that existing in any modern city. On the other hand, (1) the contrast between wealth and poverty was less glaring than it is now ; (2) the gratuitous distribution of corn by the Government or by private persons prevented the pauperism of the masses with which modern charity has to contend ; (3) the climate round the shores of the Mediterranean, which were the home of the countries of ancient civilisation, made the struggle for existence less severe than it is in more northern climes.

In our own times the miseries of the poor are being aggravated by the growth of large towns, from which the rich escape by railway into the suburbs, while the poor remain crowded together in the back and often unhealthy streets, their wretchedness not even being brought under the notice of the rich, who are thus removed from the sight of it. Lazarus is no longer laid at the door of Dives, and Dives is too apt to forget his existence.

With the Romans liberality to the poor took the form, for the most part, of cheap, or even gratuitous, distribution of bread by the State or by individuals. But relief of the poor was not the main object, for it was not the poor alone who took the doles. The motive was, as a rule, a selfish one—policy, ambition, or ostentation. In later times, owing chiefly to the influence of the Stoic philosophy, liberality was based on humanity. Horace (Sat., ii. 2. 203) says, " Cur eget indignus quisquam te divite ?" Seneca, "Dat ut homo homini." Such sentiments, however, exercised influence over only a small portion of the community ; and on the whole it is true, as has been said, that Christ found "a world without *caritas*, though not without *liberalitas*." He, by such teaching as is contained in this story, made the relief and elevation of the poor no longer a mere kindly instinct, but an all-embracing principle. Christianity has connected religious worship with the relief of the poor. There was no such connection in the mind of the Roman. The public worship in the Temple was conducted by the priest alone : the people had no part in it. Hence it had no tendency to bind rich and poor together in one community.—(Uhlhorn.)

20. Λάζαρος.—A contracted form of the commoner Eleazar. It comes from Eli-ezer, " helped of God." The Lazarus of the parable has probably nothing to do with the Lazarus of the fourth Gospel. This is the only parable in which a proper name occurs : perhaps the only reason for its occurring here is, that a name was necessary for the dialogue that follows between Abraham and the rich man. Some, however, have thought that Jesus, in giving the poor man this significant name, meant to imply that he was pious; but an epithet would have been a more natural way of describing his piety, which, besides, is inferred by his being carried after death to Abraham's bosom. His piety is not dwelt on, because poverty, not piety, constituted his claim on the humanity of the rich man. Not, however, that either Jesus or the early Christians looked upon undeserving poverty as an object for alms. This appears from a passage which occurs in the recently discovered " Teaching of the Apostles," a work probably as old as the beginning of the second century—" Let thine almsgiving drop [lit. sweat] into thy hands, *so long as thou knowest to whom thou givest.*" It is possible that this, though not recorded in the Gospels, may be a saying of Christ Himself. In the " Teaching of the Apostles," the idler who seeks to live upon Christian charity is called a " Christ-trafficker." —(Farrar, in the 'Contemporary Review.')

ἐβέβλητο.—Cf. Matt. viii. 6, ix. 2, whence it appears that the verb does not necessarily mean more than "laid." Edersheim thinks it implies that his bearers were glad to get rid of an unwelcome burden.

πυλῶνα.—The range of pillars enclosing the court of the palace through which the door entered into it. Lazarus would here be in full view of the rich man whenever the latter went in or out of his mansion. The termination -ών, like the Latin -etum (as in *quercetum*), implies a collection : we have θύραν τοῦ πυλῶνος in Acts xii. 13.

εἰλκωμένος—*v. l.*, ἠλκωμένος, for which, however, there is little authority. In Eur., Alc., 878, we have ἤλκωσεν. This word (from ἑλκόω) was probably formed by St Luke after the analogy of ἕλκω and ἑλκύω. The term is a medical one, characteristic of Luke the physician.

21. **ἐπιθυμῶν.**—The law of Moses distinctly bade the rich man to attend to him, Deut. xv. 7, 8. He must have been acquainted, too, with the example of Job (xxxi. 16-22), who could protest that he had not withheld the poor from their desire, or seen any stranger to whom he had not opened his doors.

ἀλλὰ καί.—"Nay more," like the Latin *quin et.*

οἱ κύνες.—As an aggravation of his sufferings, the dogs whom he had not strength to drive away came and licked his sores. Dogs were regarded by the Jews as unclean, and, as a rule, they had not masters as among us, but wandered about the fields and streets of the cities, devouring dead bodies and other offal. Cf. the fate of Jezebel, 2 Kings ix. 35. It is quite possible, however, that the rich man possessed dogs. Cf. Isa. lvi. 10 ; Matt. xv. 27. In the last passage, the diminutive κυνάριον is used, which may possibly imply affection, and therefore domestication, and hence · be distinguished from κύνες.

22. **τὸν κόλπον 'Αβραάμ.**—The picture seems to be that of a banquet presided over by Abraham, at which Lazarus, as the newest comer, and in requital for his sufferings, has the place of honour on the bosom of the host, just as John lay on Jesus' bosom, John xiii. 23. Cf. John i. 18. The idea is frequently found in the Rabbinical writings. "This day," says Rabbi Judah the holy, "he sits in the bosom of Abraham"—*i.e.*, is dead. Cf. 4 Macc. xiii. 16, οὕτως παθόντας ἡμᾶς 'Αβραάμ καὶ 'Ισαὰκ καὶ 'Ιακὼβ ὑποδέξονται. St Augustine says of his dead friend Nebridius : "Nunc ille vivit in sinu Abraham. Quicquid illud est quod illo significatur sinu, ibi Nebridius meus vivit."

Jesus adopts the Jewish method of speaking of the future world, but the language is figurative, and cannot be pressed literally. He frequently speaks of the kingdom of heaven as "a feast," just as from a lower point of view we speak of "a feast of reason and a flow of soul." Cf. Matt. viii. 11 : "Many shall come from the east and west, and shall recline ($\dot{a}\nu a\kappa\lambda\iota\theta\dot{\eta}\sigma o\nu\tau a\iota$) with Abraham, and Isaac, and Jacob, in the kingdom of heaven."

$\dot{\epsilon}\tau\dot{a}\phi\eta$.—Nothing is said of the burial of Lazarus ; no one troubled to give him a funeral. See pp. 185, 186.

23. $\dot{\epsilon}\nu$ $\tau\hat{\omega}$ $\dot{a}\delta\eta$.—Not "hell" but "the unseen place," or "Sheol," Lat. "Orcus." In the Creed the Greek is $\kappa a\tau\hat{\eta}\lambda\theta\epsilon\nu$ $\epsilon\dot{\iota}s$ $\dot{a}\delta ov$, the Latin "descendit ad inferna," or "ad inferos." "Hell" =A.S. *helle*, Goth. *halja*=Lat. *cella*, Gk. $\kappa a\lambda\iota\dot{a}$ (a cabin). The root is $\kappa a\lambda$—Lat. *cel-are*, *domi*-cil-*ium*. Cf. the Old Norse goddess Hel (of death).

The Jews looked for a state immediately after death, which they thought would be underground, and called Sheol or hell, where the just were in a state of happiness, the unjust in a state of misery. This is not to be confounded with the state after the resurrection of the body.

$\beta a\sigma\dot{a}\nu o\iota s$.—This, of course, is figurative. If we regard the rich man as a disembodied spirit—which we may well do, as nothing is said about a resurrection—we may find a great principle in the description of his torments. In life he had given himself up solely to the indulgence of his bodily appetites ; and now that he has no senses to indulge, he suffers as Tantalus did, for he has no other avenues to enjoyment, no moral or spiritual tastes.

Sensation is ascribed to a disembodied spirit in Cardinal Newman's "Dream of Gerontius":—

> " Hast thou not heard of those, who, after loss
> Of hand or foot, still cried that they had pain
> In hand or foot, as though they had it still ?
> So is it now with thee, who hast not lost
> Thy hand or foot, but all which made up man :
> So shall it be, until the joyous day
> Of resurrection, when thou shalt regain
> All thou hast lost, new-made, and glorified."

Virgil places in Tartarus those who had not shared their riches with their relations :—

> " Aut qui divitiis soli incubuere repertis,
> Nec partem posuere suis."—Æn., vi. 610.

$\dot{a}\pi\dot{o}$ $\mu a\kappa\rho\dot{o}\theta\epsilon\nu$.—The $\dot{a}\pi\dot{o}$ is redundant. Cf. Il. viii. 365, $\dot{a}\pi'$ $o\dot{v}\rho a\nu\dot{o}\theta\epsilon\nu$. We have a similar redundancy in our word "lesser," and the phrase "from thence."

ἐν τοῖς κόλποις.—The plural, as compared with the sing. of ver. 22, seems to contain a notion of comprehension, and an allusion to the company. Cf. ἀνατολαί, δυσμαί, in Matt. viii. 11; γάμοι, Matt. xxii. 2; οὐρανοί, *passim*.

24. Dialogues of the dead are found in the writings of the Rabbis.

Λάζαρον—whom alone among the poor he recognises. The position of the rich and poor is reversed. The rich man is now the beggar, and his prayer unheard.

τὸ ἄκρον τοῦ δακτύλου.—He prays for the smallest boon, just as Lazarus had desired merely "what fell from his table."

ὕδατος.—"In some water." A remarkable example of the genitive of the part touched: it comes under the heading of the genitive of ablation, implying a partial separation. Cf. Arist., Acharn., 184, εἰς τοὺς τρίβωνας ξυνελέγοντο τῶν λίθων—"were gathering *some* stones into their cloaks."

τὴν γλῶσσαν.—The tongue and palate, which had been pampered by riotous living, are now the chief instruments of retribution. Cf. "King Lear," v. 3—

> "The gods are just, and of our pleasant vices
> Make instruments to scourge us."

ὀδυνῶμαι.—"I am in anguish." Cf. ii. 48.

25. τέκνον.—Cf. xv. 30. This is a term of pity and tenderness: the Jewish relationship to their father Abraham is expressed by υἱὸς in chap. xix. 9. τέκνον is used in affectionate remonstrance in xv. 31; τέκνια to the disciples in John xiii. 33.

ἀπέλαβες.—"Didst receive to the full." Cf. Matt. vi. 2, 5, 16. The Rabbis said, "As in the next world the good receive a reward for the most trivial good work that they have done, so in this world the wicked receive the reward for the most trivial work they do."

τὰ ἀγαθά σου—*i.e.*, "what you thought good."

παρακαλεῖται.—Cf. Matt. v. 4 ; 2 Thess. ii. 16.

26. χάσμα.—Translated "gulf" in our version: a word of ambiguous meaning. When the authorised version was published, the word "chasm" did not exist in English. Deep chasms and steep rocks were common in the landscapes of Palestine. In 2 Sam. xviii. 17, Absalom is said to be taken and cast into a χάσμα μέγα. The Rabbis speak of the separation between the

two portions of Hades sometimes as "a wall," sometimes as consisting only of the breadth of a hand, or even of a thread. The figure here simply implies the impossibility of communication.

ὅπως.—" In order that."

27. οὖν.—If he cannot come to me here, he may yet perchance be my messenger to earth. The rich man addresses Abraham as his "father," as if in submissive reliance on his sympathy; and his words may perhaps imply that he was not entirely selfish, or that his discipline was awakening him to unselfish feelings. They are not, however, indicative of moral tone. His prayer is not for his brothers' repentance, but for precaution against their future discomfort. The tone of the story is throughout that of menacing severity against selfish conduct and selfish motives.

28. διαμαρτύρηται.—Notice the prep., " Bear solemn witness to them." See note on chap. xv. 2.

29. Μωυσέα καὶ τοὺς προφήτας.—In the Jewish canon, the Old Testament books were in three divisions : (1) The Law, or Thorah, containing the Pentateuch ; (2) the Prophets (Nebiim), containing the prophetical books (exclusive of Daniel), and also Joshua, Judges, the two books of Samuel, and of Kings—these latter were included in this division as leading up to and containing the history of prophets who did not write ; (3) the "Writings" or "Scriptures," in Hebrew Ketubim, in Latin Hagiographa—these are by some supposed to have been called " Psalms " (Luke xxiv. 44), because that book commenced the series, but this is doubtful : besides the Psalms, this division comprised Proverbs, Job, Ruth, Lamentations, Daniel, Ezra, Nehemiah, and the two books of Chronicles. The canonicity of the books of Esther, Canticles, and Ecclesiastes seems to have been a disputed point in the Apostolical age. The New Testament never refers to them. The Law and the Prophets, but not the Hagiographa, were read regularly in the synagogue.

What is it that the five brethren are to learn from the Law and the Prophets ? Clearly that they will gain admittance into the kingdom of Love only by the claim of possessing loving tempers. The Old Testament Scriptures are full of passages connecting religion and charity. Cf. Lev. xix. 18, "Thou shalt love thy neighbour as thyself ; " and the description of the righteous man in Ps. cxii. 4, 9, "He is gracious, and full of compassion, and righteous. . . . He hath dispersed, he hath given to the poor,"—

passages which correspond to the description of the attributes of God in Ps. cxi. 4, 9.

30. οὐχί.—Cf. ναίχι, for ναί, "yes." It is a classic form, more emphatic than οὐ: it occurs followed, as here, by ἀλλά in chap. i. 60, xiii. 3, 5 ; John ix. 9 ; Rom. iii. 27; 1 Cor. x. 29.

μετανοήσουσι.—This is an improvement on the moral tone of ver. 27. The change of expression, however, may have a no higher motive than a desire to persuade Abraham. There is no sign that the rich man cares for his brothers' repentance for any nobler reason than to save them from pain.

31. The faith that comes from ghosts is the faith of devils that believe and tremble. Fear cannot produce unselfishness, for it is itself a selfish emotion. The faith the rich man lacked was the faith in a loftier ideal of happiness than that which is produced by pleasure or self-seeking—the faith in the great principle of Jesus, " Learn of me ; for I am meek and lowly in heart : and ye shall find rest unto your souls "—Matt. xi. 29. The rich man might have derived a kindlier spirit from the examples set before him in the Old Testament. He might have read of the kindly Abraham's dealings with Lot ; of much that was kindly even in selfish Jacob, and of his lifelong punishment for his selfishness ; of Joseph's love for his selfish brethren ; of meek Moses and chival- rous David. These men had shown loving spirits without the in- tercession of ghosts to bid them, and indeed with little thought, if any, of immortality, which, as St Paul says, was brought to light through the Gospel—2 Tim. i. 10.[1] It was enough for them to live in the sight of God in this world, and they never had any doubt whether it were better to be good or evil—to be humane and merciful, or to be sordid, selfish, and heartless. Even if they knew certainly that there was no hell to fear, they could not have lived as this rich man had done—it would have been hell enough to them to attempt it.

οὐδέ.—" Not even."

πεισθήσονται.—Abraham does not say μετανοήσουσι, or even πιστεύσουσι. The rich man asserts that his brethren will *repent* if one *go* to them *from* the dead. "Nay," Abraham replies, in terms each phrase of which is a strong denial of the rich man's phrases,

---

[1] For the views of the Old Testament writers on the future after death contrast Ps. xlix. 14, lxxiii. 24 ; Isa. xxvi. 19, with Ps. vi. 5, xxx. 9, lxxviii. 10-12, xciv. 17, cxv. 17 ; Job xvi. 22 ; Isa. xxxviii. 11, 18, 19 ; Jer. li. 19.

" they will not even be *influenced*, even if one rise *up out from the dead.*"   The story ends as it began, in a warning against selfishness.   Selfish pursuit of pleasure had brought the rich man into torment. Selfish avoidance of pain will not save his brothers from it. The former part of the story is a warning against worldliness, the latter against what has been called other-worldliness.   It is a prophetic protest against selfish works of mercy done for the sake of the doer's own salvation, his release from purgatory, or a high degree of eternal happiness,—motives which tainted so much of the Christian charity of the middle ages, and still taints much of our own time.   Charity thus bestowed, having in view the well-being of the donor rather than the circumstances of the recipient, has led to more beggary and misery than it has relieved.

LESSON XXIX.

The Parables of the Importunate Widow and of the Pharisee and the Publican—St Luke xviii. 1-14.

1-8. *The Parable of the Importunate Widow.*

1. πάντοτε.—See p. 66. The precept here seems to refer to urgency in prayer under all circumstances, however adverse.

ἐγκακεῖν.—A military term, from κακός, cowardly.   Cf. 2 Cor. iv. 1, 16.   " To turn cowardly while engaged in any course of action," hence " to give up through the weight of overpowering evil."   The word is peculiar to St Luke and St Paul.

2. κριτής.—Among Eastern nations judges were regarded as the representatives of heaven, and so sacred was their function that the title " gods " was given to them. Cf. Judges v. 8; Ps. lxxxii. 6; John x. 34, 35.   Bringing a case to trial before a judge is called " inquiring of God,"—Exod. xviii. 15.   The judges, as a rule, were not paid, but there were two stipendiary magistrates in Jerusalem.   As one man could not form a Jewish court, this man must be regarded as appointed by Herod or the Romans.—(Edersheim.)

τὸν θεὸν μὴ φοβούμενος.—A common form of expression for

an unscrupulous person. Cf. Sallust, Cat., 15, "Animus impurus, dis hominibusque infestus;" Livy, iii. 57, "Decemvir ille deorum hominumque contemptor." For the opposite character cf. 2 Cor. viii. 21—"Providing for honest things, not only in the sight of the Lord, but also in the sight of men." In classic Greek we should have οὐ φοβούμενος. Cf. Matt. xxii. 12.

ἐντρεπόμενος.—"Standing in awe of." Cf. xx. 13; Matt. xxi. 37. In classic Greek more frequently found with a genitive.

3. χήρα.—Widows under the law of Moses had no legal provision made for their maintenance, and they were discouraged from marrying again unless they allied themselves to their deceased husband's brother. They were left dependent partly on the affection of relations, more especially of the eldest son, whose birthright or extra share of the property imposed on him the duty of providing for his mother, and partly on certain privileges accorded to them with other distressed classes. A portion of the spoil taken in war was assigned to them (2 Macc. viii. 28-30); a special prohibition was laid against taking a widow's garment in pledge (Deut. xxiv. 17), and this was practically extended to other necessaries (Job xxiv. 3); the widow was commended to the care of the community, and any neglect or oppression of her was strongly reprobated. The judge must therefore, if he were a Jew, have been utterly shameless to neglect to give a decision in this widow's case. Cf. Isa. i. 23. If, on the other hand, he were a Roman, he must have been very insolent so utterly to outrage the religious feelings of the nation.

ἤρχετο.—"Kept constantly coming"—*ventitabat*.

ἐκδίκησόν με ἀπό.—Cf. Rev. vi. 10, where the souls under the altar are represented as crying out, Ἕως πότε, ὁ δεσπότης ὁ ἅγιος καὶ ὁ ἀληθινός, οὐ κρίνεις καὶ ἐκδικεῖς τὸ αἷμα ἡμῶν ἀπὸ τῶν κατοικούντων ἐπὶ τῆς γῆς; The word is late Greek. It occurs in LXX. with ἐκ. Cf. Judges xi. 36; 2 Kings ix. 7.

The phrase contains a *constructio pragnans*—"Do me justice, and obtain what is due to me from my adversary."

The translation "avenge" is unfortunate: it is not so much the vengeance on the wronger that is dwelt on, as the righting of the wronged.

ἐν ἑαυτῷ.—Lat. *secum*, Eng. "to himself." Soliloquies are a characteristic of the parables recorded by St Luke. Cf. ver. 11, xv. 17, xvi. 3.

4. **ἐπὶ χρόνον.**—" For a time,"—*i.e.*, " for some time." Cf. Il., ii. 299 ; Od., xiv. 193.

5. **διά γε.**—Cf. xi. 8.

εἰς τέλος.—Either (1) " coming to the end," " never ceasing to come," " coming for ever," or (2) " at the end," " finally."

ὑπωπιάζῃ.—This word means literally " to wound under the eye," to " bruise." St Paul uses it in 1 Cor. ix. 27, where the revised version translates " buffet " or " box." Aristotle, in the Pax, 541, speaks of πόλεις ὑπωπιασμέναι, where the cities are personified and spoken of as " beaten black and blue." If we take it in this literal sense, we may regard the judge as speaking mockingly— " The woman will become desperate, and lay violent hands on me."

Others have taken the word metaphorically as meaning " to harass," " annoy " ; but there is no authority for this usage. In its favour, however, is the fact that the Latin *obtundo* is used in this sense. Cf. Ter., Adelph., i. 2. 33, " Ne me obtundas de hac re saepius," and Livy, ii. 15 ; and the verb σκύλλω has passed through a similar change of meaning from " rend " to " annoy." Cf. viii. 49.

6. **ὁ κύριος.**—This phrase is not used once of Jesus as a nominative in the correct version of St Matthew or St Mark. In St Luke it is used about twelve times, always in prefaces or other passages peculiar to that evangelist. This usage probably indicates that the Gospel of St Luke, like that of St John, was written later than the other two, at a time when the memory of Jesus as He had lived on earth among His disciples was fading, and a greater reverence for Him was taking the place of the tender feelings connected with those recollections.

ὁ κριτὴς τῆς ἀδικίας.—Cf. xvi. 8.

7. **ἐκλεκτῶν.**—In the Epistles this word means " those called out of the world to be disciples of Christ." Cf. 1 Thess. i. 4, εἰδότες . . . τὴν ἐκλογὴν ὑμῶν, κ.τ.λ. ; and 1 Cor. i. 26, 27, βλέπετε τὴν κλῆσιν ὑμῶν, . . . τὰ μωρὰ τοῦ κόσμου ἐξελέξατο. Peter addresses whole Christian communities as ἐκλεκτοί (1 Pet. i. 1).

βοώντων.—" Cry aloud," a strong expression, used in Gen. iv. 10, of Abel's blood crying from the earth ; and in Jonah iii. 8, of the men of Nineveh. Cf. James v. 4.

καὶ μακροθυμεῖ ἐπ' αὐτοῖς.—(1) " Does he delay his vengeance in their case ? " or, (2) taken with βοώντων, " who cry to him day and night, and yet he delays interposing in their cause." There is a *v. l.*, μακροθυμῶν.

For the construction with ἐπί cf. Matt. xviii. 26, μακροθύμησον ἐπ' ἐμοί, and Acts xi. 19, θλίψεως τῆς γενομένης ἐπὶ Στεφάνῳ.

There is a curious parallel to the passage in Ecclus. xxxv. 18 (in LXX., xxxii. 18), ὁ Κύριος οὐ μὴ βραδύνῃ, οὐδὲ μὴ μακροθυμήσει ἐπ' αὐτοῖς ἕως ἂν συντρίψῃ ὀσφὺν ἀνελεημόνων· καὶ τοῖς ἔθνεσιν ἀνταποδώσει ἐκδίκησιν.

μακροθυμία is one of the attributes ascribed to God in the vision of Moses—Exod. xxxiv. 6. It is alluded to in the parable of the Barren Fig‑tree—Luke xiii. 9. It has been defined as "that clemency by which you put a restraint on your anger, and do not immediately punish an offence, but leave the offender an opportunity to repent."

The *a fortiori* mode of argument contained in this verse is very common in Jewish parables, and is called *Kal-va-Chomer*, or "light and heavy." Cf. the πόσῳ μᾶλλον in Matt. vii. 11, x. 25, xii. 12, and the note on chap. xvi. 12, *sub. fin.* Instances of it in the Old Testament are Gen. xliv. 8; Deut. xxxi. 27 (Edersheim)—this last may be compared with ver. 8, " Behold, while I am yet alive with you this day, ye have been rebellious against the Lord ; and how much more after my death ?" There is a Rabbinical parallel to ver. 7 in a commentary on the Book of Jonah, "The bold (*i.e.*, the unabashed) conquers even a wicked person (*i.e.*, prevails on him to grant his request); how much more the All-Good of the world ?"—(Edersheim.)

8. πλήν.—" And yet," an adverbial form (acc. fem. of πλέ-ον).

τὴν πίστιν.—Note the article, which implies (1) the faith generally—*i.e.*, Christian faith ; or (2) the faith referred to in the parable—*i.e.*, the faith that persists in prayer, without fainting.

9-14. *The Parable of the Pharisee and the Publican. — The Thanksgiving of the Self-Satisfied for the sins of others.—The Prayer of the Contrite for Mercy on his own.*

9. πρός.—Probably simply " to," since τινας follows, though others take it to mean " with reference to."

τινας.—Probably some among the disciples, not Pharisees. He would not tell Pharisees a parable about Pharisees.

ἐξουθενοῦντας.—A late form for ἐξουδ.—in the New Testament confined to St Luke and St Paul.

10. ἀνέβησαν.—Up the hill on which the Temple stood, and up the steps and terraces,—see p. 19. The Pharisee would wear

his fringe and phylacteries on brow and shoulder; the publican would be in his common working dress, with no outward sign that he was an Israelite.

11. **σταθείς.**—This word is always used in the New Testament of taking up a position in preparation to making a formal or set speech, as in Luke xviii. 40, xix. 8; Acts ii. 14, v. 20, xi. 13, xvii. 22, xxv. 18, xxvii. 21. For another instance of prayer in the Temple, cf. Luke ii. 27.

It was unlawful to sit in the Temple (cf. Matt. vi. 5; Mark xi. 25). Hence ταῦτα πρὸς ἑαυτόν is a more probable reading than πρὸς ἑαυτὸν ταῦτα.

Observe that ἑστώς, a less forcible word, is used of the publican (ver. 13), who did not pose himself.

πρὸς ἑαυτόν.—To be taken with προσηύχετο, " with himself "—*i.e.*, mentally. He would not have uttered such a prayer aloud. Cf. διελογίζετο ἐν ἑαυτῷ in chap. xii. 17. Cf. 2 Macc. xi. 13. The classical Greek for " standing by himself " would be καθ' ἑαυτόν. Cf. Acts xxviii. 16 ; James ii. 17.

εὐχαριστῶ.—He utters no prayer, but a thanksgiving to God for the shortcomings of other men—to the heavenly Father for the blemishes of His children ! Contrast the profession of Paul, the Christian Pharisee, in 1 Cor. xv. 9, 10 : " For I am the least of the apostles, that am not meet to be called an apostle, because I persecuted the church of God. But by the grace of God I am what I am : and His grace which was bestowed upon me was not in vain ; but I laboured more abundantly than they all : yet not I, but the grace of God which was with me."

Οἱ λοιποὶ τῶν ἀνθρώπων.—He divides men into two classes; in the one is himself, in the other the rest of mankind.

The Rabbis described the majority of their fellow-countrymen as accursed for not knowing the Law (John vii. 49). They divided men into " people of the earth " and " fellows "—*i. e.*, educated men. A saying of the Rabbis is quoted, " No brutish man is sin-fearing, nor is one of the people of the earth pious."

οὗτος.—Contemptuously. Cf. xv. 30.

12. **νηστεύω.**—The Law only required one fast, and that on the great day of Atonement. The Hebrew word for fasting does not occur in the Pentateuch. The term used is " afflicting the soul," ταπεινοῦν τὴν ψυχήν, Lev. xvi. 29-31. The Pharisee certainly does not seem to be doing this, and it is difficult to refrain

from supposing that our Lord may have had this usage of the word ταπεινόω in His mind in ver. 14. In Ezra ix. 5, 6, Ezra, the greatest of all the Scribes, is said to rise up from his " heaviness " —*i.e.*, " affliction," or " fasting "—and pour forth a prayer of an exactly opposite character to that of the Pharisee, commencing, " O my God, I am ashamed and blush to lift up my face to Thee, my God : for our iniquities are increased over our head, and our trespass is grown up unto the heavens." The word " affliction " is commonly used to denote fasting in the Talmud, and is the title of one of its treatises. Cf. Ps. xxxv. 13, " I afflicted my soul with fasting."

From Zech. vii. 1-7, viii. 19, it appears that the Jews during the captivity observed four annual fasts, in the fourth, fifth, seventh, and tenth months. Zech. vii. 5 and 9 contain an anticipation of our Lord's teaching on the subject.

After the captivity the fasts were multiplied to twenty-eight annual and two weekly ones. The latter were observed on the 2d and 5th days of the week—*i.e.*, Monday and Thursday, because Moses was believed to have ascended Mount Sinai on a Thursday and returned on a Monday. It is probable that these fasts were no very great hardship, because the day ended at six, and the great meal of the day would be in the evening.

The object of fasting is to produce the very opposite feeling to that to which the Pharisee gives utterance—the feeling of humility and entire dependence on God. Similarly the payment of tithes is an outward expression that we owe everything to God, and are but His stewards in our possessions.

σαββάτου.—From a Hebrew word signifying—(1) "rest " ; (2) the "Sabbath-day,"—is used in the plural frequently, in the singular rarely, for "a week," as the Hebrew word is in Lev. xxiii. 15.

τοῦ σαββάτου.—Distributive = " every week."

ἀποδεκατεύω.—An Alexandrine word.

At least two tithes were required by the Law. One-tenth of the whole produce of the soil was assigned for the maintenance of the Levites, out of which the Levites were to dedicate a tenth to God, for the use of the priests. A tithe, in all probability a second tithe, was to be applied to festival purposes. In every third year either this festival tithe or a third tenth was to be eaten in company with the poor and the Levites. It appears from chap. xi. 42, that the Pharisees, from ostentation or over-scrupulousness, paid tithes on vegetables that scarcely came within the scope of the Law.

As the object of the second tithe was mainly to promote charity and brotherly feeling by enabling every third year the stranger, the fatherless, and the widow to partake of the festival with the Levites, it is obvious that, while fulfilling the letter of the institution, the Pharisee was neglecting its spirit.

We find indications of the custom of paying tithes during the captivity in Tobit i. 7.

κτῶμαι.—"I gain," not "I possess," which would be κέκτημαι.

With this so-called prayer of the Pharisee and its presumptuous boasting we may contrast the beautiful prayer in Ps. cxxxix. 23, 24: "Search me, O God, and know my heart ; try me, and know my thoughts ; and see if there be any wicked way in me, and lead me in the way everlasting."

13. μακρόθεν.—Afar off from what ? If he were not an Israelite, he would be in the Court of the Gentiles ; but then the Pharisee would not have seen him. It is better to regard him as an Israelite, and to take the word to imply that he did not press forward to the holy place as one whose character gave him a right to do so, and as the Pharisee did. He stood aloof, as in some dark remote corner of a great cathedral.

Probably the publicans, being sinners but not hypocrites, would not often be seen in the Temple, where they would encounter the chilling glances of the Pharisees ; so that this man's presence there is a token of religious earnestness and a longing for repentance.

οὐδὲ τοὺς ὀφθαλμούς.—The Jews usually stood when praying with arms outspread, the palms turned upward, and the eyes raised. Cf. 1 Tim. ii. 8, ἐπαίροντας ὁσίους χεῖρας. οὐδέ = "not even"—i.e., "to say nothing of his head and hands."

ἔτυπτε τὸ στῆθος.—Note the imperf., "never ceased while praying." Cf. οὐδεὶς ἐδίδου αὐτῷ, chap. xv. 16. The action is an expression of intense sorrow : it is still used by the Jews in the most solemn part of their confession on the Day of Atonement. Cf. xxiii. 48 ; Æn., i. 481, "Suppliciter tristes, et tunsæ pectora palmis."

Physiologically, the action is an instinctive mode of ministering relief to the tension at the heart. Here it is a contrast to the calm fixed attitude of the Pharisee.

τῷ ἁμαρτωλῷ.—"The sinner"—*i.e.*, "sinner that I am," implying not comparison with others, but deep self-abasement. Cf. 1 Tim. i. 15, "Sinners, of whom I am chief," the self-estimate of the great Christian Pharisee. It is in accordance with the spirit of this prayer that the Confessions stand at the beginning of the English Church Service—a practice derived from the early Church.

14. **δεδικαιωμένος.**—Every Jew is said in the Talmud to go away justified after offering sacrifice. The idea first occurs in Gen. xv. 6, "Abram believed in the Lord ; and He counted it to him for righteousness." As the self-sufficiency of the Pharisee is a great contrast to the implicit trustfulness in God of the great father of his race, so the publican shows some germs of the faith of Abram in acknowledging that he has come far short of the divine ideal in goodness, and clinging to God's mercy to help him to improve.

γάρ is made up of γε, verily, and ἄρα, therefore. Here the meaning of γε prevails.

With the idea cf. Matt. xxi. 31. The publican "knew himself," the Pharisee did not. Therefore the former was susceptible to good influences, the latter had made his own pride proof-armour against them. Hence, while the publicans as a class are often mentioned as being attracted to and listening to Jesus, the Pharisees as a class wilfully shut their eyes to His greatness and goodness.

So great has been the influence of this parable on men's minds, that it is perhaps now quite as common for men to say to themselves, "Thank God, I am not as that Pharisee," as to say, "Thank God, I am not as that publican." It is possible, too, for a man to be proud of his humility. Hence Jeremy Taylor says, "Make no reflex acts upon thy own humility, or upon any other grace with which God hath endowed thy soul."

ταπεινωθήσεται.—A kindred sentiment to this is reported to have fallen from the lips of Rabbi Hillel : "Humilitas mea est elevatio mea, et elevatio mea humilitas mea." Cf. Ezek. xxi. 26.

The best illustration of the principle is to be found in the magnificent passage on our Lord's self-abasement in Philip. ii. 8, 9.

The future tense may be regarded (1) as the assertion of a law ; (2) as a prophetic and authoritative promise.

The sentiment occurs also in Matt. xxiii. 12 and Luke xiv. 11.

The first passage and the one before us seem to come under (2), the second under (1).

It was one of our Lord's gnomes by which He expresses the influence of humility, meekness, and gentleness on the world, and their greatness in the sight of God. The idea is conveyed in the Old Testament in the vision to Elijah of the still small voice, and is best illustrated from the New Testament by the influence the Gospel of the loving John has had upon the world. We can discover the truth of it in ordinary life by observing the influence those who are known to be unselfish and moderate in speech gain even among the pushing and noisy.

The following illustrations of this parable are from Edersheim's 'Sketches of Jewish Life':—

"We read in the Talmud that a celebrated Rabbi was wont every day, on leaving the academy, to pray in these terms: 'I thank Thee, O Lord my God, and God of my father, that Thou hast cast my lot among those who frequent the schools and synagogues, and not among those who attend the theatre and the circus. For both I and they work and watch—I to inherit eternal life, they for their destruction.''

The following anecdote, of an arrogance almost inhuman displayed by a Scribe, comes from a Rabbinical work :—

"Rabbi Jannai, while travelling by the way, formed acquaintance with a man whom he thought his equal. His new friend invited him to dinner, and liberally set before him meat and drink. But the suspicion of the Rabbi had been excited. He began to try his host successively by questions upon the text of Scripture, upon the Mishna, allegorical interpretations, and Talmudical lore. On none of these points could he satisfy the Rabbi. When dinner was over, Jannai called upon his host, as customary, to take the cup of thanksgiving and return thanks. But the latter was sufficiently humiliated to reply, with a mixture of Eastern deference and Jewish modesty, 'Let Jannai himself give thanks in his own house.' 'At any rate,' said Jannai, 'you can join with me.' And when the latter had agreed to this, Jannai said, 'A dog has eaten of the bread of Jannai.'"

LESSON XXX.

THE PARABLE OF THE MINÆ—St Luke xix. 11-27.

THE ABSENCE OF THE LORD OF THE KINGDOM A TEST OF ITS FRIENDS AND OF ITS FOES.

11. προσθεὶς εἶπεν.—The translation of a Hebraistic expression = "continuing." In classical Greek it would be προσθεὶς παραβολὴν εἶπεν.

Jesus had been accompanied in His last journey from Galilee by an excited and ever-increasing multitude, who were expecting a glorious manifestation of the King-Messiah at Jerusalem, which He was now approaching. Jericho, which He seems to have just left, was within fifteen miles of the holy city. In the following parable Jesus designs to show that the kingdom is not to be established now, or in the way His followers expect.

The parable that follows, though it has many points of resemblance with, has many points of difference from, that of the Talents (Matt. xxv. 14-30). This parable is designed to represent different degrees of zeal in the management of one and the same thing intrusted to all alike; that of the Talents, to show that in the kingdom of God a man's acceptance does not depend upon his powers, or the extent of the sphere of his labour, but upon faithfulness of heart: *motive* is the burden of the latter, *zeal* of the former. Cf. p. 215.

ἀναφαίνεσθαι.—"Openly proclaimed." Cf. Eur., Bacchæ, 529, ἀναφαίνω σε τόδε Θήβαις ὀνομάζειν: Hdtus., iii. 82, ἀναφανῆναι μούναρχος.

12. εὐγενής.—There is probably a reference to the journey of Archelaus to Rome after the death of Herod the Great, to receive at the hands of Augustus the confirmation of his father's will, by which he was made tetrarch of Samaria, Judea, and Idumea. The Jews sent a deputation after him to protest against his succession to the throne, and against kingly power altogether. Archelaus had a magnificent palace at Jericho.

εἰς χώραν μακράν.—A contrast to the παραχρῆμα of ver. 11.

13. δέκα.—Not "his ten slaves," but "ten slaves of his." A rich man would have many more than ten. It was not at all

uncommon for a property owner to make his slaves agents in his absence, either leaving them to till his land and sell his produce, or lending them money to trade with.

μνᾶς.—Between £3 and £4 of our money : 100 Attic drachmas. The word is a corruption of the Hebrew *manch* (2 Chron. ix. 16). In our money a mina would be to a talent what a threepenny-piece is to a sovereign. A small sum of money for trading purposes, but so much more striking is the greatness of the recompense for "faithfulness in that which is least." It here stands for the powers bestowed upon us for use in Christ's service, and symbolises the lowly lot of the ordinary Christian disciple, who is expected greatly to execute small tasks.

πραγματεύσασθαι.—This verb means (1) to take trouble about; (2) to employ by way of commerce or usury. πραγματεία occurs in 2 Tim. ii. 4. For the reading, πραγματεύσασθε, cf. chap. xiv. 17. **ἔρχομαι**—"come back." Cf. John iv. 16.

14. **οἱ πολῖται.**—"His fellow-citizens." Cf. Gen. xxiii. 11. The modern Greek Test. has συμπολῖται. Here the Judæan opponents of Jesus are meant, in contrast with the δοῦλοι, His Galilean disciples.

ἐμίσουν . . . ἀπέστειλαν.—Note the tenses : the hatred was permanent, the "sending after him" a single act. Cf. Matt. xxv. 5.

οὐ θέλομεν.—Compare the cry of the Jews at the trial of Jesus, "We have no king but Cæsar," and their saying to Pilate, "Write not, The King of the Jews,"—John xix. 15, 21.

15. **καὶ ἐγένετο . . . καὶ εἶπεν.**—This is a Hebraism. The second καί shows that εἶπε is contemporaneous with ἐγένετο. **γνοῖ**—late form for γνῷ, as if from γνόω. Cf. Mark v. 43, ix. 30.

διεπραγματεύσαντο—*v. l.*, τίς τί διεπραγματεύσατο. διά implies either completion, or "during the time" = "what business they had finished *or* had carried on during his absence." For the idea of trading with the Word of God, cf. 2 Cor. ii. 17, οὐ γάρ ἐσμεν, ὡς οἱ πολλοί, καπηλεύοντες τὸν λόγον τοῦ Θεοῦ. Cf. also Eph. v. 16, ἐξαγοραζόμενοι τὸν καιρόν.

16. **σου.**—He modestly refers his success to his master's gift, not to his own diligence.

17. **ἐγένου.**—"Didst prove thyself." The reward does not consist in some external or material gain, but in enlarged service. This is the light in which true Christians endeavour to regard earthly promotion,—not as bringing in greater

income, but as involving greater responsibility, and therefore at once harder work and a greater scope for their faculties. Their reward is ever with them, comforting and supporting them. The freedom from the distraction caused by mixed motives, and the sobriety and calmness resulting from perfect confidence in God's love, enable them to develop their powers for extended work without interruption or intermission.

δέκα πόλεων.—After receiving a kingdom, the εὐγενής would be able to distribute such rewards. We may compare the assignment to Themistocles by the King of Persia of the revenues of Magnesia for his bread, Myus for his condiments, and Lampsacus for his wine.—(Thucyd., i. 138.) But in that case Themistocles had no responsibilities toward those cities.

Josephus tells us that Archelaus did actually reward his faithful adherents by placing them over cities.

19. The second servant is not praised; he has shown no excessive zeal.

20. εἶχον.—" Kept," and did nothing else with it.

ἀποκειμένην refers to the common practice of hiding treasures in unsettled countries, where there are no banks and few investments.

σουδαρίῳ.—The Latin word *sudarium*, a cloth with which to wipe off the perspiration (*sudor*): then the meaning was extended to that of a napkin or linen cloth of any kind. From the Rabbinical writings we gather that the Jews often hid their money in these σουδάρια. The talent was too large to be so concealed: it is represented as being buried in the earth—Matt. xxv. 25.

21. Eastern despots did not scruple, nor do they scruple now, to appropriate the earnings of their servants and their subjects. Moreover, if the servant had by misadventure lost the money intrusted to him, it might, he believed, be required of him again. If the cause be not false, and a mere covering for sloth, it may depict the moral cowardice and distrust of those who are afraid of labouring actively for the good of others, lest contact with the world should stain the purity of their souls. Cf. the saying of Seneca (Ep. vii.), quoted in the ' De Imitatione Christi' (i. 20), " Quoties inter homines fui, minor homo redii." And Tennyson's " Holy Grail "—

> " Leaving human wrongs to right themselves,
> Care but to pass into the silent life."

αὐστηρός.—αὔω = dry ; properly used of astringents that make the tongue dry. Cf. Cowper's "sloes austere." In 2 Macc. xiv. 30 it is translated "churlish." It may here be rendered "strict." Cf. note on σκληρός, Matt. xxv. 24.

The bad servant thinks of the work, and has hard thoughts of the master ; the good servant thinks of the master, and has pleasant thoughts of the work.

αἴρεις.—*I.e.*, "Thou wouldest have exacted in hard unmerciful justice, from my property, the equivalent of the sum of money, if I had lost it in trading."

23. ἐπὶ τράπεζαν.—"Into a bank."

This may be interpreted of any Christian work to which aid is rendered without any personal exertion, as, *e.g.*, subscribing to churches or charitable organisations ; or Jesus may be gently advising timid Christians, who are not adapted for independent labour in the kingdom of God, at least to associate themselves with persons of greater strength, under whose guidance they may apply their gifts to His service.

There was a saying traditionally ascribed to Jesus—γίγνεσθε δόκιμοι τραπεζῖται, "Show yourselves approved money-changers."

τόκῳ.—Cf. Shakespeare's "breed of barren metal." *Fœnus* is connected with the obsol. *feare* = *gignere*.

26. It is not an arbitrary rule, but a principle running through life, that he who has obtains more, and he who has not, or obtains not, loses. In the body we all lose many capacities from not using them : men may even lose the use of limbs altogether from ceasing to exercise them ; and every one loses the use of many tissues and blood-vessels. Again, if a man has learnt to observe for one purpose, he will observe for another with the greater quickness ; the habit of attention in one subject will easily be directed to another : and the same principle holds in all mental faculties, as taste, judgment, &c. So money begets money ; and the richer a man is, the more speedily can he increase his riches. It has even been asserted that the more friends a man has, the more intensely he can love each of them ; and this would certainly almost seem to have been the case with St Paul. See his list of friends in Rom. xvi. 3-16.

27. τοὺς ἐχθρούς.—No longer πολῖται, as in ver. 14. Jesus here seems to be speaking austerely, almost bitterly. He was, however, speaking as a prophet foreseeing the destruction of the nation which refused for its Messiah the Greatest and Best of the time. He said elsewhere, "Where the carcass is, there will the

vultures be gathered together " (Matt. xxv. 28)—*i.e.*, whenever a nation has fallen into moral decay, destruction will soon overtake it ; and so here He is plainly foretelling to the Scribes and Pharisees, who were sinning against light in refusing to accept Him, though they must in their hearts have felt His goodness, that destruction will come upon them—the downfall of their nation in this world, their banishment from the kingdom of Love in the next. In the parable this punishment is inflicted by the arbitrary will of the tyrant ; in the kingdom of God it follows by a natural law : the nation falls because it is rotten ; the hating soul voluntarily exiles itself from the kingdom of Love. We may apply to the last addresses of Jesus to His countrymen the saying of Hyperides to the Athenians, quoted in Plutarch's ' Phocion,'—"Examine not whether I am severe upon you, but whether I am so for my own sake."

Additional Note on the Compatibility of the Practice of Usury with the Christian Profession.

In ver. 25 Jesus alludes, without reprobation, to the taking of interest for money. In the Sermon on the Mount, He had bidden His disciples not to turn away from those who wished to borrow of them (Matt. v. 42). The question arises, Did He or did He not regard the taking of interest for loans as permissible ? For many centuries the Christian Church regarded such a practice as contrary to the principles of Christianity. In the English Church, Latimer protested against the laws that allowed usury before the time of Edward VI. ; the Act of Henry VIII., restricting the rate of usury to 10 per cent, was repealed in 1552 by an Act of Edward VI., which declared that "usury is by the Word of God utterly prohibited." Under Elizabeth the Act of Henry VIII. was revived with some restrictions. Bishop Andrewes wrote an elaborate treatise to prove that no Christian may take interest for loans. It is only during the present reign that restrictions on the rate of interest have been removed.

The Jews were forbidden by the law of Moses to take interest from one another, though not from foreigners. No legal penalty, however, was affixed : the injunction was merely a moral precept. Thus Exod. xxii. 25, and Lev. xxv. 35-37, exhort men not to exact interest from their countrymen who are poor ; Deut. xxiii.

20, distinctly states that to a stranger money may be lent on usury. That the law was not invariably or even ordinarily observed appears from Ps. xv. 5; Ezek. xviii. 8, 13, xxii. 12,—in which especial praise is bestowed on those who have observed it.

With regard to the teaching of the Old and New Testaments, on this as on other topics we must distinguish between the precept which relates to particular times and places, and the principle or spirit of the precept which has a universal application.

When the law of Moses was imposed, the Jews were a purely agricultural people, and had no commercial transactions.

In ancient times money, when borrowed on usury, was for the most part borrowed not for the systematic prosecution of commerce, but for the temporary aversion of some pressing want. Usurers traded on the needs of desperate men. In small states, again, where men knew one another and felt the claims of neighbourhood, usury was regarded as a selfish encroachment upon the province of neighbourly friendship.

Again, while slavery was permitted, the harsh creditor was a gainer by his harshness; now he is apt to be a loser. Then he could reduce his debtor to slavery, and so gain a slave. Now this temptation to charge exorbitant interest no longer exists; undue harshness is apt to diminish the chances of payment.

Moreover, history has proved the legal prohibition of usury a failure. Thus Adam Smith, in his 'Wealth of Nations,' says: "In other countries [besides England] where the interest for money has been prohibited by law, it has been found by experience that the evil of usury has increased, the debtor being obliged to pay not only for the money, but for the risk which his creditor runs by accepting compensation for the use of it." The wise Tacitus seems to refer to the same failure, when he says in reference to the Germans: "Fœnus agitare et in usuras extendere ignotum; ideoque magis servatur quam si vetitum esset." At Rome the legal rate was successively lowered, but the restrictions were constantly eluded.

Since, then, the teaching of history shows that the attempt to prohibit the taking of money as interest has been a failure, and has also been an impediment to the progress of commerce, and therefore of the welfare of nations; since Jesus, in the passage above, refers without reprobation to the practice; since, now that slavery is abolished, the usurer may often be a friend in need,—we may, it seems, conclude that there is nothing in the principles of Christianity to prevent men from being usurers. Both the spirit and precepts of Jesus, however, distinctly forbid men to use the power of superior wealth to oppress the poor or to be grasping. In the parable of the Talents, we are taught that by the code of Jesus we hold all our wealth in trust for God. (See the Essay, p. 214.) The spirit of the teaching of Jesus on the subject of usury is perhaps best carried out by such Acts as the Bankruptcy Act passed in 1861, by which imprisonment for debt was abolished, except in the case of fraudulent debtors.

LESSON XXXI.

THE PARABLES OF THE TWO SONS AND OF THE WICKED HUSBANDMEN—St Matt. xxi. 23-46.

THE REJECTION BY ISRAEL, AS A NATION, OF THE MORAL CLAIMS OF THE KINGDOM.

23. ἐλθόντος αὐτοῦ . . . αὐτῷ διδάσκοντι.—An anacolouthon, due to the simplicity of the narrative : notice the change of tense —"After He had come in ;" "while He was engaged in teaching."

οἱ ἀρχιερεῖς.—This term probably included the heads of the twenty-four courses, and some of those who had been high priests. The deputation seems to have been sent by the Sanhedrim, and to have consisted of members of that body. Their object was apparently to find a pretext for excommunicating Jesus. A similar deputation had waited on John the Baptist—John i. 19.

ἐξουσίᾳ.—Without authorisation from the Scribes, no one could *teach authoritatively*, though he might be a popular expositor, preacher, or teller of legends.—(Edersheim.)

ταῦτα probably refers to all that Jesus up till that moment had done and was still doing in Jerusalem,—the triumphal entry, the cleansing of the Temple, and the teaching in it. By all this course of conduct Jesus was putting forward a claim to be the Messiah.

25. τὸ βάπτισμα τὸ Ἰωάνου—v. l., Ἰωάννου. Baptism was the chief symbol of John's doctrine, the outward sign of the repent-

ance which he taught. John had acknowledged Jesus to be the Messiah, and his influence with the multitude had been very great. He, too, had condemned the ecclesiastics, as Jesus had done, terming them, in language borrowed from the desert imagery, "broods of vipers." He, too, had preached righteousness as the true claim of sonship with God. "Think not to say within yourselves, We have Abraham for our father : for I say unto you, that God is able of these stones to raise up children unto Abraham." He, too, had forecast the downfall of his country unless a moral and spiritual reformation took place in it. "The axe is laid unto the root of the trees : every tree, therefore, that bringeth not forth good fruit, is being hewn down and cast into the fire "— Luke iii. 7-9.

If, therefore, the deputation acknowledge the authority of John, they must necessarily acknowledge that of Jesus.

ἐν ἑαυτοῖς.—Cf. Matt. xvi. 7, "among themselves." There is, however, a various reading, παρ' ἑαυτοῖς, where the pronoun may stand for ἀλλήλοις. Cf. Xen., Mem., ii. 6—φθονοῦντες ἑαυτοῖς μισοῦσιν ἀλλήλους.

27. ἔφη αὐτοῖς καὶ αὐτός.—Both pronouns are emphatic. "He declined to answer them, as they Him."

The deputation, by professing their incompetence to decide about John, admitted their incapacity to judge about Jesus. Their formal attempt to degrade Jesus in the eyes of the multitude had resulted in their placing themselves in a position of degrading imbecility. Their dishonesty had constrained them to declare that they, the authorised judges of false prophets, could express no opinion on John, who had been the foremost religious teacher of the time. With what face, then, could they pronounce against Jesus, whom John had publicly proclaimed his superior, and whose greatness had already eclipsed the fame of His forerunner ?

28. τέκνον.—The term implies affection. In English the Christian name would be used.

29. ἐγώ.—Emphatic, in contrast to the brother's οὐ θέλω, "I won't." It almost = "You may depend on me." So in 1 Sam. iii. 4, 6, when the Lord calls Samuel, he answers ἰδού, ἐγώ : and in Gen. xxii. 1, when God called Abraham, he replied, ἰδού, ἐγώ.

30. μεταμεληθείς.—μετάνοια is the change of mind consequent upon "after-knowledge," and so a change of life : μεταμέλεια, the selfish dread of consequences, or "after care." μεταμεληθείς is

used of the remorse of Judas—Matt. xxvii. 3 : μετανοέω in the New Testament usually refers to a change of the whole life; μεταμέλομαι, to single actions.

31. προάγουσιν.—He does not say it is too late for them to follow.

32. ἐν ὁδῷ δικαιοσύνης.—*I.e.*, conducting himself as a strict Jew, paying minute obedience to the Law, fasting, praying, and giving alms. The phrase may, however, mean, "as a teacher of righteousness."

John was the son of a priest, and would therefore be thoroughly initiated in the Temple ritual ; and he would have had the Law expounded to him by the Scribes. His disciples had been perplexed at the contrast presented by the conduct of Jesus and His disciples in the matter of fasting with that of themselves and the Pharisees—Matt. ix. 14.

ἰδόντες.—" When *or* though ye had seen."

33-46. *The Parable of the Wicked Husbandmen.*

In this parable Jesus very plainly announces to the deputation from the Sanhedrim that He foresees they intend to compass His death, and that He must fall by the hands of His countrymen, as the prophets before Him had done. It may be that He had thought it not impossible that the public feeling in the capital might yet cause the nation and its rulers to turn to Him as the spiritual Messiah. Their King-Messiah, in the external and political sense, He will not be. But by this time all such hopes had left Him. His own disciples, indeed, had welcomed Him into the capital, but the rulers had kept aloof, and had sullenly rebuked Him for permitting the children to greet Him with their hosannas. After He had purged the Temple of the sacrilegious traffic, instead of recognising this act as a Messianic one, or at least as one in which any righteous zealot would have been justified, they had attempted violence against Him, and were restrained only by the enthusiasm of the people, who were hanging on His lips—Luke xix. 48, 49. Though He must have seemed to them at the least the noblest and the best of His time ; though John, whom all the people recognised as a prophet, had borne witness to Him ; though His life was stainless, and spent in acts of love and beneficence ; though none could listen to Him without being fascinated, and many regarded Him as John the Baptist, many as Elijah, many as Jeremiah, or some other of the prophets, many as the Messiah, and a few as the Son of God,—the Pharisees and priests had resolved He should die. In this parable the victim calmly tells his slayers he sees their intention. But Jesus sees beyond His death to His influence afterwards, and His country's downfall. Had the Jews accepted Him as the spiritual Messiah, the history of the world might have been changed. The yoke of Rome would not, indeed, have been violently shaken off, but Jerusalem might have continued to exist, and the Jews have exercised over the Romans a spiritual influence similar to the intellectual influence exercised by the Greeks. But in their narrow patriotism they would not have it so: the spirit of Leviticus and the Maccabees was destined to prevail over the spirit of Isaiah; and the impetuosity and vindictiveness of the zealots was doomed to bring the country to an untimely end, from which the gentler spirit of Jesus alone could have saved it. Nothing but His spirit, indeed, could have saved the "place and nation" from being taken away by the Romans. And hereafter, through Him as its representative, the nation was to enjoy a supremacy over the spirits of mankind of which none even of His most intimate disciples were dreaming.

33. ὅστις, κ.τ.λ. — "A housemaster of the class of vineyard planters." The parable refers to Isa. v. 1-6, where the prophet, speaking of God as his friend, laments the unfruitfulness of his friend's vineyard in the form of a song which has been thus translated :—

> "A vineyard had my dear friend,
>   Upon a richly fruitful height ;
> And he digged it over, and cleared it of stones,
>   And planted it with choice vines,
> And built a tower in its midst,
>   Hewed out also a wine-press in it,
> And he hoped that it should bear grapes,—
>   But it bore wild grapes."

The words φραγμὸν περιέθηκα, πύργον ᾠκοδόμησα, and προλήνιον ὤρυξα, all occur in the above passage, and the vineyard is explained as the house of Israel.

The reference by Jesus to this passage would be full of significance to His hearers, who would think, before He continued His parable, of the continuation of that of the prophet—"Let me tell you what I will do to my vineyard : take away its hedge, that it become grazing-land ; break down its wall, that it serveth for trampling upon : make a desolation of it."

This was the first threat against the holy city, uttered in the beginning of his career by the most brilliant of their prophet-poets. Jesus' hearers could look back upon its fulfilment, and would be constrained to listen with gloomy foreboding to the revival of it by the new Prophet of Nazareth—this terrible Messianic message of the claimant to the Messiahship—as He fixed upon them His eyes which seemed now to be gazing at and beyond death, while He calmly told His would-be murderers what their deeds should be.

ἀμπελών.—No possession was more valuable, none required greater care. In Ps. lxxx. 8, Israel is spoken of as a vine brought out of Egypt. That can hardly be the meaning here, for in ver. 43 the vineyard is said to be given over to another nation. It is best, probably, to interpret the vineyard as the kingdom of God, which at first was identical with Israel, but was subsequently extended to the Gentiles. The ἀμπελών may then be regarded as the mass of the people to be guided and instructed : the γεωργοί as the regularly constituted instructors and guides who in successive ages were—(1) the priests and Levites ; (2) the king with his ministers and the priests ; (3) the priests and the Scribes. The δοῦλοι would be the extraordinary messengers— the prophets. The γεωργοί and the δοῦλοι were sometimes merged as priests, were sometimes prophets. But the priests as priests never protested against the sins of idolatrous kings, but became sharers in the worship of Baal, of the sun and moon, and of the host of heaven. The priests, again, never of their own accord introduced reform—see p. 203. The prophets are called δοῦλοι in the summary of the history of the ten tribes in 2 Kings xvii. 13. Cf. Jer. xxxv. 15 (English version). It is the chief priests who take the lead in causing Jesus to be put to death. It is to them Judas goes—Matt. xxvi. 3-14.

φραγμόν.—This refers (1) to the physical boundaries of the Holy Land, which are thus described in Ps. lxxx. 10, 11: "The hills were covered with the shadow of it, and the boughs thereof were like the goodly cedars. She sent out her boughs unto the sea, and her branches unto the river "—see pp. 2, 3: (2) to the Law, which was a fence that guarded them against impurity. The word φραγμός would recall to the listeners the famous saying of the Great Synagogue, " Make a fence to the Law "—*i.e.*, impose additional injunctions, so as to keep at a safe distance from forbidden ground. In Eph. ii. 14, the Law is called a μεσότοιχον τοῦ φραγμοῦ —*i.e.*, the middle wall of the fence between Jew and Gentile.

" The elevation of the hills and table-lands of Judea," says Dean Stanley, "is the true climate of the vine. Enclosures of loose stones, like the walls of the fields in Derbyshire or Westmoreland, everywhere catch the eye on the bare slopes of Hebron, Bethlehem, and Olivet, and at the corner of each rises its square grey tower." The φραγμός would be of stone, or of stone and baked mud. Sometimes, however, thorny shrubs were added or intermingled.

ὤρυξεν.—This does not refer to digging out soil, but to scooping out a wine-press in the limestone-rock. Tristram gives the following description : " A flat or gently sloping rock is used for their construction. At the upper end a trough is cut about 3 feet deep, and $4\frac{1}{2}$ by $3\frac{1}{2}$ in length and breadth. Just below this in the same rock is hewn out a second trough 14 inches deep, and 4 feet by 3 in size. The two are connected by two or three small holes bored through the rock close to the bottom of the upper trough, so that the grapes being put in and pressed down, the juice streamed into the lower vat."

πύργον.—A watch-tower for the purpose of guarding the grapes, a place to store the wine, and a residence for the workmen. If we are to regard the detail as having any significance, we may perhaps in interpreting think of the Temple.

ἐξέδοτο.—It would seem that they undertook to give the owner a certain fixed quantity yearly for the produce of the vineyard, and all that was over was to belong to them. This appears more plainly in Mark xii. 2. Cf. 2 Sam. ix. 10, where Ziba tills the land and brings in the fruits to Mephibosheth. This is the most prevalent system of land-tenure in a great part of Italy now.

ἀπεδήμησεν.—" Went abroad." In the interpretation it refers to the invisibility of God, who is, however, regarded as manifesting Himself in special national crises, as in the planting the Israelites in Canaan, the sieges of Jerusalem, and the carrying away into captivity.

35. ἔδειραν.—δέρω properly means " to flay." It is used of beating, apparently in a slang way, like our word " hide," in Aristoph., Ranæ, 619. There is a climax in the three phrases—scourging,

killing, stoning. St Mark's gradation is (1) scourging, (2) stoning, beating on the head, and outraging, (3) killing. St Luke's narrative reserves the killing for the son. The divergency shows that Jesus was not regarded as referring to particular cases of the martyrdom of the prophets, but as summing up the history of their treatment.

In Jer. xxxvii. 15, we read how that prophet was " smitten and cast into a dungeon ; " in 2 Chron. xxiv. 21, of the stoning of Zechariah, the son of Jehoiada. In 2 Kings xxi. 16, Manasseh is said to have shed much innocent blood ; and it is probable that Isaiah perished with others in that time of persecution. There is a not improbable tradition that Jeremiah was stoned by his own countrymen in Egypt. The speech of St Stephen recorded in Acts vii. is a commentary on and development of this parable.

36. πλείονας.—Some take this to mean " better," " of more importance."

38. σχῶμεν τὴν κληρονομίαν.—The vineyard had been planted to produce moral fruits. The Israelites had again and again been warned by the prophets that the retention of their land depended on their maintaining the union of religion and morality. After the Babylonish captivity the pious alone for the most part would have sufficient enthusiasm to face the perils and difficulties of the return. Hence piety and holiness would more than ever be regarded as the true conditions of heirship. In the time of Jesus the conscience of the nation was sufficiently well trained to know who was the holiest, and therefore who the truest Heir. But Jesus refused to promote, as the Heir, the aspirations of the majority of His countrymen for material power, while He excited the jealousy of their ecclesiastical rulers by the spiritual sovereignty He was winning over the noble minority, the true and spiritual Israel. Hence the rulers sought His death, and the worldly-minded mob were willing to abet them. The ecclesiastical rulers knew that He was stealing away from them the allegiance of the devout, and they did not dispute the authority of John the Baptist who had borne witness to Him. When, therefore, He spoke of Himself as the Heir and the Son, they must have understood Him, though the Messiah is nowhere in the Hebrew Scriptures clearly and explicitly spoken of as " the Son of God," nor was the title recognised by the Jews of the time as belonging to the Messiah.

They were, then, seeking to take the inheritance when they were endeavouring to keep to themselves the kingdom of God— *i. e.*, all the light, knowledge, and privileges which they had heretofore exclusively enjoyed, but which Christ intended, not indeed to take from them, but to extend to other nations. This, however, in their jealous exclusiveness, they regarded not as extending the empire of the kingdom, but as limiting their own control over its affairs. They were like ministers conspiring against their king while on the eve of making fresh conquests, through apprehension lest they should be superseded in their office by rivals from among his new subjects.

39. ἐξέβαλον ἔξω.—This has been regarded as containing a reference to the fact that Jesus suffered outside Jerusalem ; but as the vineyard refers to the whole of the Holy Land, it will be better, if we press any interpretation of this detail, to refer it to His excommunication.

41. λέγουσιν. — The substance of the words that follow is ascribed by St Mark and St Luke to Jesus Himself. It seems very unlikely that the chief priests and Pharisees, to whom ver. 45 represents the parable as having been addressed, should have used them. If they did, then we must suppose that they were constrained by the presence of the bystanders, and the calm searching manner of Jesus, to make some reply, and answered as though in continuation to a story with which they were not concerned. The position in that case would be as ironical as the self-condemnation of Œdipus.

κακοὺς κακῶς.—Cf. Hec., 903, τὸν μὲν κακὸν κακόν τι πάσχειν: Persæ, 1020, δόσιν κακὰν κακῶν κακοῖς: Ajax, 866, πόνος πόνῳ πόνον φέρει: Catullus, iii. 13, " At vobis male sit, malæ tenebræ, Orci." In the Rheims version it is translated, " The naughtie man he will bring to naught." Another suggestion is, " The wretches, he will wretchedly destroy them."

42. λίθον.—The antecedent is here attracted into the case of the relative, as in Shakespeare's " Coriolanus," v. 6. 5, " Him I accuse the city ports by this hath entered ; " " Ant. and Cleop.," iii. 1. 15, " Him we serve 's away. Æn., i. 573, " Urbem quam statuo vestra est." The passage comes from Ps. cxviii., which is thought to have been sung for the first time at the dedication of the second Temple—Ezra vi. 15-18. There may have been some reference to a dispute as to which stone was to be used for the

future corner-stone at the top, and the priests may have selected a stone rejected by the builders.

εἰς κεφαλὴν γωνίας.—"Became for the head of a corner,"—*i.e.*, the top stone at an angle of the building, of great weight and importance in their roofs, which were built of solid flat stones, to admit of being walked on. In the psalm the restored Jews are represented as triumphantly declaring that their nation, discarded in its captivity by all other nations, had become the corner-stone of all the nations—*i.e.*, they foresaw for themselves, in their exultation, universal dominion. They may have been then referring to Jer. li. 26, where the prophet of the captivity had declared of Babylon, " They shall not take of thee a stone for a corner, nor a stone for a foundation, but thou shalt be a desolation." Peter, perhaps specially delighting in referring to this passage, on account of its allusion to his own name, quotes it—Acts iv. 11, and 1 Pet. ii. 4-8. In the last passage he combines it with Isa. viii. 14. The Rabbis referred the passage to the Messiah, so that His listeners would here understand Jesus as claiming the Messiahship. St Paul expands the metaphor in Eph. ii. 19 : " Ye are fellow-citizens with the saints, and of the household of God ; built upon the foundation of the apostles and prophets, Jesus Christ Himself being the chief corner-stone ; in whom all the building being fitly framed together groweth unto an holy temple in the Lord." Jesus, as the corner-stone, united all men in one brotherhood. Practically He says : " As a nation you were rejected and despised by other nations when you were carried into captivity, and your Temple was laid in ruins. Yet you returned, your Temple was rebuilt, and you seemed to yourselves destined for universal dominion through your Messiah. You are now rejecting me, but I am destined to be that head-stone of the corner the Psalmist alluded to. I shall be the corner-stone of a great spiritual Temple, whose influence shall be infinitely greater than that of this material one."

There was great propriety in Jesus quoting this psalm on this occasion, as He had been greeted with quotations from it as He entered the city on the preceding day (ver. 26).

αὕτη.—The fem. is used because the passage is a direct translation from the Hebrew, in which language there is no neuter. Cf. Ps. xxvi. 4, μίαν ἠτησάμην παρὰ Κυρίου—" I have asked one *thing* from the Lord."

43. **διὰ τοῦτο.**—"Because ye are rejecting this stone."

ἔθνει.—No particular nation, but the ideal nation of the future, whose invisible king is Christ; the ἔθνος ἅγιον.   Cf. 1 Pet. ii. 9.

ποιοῦντι.—The pres. = "who are producing its fruits, and so anticipating its establishment."   They are the καρπὸς τοῦ πνεύματος of Gal. v. 22.

44. **συνθλασθήσεται.**—A late poetic word.   This verse occurs in St Luke immediately after the κεφαλὴν γωνίας of ver. 42, which seems its natural place.   It has been proposed, therefore, to transpose vers. 43 and 44.   The passage, however, as it stands, is in accordance with the laws of Hebrew parallelism, and is an illustration of the figure chiasmus (see p. 37). The first couplet, from λίθον ὅν to γωνίας, is connected with the fourth, καὶ ὁ πεσών to λικμήσει αὐτόν; and the second couplet, παρὰ Κυρίου to ἡμῶν, with the third, διὰ τοῦτο to αὐτῆς.   Thus due prominence is given to the head-stone, which occurs first and last.   Moreover, the passage as it stands is a climax : the taking away of the kingdom is particular, and refers to the Jews ; the stumbling on the stone, and being ground to powder, is universal, and refers to all mankind.   It is, however, not quite certain that the passage is genuine here.   It is probably an early addition.

The stone is first regarded as lying at rest, and therefore a stone on which some one falls and breaks his limbs, as in Isa. viii. 14, 15 ; then as lifted to its place, and rolling down on those below with crushing force.   The word λικμάω occurs in Theodotion's version, Dan. ii. 44, where the great image seen by Belteshazzar in a vision has its feet broken to pieces by a stone made without hands, and the stone becomes a great mountain, and fills the whole earth ; and Daniel is represented as interpreting this stone of a kingdom set up by God which shall never be destroyed, but shall λεπτυνεῖ and λικμήσει all these kingdoms, and shall itself stand for ever.   The word λικμάω means primarily "to winnow corn," Il., v. 499 ; secondarily, "to disperse" and "bring to naught,"—Job xxvii. 21, ἀναλήψεται δε αὐτὸν καύσων καὶ ἀπελεύσεται, καὶ λικμήσει αὐτὸν ἐκ τοῦ τόπου αὐτοῦ.   In the LXX. version of Daniel, λικμήσει is rendered by ἀφανίσει, "destroy," and this will explain the meaning of λικμήσει here.

The stone on which men fall is Jesus in His humiliation; the stone which falls on man is Jesus triumphant.   Peter in his repentance is the best example of the former.   The word *contrition* illustrates its meaning. The illustration of the latter can be found in the history of the world since the parable was uttered. The Jews who crucified Jesus soon after ceased to have any local habitation, and their Temple was so utterly destroyed that few traces of it are left. The Roman empire, which rejected His precepts, fell into decay under its own vices. On the other hand, the nations which have acknowledged Him as their head have up to this time been the progressive nations of the world. Since His precepts are those of love among men, and trust in the heavenly Father, it is natural that those who follow Him should prosper, since their efforts after progress are fostered by unity and stimulated by hope, while those who reject Him are rejecting the noblest incentives to both.

LESSON XXXIII.

THE PARABLE OF THE MARRIAGE OF THE KING'S SON— St Matt. xxii. 1-14.

THE REJECTION BY ISRAEL, AS A NATION, OF THE JOYS OF THE KINGDOM.

2. γάμους.—Plural, because the festivities lasted several days. Cf. our word "nuptials." So Athens, Philippi, Colossæ, and other towns are plural, because they originally consisted of several settlements. ποιεῖν γάμους = "to prepare a marriage - feast." Jesus had already compared Himself to a bridegroom. Cf. Mark ii. 19. See also chap. xxv. 1.

This parable resembles that of "The Great Supper" in Luke xiv., but there are several obvious points of difference. See the notes there.

Here the marriage-feast represents the happiness which the royal Father has prepared for those who are faithful to His Son. Jesus wooed humanity as a bridegroom, that it might with Him enjoy the Father's love.

3. τοὺς δούλους.—These would correspond to the Roman *vocatores* or *invitatores*. In the East it is still customary to send round servants to inform the invited guests when all things are

ready.   By the δοῦλοι are probably meant the prophets. See note on Luke xiv. 17.

οὐκ ἤθελον.—" They refused, one after the other : " this is the force of the imperfect.

4. ἄριστον.—A meal corresponding to the French *déjeuner* and our luncheon.   The Jews, like the modern Turks, appear to have had only two meals a-day, the smaller one between ten and eleven o'clock in the morning, the second and larger one after sunset. This early meal commenced the series of feasts connected with the marriage

ἡτοίμακα.—Perf., " I have it prepared." Cf. Zeph. i. 7, "The Lord hath prepared (ἡτοίμακε) His sacrifice, He hath bid His guests.

5. ἀμελήσαντες.—" Having paid no attention."

ἴδιον.—A late usage : the word is simply equivalent to the possessive pronoun.

6. ὕβρισαν.—The verb implies injury accompanied with insult. In 1 Thess. ii. 2, it is translated "entreated shamefully." Cf. Chaucer, " Lamentation of Marie Magdalene " :—

> " With their vengeance insatiable
> Now have they him intreated so
> That to report is too lamentable."

7. στρατεύματα.—" Troops," a late usage. Cf. Luke xxiii. 11. The reference is probably to the Roman armies. So in Isa. x. 5, the Assyrian is spoken of as " the rod of God's anger ; " and in Jer. xxv. 9, Nebuchadnezzar as " God's servant."

Jesus foresaw that since His nation would not accept Him as its regenerator, its doom was sealed. There was no hope of contending successfully with the power of Rome ; nevertheless, the narrow spirit of Pharisaism, combined with the violence of the zealots, was inevitably leading to that hopeless struggle.

8. Cf. Acts xiii. 46, where Paul and Barnabas say to the Jews at Antioch in Pisidia, " It was necessary that the word of God should first have been spoken to you : but seeing ye put it from you, and judge yourselves unworthy of everlasting life, lo, we turn to the Gentiles."

9. διεξόδους τῶν ὁδῶν. — Cf. Ps. i. 3, διεξόδους τῶν ὑδάτων. Since the city was destroyed, this must refer to the crossings of the country roads, where the people were in the habit of congre-

gating most. In the interpretation, the reference is to the calling of the Gentiles in places outside the holy city, as Antioch, Ephesus, or Rome.

10. πονηρούς τε καὶ ἀγαθούς.—Those who had led wicked lives —the publicans and harlots—as well as those who were outwardly respectable and irreproachable in conduct, obeyed the call of Jesus and His apostles. Such persons attached themselves to Jesus and His teaching from mixed motives,—some because He seemed to satisfy their souls with the ideal of a nobler life that He set before them, and because His life and teaching from its novelty and lovingness attracted them ; others because they hoped to derive some worldly benefit from Him. These last are alluded to in the representation of the man "who had not on the wedding-garment." Cf. the parable of the Drag Net (xiii. 47, 48) ; and see St Paul's description of the Christian converts at Corinth in 1 Cor. vi. 9-11. ὁ νυμφών—v. l., ὁ γάμος.

11. That the Eastern host presented wedding-garments on such occasions cannot be determined; but in any case the parable assumes that the man could easily have procured one, and according to etiquette should have done so.

γάμου is the genitive of the characteristic. Cf. Luke xvi. 9, μαμωνᾶ τῆς ἀδικίας. Cf. Zeph. i. 8, ἐκδικήσω . . . ἐπὶ πάντας τοὺς ἐνδεδυμένους ἐνδύματα ἀλλότρια. What this garment was is best explained by Rev. xix. 7, 8, which seems to refer to this passage —"Let us be glad and rejoice, and give honour to Him : for the marriage of the Lamb is come, and His wife hath made herself ready. And to her was granted that she should be arrayed in fine linen, clean and white: *for the fine linen is the righteousness of the saints.*" The guest without the wedding-garment is the man who has accepted Christ's invitation, but has not understood or imbibed His spirit. He misunderstood the nature of the feast ; his thoughts were of a Mohammedan paradise, not of a banquet of love and purity: since he has not the garment of love and purity, he is not fit for the feast. The Israelite was reminded that he belonged to God by the distinctive badge of dark blue upon the fringes at the four corners of his garment (Num. xv. 38). St Paul describes the wedding-garment fully in Col. iii. 12. The metaphor is common in LXX. Cf. Job viii. 22, "They that hate thee shall be clothed with shame ;" xxix. 14, "I put on righteousness, and it clothed me." Cf. 1 Pet. v. 5, τὴν ταπεινοφροσύνην ἐγκομβώσασθε, "Put on humility as a slave's apron."

12. ἑταῖρε.—A mild way of introducing a rebuke, like "good friend," "my good man." Cf. xx. 13, xxvi. 50.

πῶς.—Expressive of astonishment, not of bare inquiry.

μὴ ἔχων.—In classic Greek, and probably here, this means "though thou hast not." But Hellenistic Greek does not invariably maintain the difference between οὐ and μή. From the frequent use of μή with the participle, the New Testament writers seem to have derived an instinctive use of it even where a fact was denied. See Luke iv. 35, τὸ δαιμόνιον ἐξῆλθεν ἀπ' αὐτοῦ, μηδὲν βλάψαν αὐτόν.

ἐφιμώθη.—As if he had been gagged. Cf. ver. 34; 1 Pet. ii. 15. The word is used figuratively only in Hellenistic Greek. Jos., Bell. Jud., i. 22, ὁ μὲν ἐπεφίμωτο τοῖς ἱμέροις, "he was silent through love." φιμός is used of the nose-band of a horse in Æsch., Theb., 463.

13. διακόνοις = the angels, not the same as the δοῦλοι.

ἐκεῖ, κ.τ.λ., appears to be a comment of Jesus on τὸ σκότος τὸ ἐξώτερον, not the words of the king. The "outer darkness" of the parable was the contrast to the lights of the marriage-feast, which the many delays had caused to be prolonged till night; the "gnashing of teeth," to the mirth and music of those who had not been excluded.

The parable refers to the self-imposed exclusion of the Jews from the kingdom, and their downfall as a nation ; and secondly, to the calling of the Gentiles, or rather of such a portion of them as responded to the invitation, and complied with its conditions.

The preceding parable, that of the Wicked Husbandmen, was a parable of the Old Testament history,—the Son Himself appearing as the last and greatest in the line of its prophets and teachers, the crown and completion of them. In that parable God appears as demanding something of men ; in this, as giving something to men. There He is displeased that His demands are not complied with ; here, that His goodness is not accepted: there He requires, here He imparts.

The two favourite images under which the prophets of the old covenant set forth the blessings of the new, and of all near communion with God, that of a festival and a marriage (Isa. xxv. 6, lxv. 13 ; Song of Sol. v. 1), meet in this parable of the marriage-festival.

There was always a marriage-feast after a wedding among the Jews. For this reason marriage was not celebrated either on the Sabbath or on the day before or .after it, lest the Sabbath rest should be endangered. The Rabbis describe Moses as " the friend of the Bridegroom," who leads out the bride ; while Jehovah, as the Bridegroom, meets His Church at Sinai.

In Ps. xlv. we have a royal marriage psalm, or " Song of Loves," as the superscription in the Bible has it, apparently celebrating the entrance of the bridal procession into the palace of the royal bridegroom.

LESSON XXXIV.

The Parable of the Ten Virgins—St Matt. xxv. 1-13.

THE TESTING OF THE MEMBERS OF THE KINGDOM BY THE POSTPONEMENT OF ITS CROWNING JOYS.

1. ὁμοιωθήσεται.—" Shall be made like "—*i.e.*, the condition of Christians at the coming of Jesus will resemble the condition of these virgins.

δέκα.—Cf. the ten slaves in Luke xix. 13. Ten was a favourite number with the Jews. Thus it was ruled that whenever there were ten Jews living in one place there was a congregation, and there a synagogue ought to be built. The common occurrence of the number ten owes its origin simply to the fact that there are ten fingers on both hands.

παρθένοις.—We too have our " bridesmaids." Cf. Ps. xlv. 15, where the queen is brought home to the royal bridegroom accompanied by her virgin friends. So in Theoc., xviii. i., twelve Spartan maidens serenade the home of Menelaus after his marriage with Helen ; and in Catull., lxi., the virgins at a wedding sing a song to Hymenæus. Pindar, too, Pyth., iii., speaks of the παρθένοι ἑταῖραι of the bride as serenading their friend on the morning of her wedding.

The fitness of maidens for the office arises from their being young, pure in heart, and free from the cares of the world. So the heavenly Bridegroom desires for His festival those whose hearts are young and pure, and whose trust in Him has kept them from the μέριμναι of the world. Cf. Matt. xiii. 22.

αἵτινες—not αἱ, because their character is described.

τὰς λαμπάδας.—Jesus had already used this word symbolically in Matt. v. 16. In classic Greek this word means "torches." We find mention of torches at weddings in Il., xviii. 492, Νύμφας δ' ἐκ θαλάμων δαΐδων ὕπο λαμπομενάων 'Ηγίνεον ἀνὰ ἄστυ.

In Rome the bride was brought down from her father's house to that of the bridegroom in the evening by torchlight. Cf. Ter., Adelph., viii. 9, " Missa hæc face, Hymenæum, turbas, lampadas, tibicinas."

That torches might be fed by oil is evident from the following passage in Elphinstone's India : " The true Hindoo way of lighting up is by torches held by men, who feed the flame with oil from a sort of bottle (ἀγγεῖον) constructed for the purpose."

But perhaps λαμπάς is here used for λύχνος, a lamp, and these were lamps, probably attached to stands (ἀγγεῖα), and fed with oil.

Weddings among the Jews took place by night.

εἰς ὑπάντησιν.—They were probably in the house of the bride, where the marriage was to take place on the arrival of the bridegroom.

2. **φρόνιμοι.**—" Prudent."   Cf. Matt. vii. 24 ; Luke xvi. 8.

5. **ἐνύσταξαν καί, κ.τ.λ.**—Notice the change of tense (cf. Luke xix. 14), " They nodded the head, and began to sleep soundly." The combination occurs in the LXX. version of the murder of Ishbosheth, 2 Sam. iv. 6: καὶ ἰδοὺ ἡ θυρωρὸς τοῦ οἴκου ἐκάθαιρε πυροὺς, καὶ ἐνύσταξε καὶ ἐκάθευδε.   " The porteress was sifting wheat," &c.

6. **γέγονεν.**—Preteritive, " there ariseth."   Cf. Rom. xiii. 11.

κραυγή.—A cry of joy raised by the people, who see him coming a little way off.   They are made aware of his approach from seeing the light of the torches or lamps carried by those who accompanied him in the procession.   The connection of God with His faithful worshippers is compared to that of a bridegroom with his bride in Isa. lxii. 5: " As a young man marrieth a virgin, so shall thy sons marry thee : and as the bridegroom rejoiceth over the bride, so shall thy God rejoice over thee."

7. **ἐκόσμησαν.** — By pouring on fresh oil, and removing the

fungi about the wick. For the latter purpose a sharp-pointed wire was attached to the lamp, and this is still seen in the bronze lamps found in sepulchres.

8. σβέννυνται.—" Are just on the point of going out."

9. Translate μήποτε οὐ μὴ ἀρκέσῃ, κ.τ.λ.—" Never (shall we give you of our oil) : there will certainly not be enough for us and for you." Others translate (after the Vulgate), " Lest there be not enough for us and you ; go rather to them that sell," &c. (οὐ μή being simply a strengthened negative). There is a *v. l.*, οὐκ ἀρκέσῃ.

Each believer must be personally ready. He must not think that the piety of the congregation or community to which he belongs will conceal his own defects. This interpretation is sanctioned by a passage in the recently discovered " Teaching of the Apostles" : " Watch for your life. Let your lamps not be quenched, and your loins not be unloosed, but be ye ready ; for ye know not the hour in which your Lord cometh. Ye shall frequently gather yourselves together, seeking the things that are profitable for your souls ; *for the whole time of your faith shall not profit you unless in the last season ye be found perfect.*"—(Farrar's translation, in the ' Contemporary Review.')

With the whole narrative we may compare 1 Macc. ix. 37— " After this came word to Jonathan and Simon his brother that the children of Jambri made a great marriage, and were bringing the bride from Nedabetha with a great train, as being the daughter of one of the great princes of Canaan. Therefore they remembered John their brother, and went up and hid themselves under the covert of the mountain : where they lifted up their eyes and looked, and behold there was much ado, and great carriage ; and the bridegroom came forth, and his friends and brethren, to meet them with drums, and instruments of music, and many weapons."

Milton has a beautiful allusion to the parable in his ninth sonnet, addressed " To a Virtuous Young Lady " :—

> " Thy care is fixed, and zealously attends
> To fill thy odorous lamp with deeds of light,
> And hope that reaps not shame. Therefore be sure
> Thou, when the bridegroom with his feastful friends
> Passes to bliss at the mid hour of night,
> Hast gained thy entrance, virgin wise and pure."

LESSON XXXV.

THE PARABLE OF THE TALENTS—St Matt. xxv. 14-30.

THE TESTING OF THE MEMBERS BY THE MORAL CLAIMS OF THE KINGDOM.

14. ἰδίους.—Cf. chap. xxii. 5.

δούλους.—"Slaves," not "servants."   Slaves in antiquity were often artisans, or were allowed to engage freely in business (as was the case with serfs in Russia and slaves in America), paying some fixed yearly sum to their master ; or they had money committed to them with which to trade on his account, or with which to enlarge their business, bringing him in a share of the profits. The share they were allowed to keep to themselves was called "*peculium*."   The Romans carried on many lucrative businesses by means of their slaves which they could not or would not have carried on themselves.   Cicero tells us a good slave could purchase his liberty in six years.

15. πέντε—about £1170 ; δύο, about £460.

16. εὐθέως with πορευθείς expresses the promptitude with which the servants set to work.   Some, however, take it with ἀπεδήμησεν, in which case it expresses the absolute independence permitted to them ; and we may illustrate it by the haste with which the Duke leaves, in "Measure for Measure," Act I. sc. i. 5, and Angelo's expostulation, "Now, good my lord, let there be some more test made," &c.   εἰργάσατο ἐν.—Quite classical = " trafficked with them."   Cf. Luke xix. 16.

ἐκέρδησεν—*v. l.,* ἐποίησεν, which would have the same meaning. *Facere* is similarly used.

18. The talent, being large, is buried in the earth—a common practice in Palestine, where property was insecure on account of the constant insurrections, and the existence of brigands.   Cf. the parable of the Hid Treasure in Matt. xiii. 44.   The smaller *mina* was placed in a napkin.

19. πολὺν χρόνον.—This delay makes the fidelity of the first two more marked, since, in spite of it, they had not been careless, and increases the guilt of the third, who had been idle so long. συναίρει λόγον.—Cf. xviii. 23.

21. εὖ may be taken (1) by itself, as in E. V., but the classic form in this case would have been εὖγε: or (2) with the verb, "Thou wast admirably faithful," &c.

ἐπ' ὀλίγα and ἐπὶ πολλῶν. — This variety in the case is quite common, and seems to imply no distinction. We might, however, translate, "Thou hast shown faithful activity over a few things; I will establish thee in superintendence over many."

εἴσελθε εἰς. Cf. Ps. xcv. 11, "Enter into my rest;" Num. xiv. 30; Heb. iii. 11. τὴν χαράν.—Cf. Rom. viii. 17, "Joint heirs with Christ: if so be that we suffer with Him, that we may be also glorified together." Heb. xii. 2, "For the joy that was set before Him, endured the cross, despising the shame, and is set down at the right hand of the throne of God." Among modern Greeks χαράν denotes simply a feast: the Syriac translation has "feast" as its meaning here.

Archbishop Leighton says: "It is but little we can receive here,—some drops of joy that enter into us; but there we shall enter into joy, as vessels put into a sea of happiness."

24. ἔγνων σε ὅτι.—In English we should usually have the σε the nominative of the following verb. Cf., however, Shakespeare, "Richard II.," iii. 3. 49, "March on, and mark King Richard how he looks."

σκληρός (in Luke xix. 21 the word is αὐστηρός), from σκέλλω, σκλῆναι, "to make dry." It signifies that which, through lack of moisture, is hard and dry, and thus rough and disagreeable to the taste, and even warped and untractable. Hence it expresses roughness, harshness, and untractability in the moral nature of man. It is applied to Nabal in 1 Sam. xxv. 3, ἄνθρωπος σκληρὸς καὶ πονηρὸς ἐν ἐπιτηδεύμασι. The image in σκληρὸς is derived from the touch, in αὐστηρός from the taste. σκληρός is a much stronger word than αὐστηρός, and may be translated "harsh, inhuman, uncivil."

συνάγων, κ.τ.λ.—"Gathering with the rake where you have not scattered with the fan" (with reference to the threshing-floor of another man's farm). διασκορπίζω is used of winnowing in Ezek. v. 2, τὸ τέταρτον διασκορπιεῖς τῷ πνεύματι.

φοβηθείς.—Afraid of losing the talent in business, or of not being able to satisfy thee. This man represents those Christians who shun active work for God, either because they have not courage to face the difficulties and temptations of mixing in the world, or because, regarding God as a hard taskmaster rather than as a loving Father, they are not stimulated by love for Him to any active service. They are willing to indulge in sentimental piety; they carefully guard their characters from contamination; but they will not strengthen them by energy. They rust out rather than wear out. The foolish virgins erred through presumption, the slothful servant through diffidence. They counted it too easy, he too hard, to serve the Lord. They were sanguine, he melancholic.

27. βαλεῖν apparently means simply "to put," without any idea of flinging. Cf. Luke x. 35, where the good Samaritan is spoken of as ἐκβαλών δύο δηνάρια, "taking out two shillings"; and cf. note on Luke xvi. 20.

τραπεζίταις — from τράπεζα, because the bankers had tables before them. See note on Luke xix. 23.

There is a saying traditionally assigned to our Lord, but nowhere found in the New Testament, which may have originated from this,—γίνεσθε τραπεζῖται δόκιμοι, "Be ye approved money-changers." But that passage seems to mean, "Be as experienced money-changers, who readily distinguish good coin from bad;" and seems rather to have arisen out of 1 Thess. v. 21, 22, πάντα δοκιμάζετε, τὸ καλὸν κατέχετε.

τόκῳ.—Cf. Shakespeare's "breed of barren metal." The rate of interest in antiquity was very high—among the Romans 12 per cent. See note at the end of Lesson XXX.

Seneca, Ad. Marc., 10, says: "We have received our good things as a loan. The use and advantage are ours, and the duration thereof the divine Disposer of His own bounty regulates. We ought to have in readiness what He has given us for an uncertain period, and to restore it, when summoned to do so, without complaint."

Augustine, preaching on the anniversary of his exaltation to the episcopate, uses this parable in speaking of a temptation which he felt to withdraw from active labour in the Church, and cultivate a solitary piety. Again he says: "If you are cold, faint, looking to yourself alone, and as it were self-sufficient, and saying in your heart, 'What have I to do with caring for the sins of others? my own soul is sufficient for me, that I should keep it unharmed for God'—does there not occur to your mind that slave who hid his talent and would not spend it? for, was the accusation brought against him that he had lost and not rather that he had saved it, and gained nothing ? "

29. See note on Luke xix. 26.

30. ἐξώτερον.—There seems to be no special force in the comparative, for in Cho., 1023, ἐξωτέρω is used in the same way as ἔξω in Prom., 883. In the one case we have ἐξωτέρω δρόμου, in the other ἔξω δρόμου. So in 3 Kings vi. 29, we have τῷ ἐσωτέρῳ καὶ τῷ ἐξωτέρῳ, in our version translated " within " and " without."

ὁ κλαυθμός.—The article implies the *ideal* weeping—*i. e.*, weeping and gnashing of teeth, in comparison with which none other can be regarded as such. Cf. Matt. xiii. 42.

The use of the word *talent* for ability is due to this parable. In Middle English it meant " will or inclination," from the figure of the inclination or tilting of a balance. Chaucer speaks of beasts that have " talente [will] to flien, or to desiren any thing."

LESSON XXXVI.

The Allegory of the Good Shepherd—St John x. 1-16.

The verses from 1-16 form a triptych, or picture in three compartments : (1) ver. 1-6, which may be called " The Shepherd," describes the forming and departure of the flock in the morning ; (2) ver. 7-10, " The Gate," describes the life and activity of the flock in the middle of the day ; (3) ver. 11-16, " The Good Shepherd "—or rather " The Ideal Shepherd "—describes the return of the flock as the shades of evening are coming on.

1-6. The Shepherd.

1. ἀμὴν ἀμὴν.—This double ἀμὴν does not occur in other parts of the New Testament, but we find it twenty-five times in St John, and only in the mouth of Jesus. Cf. note on Matt. v. 18. What the θύρα is, Jesus explains in ver. 7.

ἀναβαίνων.—The fold was not covered in, but surrounded by a low wall or fence.

ἀλλαχόθεν = the classic ἄλλοθεν, " from elsewhere "—*i.e.*, from another direction than that indicated by the gate.

κλέπτης — who seeks to avoid detection ; λῃστής, who uses open force to secure his ends.

2. ποιμήν.—"A," *not* "the shepherd." The absence of the article fixes attention on the character as distinct from the person. Several flocks were often gathered into one fold for protection during the night. In the morning each shepherd passed into the fold to bring out his own flock ; and he entered by the same door as they.

3. ὁ θυρωρός.—The under-shepherd who had charge of the sheep during the night. Various interpretations have been suggested of the phrase, but it is perhaps best simply to regard it as part of the description of the legitimate mode of entering.

φωνεῖ.—A word signifying personal address rather than general or authoritative invitation (καλεῖ).

κατ' ὄνομα.—All that are gathered within the fold listen to his voice as a shepherd's voice, even though they are not peculiarly his own sheep. But the shepherd of each flock calls his own sheep by name, and leads them out. It was not an unusual custom among the shepherds of ancient times to give individual sheep a name. Names of a sheep and a ewe are given in Theoc., Idyl., v. 102. "Calling by name" is a phrase used in the Old Testament to express God's care or favour. Cf. Isa. xliii. 1, "I have called thee by name ; thou art mine." Cf. Rev. iii. 5. The phrase, "to be known of God," corresponds with this image. Cf. 1 Cor. xiii. 12.

4. ἐκβάλῃ.—Cf. Luke x. 2. A more forcible word than ἐξάγειν. He puts them forth with a loving constraint. Perhaps there is a reference to the separation of the members of the new kingdom from the old theocratic fold of Israel.

πάντα.—He is careful to leave none behind.

5. οὐ μὴ ἀκολουθήσουσι. — For the classic ἀκολουθήσωσι. "They *certainly* will not follow him."

6. παροιμία.—A translation of the Hebrew *mâshâl*. See on Luke xiv. 7.

7-10. *The Gate.*

7. τῶν προβάτων.—" Of the sheep "—*i.e.*, by which they as well as the shepherd enter the fold. Henceforth Christianity was to take the place of Judaism by absorbing it.

8. πρὸ ἐμοῦ.—Omitted in an important group of early authorities.

This is a very hard verse. Could Jesus mean to say that all the teachers, kings, and prophets in Israel before Him had been thieves and robbers? This cannot be, for in this same Gospel He is represented as alluding to the authority of Moses, chap. vii. 19; of the Scriptures, v. 39; and to salvation as coming from the Jews, iv. 22.

In the English version the passage gains an additional emphasis by the translation, ' All that *ever* came before me." But the word "ever" is not in the Greek.

It is probably best to interpret by the technical signification of ἦλθον, as referring to the Messiah. Cf. Matt. xi. 3, σὺ εἶ ὁ ἐρχόμενος: John vi. 14, ὁ προφήτης ὁ ἐρχόμενος εἰς τὸν κόσμον: Dan. ix. 26, where Messiah is spoken of as " the Prince that shall come": Mal. iii. 1, " The Lord, whom ye seek, shall suddenly come to His temple."

Jesus is then probably alluding to the false pretenders to the Messiahship, and others who, in His own time or shortly before Him, attempted by intrigue or force to restore the kingdom to Israel, and His assertion here is that such men had shown themselves not shepherds to the sheep, but thieves and robbers.[1]

Among these self-seeking leaders of the people and false Messiahs was Athronges, a shepherd who rose against the Romans in the south of Judæa with some success, but displayed great cruelty to his own countrymen. Josephus says of him and his followers that they slew some out of the hopes of gain, and others from a mere custom of slaying men—Ant., xvii. 10. 7. Simon, who had been a slave of Herod's, also caused himself to be proclaimed king, and won many people over to him by false hopes, but effected nothing but plundering and burning. Judas the Gaulonite also headed a sedition against the Roman government in A.D. 6. This man's avowed object was to restore the theocracy (" *the fold of Israel* "), and he began his operations by resisting Gentile taxation. Cf. Acts v. 37. Herod himself had sought to lay claim to the Messianic crown by fulfilling the prophecy of Zechariah, that at that time the Temple should be rebuilt.

---

[1] We may find a similar contrast in the title of ποιμένα λαῶν, given by Homer to Agamemnon, and that of κλέπτης, which Aristophanes represents Cleon as proudly assuming in the famous line—

" κλέπτης μὲν οὐκ ἄν μᾶλλον, εὐτυχὴς δ'ἴσως."—Eq. 1252.

All these men had aimed at constituting themselves gates for the sheep to enter into the fold of Israel as a restored kingdom. But they were seeking their own good, and not that of the sheep; and we learn of them all that, like the bad shepherds of Ezek. xxxiv. 4, while they had any power they "ruled the sheep with force and with cruelty."

Jesus declares that He is, in comparison with them, the true Shepherd of the sheep of Israel, and that they who have sought to enter the fold in other ways than His—the way of love and self-sacrifice—have proved themselves thieves and robbers,—have been seeking, by intrigue and violence, to enrich themselves at the expense of the sheep.

Nor from the number of these "thieves and robbers" can we omit the Pharisees, who, while they feigned a desire to let the sheep into the theocratic fold, were at once enriched by them and contemptuous of them ; while as to the true fold—the kingdom of heavenly Love—that they neither entered themselves nor suffered others to enter.　They had taken away the key of the knowledge of it—Luke xi. 52.　They even turned the sheep out from it, as in the case of the blind man, chap. ix. 34.　This outcast, so expelled from their narrow Jewish fold, the Good Shepherd had received into the ampler fold of the Son of man, chap. ix. 35.

9. ἐγώ εἰμι ἡ θύρα.—The reiteration adds a solemn emphasis. Cf. the repetition of ὁ ποιμὴν ὁ καλός in ver. 11, 14, and of οὐ δύναταί μου μαθητὴς εἶναι in Luke xiv. 26, 27, 33.　For the meaning, cf. Matt. vii. 13, 14; Eph. ii. 18.

εἰσελεύσεται καὶ ἐξελεύσεται.—This is a reference to Numb. xxvii. 16, 17, " Let the Lord, the God of the spirits of all flesh, set a man over the congregation, which may go out before them, and which may go in before them, and which may lead them out, and which may bring them in ; that the congregation of the Lord be not as sheep which have no shepherd."　The figure refers to the free use of an abode as one's home.　The sheep can go freely into the fold when they need rest, and freely out of it when they need nourishment.　The phrase is common in the Old Testament — cf. Deut. xxviii. 6, xxxi. 2 ; Jer. xxxvii. 4 ; Acts i. 21.

νομήν.—The flock are to find through Jesus safety, liberty, and food.　"The Christian may exercise the sum of all his powers, claiming his share in the inheritance of the world, secure in his home."—Westcott.

10. **θύσῃ**.—See note on Luke xv. 23 ; and cf. the use of the Latin *macto* in Ov., Met., viii. 684, 685, "Unicus anser, quem mactare parabant."

ἀπολέσῃ.—A shepherd who rules the sheep for selfish ends, whether he be regarded as a teacher or a governor, will necessarily cause destruction. So the Roman oligarchy, when they had become selfish and demoralised, fell before Julius Cæsar, the Roman Empire before the Barbarians, the French Monarchy under the Revolution.

ἦλθον.—"Came," not "am come."

περισσόν.—"Abundance," in addition to life. The ζωήν is opposed to θύσῃ, the περισσόν to ἀπολέσῃ. See note at the end of the chapter.

11-16. *The Good Shepherd.*

11. **ὁ ποιμὴν ὁ**.—The repeated article gives additional emphasis. Cf. τὸν μόσχον τὸν σιτευτόν, Luke xv. 23.

ὁ καλός, not ὁ ἀγαθός.—Good as *seen*, not merely good inwardly ; such goodness as by its moral beauty will claim all men's admiration. A man must be very base not to admire self-sacrifice when he sees it. "We needs must love the highest when we see it." Cf. "the staff Beauty," Κάλλος, in Zech. xi. 7. In classical Greek καλός is used of men in a moral sense only in the phrase καλὸς κἀγαθός, which occurs in LXX., in Tobit vii. 7 ; 2 Macc. xv. 12. We have καλὸς with διάκονος in 1 Tim. iv. 6 ; with στρατιώτης, 2 Tim. ii. 3 ; with οἰκονόμοι in 1 Pet. iv. 10.

τὴν ψυχὴν τίθησιν.—The phrase is peculiar to St John, in the New Testament, and does not occur elsewhere. Cf. vers. 15, 17, xiii. 37, xv. 13 ; 1 John iii. 16. It means either (1) "*pays down.*" Cf. Matt. xx. 28, ὁ υἱὸς τοῦ ἀνθρώπου ἦλθε δοῦναι τὴν ψυχὴν αὐτοῦ λύτρον ἀντὶ πολλῶν. Demosthenes uses the word in this sense. Or (2) "puts off and lays aside as a robe," as in John xiii. 4, τίθησι τὰ ἱμάτια. Cf. Luke xxiii. 46, πάτερ, εἰς χεῖράς σου παρατίθεμαι τὸ πνεῦμά μου : xix. 21, αἴρεις ὃ οὐκ ἔθηκας—where the idea is of temporary deposition. Cicero uses "ponere vitam," Ep. ad Fam., ix. 24.

There is probably a reference throughout the passage to Isa. liii., and, in this clause, to ver. 10, "Thou shalt make his soul an offering for sin," which Cheyne translates, "If he were to lay down his soul as an offering for guilt."

12. σκορπίζει—*i.e.*, "the flock." Individuals perish : the society is broken up.

13. In many MSS. this verse begins with ὁ δὲ μισθωτὸς φεύγει.

16. ἄλλα—*i.e.*, the Gentiles. Cf. Matt. viii. 11, 12. τῆς αὐλῆς ταύτης—the organisation of the Jewish theocracy. ἀγαγεῖν = "make myself leader of." μία ποίμνη, εἷς ποιμήν.—Cf. Ezek. xxxiv. 23, "And I will set up one shepherd over them, and he shall feed them."

μία.—Cf. xi. 52. As several flocks were gathered into one fold, the sheep of the One Shepherd might be in several folds. So the sheep of the Good Shepherd are gathered from many nationalities and diverse religions.

ποίμνη, not αὐλή.—Unity, not uniformity ; unity in life, not in organisation merely. The reference is to what St Paul calls the πλήρωμα τῶν ἐθνῶν, Rom. xi. 25—the uniting all nations into one brotherhood, acknowledging Jesus, the self-sacrificing Shepherd, as their head. Cf. the beautiful passage in Eph. ii. 11-22.

ADDITIONAL NOTE ON VERSES 9, 10.

Fully to appreciate the meaning of these verses, we must picture to ourselves the life of a pious Jew who in the time of Jesus attempted to follow out the precepts of the Rabbis. Such a man would have no choice or freedom in any of the details of life. Every action at every moment was practically arranged for him, and no time was left for the entrance of new thoughts. He could learn nothing from any other nation, for if he associated with men of other nations he was polluted. Not for him were the treasures of literature, science, and art ; nor could he enter with loving interest into the thoughts and feelings of men of other nations if he became acquainted with them. For him the discovery of America, the revolution effected in astronomy by Galileo, the discoveries of Isaac Newton, the literature of Shakespeare, would have been equally uninteresting. "All actions, studies, and words," says Josephus, "have with us a reference to piety towards God ; for the giver of the law has left *nothing* in suspense or undetermined, beginning immediately from the earliest infancy, and the details of the domestic life of every one ; He left nothing even of the very smallest consequence to the disposal and arbitration of those for whom He gave laws. Accordingly, He made a fixed rule of law what sorts of food they should abstain from, and what sorts they should use ; which were the persons with whom they should maintain intercourse ; what diligence they should use in their occupations, and what times of rest should be interposed, in order that one living under it, as under a father and guardian, might neither voluntarily nor out of ignorance be guilty of any sin."—Apion, ii. 18. " No one could be born, circumcised, brought up, educated, betrothed, married, or buried—no one could celebrate the Sabbath or other feasts, or begin a business, or make a contract, or kill a beast for food, or even bake bread, without the advice or presence of a Rabbi." The words of Christ respecting binding and loosing were a proverb of the Rabbis. They bound and they loosed as they thought fit. What they loosed was permitted ; what they bound was forbidden. They were the brain, the eyes, the ears, the nerves, the muscles of the people, who were mere children apart from them.

To the sheep thus rigidly governed Jesus gave new pasture by breaking down the barriers of hate which separated the unpolluted Jew from the polluted, Jews from Samaritans, and both from Gentiles. So that in after-years His great disciple St Paul could say, " There is neither Greek nor Jew, circumcision nor uncircumcision, Barbarian, Scythian, bond nor free : but Christ is all, and in all "—Col. iii. 11. The boundaries of the pastures being thus enlarged, the sheep of the fold have had " life and abundance," because they have had wider sympathies, and though gathered from many nations and speaking many languages, have been enabled to interchange their thoughts freely on all subjects.

Again, Jesus gave life and abundance, because, owing to His influence, women have gained a nobler position, and slaves their liberty. The picture of the Good Shepherd is a favourite one in the Roman catacombs ; and, among other illustrations, the dead are represented as standing before the Good Shepherd, and presenting to Him the slaves they liberated in their lifetime.

Again, Jesus gave life and abundance by affording new hopes to the weak and oppressed, the sinful and the erring. The false shepherds destroyed the life and spirit of such by despising them. Jesus gave them new life and spirit by associating with them, bringing out what was good in them, enabling them to recover their self-respect ; and He has led His disciples in all ages to follow His example, and to act and teach on the conviction that men can do something to save one another from sinful habits, and are bound in loyalty to Him to make the effort.

Again, He gave life and abundance by giving men new power against evil thoughts which deaden their faculties for action, by leading them to think of Him as ever present to keep them and save them from their worse selves, and binding them together in a society whose object is to deliver each member from these evil influences, and to aid him against them.   Cf. 1 John v. 18.

Again, He gave life and abundance by giving men a new object for their love and loyalty; so that the lonely and oppressed have always some One on whom to fix their affectious, and to whom they may look up.

In fine, Jesus has given life and abundance to men, because through Him the paralysing fear of God and of the future has given place to a trust, and faith, and hope, that stimulate to energy and strengthen in endurance: because through Him the life of every human being has come to be regarded as an existence of eternal value and eternal destiny: because He has widened the range and intensified the activities of men's love and of their sympathies; has diffused sacred and ennobling sentiments, before unknown, round their homes and their labour; has elevated the study of the beauties and laws of the natural world into the study of the attributes of the heavenly Father and of the character of the heavenly Home; has vindicated for weakness, and suffering, and deformity, a claim to love and to be loved, to serve and to be served amidst the human brotherhood ; and has set the virtue of amiability on a throne as consort with the virtue of manliness. For the death of despair, of contempt, of hate, of lust, of ignorance, of loathing, of humiliation, He, the Ideal Shepherd of the human race, came to give the life of hope, of sympathy, of love, of family affection, of knowledge, of pity, and of self-respect.

LESSON XXXVII.

THE PARABLE OF THE BODY: THE USE OF CHRISTIAN GIFTS.—1 Cor. xii. 12-31.

12. For this "Parable of the Body" cf. the Fable of Menenius Agrippa, as told in Livy, ii. 32, and in Shakespeare's "Coriolanus," Act I. sc. 1. Marcus Aurelius says, "We are made for co-operation, like feet, like hands, like eyelids, like the rows of the upper and lower teeth."

ὁ Χριστός—*i.e.*, the spiritual body of Christ, which includes all Christians as contained in Christ, their head and representative.

13. εἰς ἓν σῶμα.—"With a view to forming one body."

ἐποτίσθημεν.—"Were all drenched with one spirit,"—*i.e.*, in the spiritual gifts we received at baptism.

14. καὶ γάρ.—For the body also consists, not of one limb, but of many, even as the body of Christians, though baptised with one Spirit, received many different gifts.

15. παρὰ τοῦτο—"on account of this." Cf. our vulgarism, "along of this."

18. νῦν.—Logical, "but as it is."

20. "Many members, yet one body."

21. The superiors in the Christian community cannot afford to despise the inferiors.

23. περιτίθεμεν—*i.e.*, by dress.

περισσοτέραν—*i.e.*, in dress.

24. τὰ δὲ εὐσχήμονα.—"Whereas our comely parts."

ἀλλὰ ὁ θεός.—"But the truth is, it was God whose."

τῷ ὑστερουμένῳ.—The middle expresses consciousness—"that which feels its own shortcomings."

25. μεριμνῶσι.—Cf. 2 Cor. xi. 28, 29, "That which cometh upon me daily, the care (ἡ μέριμνα) of all the churches. Who is weak (τίς ἀσθενεῖ), and I am not weak? Who is offended, and I burn not?"

τὰ μέλη.—The members of the body are here personified: the figure expresses the sympathy they have with one another. "The mouth speaks, and the eyes laugh and sparkle."

27. ὑμεῖς—*i.e.*, the Christians at Corinth. According to St

Paul, every single church is the ideal body of Christ, as it is the ideal temple of God (iii. 16). Cf. note on ἐκκλησία, p. 294.

ἐκ μέρους.—Either (1) "in particular," as having special functions in the Church ; or (2), in accordance with the use of the phrase in the next chapter, "members of a part"—*i.e.*, the earthly and rudimentary, as opposed to the heavenly and perfect. Cf. xiii. 10.

28. προφήτας.—The preposition πρό means "instead of." A prophet is one who speaks instead of God : the word does not necessarily imply prediction. As appears from xiii. 3, "He that prophesieth speaketh unto men, to edification, and exhortation, and comfort." See note on Matt. vii. 22.

ἀντιλήψεις.—As, *e.g.*, tending the sick and the poor.

κυβερνήσεις.—As, *e.g.*, the administrative functions of the episcopate.

The knowledge of Christianity, and the enthusiasm it stirred, brought with it new powers, which the Apostle calls χαρίσματα, or gifts. We need not enter into their nature. Most of them have passed away. While the Apostle congratulates the Corinthians on these new powers, he deprecates the misuse of them. The Corinthians were excited about them, and disposed to make a parade of them. The Apostle urges them rather to turn them to profitable use, and to prefer those which were useful to those which seemed more wonderful, and, so to speak, sensational.

Strange to say, the possession of these spiritual gifts led to quarrelling, to euvy, and factions. Those who possessed the loftier gifts looked down on those less highly endowed, and those who possessed only the meaner were disposed to envy the more highly favoured. To check this spirit, the Apostle first of all relates the "Parable of the Body," insisting on the unity of the Church, and the sympathy that ought to exist between its various members, as between the various members of the body : and then he hurries on to "the Praise of Love,"—that Love without which all other gifts are vanity.

There comes a time to most people, usually in boyhood, when they become conscious of the possession of gifts—the power of language, of seeing through problems, of reasoning, of memory, or of wit. The first impulse on this discovery is to take a childish pride in the newly found gifts, as the Corinthians did, to use them for display, and to show our superiority to others.

The Apostle here calls us to a soberer use of them : they are intended for the service of Christ and of our fellow-Christians, who are members, with us, of His body. Their exercise will be none the less delightful because they are made to minister to the community in which we live ; and if we make the experiment, we shall find the irony of concealing our serviceableness more truly delightful than the praise and admiration won by displaying it.

In the little world of school, as in the larger spheres of Christianity, we are all members of one another, all exercise subtle influence on one another, and are affected by one another's good or evil deeds.

The words of the Apostle are especially cheering to those whose gifts are small. A boy who appears to be dull may, by patient industry and a loving disposition, be more useful to the community than the member who is quick and smart, but selfish and forward. The Apostle teaches that the Great Master, Christ, regards the humblest of such members as part of His Body, as much as the comeliest or most renowned.

LESSON XXXVIII.

THE PRAISE OF LOVE : ON CHRISTIAN LOVE.—1 Cor. xiii.

1. **καθ' ὑπερβολήν.**—An adverbial substantive used for an adjective. "A surpassing or *par excellence* way."

ὁδόν.—Way of life : so ἡ ὁδός = Christianity in Acts ix. 2, xix. 9, 23, &c. Cf. Cebetis Tabula, οὐχ εὑρίσκουσι ποία ἐστὶν ἡ ἀληθινὴ ὁδὸς ἡ ἐν τῷ βίῳ ; and Philo, De Vict., p. 841 A, ἐκτραπόμενος τῆς ἐπ' ἀρετὴν καὶ καλοκἀγαθίαν ἀγούσης ὁδου ; and cf. Matt. vii. 13, and Ps. xviii. 21, "the ways of the Lord"; Ps. i. 1, "the way of sinners"; Gen. vi. 12, "all flesh had corrupted his way."

δείκνυμι.—The imperfect present. "I proceed to show you." The tense is a vivid one, and expresses the eager haste with which Paul hastens to the congenial subject of ἀγαπή, or Love.

ἐάν. — "If circumstances were such that I should speak." Paul does not lay claim to all that follows.

ταῖς γλώσσαις.—This is put first, because this was the χάρισμα of which the Corinthians were most proud. Cf. Il., ii. 489, for a weaker parallel, εἴ μοι δέκα μὲν γλῶσσαι δέκα δὲ στόματ' εἶεν.

τῶν ἀγγέλων. — The separation of this word from τῶν αν- θρώπων gives it additional emphasis. "Ay, or even of angels" —*i.e.*, of "angels to angels"—all that both words could express of great and glorious.

ἀγάπην.—This substantive is unknown to classical Greek, though the verb ἀγαπάω is frequent. It is first found in the LXX., where it is used (1) of conjugal affection ; (2) of friendship ; (3) of the devotion of man to God ; (4) the love of God for the chosen people.

The word used by the Greeks for (2) was φιλία, and this gave its name to affection generally. They knew but little, strictly speaking, of domestic and conjugal affection. The word ἔρως, which most nearly approaches to the modern notions of love, ex- pressed either a merely sensual admiration of physical beauty or an intellectual admiration of ideal beauty.

It is impossible to define the word ἀγάπη as used by St Paul in this passage by any single word or phrase. It has been said that it is at once love to man for the sake of love to God, and love to God showing itself in love to man. Describing it by the contents the Apostle assigns to it, we find it includes patience, generosity, humility, dignified demeanour, peaceableness, good temper, inno- cence and unsuspiciousness, and love of realities.

The word was translated *caritas* by Jerome in the Vulgate ; probably he did not like to use *amor*, which has a fleshly meaning. Wycliffe rendered it by *charity*, as did the Rheims version : Tyn- dale, Cranmer, and the Geneva Bible by *love*, which the Revised Version has restored in the place of *charity*.

The objection to the word *charity* is, that it is now associated with the idea of mere almsgiving and tolerance ; to *love*, that it is a word associated with the affection between persons of different sexes. The word *passion*, however, is used of the lower form of this feeling. In 1 John v. throughout, ἀγάπη is rendered "love," where it is used of the affection of Christians towards one another as well as of their love to God, and the love of God and Christ towards them.

The word *love* has been consecrated to the service of religion in the 'Imitatio Christi' of Thomas à Kempis (Parker's translation), especially in Bk. III., caps. 5, 6, which contains an expansion of this chapter : "Love [in the Latin *amor*] feels no burden, thinks nothing of trouble, attempts what is above its strength, pleads no excuse of impossibility ; for it thinks all things lawful for itself, and all things possible.   Love is active, sincere, affectionate, pleasant, and amiable ; courageous, patient, faithful, prudent, long-suffering, manly, and never seeking itself.   Love is circumspect, humble, and upright ; not yielding to softness or to levity, nor attending to vain things : it is sober, chaste, steady, quiet, and guarded in all its senses."

The word was consecrated, too, for many centuries in the allegorical interpretation of the Song of Solomon, which was supposed by the Jewish Rabbis to express the mutual love between God and His people, and by the Christian Fathers the love of the Church for Christ, and of Christ for the Church.

It is a much tenderer word than charity, and tenderness and delicacy of feeling are breathed throughout the chapter.

χαλκὸς ἠχῶν.—"Ringing metal" generally ; κύμβαλον ἀλαλάζον, the particular instance, "a clanging cymbal."   In Ps. cl. 5, we have κυμβάλοις ἀλαλαγμοῦ.   The epithet refers to the unmeaning character of the sound of cymbals (which were mere metal basins, always in a pair, and struck together with the hands), as compared with the significance of real music.   Cymbals appear to have been used in the Temple worship to beat time at the right places.

2. προφητείαν.—See note on chap. xii. 28.

τὰ μυστήρια.—Notice the article.   "The whole range of God's secrets."   εἰδῶ is used in zeugma with γνῶσιν for "have."

ὥστε ὅρη μεθιστάνειν.—"Enough to remove mountains."   This is an allusion to the words of our Lord in Matt. xvii. 20, xxi. 21. The phrase "to remove mountains" was common amongst the Rabbis for clearing away difficulties, and hence the most distinguished teachers were called "uprooters of mountains."   μεθιστάνειν is a late form : there is a *v. l.*, μεθιστάναι.

οὐθέν.—Late form for οὐδέν.   Cf. ἐξουθενοῦντας, Luke xviii. 9.

3. ψωμίσω. — "Dole away in mouthfuls all my property or estates."   The word occurs in Rom. xii. 20, "If thine enemy hunger, feed him"—ψώμιζε αὐτόν.   ψώμιον is the word translated "sop" in John xiii. 26, 27, 30.   The idea is, that the whole of the property is given away for the benefit of the largest number.

παραδῶ.—Cf. Dan. iii. 28 ; Acts xv. 26. Clemens Romanus alludes to heathen examples of kings and rulers who delivered themselves up to save their subjects, and to Christians παραδεδωκότας ἑαυτούς to chains in the place of prisoners, or selling themselves as slaves to obtain the means of feeding the poor (ψωμίζειν). Certainly those Christians who have devoted themselves to the care of lepers, and of others afflicted with loathsome and infectious diseases, may be said to have "given their bodies" in charity.

καυχήσωμαι (v. l., κανθήσωμαι).—The yielding up of the body is a climax to the yielding up of the goods : the low motive, ἵνα καυχήσωμαι, neutralises the virtue of both. Ver. 2 alludes to a faith towards God which is worthless, because unaccompanied by love : ver. 3 to an apparent love towards man which is worthless, because its motive is ostentation.

The v. l., κανθήσωμαι, probably arose (1) from the familiarity with Christian martyrdom by fire ; (2) from a resemblance to Dan. iii. 28, καὶ παρέδωκαν τὰ σώματα αὐτῶν εἰς πῦρ ; (3) from the unfamiliar absolute use of παραδίδωμι.—(Westcott.)

In the after-days of Christianity the high honours paid to the martyrs after death induced many men, little conspicuous for the practice of Christian virtues, to court martyrdom for self-glorification. Reputation, not love, had, consciously or unconsciously, been their aim in professing the faith. To such men the unnoted and persistent practice of Christian love had no charms in comparison with the one supreme act of courage in death, displayed before the whole society, and winning for their remains a reverence often amounting to worship. The sentiment of St Paul is a prophetic warning against such selfish sacrifices, which were destined to bring more dishonour to the faith than honour to those who offered them.

The story of Sopricius of Antioch is a good illustration of this spirit of boastful martyrdom unaccompanied by love. He, at first, showed a willingness "to give his body" for the Christian faith, and was condemned to death for professing it : that he had not ἀγάπη he showed by refusing to forgive his enemy while on the way to execution. In his case, however, even his temporary courage, apart from love, availed him nothing. For at the last moment he recanted and abjured the faith.

4. With this personification of Love we may compare the per-

sonification of Wisdom in the Book of Wisdom, chap. vii. 22-30, and in the Epistle of James, iii. 17.

μακροθυμεῖ—*i.e.*, "is slow to take offence, or resent a slight."

χρηστεύεται.—Mid. voice: *not* "shows kindness," but "shows itself kind"—*i.e.*, "is gracious in demeanour."

περπερεύεται.—Derived from the old Latin word *perperus*, "a braggart"; or, perhaps, the Greek πέρ-περ-ος is the original, akin to πέραν, πέρα, &c. Polybius seems to be the first author to use the adjective (B.C. 165). The verb means, "does not show itself off." It occurs in Epictetus, and in Cicero's letters to Atticus, i. 14, "Quo modo ἐνεπερπερευσάμην novo auditori Pompeio"; it is not found in classical Greek.

φυσιοῦται.—Either passive, "is inflated with vanity"—cf. viii. 2—or middle, "does not swell and swagger."

5. ἀσχημονεῖ.—We might almost render, "does not behave vulgarly"; so that οὐκ ἀσχημονεῖ would express the conduct of a Christian gentleman—*i.e.*, of one who assumes no airs of superiority, and shows a deference to the opinions of others, not merely out of cold politeness, but because he recognises all men as brothers in Christ, and has learnt from true humility to repress selfishness even in the smallest details of conduct. In conversation he is a listener rather than a talker; if he sees reason to contradict, he does so without dogmatising; he will let another precede him into a room rather than push forward himself, and so on.

οὐ ζητεῖ τὰ ἑαυτῆς.—ζητέω here means "to seek," in the sense of "to strive after," so that the phrase means, "strives not after her own interests." Cf. 1 Cor. x. 24, μηδεὶς τὸ ἑαυτοῦ ζητείτω, ἀλλὰ τὸ τοῦ ἑτέρου; and Phil. ii. 4, 21. Note the καί in the second clause of ver. 4, μὴ τὰ ἑαυτῶν ἕκαστοι σκοποῦντες, ἀλλὰ καὶ τὰ ἑτέρων ἕκαστοι. For the connection between self-love and the love of our neighbour, see the Essay on p. 48.

The Apostle speaks hyperbolically, and his protest is against grasping in all its forms, and warns men not to allow their own interests to make them unfair in word or deed: our adjective *disinterested* expresses his meaning best. Without such love wisdom is cunning, and courage audacity. It is the quality that makes the men and women who possess it the arbitrators in the disputes of the society in which they move. It distinguishes the statesman from the mere politician, the judge from the advocate, the soldier from the bravo, the Christian minister from the professional ecclesiastic, the searcher after truth from the hireling *littérateur*.

οὐ παροξύνεται.—"Flies not into a rage"—*i.e.*, having learnt to repress self, is not hastily led into a passion by self-esteem. It is interesting as a commentary on this to read in Acts xv. 39 that there was a παροξυσμός between St Paul and Barnabas. The quarrel, however, appears to have arisen from public grounds. Chrysostom remarks, ὁ Παῦλος ἐζήτει τὸ δίκαιον, ὁ Βαρνάβας τὸ φιλάνθρωπον. St Paul thought more of the cause (τὰ Χριστοῦ) (Phil. ii. 21); Barnabas more of doing a kindness to Mark.

οὐ λογίζεται τὸ κακόν.—"Does not mentally register, put down in its mental account-book," the evil done to it—*i. e.*, neither easily takes offence, nor is with difficulty appeased.

6. **οὐ χαίρει ἐπὶ τῇ ἀδικίᾳ.**—For the construction cf. Matt. xviii. 13, where the shepherd rejoices when he has found his sheep— χαίρει ἐπ' αὐτῷ. ἀδικία is personified, and opposed to ἀληθείᾳ in the next clause. We should have expected δικαιοσύνη to be opposed to ἀδικία. But ἀλήθεια does not mean veracity, but the truth of the Gospel. The word had already been used of the Jewish religion. Cf. Ps. xxvi. 3, "I have walked in Thy truth;" lxxxvi. 11, "Teach me Thy way, O Lord: I will walk in Thy truth." It is used of *natural religion* in Rom. i. 18—τῶν τὴν ἀλήθειαν ἐν ἀδικίᾳ κατεχόντων,—spoken of the heathen who combined a knowledge of the true God with the practice of immorality.

It is used of Christianity in the catholic epistles, in the Epistles of St Paul, and is especially characteristic of the Gospel and Epistles of St John. Thus in 2 Tim. iii. 8 we read, οὗτοι ἀνθίστανται τῇ ἀληθείᾳ: in 2 Pet. ii. 2, ἡ ὁδὸς τῆς ἀληθείας: John i. 17, "Grace and truth came by Jesus Christ."

But the passage that best illustrates the contrast between ἀδικία and ἀλήθεια is John iii. 21, "He that doeth truth cometh to the light, that his deeds may be made manifest, that they are wrought in God." Cf. 1 John i. 6. "To do the truth" is a pregnant or condensed sentence for "to do what we have learnt to be right"; but it implies much more than this—(1) That right conduct is reality, and wickedness unreality, because it is in accordance with the higher part of our nature to do what is right, and we were formed to do it. So we speak of a man being true or untrue to himself, or his better nature. (2) That Christianity is *par ex-*

cellence the truth, because it is at once the highest revelation of God, and the loftiest form of morality.

"To rejoice *over* iniquity," therefore, is to exult from whatever motive at the commission of wickedness—whether because our lower nature and our bestial appetites are gratified, or because the shortcomings of others gratify our self-esteem by giving us a sense of superiority over those that have fallen. The extreme instances of such characters are described in Isa. v. 20, "them that call evil good, and good evil; that put darkness for light, and light for darkness." They are represented in Shakespeare by the witches in "Macbeth," with whom "fair was foul, and foul was fair." Cf. Eur., Hec., 608, κακός δ' ὁ μή τι δρῶν κακόν, "He that does nought base is reckoned base."

συγχαίρει τῇ ἀληθείᾳ.—Notice the change of construction from ἐπὶ τῇ ἀδικίᾳ. Truth is represented, as it were, on a triumphal progress. The triumphal car of Christian morality slowly proceeds through the world, while the better spirits rejoice around it, like the boys and girls around the Trojan horse in Æn., ii. 238, 239, "Pueri circum innuptæque puellæ sacra canunt."

Marcus Aurelius says, "When thou wishest to delight thyself, think of the virtues of those who live with thee—the activity of one, the modesty of another, the liberality of a third, and some other good quality of a fourth."

7. πάντα στέγει.—στέγω = (1) to conceal faults in a neighbour. Cf. Ecclus. viii. 17, "Consult not with a fool, for he cannot keep (στέξαι) counsel." (2) "Bearing," in the sense of being proof against,—the metaphor being taken from a ship or roof which does not leak, or troops or walls warding off an assault (cf. Sept. c. Theb., 216, πύργον στέγειν εὔχεσθε πολεμίων δόρυ), or ice bearing weight. Then it comes to mean, "is proof against affronts, slander, and similar hardships." Cf. 1 Cor. ix. 12, where πάντα στέγομεν seems to mean, "we are proof against all pressure of temptation."

The second meaning is the more probable one in this passage.

πάντα πιστεύει—i. e., is not mistrustful, the quality opposed to the cynicism which criticises and assigns interested motives to all good actions, and is always suspicious because unable to believe in the existence of good.

πάντα ἐλπίζει.—It was largely by thus trusting and believing in the good in boys, that Dr Arnold fostered and even created good in them. Such hopefulness inspires missionary efforts for the reformation of the very worst and most hardened offenders, and inspires them, too, with hopes of their own reform.

πάντα ὑπομένει.—ὑπομένει often means "to bide the brunt of encounter in battle." Here, as elsewhere in the New Testament, it refers to fortitude under tribulation and persecution, and so has a higher meaning than στέγει, which refers to minor annoyances. Cf. Rom. v. 3, ἡ θλίψις ὑπομονὴν κατεργάζεται.

8. **οὐδέποτε.**—A very emphatic word—"no never."

οὐδέποτε πίπτει.—Either (1) never falls to decay (cf. Isa. xxviii. 1, 4, where it is used of flowers; and Wisd. vi. 12, where it is said ἀμάραντός ἐστιν ἡ σοφία); or (2) remains unmoved while all things else are falling: so of Wisdom (Wisd. vii. 27) it is said that μένουσα ἐν αὐτῇ τὰ πάντα καινίζει—"remaining in herself, she maketh all things new." Cf. Luke xvi. 17; and Hdtus., vii. 18, ἄνθρωπος ἰδὼν ἤδη πολλά τε καὶ μεγάλα πεσόντα πρήγματα ὑπὸ ἡσσύνων.

9. **ἐκ μέρους.**—Emphatic by position. Notice that ἐκ μέρους is opposed to τέλειον, as νήπιος to ἀνήρ. Philo (De Cherub.) says, ἀλλὰ νῦν ὅτε ζῶμεν γνωριζόμεθα μᾶλλον ἢ γνωρίζομεν.

11. **ἐλάλουν,** not ἔλεγον, "I talked." λέγω="to speak rationally and articulately"; λαλῶ, "to talk, prate, chatter." Cf. ver. 1, where λαλῶ="I utter"; ἐλογιζόμην="I reasoned."

ὅτε γέγονα, κ.τ.λ.—"Since I have become a man I have brought to an end (have done with) the ways of an infant."

The τέλειος gives up tongues, prophecies, and partial knowledge, as the child gives up his stammering, his vague thoughts, and imperfect reasoning; but the child's faculty for loving still continues.

12. **δι' ἐσόπτρου.**—Cf. James i. 23, "by means of a mirror." The ancient mirrors were of polished metal. Those of Corinth were famous. In such mirrors the images would be blurred and indistinct.

ἐν αἰνίγματι.—In the midst of an enigma, with a problem before us and around us which we cannot solve; or perhaps ἐν is for εἰς, and we should read "on an enigma."

There is a reference here and in the next verse to Num. xii. 8, στόμα κατὰ στόμα λαλήσω αὐτῷ ἐν εἴδει, καὶ οὐ δι' αἰνιγμάτων, καὶ τὴν δόξαν Κυρίου εἶδε.

πρόσωπον πρὸς πρόσωπον.—Cf. 1 John iii. 3; Matt. v. 8 (see note there). The phrase occurs in Gen. xxxii. 30. Cf. στόμα πρὸς στόμα, 2 John 12.

ἐπιγνώσομαι.—The preposition is intensive, " I shall be known in full."

13. νυνί.—Logical, not temporal—"so now, you see."

τὰ τρία ταῦτα.—Cf. Ar., Nub., 424, τό χάος τουτὶ καὶ τὰς νεφέλας, καὶ τῆν γλῶτταν 'τρία ταύτι. Philo uses the phrase several times.

μείζων τούτων.—Love is regarded as one category, and faith with hope as another. The greater of these two categories is love.

It was said of the Apostle St John, that when he was too old and feeble to preach, he used to repeat to his disciples his Master's precept, " Little children, love one another."

THE END.

PRINTED BY WILLIAM BLACKWOOD AND SONS.

9 783744 762120